MISSION AND MEANINGLESSNESS

Also published by SPCK
LINGUISTICS AND BIBLICAL INTERPRETATION
Peter Cotterell and Max Turner

PETER COTTERELL

MISSION AND MEANINGLESSNESS

The good news in a world of suffering and disorder

First published in Great Britain 1990
SPCK
Holy Trinity Church
Marylebone Road
London NW1 4DU

Unless otherwise stated the biblical quotations in this book are from the
Holy Bible, New International Version, Copyright © 1973, 1978, 1984 by
International Bible Society, Used by permission of Hodder and Stoughton
Limited. Quotations from the Revised Standard Version of the Bible,
copyright 1946, 1952, © 1957, 1971, 1973 by the Division of Christian
Education of the National Council of the Churches of Christ in the USA, are
used by permission.

British Library Cataloguing in Publication Data

Cotterell, Peter
    Mission and meaninglessness : the Good News in a world of
    suffering and disorder.
    1. Christian theology
    I. Title
    230

    ISBN 0-281-04449-X

Typeset by Pioneer Associates Ltd.
Printed in Great Britain by
Courier International, Tiptree, Essex

Contents

Contents

Contents

Contents

Contents

Introduction

'Meaningless! Meaningless!'
  says the Teacher.
'Utterly meaningless!
  Everything is meaningless.'

What does man gain from all his labour
  at which he toils under the sun?
Generations come and generations go,
  but the earth remains for ever.
The sun rises and the sun sets,
  and hurries back to where it rises.
The wind blows to the south
  and turns to the north;
round and round it goes,
  ever returning on its course.
All streams flow into the sea,
  yet the sea is never full.
To the place the streams come from,
  there they return again.
All things are wearisome,
  more than one can say.
The eye never has enough of seeing,
  nor the ear its fill of hearing.
What has been will be again,
  what has been done will be done again . . .

. . . So I hated life, because the work that is done under the sun was grievous to me. All of it is meaningless, a chasing after the wind. I hated all the things I had toiled for under the sun, because I must leave them to the one who comes after me. And who knows whether he will be a wise man or a fool? Yet he will have control over all the work into which I have poured my effort and skill under the sun. This too is meaningless . . .

. . . Man's fate is like that of the animals; the same fate awaits them both: As one dies, so dies the other. All have the same breath; man has no advantage over the animal. Everything is meaningless. All go to the same place; all come from dust, and to dust all return.

Who knows if the spirit of man rises upward and if the spirit of the
animal goes down into the earth? . . .

. . . Again I looked and saw all the oppression that was taking
place under the sun:

> I saw the tears of the oppressed –
> and they have no comforter;
> power was on the side of their oppressors –
> and they have no comforter.
> And I declared that the dead,
> who had already died,
> are happier than the living,
> who are still alive.
> But better than both
> is he who has not yet been,
> who has not seen the evil
> that is done under the sun.

And I saw that all labour and all achievement spring from man's
envy of his neighbour. This too is meaningless, a chasing after the
wind.

(Eccles. 1.2–9; 2.17–19; 3.19–21; 4.1–4)

Seen from within the two apparent boundaries to human existence,
birth and death, life appears to be meaningless. Good things happen
to bad people; bad things happen to good people. Disease and
sudden death always threaten; accident, calamity, is an ever-present
possibility. Humanity is left with the choice of an extreme
existentialism – life *is* meaningless, too bad – or of one of the many
religions which have at least this much in common: they all believe
that life *should* make sense.

The Christian mission is charged with the task of giving meaning
to life, of giving hope in a world of suffering and disorder. But
more than that, Christian mission involves *acting* to oppose
oppression, to bring wholeness and health, to announce Good
News: reconciliation with God, and the creation of the new
community, the Church, a community of love and compassion . . .
and of power. This is the theme of this book.

2

PART ONE

Religion, Religions, and the Apparent Meaninglessness of Life

1 The Apparent Meaninglessness of Life

DISORDERED HUMAN EXISTENCE

Between the two apparent boundaries set to human existence, birth and death, life makes no sense. In 1982 the Jewish rabbi Harold Kushner crafted a moving book, *When bad things happen to good people*,[1] a book which had its origins in personal experience. His first child was afflicted with the condition known as progeria, rapid ageing. The doctor told the rabbi and his wife that their son would never grow much beyond three feet in height, would have no hair on his head or body, and would die in his early teens. Kushner comments on his reaction:

> . . . what I mostly felt that day was a deep, aching sense of unfairness. It didn't make sense. I had been a good person. I had tried to do what was right in the sight of God. More than that, I was living a more religiously committed life than most people I knew, who had large, healthy families . . . How could this be happening to my family? If God existed, if He was minimally fair, let alone loving and forgiving, how could He do this to me?[2]

The rest of his book is devoted to grappling with the problem as it is perceived from within the Jewish faith.

It is probably true that with the passing of time and with growing experience of the human condition everyone becomes aware of the unsatisfactory nature of human existence. Even where our own families are spared massive suffering, we cannot long remain unaware of its existence in the families of other people. A young medical doctor commits himself to work among Somali nomads, and as he sets up his tent surgery for the day's work is struck down by an unknown assassin, a knife through his back and into his heart. Another young doctor, expecting to fly home after short-term medical service in a remote region of a Third World country, is taken unwell at the airport, and instead of a happy reunion in her home country is buried in a foreign land. A man and woman in west London, living together, have a horrendous

5

disagreement, and when she takes their child to school he follows her, plunges a carving knife in her back and then cuts his own throat. Parents on holiday leave their little boy for just a few minutes, and he is found floating face down in a tiny paddling pool, dead.

These are just examples plucked from the memory of one individual, examples of the inexplicable nature of human existence. Between the two apparent boundaries of birth and death no meaningful profit-and-loss statement, no sensible balance sheet for the human individual, can be produced. There does not appear to be any correlation between our actions and our experiences. An apparently evil, godless, careless individual flourishes, and flourishes right through life. It simply is not true that eventually, somewhere in *this* life, he gets what is due to him. An apparently good and godly person, careful for others, experiences hardship, illness, loss, and, unlike biblical Job, does *not* find appropriate compensation in *this* life. There appears to be no *order* to the human condition.

And again, this disorder is not one only of the individual existence, but one which affects also groups of people, whole communities, even entire peoples. The six million Jews murdered under the Nazi tyranny. At least five times that number who died under Stalin's purges of the 1930s. The so-called natural disasters: the disaster in Wales, at Aberfan,[3] on 21 October 1966, when a slag heap fell on to the village, and not merely on to the village, but on to the school, where little children sat at their lessons, and one hundred and thirty-eight of them died at their little desks. The disaster of 1988 in the skies over Scotland, when a terrorist bomb blasted an American passenger aircraft into pieces which rained down on the town of Lockerbie and Scottish country people died alongside American travellers. The ninety-five football fans who went to see a football match and were crushed to death in the very eyes of the cameras of the TV companies and the nation's press. The two million and more people who starved to death in Ethiopia.

How are we to characterize human existence? John Macquarrie comments:

A question like this can, of course, be answered only by a broad empirical generalization, and such generalizations can always be challenged. Yet perhaps no one would deny that when we do look at actual human existing, we perceive a massive disorder in existence, a pathology that seems to extend all through existence, whether we consider the community or the individual, and that stultifies it.[4]

Buddhism characterizes human existence through three words: *anicca*, life's impermanence; *anatta*, contrary to the usual human perception, the impersonality of human existence; and *dukkha,* the general unsatisfactoriness of life. Trevor Ling defines *dukkha* as 'a word which is variously translated as "evil" or "ill" or "suffering", and [which] means any or all of these as they are expressions of the general unsatisfactoriness of ordinary empirical existence, the sense that things are not as they should be'.[5]

Things are not as they should be. Here is the affirmation that distinguishes the existentialist from everyone else. In existentialism the reality of *dukkha* is accepted, but the possibility of there actually being any *meaning* to life is denied: 'The existentialist believes that there is no meaning in any one thing, or in everything put together. The world is absurd and pointless. To be human is to choose in the light of the absurdity of the world.'[6]

The religions of the world have at least this much in common: they all believe that the human existence ought to make sense, that life ought to have meaning; and all religions offer an explanation of *dukkha.* We shall return to this point below.

THE POLARITIES OF HUMAN EXISTENCE

Our recognition of disorder in our lives and in the lives of our communities reflects our awareness of our own existence. We conduct dialogue with ourselves, we personalize our individualities and we may even recognize a certain internal confusion, 'I' struggling against 'myself'. In a crucial passage in his letter to Rome, Paul comments (but it could have been any one of us):

> I do not understand what I do. For what I want to do I do not do, but what I hate I do . . . As it is, it is no longer I myself who do it, but it is sin living in me . . . For I have the desire to do what is good, but I cannot carry it out.
>
> (Rom. 7.15–18)

What every individual has is an individual existence which he is able to monitor, to assess, to approve of or to disapprove of, in the light of such insights on the human existence as he might have. And he then has the potentiality for change, to struggle to bring that individual existence more into conformity with what is perceived to be appropriate. This potentiality appears to be exclusive to humanity. It is clearly not a potentiality available to the world of rocks and earth and water, nor to the world of vegetation. Nor does conscious struggle to attain some 'better' condition appear to be the concern of the animal world.

The human struggle may, of course, in some individuals, be only minimal. In the example of Paul, and in the case of Gautama, the Buddha, the struggle may be of epic proportions. But that struggle to realize a genuine potentiality inevitably encounters what Macquarrie has called 'the polarities of existence'. These polarities reflect the tensions of the human predicament, the conflicting parameters within which, somehow, the potential may be realized. He identifies four such polarities:[7]

The Polarities of Possibility and Facticity

The human mind can conceive of personal possibilities, actions, moral decisions, plans for personal development, plans for better relationships with others. But these possibilities are limited by the hard and limiting facts of the individual existence. There are issues of age, and of inherited intelligence, of education, of the ability actually to manipulate the agencies set up by the State and the Church and society to make personal choice more easy.

In conflict situations, in a famine situation, life may consist solely of the search for safety, for the basic needs of existence, with no room at all for implementing any programme of change, however theoretically possible that might be. In many parts of the world the poor may simply be defined as those who have no choices. The theoretical possibilities might be there, but the facts of the individual existence make the possibilities simply irrelevant:

No one can be sure whether the harvest will be good or bad: no one can be sure who will be alive this time next year, or even next week . . . In circumstances like this, no one can feel that man is the

8

master of his environment: nature may have a grand continuing design, but a man's life is filled with discontinuities. No peasant thinks in terms of five-year plans.[8]

At the level of the community, and even of the world community, the same conflict between possibility and facticity occurs. In the face of famine conditions in parts of Africa and Asia (The Sudan, Ethiopia, Mozambique, Bangladesh) in the 1980s, *Newsweek* magazine in an article entitled 'Feast and Famine' reported, 'The world is swimming in nearly 400 million tons of surplus grain . . . For the first time in history, there is more than enough food . . .', but had then to add a further comment: '. . . by World Bank estimates some 730 million people – one out of seven in the world population – do not get enough calories to live an "active working life"'.[9]

The Polarities of Rationality and Irrationality

On the one hand we distinguish between rational and irrational behaviour, and theoretically assume a will to act rationally. But there appear to be powers, influences, which override the rational, sometimes for the good, as when an individual sacrifices his own life in a vain attempt to save another life, sometimes for the worse, as when out of frustration minority groups give way to mass violence, knowing that what is being attacked is not, in fact, the actual cause of their frustrations. Or as when a wife protects her husband, knowing him to be a rapist, and aware of the enormous harm being done to the community by her refusal to betray her husband.

The Polarities of Community and Individuality

We have been created for community. The creation statement of Genesis 2.18, 'It is not good for the man to be alone,' is a profound comment on human nature. To be human is to be gregarious. But community introduces a conflict with our individuality. What is required by the community may well be opposed to what we desire for ourselves. The community demands our time and, in some sense, our loyalty. At the first level of community is the family, and the demands of a spouse – of a spouse who is disadvantaged in some way, for example – limit the freedom of choice open to the entire family. Even more is this true of the wider community, so that it sometimes appears that within the effective and integrated community there is little room for individual initiative at all.

The Polarities of Responsibility and Impotence

The concept of responsibility necessarily invokes some perception of conscience. The conscience is directly related to the form of intra-personal dialogue, the self-critique, to which reference has already been made. Somehow we do all have a self-perception, a view of ourselves both as we are and as we would wish to be. It is out of this self-perception that responsibility somehow emerges: a refusal to ignore a feature of life which seems to demand change, a determination to take such action as will bring about change. But this determination then encounters its relative impotence.

In Addis Ababa in the 1970s there was only the one hospital for the mentally sick in all Ethiopia, a country nearly twice the size of Texas and five times the size of the United Kingdom, and with a population of more than thirty million people. All over the country the mentally sick were untreated. If they became violent the common treatment was to tie the sick person to the centre-pole of his hut, and there he lived out his life. In the world as a whole there were sufficient doctors and nurses and financial resources to improve the situation beyond all recognition. That was the potentiality in response to my sense of responsibility. The facticity was that doctors were not prepared to work in the primitive conditions then prevalent in much of interior Ethiopia, and the facticity of the situation then led to *impotence*.

Indeed, the four polarities identified by Macquarrie combine to identify a network of opposites whose manifold tensions determine the actual nature of human *dukkha*.

SUPERFICIAL RESPONSES TO HUMAN *DUKKHA*

John 9.1–3: The Man who was Born Blind

The purpose of the pericope is to provide an illustration for John's presentation of Jesus as the light of the world, and of the conflict between Jesus and the Pharisees who consistently rejected the light. But in presenting the case of the man born blind John includes, in passing, a fragment of dialogue which illustrates the contemporary explanation of apparent *dukkha*:

> 'Rabbi, who sinned, this man or his parents, that he was born blind?'
> 'Neither this man nor his parents . . .'

That is to say, the man was not born blind as a punishment for the sins of his parents (appeal was made by the rabbis to Exod. 20.5 in support of such a view). Nor was he born blind because of his own prenatal sin.

However, we would be quite wrong to suppose that Jesus simply dismissed any relationship at all between human suffering and human sin. Commenting on the earlier healing recorded in John 5, Raymond E. Brown writes: 'Elsewhere Jesus does not accept the thesis that because a man was sick or suffering, it was a sign that he had committed sin (John ix.3; Luke xiii. 1–5). Nevertheless, on a more general scale he does indicate a connection between sin and suffering . . .'[10]

Rudolf Schnackenburg expresses the point concisely, pointing out that Jesus 'goes against the view widespread in Judaism that there was a necessary connection between illness and sin'.[11] There is no necessary connection between an individual's particular suffering and that individual's particular sin, nor any other individual's particular sin. But this does not of itself deny a more general relationship between sin and suffering.

Luke 13.1–5: Two Major Tragedies

Although the details of the two tragedies alluded to in this passage are not known to us, the main facts are reasonably clear.[12] In the first, an unspecified number of Galileans, probably at Passover (the only religious festival where Jews slaughtered their own sacrificial animals), had been killed on the orders of Pilate. The act was clearly perceived as peculiarly horrific, human blood being, perhaps literally, mixed with the animal blood of the sacrifices. Jesus then added a second example of exemplary and apparently inexplicable suffering, the occasion when eighteen men were crushed to death by the collapse of a 'tower' at Siloam.

We know that Pilate had an aqueduct constructed to carry water from Gihon to the city, and it is possible that the tower formed part of that system. It has been suggested that the construction was improperly financed from the temple tax,[13] and that in Jerusalem there was a view that those who were crushed by the tower were under the judgement of God for participating in what was an act of impiety.

The two questions asked by Jesus, 'Do you think that these Galileans were worse sinners . . .' and ' . . . do you think they were more guilty . . .?', are more than rhetorical; they reflect a contemporary rationalization. An extraordinary death demanded an extraordinary explanation, and one was found. The event described by Jesus' audience depicted a horrific death. The example added by Jesus takes the case inferred one step further, by at least providing a basis for the argument that a horrific punishment must imply a horrific sin. The argument is rejected. Death of some kind, more or less horrific, awaits everyone. And what, therefore, is required of everyone (and not merely of the gross sinner) is repentance.

Proverbs 3.9–10: A Prosperity Theology

This response to the problem posed by *dukkha* has found widespread acceptance in the rampant materialism of the last two decades of the twentieth century. At this point it is sufficient to note merely the salient points of the theology of prosperity.

A clear base to the theology is found in a number of isolated Old Testament texts:

> Honour the Lord with your wealth,
>   with the firstfruits of all your crops;
> then your barns will be filled to overflowing,
>   and your vats will brim over with new wine.
>   (Prov. 3.9–10)

But remember the Lord your God, for it is he who gives you the ability to produce wealth, and so confirms his covenant, which he swore to your forefathers, as it is today.

                    (Deut. 8.18)

. . . when you and your children return to the Lord your God and obey him with all your heart and with all your soul . . . then the Lord your God will restore your fortunes and have compassion on you . . . He will bring you to the land that belonged to your fathers, and you will take possession of it. He will make you more prosperous . . .

(Deut. 30.2–5)

And there are similar passages in the New Testament. For example:

Whoever sows sparingly will also reap sparingly, and whoever sows generously will also reap generously . . . Now he who supplies seed to the sower and bread for food will also supply and increase your store of seed and will enlarge the harvest of your righteousness. You will be made rich in every way so that you can be generous on every occasion . . .

(2 Cor. 9.6–11)

Of the doctrine that material, physical and spiritual prosperity for the individual are in precise proportion to that individual's obedience to God,[14] the first thing to be said is that it is demonstrably untrue. What is most striking is the fact that the passage taken from 2 Corinthians is set in the immediate context of an appeal on behalf of the poor Christians of Jerusalem. And that the letter itself is written by the man who confesses, 'I have laboured and toiled and have often gone without sleep; I have known hunger and thirst and have often gone without food; I have been cold and naked' (2 Cor. 11.27).

The fact is that faith as it is perceived in so pivotal a passage as Hebrews 11 is as likely to result in a violent death by wild beasts or burning flames (cf. vv. 33–4), torture, jeers, flogging, chains, and imprisonment, persecution and exile (vv. 35–8), as in an enhanced bank balance or perfect health.

This chapter has set the agenda for the book. Life is characterized by *dukkha*, the general unsatisfactoriness of life. Human existence is marked by an enormous disorder, and yet we demand that life should make sense. Within the apparent boundaries of the human existence it is impossible to make sense of life. Existentialism formally accepts the meaninglessness of life, and in its more extreme form, nihilism, denies the *reality* of anything at all. For the nihilist there are no answers to the fundamental questions that we ask about life. We are the chance products of the evolutionary process, and neither within the limitations of our own world nor in the vast spaces of the universe will any meaning be found. Jean-Paul Sartre dismissed God from the universe, and as he himself commented, '. . . there disappears with him all possibility of finding values in an intelligible heaven'.[15]

It can be argued that the world's religions take *dukkha* as a starting-point, and set about offering, more or less formally, an explanation of the origin or source of *dukkha*, and a way of restoring order to human existence. We turn now to a consideration of religion.

2 Religions in Conflict [1]

DEFINING 'RELIGION'

Although we feel that we know intuitively what we mean by religion, it is less easy to find a definition which meets with general approval.[2] A. N. Whitehead's is clearly a philosophical definition: 'religion is what the individual does with his own solitariness' – a definition which contrasts nicely with the popular perception that religion is going to church. In agreement with the popular perception, Emile Durkheim commented that religion is 'an eminently collective thing'. E. Tylor saw religion as 'The belief in Spiritual Beings', but by its very conciseness this definition seems to ignore entirely what E. J. Sharpe calls the dual aspect of religion,[3] the recognition that religion involves inward convictions and dependent outward practices.

A. Menzies understands religion as 'the worship of higher powers from a sense of need', and while his recognition of the relationship between human inadequacy and religion is obviously important, 'worship' (admittedly difficult to define – 'the appropriate response to an awareness of God', perhaps?) imports into religion what is not, in fact, necessarily there: god or the gods.

Our difficulty in defining the term 'religion' is in some sense related to Sharpe's own observation: 'It is all too easily forgotten by some western students that many languages simply do not have an equivalent of the word "religion" in their vocabulary. "Law", "duty", "custom", "worship", "spiritual discipline", "the way", they know; "religion" they do not.'[4]

Definitions may be classified as primarily tactical or as primarily defining. The former category would include Karl Marx's famous identification of religion as 'the opium of the people'. Tactical definitions are adopted usually for reasons of polemic. Those definitions which are genuinely defining are of value as much through their power to exclude as through their power positively to identify the members of a class.

The definition I use here is both tactical and defining. It is a definition which can be used to further the argument of the

15

chapter. But it is also a definition which allows us to include under the term 'religion' those entities we intuitively recognize as religions, while excluding entities of whose nature we are, through the otherwise nebulous significance of the term 'religion', uncertain:

A religion is any coherent philosophical system which attempts to answer the fundamental questions. The fundamental questions fall into three sequences:
Who am I,[5] Where did I come from, Where am I going to, Why; Who are you, Where did you come from, Where are you going to, Why; What is this world, Where did it come from, Where is it going to, Why.

It is worth noting that the Second Vatican Council characterized religions in a very similar manner:

Men look to their religions for an answer to the unsolved riddles of human existence. The problems that weigh heavily on the hearts of men are the same today as in the ages past. What is man? What is the meaning and purpose of life? What is upright behavior, and what is sinful? Where does suffering originate, and what end does it serve? . . . And finally, what is the ultimate mystery, beyond human explanation, which embraces our entire existence, from which we take our origin and towards which we tend?[6]

The definition allows us to include within a single class those systems which are monotheistic (Judaism, Islam), those which are polytheistic (Hinduism? African Traditional Religion?), those which are agnostic (Confucianism, Hinayana Buddhism), and even those which are atheistic (Marxism). On the other hand economic systems such as capitalism are excluded: a capitalist might, presumably, be a Muslim, a Jew or a Christian.

What is at once apparent is that the answers offered by the world's religions to the fundamental questions are strikingly different. Marxism sees humanity as the mere chance product of the process of evolution. Buddhism denies any meaning to *individual* existence at all. One school of Hinduism would identify humanity with 'god'. Islam sees man as having a tendency to do ill, but as capable of doing what is right, needing only the revelation that came through Muhammad to enable him to evade sin and to do what is right. Judaism would generally agree, offering a

16

sophisticated doctrine of the two *yetzer,*[7] the *yetzer ha-ra'*, the evil nature, and the *yetzer ha-tov*, the good nature. Each is created by Yahweh, and in that sense the translation '*evil* spirit' is misleading: it is a spirit, sometimes associated directly with the Satan, that is opposed to the good spirit, but it is only that spirit that makes possible essentially human activities such as procreation. Torah-law is seen as the means of directing the two spirits into harmony with the will of God. Christianity, in contrast, sees humanity as fallen, and needing salvation, deliverance, not instruction. And it would be difficult to find any way of reconciling these conflicting understandings of the human predicament.

Arguably, the one feature common to all religions as defined here is that in responding to the fundamental questions at all they exhibit the assumption that life *should* make sense. The religious system, then, has as one of its tasks the formulation of a more or less systematic explanation of the human disorder, and a more or less holistic programme for human behaviour appropriate to the explanation, Sharpe's 'inward convictions' and 'outward practices'.

To anticipate the thinking of John Hick at this point, it is perhaps worth noting that he recognizes this common core to the world's religions:

> . . . the great world traditions are fundamentally alike in exhibiting a soteriological structure. That is to say, they are all concerned with salvation . . . Each begins by declaring that our ordinary human life is profoundly lacking and distorted. It is a 'fallen' life, immersed in the unreality of *maya* or pervaded by *dukkha,* sorrow and unsatisfactoriness.[8]

In other words, religions produce a theodicy, an explanation of apparently undeserved suffering, of the apparent randomness of life, of the human disorder.

What is deeply significant is that the analyses of *dukkha* that are presented, and the outward practices that are proposed, are not merely different, but are actually irreconcilably different from one another. Or, in terms of the fundamental questions, the fundamental answers offered to the questions are not mere echoes of one another but are clearly independent voices. Religions disagree with one another not merely in the peripheral issues, but in the core issues, in the very fundamentals of life.

17

Religions such as Hinduism and Buddhism resolve *dukkha* by removing both of the apparent boundaries to human existence, birth and death, to offer a cyclic model, where the present experience, if inexplicable in terms of the present, is readily explicable in terms of the past, and the future experience will, similarly, be determined by the present. *Dukkha* is to be explained by *karma,* a cosmic law which relates human behaviour to human destiny, which sees the end of each individual incarnation as accompanied by a balancing of the human account and the calculating of a residue, a 'balance carried forward', which explains the experiences of the next incarnation.

An atheistic religion such as Marxism (which is considered in some detail in Part Three) explains *dukkha* in terms of class struggle, in terms of a society which, under a cosmic law of dialectical materialism, moves and is moved inexorably towards the establishment of a human paradise on earth. The end product is to be the classless society in which government withers away, from which *superstitious* religion has been eliminated. For the Marxist there *is* meaning in human history, and suffering is not random. For Marx meaning was to be found in a philosophy of history, in sociology,[9] but what he founded was properly a religion.

Marx would certainly not have identified his movement as a religion, but some of his contemporaries were more clear-sighted. Pierre-Joseph Proudhon wrote to Marx begging him *not* to produce such a religion:

> With all my heart I welcome your idea of exposing all opinions to the light. Let us have decent and sincere polemics; let us give the world an example of learned and far-sighted tolerance. But simply because we are at the head of a movement, do not let us ourselves become the leaders of a new intolerance, let us not pose as the apostles of a new religion – even though this religion be the religion of logic, the religion of reason itself.[10]

Christian Science deals with the problem of *dukkha* by denying the reality of suffering, of death, of disease. Mary Baker Eddy propounded four fundamentals of her religion:
1. God is all.
2. God is good.
3. God, Spirit, being all, nothing is matter.

4. God, omnipotent Good, denies death, evil, sin, disease.[11]

The illusory material world in which pain is named must be denied by the real spiritual world from which pain is dismissed: 'The fact that pain cannot exist where there is no mortal mind to feel it, is a proof that this so-called mind makes its own pain, – that is, its own *belief* in pain.'[12]

A remarkable illustration is supplied by Mrs Eddy, of a child who has 'hurt her face by falling on the carpet'. The wise mother is to respond to the child's expression of pain: '"Oh, nonsense (no-sense material)! You're not hurt, so don't think you are." Presently the child forgets all about the accident and is at play again.'[13] Lurking in the background of the illustration is a genuine insight: that many children and some adults verbalize a pain that does not correspond to any physical hurt. But the example is of a child who has 'hurt her face'. According to Christian Science the lesion on the face has no necessary correlate in an experience of pain. In theory, it seems, if the child has broken her leg in a fall and the mother is able to convince the child that the leg is not hurting her, then the child will 'forget all about the accident and play again'.

A parallel approach to suffering occurs in the Hindu classic the Bhagavad Gita, 'The Song of the Lord'. Arjuna, the young prince, rides in his chariot between the two opposing armies preparing to engage in battle. It is civil war: his own people are there on both sides. He imagines the imminent carnage, and recoils from it. But the Lord Krishna explains the reality to him:

Why grieve for those for whom no grief is due? . . . There was never a time when I was not, nor thou, nor these princes were not: there will never be a time when we shall cease to be . . . Those external relations which bring cold and heat, pain and happiness, they come and go; they are not permanent. Endure them bravely, O Prince! The hero whose soul is unmoved by circumstance, who accepts pleasure and pain with equanimity, only he is fit for immortality . . . The spirit kills not, nor is It killed . . . weapons cleave It not, fire burns It not, water drenches It not, and wind dries It not.[14]

The Song ends with the battle in which both armies are effectively destroyed. The carnage envisaged by Arjuna occurs, but is interpreted as a mere event in a long succession of incarnations for everyone involved, a carnage made necessary by the duty of the prince to rule and of the warrior to kill and be killed, so that the spirit might move onward and upward to freedom. The suffering involved is unimportant, just one aspect of the illusory material world.

Buddhism, in its fundamental statement of the Four Royal Truths, identifies suffering as the consequence of desire, the desire for things, for experiences, but above all the desire for individuality: 'What then is the Holy Truth of the origination of ill? It is that craving which leads to rebirth, accompanied by delight and greed, seeking its delight now here, now there, i.e. craving for sensuous experience, craving to perpetuate oneself, craving for extinction.'[15]

Just as religions have different explanations of *dukkha,* so they offer different responses to it. Hinduism advocates the pursuit of caste duty (Arjuna is to lead his army into battle because that is the duty of a prince) so that the law of *karma* may operate favourably and the debit balance carried forward may be reduced, taking the individual nearer to the goal of deliverance, *moksha,* from the cycle of rebirth. Buddhism explains suffering as due to desire, and the escape from *dukkha* is then the extinction of desire through the observation of the Middle Way between asceticism on the one hand and hedonism on the other. Marxism explains the apparent disorder of life as due to the ongoing class struggle, and its resolution through the triumph of the proletariat, whose duty, then, is to struggle against capitalism, to foment revolution and so end the dialectical process by exhausting the class conflict on which it feeds. Christianity explains *dukkha* in terms of a cosmic fall, in terms of human disobedience, and the solution is found not in any human effort, since human sinfulness makes such action futile, but in the intervention of God in the incarnation, in the atonement, in a process of reconciliation to God. This in turn brings to an end the conflict between humanity and God, ends the personal disorder, and contributes to a reduction in the more general disorder of the cosmos.

SEVEN APPROACHES TO THE WORLD'S RELIGIONS

How then are we to understand the world's religions? Quite clearly for the Christian a tolerance of the beliefs of others, and a rejection of all attempts to impose religious beliefs or to deny access to religious knowledge to anyone, should provide a starting-point for any response to the question.

In a valuable book edited by Owen Thomas and published back in 1969,[16] with contributions from such focal figures as Ernst Troeltsch, Karl Barth, Emil Brunner, W. E. Hocking, Paul Tillich and Hans Küng, seven possible approaches to religion are outlined.

Truth-Falsehood

This is the view that one of the many religions is true and that all others are, necessarily, false. The expectation of those who hold to this view is then that when exposed to the truth other religions would wither away or that, at least, adherents of other religions would tend to abandon them and turn to the truth. Luther from the Reformation period would hold to this position.

Relativity

Religion is related to culture, so that while Christianity might be seen as appropriate to Europe, Hinduism would be the appropriate religion for India and Buddhism for South-east Asia. Truth is then simply 'truth-for-me', and a distinction is made between religious truth and other concepts of truth and falsehood. Troeltsch propounds essentially this view.

But we must ask whether religion is simply a *constituent* of culture or even a *product* of culture, or whether religion is, in fact, the *foundation* of culture or even the *source* of culture. The first position is not infrequently assumed by those who take the relativistic position on religion. The dispersion of Christianity, for example, into every continent, so that what began in a Jewish context is happily settled in Africa, in South America and in Asia *with the fundamentals unchanged*, and the subsequent creation of new cultures (specifically *not* one new culture), suggests that the supposed existence of an ethnically determined preference for a particular religious truth-package cannot be demonstrated.

Essence

There is a plausible and widely held belief that all religions share some common essence. Indeed, the very fact that we can identify a class of 'religions' would seem to imply such a common content.

21

However, it has proved extremely difficult to discover what this supposed common element is. Religion is popularly supposed to involve a belief in God, but certainly in its earliest form Buddhism had nothing to say about the gods, either in its analysis of the human predicament or in its programme for human behaviour. Confucius, too, seemed to offer an ethical system which served as a religion but without any necessary reference to gods at all. And if Marxism is allowed to be a religion then we have one religion which is overtly atheistic and not merely agnostic. The philosopher Friedrich Schleiermacher and the theologian John Hick would take the common essence view of religion.

Development-Fulfilment

Religion is seen as part of an evolutionary process, from the 'lower' religions, such as African Traditional Religion, to the 'higher' religions, such as Christianity. Expressed in this way the sheer paternalism of the theory becomes apparent. It is difficult to identify a scientific method within which such terms as 'higher religion' and 'lower religion' could be given objective meaning.

But there is a further difficulty. The massive labours of Sir James Frazer notwithstanding,[17] it is not clear from history that there is any demonstrable unidirectional process of development in religions at all. In matters of religion it is not at all clear that the new is the better. And certainly there is no way of demonstrating that the earlier religions prepared the way for the later religions in the normal sense of any evolutionary process. Indeed those religions which stand in the closest evolutionary relationship to one another (Judaism, Christianity and Islam, or Hinduism, Buddhism and Sikkhism) would appear to display higher inter-religion barriers than those which have few such historical links (African Traditional Religion and Islam, for example).

Salvation History

All religions are seen as in some measure repositories of the grace of God. Christianity is 'the historically visible vanguard or explicit expression of that salvation which is implicit or hidden in the other religions'.[18] But the other religions are also spheres of the divine initiative. God cannot be shut out from any part of his world. The history of the human race is a salvation history, and from that central concern of God for the salvation of humanity no race is excluded.

From this viewpoint the task of mission is not to replace one religion by another, but to engage in dialogue with the religions to enable their adherents to understand their true situation, and yet to understand it from within their own religions. This is the view held by Karl Rahner, who sees the sincere followers of other religions as 'anonymous Christians', and of Hans Küng, although he rejects Rahner's notion of anonymous Christianity.

It is no accident that these two are Roman Catholic theologians, since the *Heilsgeschichte,* salvation history, approach to the world's religions was sanctioned by the Second Vatican Council.

Secularization

A more nearly contemporary view of religion sets an agenda which will effectively liberate humanity from its preoccupation with religion, so as to devote all its energies to this present world, to resolving its problems here and now, rather than in postponing solutions to some other existence or to some eschatologically determined future.

The Christian, then, should be concerned not to transfer the adherents of other religions into the Christian religion, but to set them free from all religious concerns. A Hindu would then be set free from his concerns with the samsaric cycle of birth and rebirth, would cease worrying about his *karma*, and would be free to concentrate on the present for the sake of the present life.

Revelation–Sin

This view of religions can be variously nuanced, but in its essence it sees God revealing himself to humanity through his creation, and through human conscience, so that man becomes God-conscious. However, the response to that God-consciousness is determined by an essential human sinfulness, an inner disorder. A religion of sorts is produced, but it always falls short of what the revelation demands. In fact the religion is in some sense an actual denial of the revelation.

The position is most clearly expressed in Romans 1.25: 'They exchanged the truth of God for a lie, and worshipped and served created things rather than the Creator . . .'

William Temple, in his *Readings in St John's Gospel*,[19] draws attention to the essential role of the Holy Spirit in bringing humanity to an adequate understanding of the predicament:

> The Comforter will bring evidence to prove the world wrong in certain respects . . . [namely] the three matters most important to man's life, sin, righteousness and judgement . . .
> . . . The world has to learn that its very conception of these things is all wrong. If it tries to avoid sin or to seek righteousness, it does not avoid or seek the right things; if it fears or prepares for judgement, it does not fear or prepare for the right thing.[20]

Religion, then, is a futile human construct, and not a vehicle of salvation.[21] Indeed Barth (and he together with Luther would be considered the primary exponents of this view) would identify a Christian 'religion' which, equally, is a human and futile construct, and would insist that religion must always be distinguished from the divine self-revelation, and that salvation comes through that revelation and through that revelation alone.

3 The Christian World-View

SOURCES OF THE CHRISTIAN WORLD-VIEW

The world-view of the individual, that is to say the individual's understanding of the world and his relationship to it, his behaviour in it, is in large measure determined by that individual's religion. Christian mission, however that may be defined, is clearly the consequence of a particular way of viewing the world. If this is the case, then the actual process of forming a world-view demands careful investigation.

It would be simplistic to suggest that anyone ever formulated a world-view in an entirely disinterested way. Since human nature is already disordered, and since even redeemed human nature is still part of the 'now-and-not-yet' of salvation, a process that has begun but is by no means complete, our individual world-views are in varying measure flawed.

The Christian's world-view will be formed out of three major components: his own existential awareness of the world, his understanding of Scripture, and his own self-interest. We must distinguish at this point between what is professed and what is evidenced praxeologically. Although hesitant to endorse Bonino's famed maxim that action is itself the truth,[1] we are concerned here not with a theoretical ideal, but with the reality, and the real world-view of an individual is clearly evidenced by his praxis. Millions of Christians profess a concern for those they would theoretically designate the 'lost', and the theoretical world-view associated with that concern should lead to their taking steps to reach those lost. That the vast majority take no such steps is because the theoretical world-view is seriously modified by self-interest, producing a praxeologically determinative world-view which would probably not be verbalized by the individual concerned, nor, indeed, acknowledged if it were verbalized by another person. However, since missiology is a praxis and not a theory, it must be with the praxeologically determinative world-view that we are concerned, and with no other.

The Existential Contribution to the Formation of a World-View

By this we mean that contribution to the world-view which originates in our experience within the world. Depending on the area of the world where we live, we will have some idea of the seasonal variations of summer and winter, of dry season and rainy season, of monsoon, of cold and heat. There will be a knowledge of sun, moon, stars, possibly also of eclipses and other celestial phenomena. There will be an awareness of good health and of disease. The basic facts of life will be known: birth and death, procreation. There will be some parallel knowledge of animals, and of vegetation.

There will also be a pragmatic experience of one or more cultures: that houses are built in *this* way, and that shoes are worn on *these* occasions, that greetings are exchanged, hands shaken, food offered, and so on. Inevitably, what appears to be *normal* becomes invested with a moral quality: normal actions become *right* actions. The unusual, the abnormal, may be seen as actually *wrong*.

And there will be the experience of the abnormal, the inexplicable, the frightening, the threatening. Thunder and lightning, possibly. Physical or mental disorder. Famine. A Holocaust-type situation. Religion.

These experiences lie in the first stage of the development of a world-view, the stage of *observation*, and eventually give birth to the second stage, the stage of *interrogation*, the stage which is characterized by the interrogatives Why? and How? and Who? and When?

The Contribution of Authoritative Texts to the Formation of a World-View

Since our working definition of religion is deliberately directed towards the task of answering fundamental (and existential) questions, it is to be expected that the special literatures of the world religions would provide at least some answers to the interrogatives prompted by human existence.

And this is, indeed, what we find. The *Bhagavad Gita* for Hindus, *Das Kapital* for Marxists, the Bible for Christians, the Qur'an for Muslims, *Science and Health with Key to the Scriptures* for Christian Scientists, *The Book of Mormon*, for Mormons, the *Tipitaka*, for Buddhists, all provide more or less comprehensive answers to the interrogatives raised by existential thinking, and move the thinker on towards the construction of a consistent world-view. There may be an account of beginnings: of creation. There may be an account of some ultimate consummation. There will certainly be some rationale for a particular lifestyle.

At this point we simply note the crucial issue of hermeneutics, the science of interpreting text. For the fact is that two people approaching a single text will none the less be capable of very different perceptions of the 'meaning' (whatever that means).[2] We shall return to the issue below.

The Contribution of Self-Interest to the Formation of a World-View

Although theoretically there should be a harmonious relationship between the world-view appropriate to an understanding of those texts taken to be authoritative by any individual, and the actual world-view evidenced in the life of that individual, there is always a certain discrepancy between the two. This discrepancy is due partly to the polarities identified by John Macquarrie,[3] but at least partly to self-interest. The Muslim may be required to give as *zakat* a percentage of his income, but self-interest may dictate that a lesser amount is in fact given. The Christian may be supposed to believe in hell, but concern for unconverted relatives may mean a rejection of that particular doctrine. A Marxist may be expected to demonstrate solidarity with the working classes across national boundaries, but a very bourgeois nationalism may form part of the actual Marxist world-view.[4]

THE INTERPRETATION OF TEXTS

Before we can advance towards the construction of a Christian world-view we must examine the issue of the interpretation of texts.

Meaning and Significance

This fundamental issue is discussed in some detail in *Linguistics and Biblical Interpretation*.[5] We begin by distinguishing between *meaning* and *significance*. There has been lengthy discussion of

27

the locus of meaning in a text. There are at least three obvious loci: in the text itself, in the reader of the text, or in the author of the text. The objective reality is the text itself, but the text is no more than marks on paper until a mind somewhere encounters them and processes them. Meaning is clearly a function of mind.

But whose mind? Any text begins with an author (the text might be an *oral* text) and is perceived by an auditor. It is clearly appropriate to think of both author and auditor as having some relationship to the meaning of the text. The view that the meaning perceived by the auditor may be independent of any meaning *intended* by the author effectively dismisses the author from the communication process. The author dies in the very act of producing a text.

The meaning of a text is the meaning, the sense, intended by the author. Here we recognize that the level of linguistic competence of an author might lead to ambiguity in the text, or even to an apparent contradiction between what any individual statement in the text might appear to mean and what the author clearly intended to convey.[6] We therefore make use of the term 'discourse meaning', as a reminder that meaning is not to be found in individual lexical items, nor in sentences taken in isolation, but in the larger discourse. The discourse meaning of any text is a singular meaning.[7]

But a discourse may also have 'significance' for the reader, what might be termed 'meaning-for-him'. Although the discourse has a single meaning, it has an indeterminate number of significances.[8] However, these various significances must all be related to the singular meaning of the text. They do not have an existence independent of the meaning. Thus the first task of any reader in a search for the significance of any text is the discerning of the discourse meaning.

The Presupposition Pool

In approaching any biblical text we must be aware of its historical and sociological context. It is that context which provides the 'presupposition pool' for the author. The presupposition pool is that pool of knowledge, experience and understanding assumed by the author to be appropriate to the anticipated readership. H. P.

Grice identified a number of maxims which exemplify the normal structure of conversation, among which is the 'Maxim of Quantity', that the communication should be as informative as is required and no more.[9] It is important to supply the reader with enough information so that he is able to understand the communication, but not to tell the reader what he already knows. Inevitably in the case of a text of some antiquity the presupposition pool appropriate to new readers will be very different from that of the original readers, so that what was once entirely clear is now opaque. This is certainly true, for example, of the discussion of head-covering in 1 Corinthians 11.1–16. There is considerable danger of the modern reader approaching an ancient text and assuming for the text a presupposition pool appropriate to the twentieth century, and interpreting the text accordingly.

It is of importance, here, to recognize that the writers of biblical text wrote into a world to which the contemporary scientific outlook was totally unknown. Due humility requires us to add that science is *still* in its infancy, and Bible scholars should not accord to science an infallibility, or even an objectivity, that the scientists themselves have long since abandoned. But those early writers could not take into account theories of the nature of time and space which would not even begin to be enunciated for a millennium and more. To be a timeless word, the word was necessarily an unscientific word; not that it contradicts science, but that it stands aside from what is in reality an ongoing art form. The biblical writers wrote from and into a presupposition pool, and it was from that pool that they had to dredge comprehension, a comprehension that would be effectively retained even over centuries.

Literary Genre

It is vital to identify literary genre before advancing to interpretation. Revelation 12 presents an account of a drama featuring a pregnant woman, a baby, a dragon and the *angeloi*, divine messengers. There is a war, there is a flood which is spewed out of the mouth of the dragon, a flood which is evaded by the woman who is miraculously provided with wings so that she can escape to a desert. Act One of the drama ends with the frustrated dragon left standing, expectantly, on the shores of the sea created from the flood. It is in vain that we ask where the sea was situated: it was situated nowhere other than in the remarkable allegory of which it is part. And it is as allegory that the drama must be interpreted, not as history.

The Question of Reliability

The presuppositions of any exegete determine in good measure the conclusions he will draw from the study of a text. If it is assumed that the Nicodemus pericope in John 3 is unhistorical,[10] then the interpretation of the pericope will develop appropriately. If it is assumed that genuine predictions of future events do not occur, then that presupposition will influence the understanding of, say, Daniel 11 – 12.[11] My own understanding starts from an assumption of the reliability of Scripture *properly interpreted.*

A CHRISTIAN WORLD-VIEW

Setting on one side, so far as is possible, the third contribution to the formation of a world-view, self-interest, we consider a world-view that might emerge from an existential awareness of the world and an understanding of Scripture informed by the principles discussed on pp. 27–30 above.

An awareness of the world probably precedes self-awareness in a baby. There is a real world of which I become aware through its impact on my senses. This world is not eternal, is not incidental or accidental, but is a purposeful creation. This perception does not originate with humanity, but is revealed to humanity by the Creator.

The Creator stands self-revealed as one who communicates with his creation, not as an absentee clock-maker. Through chosen individuals (Abram, Moses, David, Isaiah, Jeremiah, Paul), he has shown himself in such forensic terms as justice, judgement, righteousness and sin, and in sociological terms such as father and husband, friend and brother. He indicates his relationship with humanity in a moving vocabulary of words: compassion, love, mercy, grace, yearning, longing, tenderness.

The vocabulary reveals a tension between the Creator and the created, and in created humanity between the 'would' and the 'cannot'. A relationship between God and humanity is there in potential, but it is not regularly actualized. The human disability (which is all-pervasive) makes the relationship at best tenuous.

Humanity is perceived as a complex blend of individuality and relationship. Man and woman in a sexually determined way provide a significant unit, the family (although not by any means identical with the concept 'family' in much of Europe and North America), from which the larger and more complex assemblages of society are constructed.

Existentially, we are aware of tensions between individuals and between the societal constructs: the tensions are evidenced by disagreements, arguments, actual conflict, murder, and, on the larger scale, war. These tensions are explained in terms of a fall from an original condition of harmony, a fall characterized by disobedience to God. The text which describes the fall is significantly (from the linguistic standpoint) placed at the head of the scriptural record, subordinate only to the description of the drama of creation. It displays some of the characteristics of allegory: there is a man and a woman, and there is a garden, but there is also a 'serpent' which talks. Elsewhere the allegory is partly explained by the identification of the 'serpent' as 'the devil, or Satan' (Rev. 20.2), an Adversary who also is part of the world-view of the Christian.

The disorder that is evident throughout human society is then perceived as having its roots in a 'fall', and as being presently fomented by the Adversary, the Satan. But this explanation of the human disorder is extended to a secondary disorder observed in nature. Nature itself appears to be pitted against humanity. Weeds grow readily, but vegetables grow only if carefully tended. The seasons produce the right conditions for ensuring a harvest, but not always: there is drought and storm, flood, pestilence. This is no part of the original intention of the Creator, but is an alien disorder consequent upon the same human 'fall'.

For human existence there are two apparent termini: birth and death. Between the two termini humanity lives out a brief existence in a permanent condition of uncertainty, and death itself visits him in any one of a number of forms, many of them painful and frightening. The Scripture takes our world-view beyond one of the termini, to show a continuing life after death, at the beginning of which stands judgement, a judgement at the hands of a Judge who has a total knowledge of our lives, from whom nothing can be concealed. The charges raised against us appear to be capable of reduction to the one charge of living 'un-humanly', other than as the Creator intended. And the outcome of the judgement is eternal life or an equally eternal death, following from a verdict of acquittal or a verdict of guilty.

The forensic element of the relationship between God and his creation is notable. And since God makes demands of us, whether through the Old Covenant Torah, or through the New Covenant teaching of Jesus (equally summarized in the same terms, 'be holy, because I am holy', Lev. 11.44; 1 Pet. 1.16), without some way of dealing with human failure a verdict of guilty appears inevitable. In the Old Covenant a complex pattern of animal sacrifice was provided which in some sense provisionally covered sin, but this pattern is now explained by and superseded by the death of Jesus of Nazareth, affirmed as God incarnate through his resurrection. As God incarnate this one death merits infinite efficacy, and is the one provision made by the Creator for resolving the disorder which pervades all humanity and all creation.

The Christian world-view recognizes the existence of other orders of beings beyond those accessible to the physical senses: the messengers of God, the Satan and his messengers. And the two worlds are in constant intercommunion, although in some humans the perception of the spiritual has, for whatever reason, been all but extinguished.

It is the ultimate purpose of the Creator to bring the present mode of existence to an end, and to bring about the goal of the original creation: a community enjoying God. It is this which is the ultimate goal of history, this which should be the ultimate concern of the individual. Life does not consist in present material affluence, but in being rich towards God (Luke 12.15,21).

THE QUESTION OF TRUTH [12]

Our admittedly brief introduction to the conflicting analyses of the human predicament by the world religions, and the similarly brief characterization of the uniqueness claims of Christianity through its world-view, raises the whole question of truth. The conflict between the explanations of *dukkha,* the solutions offered to *dukkha,* and even between the supposed *histories* of the religions is admitted. But does it necessarily follow that we are forced into the position of recognizing that one or other of the religious analyses is correct, and the others incorrect, or, less belligerently, that one or the other is more or less correct, and the others more or less incorrect?

If we take the issue more generally, when Christianity claims that Jesus died on the cross, and Islam, through its understanding of Sura 4, 'Women', insists that Jesus was not crucified,[13] or when Judaism denies that Jesus was Messiah and offers to the Christian salvation through the Noahic covenant,[14] must we make a choice between the alternatives? Is truth in matters religious in some way different from truth in, say, matters of history, and is there even such a thing as 'religious history'?

The term 'history' is itself polysemous. Karl Jaspers discerns six distinct meanings of historicity:[15]

1. The infinity of all things from all times.

2. History, as presented through documentation, an endless recording of recollections from an infinite source.

3. Those events, matters, which are of concern to humanity in understanding and explaining itself, whether individually, nationally or globally.

4. Existential history: the individual's own perception of his relationship with external event.

5. The history of the universe, of space and time, even that part which is quite independent of humanity and so not open to his observation or part of his record.

6. Sacred history. Of this Jaspers comments, 'Unlike all other historic phenomena, this cannot be attested as reality. Its witnesses can only say, "We believed". The claim put forth in its behalf differs from any other.'[16]

Is history, in the sense of a certain and objective record of past events, a myth? Can *any* past event be unequivocally established as 'true', or must we surrender any idea of a relationship between history and truth?

It is the case that the majority of propositions relating to history would be difficult to substantiate.[17] If we go back to John 9 and the account of the healing of the man born blind, we note the successive difficulties of establishing the facts of the case even in its original setting. Since *a priori* a man who was born blind cannot suddenly have his sight restored, this man cannot have been born blind. He himself says that he was. And his appearance is certainly very much like that of a man who is known to have been born blind. His parents agree that he is their son, and that he was born blind. But even so the proposition 'this man was born blind' has not been established.

And there is a further proposition: God does not hear the prayers of a sinner. And yet it appears that a prayer of Jesus on behalf of the man born blind has been answered. Since Jesus is (like everyone else?) a sinner, his prayer cannot have been answered. So again either the man was not born blind or he cannot now see. The third alternative, that Jesus was not, in fact, a sinner, is not given any consideration. Neither the simple historical proposition nor the theological proposition is capable of substantiation. Of course some propositions can be verified. The proposition that the man could see could be verified in fact: a simple test could be devised to show that he had sight.

Truth claims may helpfully be divided into two categories, those claims which are verifiable as fact and those claims which are verifiable only notionally. The proposition 'Christ died for our sins' (1 Cor. 15.3) has two parts to it. The first part, 'Christ died', is in principle verifiable as fact; that is to say we could, in principle, go back to the first century to observe the event. The second part is verifiable only notionally. We cannot produce a verification programme from within generally admitted human limitations which would show that Christ died 'for our sins'.

If the differences between the world's religions consisted entirely of propositions which could only be verified notionally, then we might well be forced into admitting that truth is simply not available to us. But where the conflicting propositions are susceptible of verification as fact, at least in principle, then they cannot simply be reconciled to one another by labelling them 'religious truth'.

To return to the issue of the crucifixion, Christianity has developed an entire theology based on the premise that Jesus of Nazareth, the Messiah, was crucified, died, was buried, and was raised to life again. Islam denies that he was crucified. In principle the two propositions could be subjected to a verification process. And only one could be found to correspond to concrete historical fact, only one could be true. And that 'truth' must be true for all observers, it must be true for everyone, for that is the meaning of truth. It is meaningless to suggest that both are 'religiously true'.

If this is so, then it follows that it is simply not possible to maintain the view that there is an underlying unity in religions. To quote John Kane, 'Detailed scholarly work in the history of religions has shown such facile assertions of unity to be without basis.'[18]

It does no credit to scholarship to do other than admit to the fundamental and irreducible contradictions that exist among the myriad propositions of the world's religions. Indeed, while academics may pretend to find unity among the religions, the committed members of the religions are quite clear in rejecting such spurious unity. Rabbi Forta, on behalf of Orthodox Judaism, says: 'At the most elemental level of all . . . Judaism and Christianity stand poles apart . . . Those who work with the community . . . must never lose sight of the unbridgeable chasm separating Judaism and Christianity at the very core of both belief systems.'[19] And in the same vein Seyyed Hossein Nasr writes:

> Islam does not accept the idea of incarnation or filial relationship. In its perspective Jesus . . . was a major prophet and spiritual pole of the whole Abrahamic tradition but not a god-man or the son of God. The Qur'an does not accept that he was crucified, but states that he was taken directly to heaven. This is the one irreducible 'fact' separating Christianity from Islam, a fact which is in reality placed there providentially to prevent a mingling of the two religions.[20]

4 The Problem of Particularity

THE PROBLEM STATED

Religion is not a modern phenomenon. Hinduism, through its Vedic literature, goes back at least three thousand years, and other traditional religions (African, South American Indian, Arab), have equally long pedigrees. Through these millennia the religions have tended to be ethnic: their adherents lived essentially in ignorance of the religions of the other peoples of the world.

The linguistic studies of Malcolm Guthrie[1] have provided us with a relatively clear view of the relationships between the various Bantu groups and their languages, and of their histories, taking us back two thousand years and more. And for most of that time the Bantu peoples of Africa had no knowledge of and no possibility of knowing about Christianity or its parent Judaism. Today, in the People's Republic of Mongolia there are no known Christians and no Christian missionaries. Throughout history the vast majority of humanity has known nothing of the particular teachings of the Judeo-Christian tradition which is supposed to offer the only valid world-view, the only valid way of looking at the present life and of preparing for the life still to come.

For the thinking person it is extremely difficult to maintain a belief in the uniqueness of the Christian way of salvation when confronted with the reality of religious pluralism and the implications of that pluralism. John Hick comments:

> Again, it is a fact evident to ordinary people (even though not always taken into account by theologians) that in the great majority of cases – say, 98 or 99 per cent – the religion in which a person believes and to which he adheres depends upon where he was born . . . Any credible religious faith must be able to make sense of this circumstance.[2]

Of course it is not difficult to identify individuals who have made the transition from one religion to another. However, this does not affect the general validity of Hick's observation. And if we

36

hold to the view of the sole salvific validity of Christianity (or, indeed, of any other religion), we are confronted with the question of the moral character of a God who allows for and even wills the birth of these myriads of individuals in such circumstances that through no fault of their own they must die without having had access to the way of salvation. The very terms used to designate the God of Christianity, loving, gracious, good, just, righteous, are necessarily called into question by the injustice which we can readily perceive. Granted that God has a universal salvific purpose, that purpose appears to have no apparent means of fulfilment in the real world.

The response to the problem has taken four forms. The first may be characterized as *inclusivist*, to find salvation *within* each religion, while allowing for some unique status for Christianity. This has tended to be the dominant Roman Catholic view since the Second Vatican Council, and is especially associated with the names of Karl Rahner and Hans Küng.

Secondly there is the *pluralistic* response, which suggests that there is, in fact, a common content to the world's religions and that each in its own way is salvific without any reference to Christianity at all. This has been the pathway taken by John Hick.

Thirdly there has been the reaffirmation of the traditional evangelical view: salvation *does* depend on an overt knowledge of Christ, myriads have *not* heard of him, and unless the Christian mission is furthered as a matter of urgency myriads more will join them in 'a lost eternity'.

A fourth view is that although salvation is not supplied *by* the non-Christian religions, still salvation may be found by those who are within them, through the threefold programme of an inward Logos illumination, general revelation, and the saving work of Christ.

JOHN HICK'S COPERNICAN REVOLUTION: PLURALISM

Hick has criticized traditional Christian thinking because it dogmatically placed Christianity at the centre of the universe of faiths[3] and located other religions in orbits around this 'sun', depending on their supposed closeness to Christianity. Thus Judaism would have a lower orbit than Islam, which would, however, be closer to the sun that is Christianity than Hinduism. Hick saw this as a Ptolemaic model. In its place he has proposed a succession of more and more refined models which in some sense parallel the Copernican revolution which transformed our understanding of our planetary system. His general critique of the traditional view of a unique Christianity is investigated in depth in two important books by Gavin D'Costa, *Theology and Religious Pluralism*[4] and *John Hick's Theology of Religions,*[5] and is conveniently summarized in Hick's own chapter, 'The Non-Absoluteness of Christianity', in *The Myth of Christian Uniqueness.*[6]

Whatever else may be accomplished by that chapter, Hick makes it quite clear that as a religion, as an exclusivist religion, and as an intolerant religion, Christianity has a history of which it cannot always be proud. It must be quite clear that whatever claims might be made for the uniqueness and superiority of Christianity, those claims cannot rest on the political history of so-called Christian nations, nor on the praxis of state churches, nor even on the suggestion that Christianity produces people of great moral stature.[7] It may indeed do so, but some 'Christians' have lived debased lives, and many non-Christians have lived morally elevated lives.

Hick makes it clear that as he has himself rejected the inclusivist position and moved across to the pluralistic position, so he expects this to be, ultimately, the position taken by the Church of the future.

The obvious first move was to replace Christianity as the centre of the system, to place God at the centre, and have Christianity join the system of circling planets. This certainly disposed of any absolute role for Christianity, but provided the system with a nucleus appropriate only to theistic, and arguably only to monotheistic, religions. This limitation has been removed to some extent by the substitution of a nebulous Absolute for the nuclear God, an Absolute which may be more or less accommodated to Hinduism and Buddhism as well as to the monotheistic religions. But this can be done only by speciously dismissing the objections of the Hindu or Buddhist, on the one hand by restating their respective theologies so as to conform to the proposed common Absolute, and on the other hand by gratuitously insisting their incompetence as exponents of their own religious systems.[8]

But even the proposition that there is a common 'god' at the centre of the theistic religions is not without objection. Certainly there is a strong case to be stated for the proposition that the God of the Old Testament and the God of the New Testament are one and the same, and a less strong case for the proposition that this is the same as Allah of the Qur'an. However, the question may be differently formulated and might then have a different answer. Is the 'god' of, say, Reform Judaism the same as the 'god' of New Testament Christianity, and is the 'god' of modern fundamentalist Shi'a Islam the same as either? Or yet again, was the 'god' of the rabbinic Judaism of Jesus' day the same as the 'god' of the Old Testament?

To answer such questions it is not sufficient to point either to a common name (as in the case of Judaism and Christianity) or a supposed common descent (as in the case of Judaism and Islam), nor even to some common denominator of the expression 'god' (e.g., that he is, in each case, seen as the creator of the universe).

The questions can only adequately be answered by a full consideration of the *referent*[9] of each term. And when we consider the three referents ('god' in Islam, in Judaism and in Christianity) it is by no means clear that they are, in fact, one and the same. The issue is, of course, the place given to Jesus[10] in each case. Judaism denies that Jesus is in any sense the Messiah. Islam accepts that he is Messiah, but denies that he is Son of God. Neither gives to Jesus any place in the godhead. Neither would accept a sound New Testament designation of God as 'the God and Father of our Lord Jesus Christ' (Eph. 1.3). In fact, in each of the three monotheistic religions[11] there is a developed theology based on authoritative texts which so defines the godhead as to make any attempt at constructing a common referent misplaced.[12]

This does not resolve the tension between the nature of the deities in, say, Christianity and Islam, the one trinitarian and the other uncompromisingly monotheistic. Hick has, therefore, moved to reinterpret trinitarian Christology in terms of an inspiration Christology.[13] Of this he admits:

An inspiration christology coheres better with some ways of understanding trinitarian language than with others. It does not require or support the notion of three divine persons . . . so that one could speak of the Father, the Son and the Holy Spirit as loving one another within the eternal family of the trinity, and of the Son coming down to earth to make atonement on behalf of human beings . . . An inspiration christology is, however, fully compatible with the conception of the trinity as affirming three distinguishable ways in which the one God is experienced as acting in relation to, and is accordingly known by, us – namely, as creator, redeemer, and inspirer.[14]

This appears to be a reformulation of the third-century heretical modalism of Sabellius.[15] This view was rejected by Chalcedon precisely because it does not do justice to the biblical evidence.

On this point Hick comments:

Atonement theory has also taken a number of forms, some cohering better than others with an inspiration christology and an economic or modal trinitarianism. As in the case of christology, the kind of atonement thinking most hospitable to religious pluralism is nearest to what appears to have been the teaching of Jesus himself.[16]

He goes on to quote as a source for what Jesus himself taught, the parable of the prodigal son, and observes that 'the father in the parable did not require a blood sacrifice to appease his sense of justice'.[17] The comment is simply unworthy of the weighty matter being discussed. It is precisely the cumulative weight of the teaching of Jesus that drove the early Church to the kind of exclusivist theology it ultimately recognized. To extract one strand of that teaching, to identify that as 'the teaching of Jesus himself' as though there is some objective way of showing that *this* and no other was the authentic teaching of Jesus, is a prostitution of scholarship. Indeed the weakest part of Hick's presentation of his pluralism is that part which treats of a biblical basis. His phenomenology is convincing, but his exegesis is not.

INCLUSIVISM: RAHNER AND KÜNG

If the pluralist approach to the problem posed by the continuing pluralism in religions is unsatisfactory in so far as it is unable to provide any convincing demonstration of some common focus (other than the recognition of *dukkha*) for them, is it possible that some legitimacy can be given to those religions through the inclusivist approach? Inclusivism finds a modified and limited salvific value in the world's religions, while retaining in some sense the uniqueness of Christianity. This has increasingly become the position of the Roman Catholic Church and of its theologians, particularly of Karl Rahner and Hans Küng. We consider first of all the very important role played by the Second Vatican Council in legitimizing a move from the traditional *extra ecclesiam nulla salus*, 'no salvation outside of the Church', to a very much more open and pragmatic understanding of other religions.

The Second Vatican Council and Beyond[18]

The second Vatican Council was held in Rome from 1962 to 1965, and produced a plethora of documents.[19] There are four conciliar documents with passages which relate to our theme. These are: *Lumen gentium*, 'Dogmatic Constitution on the Church'; *Nostra aetate,*[20] 'Declaration on the Relationship of the Church to Non-Christian Religions'; *Gaudium et spes*, 'Pastoral Constitution'; and *Ad gentes*, 'Decree on the Church's Missionary Activity'.

In paragraph 15 of *Lumen gentium* a revolutionary new assessment is given of the position of peoples who stand knowingly outside the Roman Catholic Church: 'The Church knows that she is joined in many ways to the baptized who are honoured by the name of Christian, but who do not however profess the Catholic faith . . .'

Such people are 'in some real way' joined to the Catholic Church in the Holy Spirit. But that is by no means all. The following paragraph deals with the Jews, and the Muslims, 'who profess to hold the faith of Abraham, and together with us they adore the one, merciful God, mankind's judge on the last day'. And still that is not all: 'Those who, through no fault of their own, do not know the Gospel of Christ . . . but who nevertheless seek God with a sincere heart, and . . . try in their actions to do his will . . . those too may achieve eternal salvation.' As Rahner comments, in the light of these dramatic new statements of Catholic doctrine

41

We can only wonder how few controversies arose during the Council with regard to these assertions of optimism concerning salvation, and wonder too at how little opposition the conservative wing of the Council brought to bear on this point . . . even though this doctrine marked a far more decisive phase in the development of the Church's conscious awareness of her faith than, for instance, the doctrine of collegiality in the Church, the relationship between scripture and tradition, the acceptance of the new exegesis etc.[21]

In *Nostra aetate* the attitude of the Catholic Church towards other religions is summed up succinctly: 'The Catholic Church rejects nothing of what is true and holy in these religions. She has a high regard for the manner of life and conduct, the precepts and doctrines which . . . often reflect a ray of that truth which enlightens all men.'[22] The summary importantly continues: 'Yet she proclaims and is in duty bound to proclaim without fail, Christ who is the way, the truth and the life (Jn. 14:6).[23] In him, in whom God reconciled all things to himself . . . men find the fulness of their religious life.'

The questions left unresolved by these multiply ambiguous statements by the Council are numerous. It is clearly important to recognize that in Catholic teaching the Christian is not saved, he is only more or less likely to be saved; and Rahner would suppose that the Catholic is more likely, and the non-Catholic Christian less likely, and the member of a non-Mosaic and non-Christian religion least likely, with perhaps those who have overtly and knowingly and intelligently rejected Christianity being unlikely, to be saved. With such a spectrum in its view, the position of the Council becomes, perhaps, a little more understandable. Whether that view is, in fact, conformable to Scripture is another matter which will be considered below.

Knitter's Five Stages in Catholic Soteriology

In an important article, 'Roman Catholic Approaches to Other Religions: Developments and Tensions', the Catholic theologian Paul Knitter has identified five stages in the development of the Catholic theology of religions.[24] His first period takes the Church through two stages, from *exclusive ecclesiocentrism* to *inclusive ecclesiocentrism*. The Council of Florence in 1442 articulated the exclusive position, that outside the Roman Catholic Church there was no salvation. The Council of Trent a century later (1545–63) opened the way for the incorporation into the Church (in an undefined way) of 'pagans' who lived a moral life but were not, for whatever reason, formally baptized into the Church.

Knitter labels the third position *constitutive Christocentrism*, which is seen as the focus of the ideas of the Second Vatican Council and of Karl Rahner. The attention is turned away from the Church towards Christ as the new focus. If it was evident that the Church was not to be found in the world's religions, at least it could be asserted that Christ could not be excluded from them. Thus a new and entirely innovative optimism so far as the world's religions was concerned became acceptable doctrine for world Catholicism.

The fourth position represents a reaction against the perceived imperialism of Rahner's 'anonymous Christianity', and is characterized as *normative Christocentrism*, with Christ no longer *within* other religions, and so disturbing their autonomy, but above them. Hans Küng, therefore, allows religions even without Christ in them, even without Rahner's 'grace gifts' in them, to function as vehicles of salvation, as the *ordinary* way of salvation for most peoples. For some Catholic theologians, although not for Küng, mission might then mean encouraging Buddhists to be 'better' Buddhists.

And finally a minority view is identified by Knitter as *dialogical theocentrism*, a view in which there is a return to early distinctions between the historical Jesus and the Logos of God. Jesus was a historical manifestation of the Logos, but according to Raimundo Panikkar and Gregory Baum and others we must not absolutize this event, nor deny the possibility of other salvation paradigms in addition to the Christian paradigm. This is a Catholic parallel to some, at least, of the ideas of John Hick.[25]

Anonymous Christianity[26]

The Four Theses

Karl Rahner was an influential Roman Catholic theologian whose views informed and influenced the thinking of the Second Vatican Council,[27] at which he was an official adviser.

Although the definitive exposition of Rahner's concept of the 'anonymous Christian'[28] appears in his *Theological Investigations*[29] a decade after the Council, the basic ideas were worked out much earlier, and certainly the central four theses were included in a lecture given by Rahner in April 1961.[30]

Rahner himself defines what *he* means by the term anonymous Christian: he is 'the pagan after the beginning of the Christian mission, who lives in the state of Christ's grace through faith, hope and love, yet who has no explicit knowledge of the fact that his life is orientated in grace-given salvation to Jesus Christ'.[31]

Explicitly Rahner identifies two parts to his fundamental concept: firstly, that there *are* individuals outside the Church who have never heard the Good News of Jesus Christ but who *are* justified. Secondly, that their justification is solely on account of Christ, the Christ of whom they have not explicitly heard. Thus the uniqueness of Christianity and the sole sufficiency of Christ is preserved by Rahner, while allowing for some of those myriads who are now (or who have been in the past) born into other religions to be saved.

He condenses his argument neatly into four theses which are formally presented in his *Theological Investigations*, volume V and chapter 6. Rahner begins by identifying the continuing pluralism of religion as a scandal, as *the* scandal: 'The fact of the pluralism of religions, which endures and still from time to time becomes virulent anew even after a history of two thousand years, must therefore be the greatest scandal and the greatest vexation for Christianity.'[32] The vexation lies not merely in the continued existence of a multiplicity of religions, but in their insistent *availability*. Christians are daily confronted by choice, by claims, by offers of salvation, as much as are members of other, traditionally *receiving* religions. Rahner is concerned to explicate these religions. What are they? Is God within them? Can people be saved through them?

His first thesis is superficially orthodox: 'Christianity understands itself as the absolute religion, intended for all men, which cannot recognize any other religion beside itself as of equal right.'[33]

The uniqueness of Christianity is rested upon the incarnation and the passion of the Word-made-flesh, God incarnate. But this uniqueness lies precisely within history. Christianity, for Rahner, has its beginning in the incarnation: 'As a historical quantity Christianity has, therefore, a temporal and spatial starting point in

Jesus of Nazareth . . .[34] Rahner goes on to declare that the incarnation invalidated the 'Mosaic religion', which thus reached the end of its period of salvific effectiveness. And a similar confrontation, although possibly at different points in history, invalidates other religions such as Buddhism and Hinduism.

But does Christianity have a starting-point in the incarnation? Christians have always perceived their faith as *continuous* with 'Mosaic religion' properly understood, and this continuity has been a principal source of friction between the two peoples. Christians are forced perennially to consider their Jewish roots, and Jews are similarly forced perennially to consider the missionizing, the evangelizing, essential to the universalism of Christianity, an enigma to the particularism of contemporary Judaism.[35] If Christianity were a *new* religion, the conflicts with Judaism would be no different from the conflicts with other religions. But Christianity insists that it is *not* a new religion: on the contrary, 'Mosaic religion' as anything other than a faith-response to a God of sheer grace was always invalid. As anything other than the precursor of and the preparation for the coming of Jesus of Nazareth it was always invalid. And conversely, 'Mosaic religion' itself consistently invalidated the religions which it encountered through its history. Christianity did not invalidate Greek mystery religions or Roman superstition at the ascension: they were already invalidated by the presence of 'Mosaic religion', properly understood.

In short, Old Testament Christianity was never invalidated. New Testament Christianity will never be invalidated. But perversions of either, the replacement of the faith-grace axis by religious systems based on legalism and self-justification, are always invalid.

The second thesis:

Until the moment when the gospel really enters into the historical situation of an individual, a non-Christian religion (even outside the Mosaic religion) does not merely contain elements of a natural knowledge of God, elements, moreover, mixed up with human depravity . . . It contains also supernatural elements arising out of the grace which is given to men as a gratuitous gift on account of Christ.[36]

45

The consequence of this second thesis is that non-Christian religions may be considered as lawful religions, as salvific religions. Now Rahner does recognize the problem involved in talking about a *religion*. A religion as such cannot be confronted with anything or anyone. It is *people* who must be considered and confronted, not religions. This is a problem which he intuitively recognizes but never really grapples with. For he now goes on to speak of the point of invalidation of a *religion* in terms of the moment when the followers of a non-Christian religion are first confronted by Christianity.[37] But in the next paragraph he is again speaking of the moment when the *religions* first came into 'real and historically powerful contact with Christianity'.[38]

Rahner's argument is simple. God wills all to be saved. That salvation is made possible only through grace and through Christ. The vast majority of people in all history, and even the majority of people today, are outside the Church. If God wills them to be saved, and if that willing has any meaning to it, then God must be at work outside the Church. But more. In all history nearly all people have been inside non-Christian religions. And perhaps we might add that this is still true if we take the view that Marxism is a non-Christian religion (Rahner does not). But if this is the case, then God must be salvifically at work inside those religions. For how else could people have been saved?

In the course of his argument Rahner appears to reject the view that those who are outside the Church are damned, because there is no hope at all of getting that view accepted by men today.[39] This may well be the case: but has that view *ever* been accepted by 'man'? And is truth necessarily palatable or acceptable?

If there is a flaw here in Rahner's grounds for seeking some kind of universalism, there is a flaw also in his logic. It is true that the vast majority of the world's peoples are in one or other of the non-Christian religions, but this does not require that God use the religions to reach them with his grace. All peoples are also in the world. All peoples are in society. May it not be that all peoples are reached by God, but precisely *not* through their religions, since it is their religions which predispose them *not* to seek after God? Rahner is clearly right in rejecting the notion that the 'pagan' is entirely abandoned by God[40] – after all, God sends the rain on the just and on the unjust, Christ sustains all things for all people – but it is not clear that he reveals himself through religion.

The third thesis starts from a characterization of religious man as the recipient of revelation 'if he has accepted God's grace as the ultimate unfathomable entelechy of his existence by accepting the inmeasurableness of his dying existence as opening out into infinity'.[41] I interpret this to mean that most pagans know that they must die, most expect some form of life after death, and that if their view of that life is entelechous then the source of their knowledge is God.

It is arguably true that in many religions the view of the future life is sombre, and that in some religions the view of life beyond death is entelechous. It might be said that this is particularly true of the Muslim view. For the Muslim, life beyond the grave offers the sensuous delights only imperfectly enjoyed here.[42] What is less clear is why this should give to, say, Islam, a grace-content denied to, say, African traditional religion, in which life beyond the grave is shadowy, fearful, uncertain.

However, Rahner does address the question of the possibility of an encounter between the Holy Spirit and the pagan. Here we are on firmer ground, since the New Testament makes clear the role of the Spirit in the process of conviction and conversion.[43] Surely rightly, Rahner comments on the 'boundless transcendental movement of the human spirit to God' that the movement is not merely asymptotic, never attaining its goal, but that God as goal is reachable. The Deuteronomist would have recognized the sentiment: 'There you will worship man-made gods of wood and stone, which cannot see or hear or eat or smell. But if from there you seek the Lord your God, you will find him if you look for him with all your heart and with all your soul' (Deut. 4.28–9).

It is in his first example of the meeting of spirit and Spirit that Rahner appears to come closest to the problem which we have been considering: the problem of the individual who has no explicit knowledge of the Good News, and yet who longs for God – the one who

cannot see how he is to include God as an entry in the accounting, as one that makes the debit and credit, the notional and actual values, come out right. This man surrenders himself to God . . . to the hope of an incalculable ultimate reconciliation of his existence in which he whom we call God dwells; he releases his unresolved and uncalculated existence, he lets go in trust and hope . . .[44]

There is a real experience of God in which, to use the phraseology of Martyn Lloyd-Jones, we 'fly to God for refuge'.[45] It is no balanced, assessed, assured decision, simply a decision to let go of rational decision-making and to hand the insoluble enigma of human life over to God. It is often the experience of the Christian. Rahner would argue that it could be the experience also of the anonymous Christian.[46]

Rahner advances from his preamble to state his third thesis: 'Christianity does not simply confront the member of an extra-Christian religion as a mere non-Christian, but as someone who can and must already be regarded in this or that respect as an anonymous Christian.'[47]

There appears to be implied in Rahner's formula a certain respect for a person's religious standing *before* he encounters Christianity which contrasts with Pauline practice. Thus in Acts 14.8–18 we have the first confrontation between Christianity and a pure non-Jewish religion, the worship of Zeus and Hermes at Lystra. Paul's address accords well with the Old Testament approach: '. . . turn from these worthless things [*mataia*] to the living God, who made heaven and earth and sea and everything in them' (Acts 14.15).

The domain of meaning of *matēn* and related terms is a clear indication of Paul's assessment of their religion. The RSV renders it 'vain' in Matthew 15.9, in Mark 7.7, and in James 1.26, and 'futile' in 1 Corinthians 3.20; 15.17 and in Titus 3.9 and 1 Peter 1.18 ('futility' in Rom. 8.20 and Eph. 4.17). The use of *mataioomai* in Romans 1.21 is particularly striking since it occurs in the context of a discussion of general revelation and the human construction of natural theology. The religion that was constructed was debased, and its adherents were subject to the wrath of God because the process of thought lying behind it all was futile.

Possibly the only example of a positive attitude towards pagan religion in the New Testament is found in Acts 17.16–34, Paul's reference to 'an unknown god'. He then identifies this unknown god as the one he is now proclaiming. This incident is immensely significant, for Paul takes a 'god' who, apparently, has no name and no characteristics, and is prepared to recognize *that*, the undefined, as God. In modern times there has been a continuing debate on the practice of using the name of a local deity to stand for 'God' in translations of the Bible. The problem is always that the name already has its properties, it already stands as a token for something, someone, with specific characteristics. The problem is particularly acute with respect to the name 'Allah'.[48] Within Islam the name already has certain features associated with it: positively he is creator, but negatively he is *not* triune, and, more importantly still, he is *not* 'the God and Father of the Lord Jesus' (2 Cor. 11.31) in any sense that conforms to the understanding of that phrase in the New Testament. It is simply the case that we cannot take a word with an established history, an agreed content, and arbitrarily end the history and change the content.[49] Paul does not take the risk of giving implicit approval to another religion by adopting a religiously identifiable deity. What is more, far from commending their religious practices, he explicitly condemns both their shrines and those who served them (Acts 17.24–5).

We may also note in passing the accusation against Paul in Acts 19.26 that he had 'convinced and led astray large numbers of people . . . [saying] that man-made gods are no gods at all'. Paul does not appear to perceive evidence of revelation in these religions, and far from merely announcing to the people that they are already 'in this or that respect' Christians, he commands them to abandon the religion they are in, which is futile, to repent, and to turn to Christ.

The world's religions continue to exist. Confronted with Christianity they do not wither away. Indeed, the contemporary experience is of the revival of religions of all categories: not merely the so-called great historical religions such as Islam, but also African Traditional Religion. How is the Christian to respond to these facts? In his fourth thesis Rahner says:

> It is nevertheless absolutely permissible for the Christian himself to interpret this non-Christianity as Christianity of an anonymous kind which he does always go out to meet as a missionary, seeing it as a

world which is to be brought to the explicit consciousness of what already belongs to it as a divine offer or already pertains to it also over and above this as a divine gift of grace accepted unreflectedly and implicitly.[50]

The Church then becomes the 'vanguard' of the redeemed, with anonymous Christians in uncountable numbers following, unknowingly, behind.

In volume XIV and chapter 17 of his *Theological Investigations* Rahner presents some 'Observations on the Problem of the "Anonymous Christian"'. He agrees first of all that it could be right to concentrate on the term anonymous Christian rather than on the term anonymous Christianity. Secondly, he admits that 'No truly theological demonstration of this thesis can be supplied here from scripture or tradition',[51] although he appeals to a history within the Catholic tradition of openness towards the possibility of salvation other than through an overt commitment to Christ. This then moves to a detailed appeal to the documents of Vatican II for support for the concept of the anonymous Christian.

Anonymous Christianity: A Summary

Four consequences appear to follow from Rahner's theses. Firstly, other religions are delivered from total rejection, and are accorded some measure of validity so that God might use them, in grace, to bring to their adherents the hope of salvation. Secondly, God is seen to be at work, salvifically, everywhere, not only in the Church but in these other religions. Thirdly, the myriads for whom there has never been any overt witness to Christ are delivered from their hopelessness: a way of salvation, founded on the sheer grace of God in Christ, is found for them. And finally, the moral character of God is rescued: the unwillingly blind are *not* condemned for their blindness, but are judged by the extent to which they longed to see.

However, as Lesslie Newbigin has commented, 'This scheme is vulnerable at many points.'[52] We here mention just three objections. Firstly, the honorary granting of Christian citizenship to those who have not asked for it, and who have, in some cases, positively resisted it (as is true of both Muslims and Jews), savours of sheer imperialism. Secondly, Rahner's position, and indeed that of the Second Vatican Council at this point, appears not merely to lack biblical support, but actually to run contrary to the teachings of both the Old and New Testaments. Thirdly, it must be said that in the contemporary debates about the world's religions the religions themselves are hopelessly idealized. The world's religions are *not* kindly debating societies, but as those of us who have lived among them for any length of time will know, they are a morass of superstition, ignorance, exploitation, oppression, fear. And to take up Barth's distinction again, this is as true of *Christianity* as a religion as it is true of any other religion. The horrors of Canaanite religion are still with us, the *shaman* still claims the power to manipulate his gods, witchcraft still flourishes, the credulous are exploited, human achievement is exalted, the rich are filled with yet more good things, and it is the poor who are sent empty away.

The fact is that religions do not prepare their adherents for the revelation of Christ. Paradoxically, the closer any religion stands to Christianity so the higher is the barrier erected by it between its own adherents and the Christian revelation. If salvation is to be found by the adherents of these religions, it may well be found while they are still in them, but it will be found not because of them, but in spite of them.

Hans Küng's Ordinary and Special Ways

Hans Küng rejects Rahner's proposals[33] but offers an alternative way of dealing with the problem of the continuing existence of a multiplicity of religions. First of all, Küng reminds us that Vatican II explicitly abandoned the traditional view that there could be no salvation outside the Catholic Church. He quotes the Dogmatic Constitution on the Church, of 21 November 1964:

> Nor is God far distant from those who in shadows and images seek the unknown God: for he gives all men life and breath and all things (cf. Acts 17.25–28), and as Saviour wants all men to be saved (cf. I Tim. 2.4). Those who through no fault of theirs are still ignorant of the Gospel of Christ and of his Church yet sincerely seek God and, with the help of divine grace, strive to do his will as known to them through the voice of their conscience, those men can attain to eternal salvation. Nor does divine providence deny the assistance necessary to salvation to those who, without having attained, through no fault of their own, to an explicit knowledge of God, are striving, not without divine grace, to lead a good life.[54]

Küng clearly recognizes the impossibility of merely incorporating people of 'good will' or who lead a 'good life' into the Church, which is necessarily the fellowship of those who believe in Christ and who confess Christ. He also admits the danger of idealizing the world's religions, of failing to see the element of disobedience and even perversion enshrined in religion: he has just such a jaundiced view of religion as Barth has expressed.[55] As Küng comments of the religious activities of those who are to be found in the other religions:

> However inappropriate that arrogant lack of understanding which rejects the world religions as simply false, it is no less inappropriate to idealize them in a utopian fashion as all in the same way perfect objectivizations of man's religious experience ... there remains a denial and flight from God: in all their hope for God's grace, a concealed self-redemption; in all their genuine conversion, an inadvertent turning away.[56]

Küng postulates two ways of salvation: the 'ordinary way', the way for the multitudes of people who have never been meaningfully exposed to Christianity, and the 'extraordinary way', available only to a comparative few who have encountered Christ:

> A man is to be saved within the religion that is made available to him in his historical situation. Hence it is his right and his duty to seek God within that religion in which the hidden God has already found him. All this until such time as he is confronted in an existential way with the revelation of Jesus Christ.[57]

It has to be said that when Küng moves on to explain how and when the other religions point to God he is less convincing. These religions teach the truth when they recognize man's need of salvation, when they identify God's grace in himself coming to us when we cannot come to him, when they hear the voice of their own prophets. But the detailed study of individual religions shows that they do not, in fact, function in these ways. If they recognize the need of salvation, they create their own way of attaining it.[58] Despite Küng's attempt to ensure that salvation is in both the ordinary and extraordinary ways through Christ alone, in conformity with John 14.6, two ways of salvation emerge, one of them the way of common religion.

5 Exclusivism and The Bible

EXCLUSIVISM AND THE BIBLE: OLD TESTAMENT

The Bible emphasizes revelation over against human insight. To the perceptive reader it is apparent that the 'great' figures of the Old Testament and, with the exception of Jesus himself, of the New Testament, are great not because of qualities inherent in themselves, but because of God's salvific activity demonstrated through them. An honest study of Moses, Jacob, David, Solomon, or Elijah, to name but five key figures of the Old Testament, or of Peter, Paul, or Timothy in the New Testament, does not leave us with a great respect for the human material with which God chose to do his work. Revelation came to them often despite their own paucity of religious faith. But it always appears to be the intention of God that this revelation made to chosen individuals should be for the benefit of others: certainly for the 'chosen people', but also for the surrounding nations.

The Bible is clearly concerned for right belief allied to right praxis. But this right belief comes only through revelation, a fact which is demonstrated by the plight of those who do not have it. It seems to be for this reason that sheer iconoclasm marks the Old Testament attitude towards other religions, summed up by Deuteronomy 7.1–6:

> When the Lord your God brings you into the land you are entering to possess and drives out before you many nations . . . and when the Lord your God has delivered them over to you and you have defeated them, then you must destroy them totally. Make no treaty with them, and show them no mercy. Do not intermarry with them. Do not give your daughters to their sons or take their daughters for your sons, for they will turn your sons away from following me to serve other gods . . . This is what you are to do to them: Break down their altars, smash their sacred stones, cut down their Asherah poles and burn their idols in the fire.

These words represent a clear religio-political stance for the emerging nation, Israel. There is no suggestion here of tolerance of or of accommodation with the religions to be found in abundance in the contemporary Near East.

It is true that the law made provision for the expression of a proper concern for the stranger, the non-Israelite, who for whatever reason found himself sharing the same socio-economic milieu with the people of God. The *zarim* were temporary sojourners only, and appeared primarily in the interest of trade. The *gerim* were different: they settled in the land, and came under the same law as did Israel. But they were clearly differentiated from the Israelite, perhaps nowhere more revealingly than in the provision of the Deuteronomic code allowing them to eat meat which would be forbidden to the true son of the law (cf. Deut. 14.21).[1] But although the stranger was, in accordance with the customs of the time, well cared for, there appears to have been little if any overt concern to convert him to the worship of Yahweh.

This is, perhaps, surprising, in that the original covenant with Abram had apparently envisaged a blessing reaching out to all the peoples of the earth (Gen. 12.1–3). It is, of course, entirely possible that the 'blessing' (Heb. *berakah*) promised would be material prosperity, and that those who acted rightly towards Abram would be rewarded appropriately but materially. If the intention was *spiritual* enrichment, there is little in the Old Testament to show that Israel felt any obligation positively to reach out with that enrichment to the neighbouring nations. The expectation was centripetal, not centrifugal: the nations might be drawn in to Jerusalem and there encounter God, but there could be no expectation that Israel might send out her own spiritual emissaries. Perhaps it is fair to say that in the social and political context of the day that would scarcely have appeared a credible programme for any minority people.

The exclusivism inherent in Israel's religion is well illustrated in Joshua 24.14ff: 'Throw away the gods your forefathers worshipped beyond the River and in Egypt, and serve the Lord.'

Isaiah represents a different and more hostile attitude towards the religions of the nations:

> Bring in your idols to tell us
> what is going to happen.
> Tell us what the former things were,
> so that we may consider them

and know their final outcome.
Or declare to us the things to come,
   tell us what the future holds,
   so that we may know you are gods.
Do something, whether good or bad,
   so that we will be dismayed and filled with fear.
                                                   (Isa. 41.22–3)[2]

But there *is* a recognition in Isaiah that Yahweh relates in some way to all the nations of the earth, and that only in Yahweh can they hope to find salvation: 'Turn to me and be saved, all you ends of the earth; for I am God, and there is no other' (Isa. 45.22). And what is more, Israel is the servant who is to bring salvation to the whole earth:

It is too small a thing for you to be my servant
   to restore the tribes of Jacob
   and bring back those of Israel I have kept.
I will also make you a light for the Gentiles,
   that you may bring my salvation to the ends of the earth.
                                                   (Isa. 49.6)

EXCLUSIVISM AND THE BIBLE: NEW TESTAMENT

The New Testament offers a very similar assessment of contemporary religions. In Ephesians 2.11–13 we have a paradigmatic expression of the true condition of those who espouse religion without revelation: they are separate from Christ, excluded from citizenship in Israel, foreigners to the covenants of promise, and consequently without hope and without God. This last statement is particularly important. The people are *atheoi*, without God, not in the sense that they lack religion,[3] but in the sense that their religion lacked God. Or, what amounts to the same thing, that their humanly constructed religion, far from leading them to God, led them away from him.

We must at this point consider the two crucial statements of John 14.6 and Acts 4.12. In the former Jesus tells Thomas, 'I am the way and the truth and the life. No-one comes to the Father except through me.' In the latter, Peter, speaking of Jesus, tells a gathering of the Jewish religious leaders, possibly a formal assembly of the Sanhedrin: 'Salvation is found in no-one else, for there is no other name under heaven given to men by which we must be saved.'

Although these two verses of the New Testament are in a sense isolated verses, they are entirely in accord with the thrust of New Testament teaching in general. They cannot be dismissed as mere eccentricities. It simply will not do to import into the Bible the modern reluctance to believe in absolutes. We may decide to reject absolutes ourselves, but we must do that for ourselves and by ourselves. We cannot claim biblical support for our decisions. In any event, the two verses are there, in the New Testament, and those who reject what the verses appear to imply have usually attempted to find some way of reinterpreting them. Thus, in *No Other Name?*, in a chapter entitled 'How is Jesus unique?', Paul Knitter writes:

> In Acts 4:12, the apostles, after having cured the lame man in the name of Jesus, cried out 'there is no other name by which we can be saved,' not to rule out the possibility of other saviors, but to proclaim that this Lord Jesus was still alive and that it was he, not they, who was working such wonders in the community.[4]

To say the least, this is an extraordinary piece of textual interpretation. The equation 'there is no other name by which we can be saved' equals 'Jesus is still alive and it is through him, not us, that this man has been healed' requires some justification, and a very special hermeneutic. And when Knitter goes on to say that the text is abused if it is used as a starting-point for evaluating other religions, he is on the one hand condemning himself for a gross abuse of the text and on the other hand misrepresenting the use made of the text by conservative theologians. The text is not a starting-point in our evaluation of other religions, but it is certainly one of several stopping-points along the way.

Peggy Starkey examines both of the relevant texts in her article 'Biblical Faith and the Challenge of Religious Pluralism'.[5] Methodologically, it is clear that the purpose of the examination is *not* the scholarly exegesis of the texts and their cotexts, but a justification of a denial of the exclusivism evident in them. In dealing with the Acts statement Starkey has three comments to make. The first comment is on the redactional activity of Luke.

This is seen in terms of a tension between a recognition of the uniqueness of Jesus and an acceptance by God even of those who do not belong to the group of Jesus' disciples (Luke 9.49–50). But the passing reference to Luke 9 allows Starkey to import into the incident a meaning that is simply not there. The disciples of Jesus *are* denied the luxury of putting a stop to the exorcizing activities of others outside their own coterie, but this is not at all the same thing as suggesting that such exorcists are also in the Kingdom of God.

Secondly, she rightly observes that the verb *sōzein* is used both of physical healing and of salvation. It is in the name of Jesus that this man has been physically healed. There is then an attempt to separate the *name* of Jesus from the *person* of Jesus: 'This statement is an affirmation of the community of believers that Jesus Christ is the name through which they have experienced salvation.'[6] But this is a clear example of synecdoche, the name of Jesus being seen not as a mere magical symbol, efficacious of *itself*, but as representing all that Jesus had done, was doing, would do, and was in *himself.*

Thirdly, she appeals to Krister Stendahl's dictum that confessional language is not metaphysical language. Christians using confessional language are not to be seen as making absolute, final statements about the nature of reality. But Stendahl is simply falling into the error of positing two kinds of truth, historical truth and religious truth. Confessional language is still language, it still makes statements which must be perceived using the same criteria as are used in perceiving all language.

It is arguable that the Acts pericope leaves room for the possibility of a person being *physically* healed by some other name, but as F. F. Bruce points out, there is a transition in the use of *sōzein* at verse 12, to *salvation*, with an emphasis placed on *to dedomenon* by the definite article, so that the givenness of Jesus is accorded prominence.[7] There is *no salvation* to be found elsewhere.

On John 14.6 Starkey comments of John's Gospel in general: 'This is not "scientific" history, but interpretative history. The author's purpose is theological, not chronological.'[8] Two things must be said in response: firstly, that it has long been accepted that the very notion of 'scientific' history is unreal. All historical records are interpretative: science itself is unscientific when it comes to describe itself. K. R. Popper reminds us that 'all scientific descriptions of facts are highly selective, that they always depend upon theories',[9] and he goes on to show how this is true of all histories. But secondly, we have to say that we do not accept that chronology can simply be dismissed from our consideration of John's Gospel. Anyone who has wrestled with the question of the dating of the Upper Room meal and of the crucifixion itself will know the temptation to take this draconian line, and the need to resist the temptation. What Starkey appears to be saying is not merely that John's concern is not with chronology, but that John is quite prepared to fabricate events and speeches in the interest of the furtherance of his particular theology. Thus when Starkey comments, 'John states that there is no access to God . . . except through the historical reality of Jesus',[10] she is intentionally eliminating Jesus from the authorship of the *logion*, and making 'John' the author (not the apostle of that name, but 'an unknown author' who produced the Gospel between AD 90 and 100.[11] Thus the dominical character of the saying is dismissed.

The next step is to appeal to Gregory Baum's characterization of such language as that of John 14.6 as 'survival language' which 'always modifies the truth'.[12] Baum is a Roman Catholic theologian, with a Jewish family background, and is strongly committed to ecumenism in its broadest sense. His radical view is that the Christian proclamation should have as its goal precisely not the conversion of Muslims and Hindus and Jews to Christianity, but the creation of 'theological space' for the world religions.[13] He is ideologically committed to a relativistic position, and that position certainly requires a reassessment of what he himself identifies as the 'exclusivist claims' of the New Testament. But once we recognize that these *are* exclusivist claims, it becomes difficult to justify an entirely contrary 'reinterpretation'. They *are* exclusivist. We may not like it. We may refuse to accept it. But John quite clearly does record the words he attributes to Jesus. To deny that Jesus said anything of the sort, to deny that *John* wrote anything of the sort, to suppose that someone else wrote it to bolster the threatened faith of a minority community, and to deny that the words meant then or mean now what the naive reader perceives them to mean is simply unscholarly. Starkey quotes C. K. Barrett, and we may safely conclude this section with his comment on the relevant words:

> If John, here and elsewhere, used some of the notions and terminology of the religions of his day, and there are many indications that he was not unfamiliar with them, he was quite sure that those religions were ineffective, and that there was no religious or mystical approach to God which could achieve its goal.[14]

And we would want to add: he knew it because he knew that Jesus had said it.

We must now turn to a positive exegesis of John 14.6, since if we accept the historicity of the Johannine Last Discourse the exclusivist statement of Jesus predates, and presumably informs, the later and similar exclusivist statement by Peter.

The statement itself is given a peculiar authority by the introductory phrase *egō eimi*. This phrase is important, because by it we are shown not what Jesus *does*, but what Jesus *is*. It is not that Jesus *knows* the way, or that he *shows* the way, but that he *is* the way.[15] There follows a significant sequence of three predicates co-ordinated by *kai*, but with the emphasis on *hodos*, 'the way', ensured by its being fronted. As Rudolf Schnackenburg notes, this emphasis is confirmed by the *di'emou*, 'through me', in the second part of the affirmation.[16] Thus the primary concern of the statement is not *truth*, nor is it *life*, but the *way to the Father*. The other two terms are by way of being themes for the Fourth Gospel, but *hodos* occurs only here and in 1.23 (and there in a quotation from Isa.40).

The word must be explicated in terms of the immediate context. Jesus already knows that he is about to complete his mission on earth. The disciples are to be left behind. How can his role of rabbi and Lord be continued? The answer is developed in a lengthy section reaching from 13.31 through to 14.31, a section which is marked in typical discourse style by the departure of Judas and a deeply suggestive comment with the form of a mere time indication, 'it was night' (13.30). Now attention moves from the duologue between Jesus and Judas to a broader dialogue involving Jesus and the eleven. The topic of the dialogue is set by Jesus: 'Where I am going' (13.33), and this stands at the head of a pericope which is most unfortunately interrupted by the entirely unwarranted and intrusive chapter division.

Peter begins by promising to walk in Jesus' way. Rashly, he believes that he is willing, if necessary, to lay down his life for his Lord. There are two comments to be made on this: firstly, that Peter does not have the resources in himself to take this way. Secondly, he does not really understand what the way *is*. The way in question was more than a walk on earth: it was of essence a walk whose end, whose goal, was God. Jesus was about to walk that way, but it was a walk and a way *via* the cross. There can be no other way to God. *That* is what Jesus is speaking about.

But the metaphor takes us further than this. Metaphorically, Jesus himself *is* the way. It is not merely a matter of walking behind Jesus so as to emulate him, as is required of a Muslim's walk behind Muhammad. Jesus is more than a mere exemplar. 'No-one comes to the Father except *di'emou'*, *through* Jesus, *by* Jesus. It is *through* him, through an acknowledgement of who he is, that one may come to the Father: 'I am in the Father' (14.11). Of course it is true, as J. H. Bernard points out in his commentary, that 'To walk in God's way has been the aspiration of pious men of every race';[17] but that is precisely *not* what the statement is about: it is walking *to* God. And no one can get there other than through Jesus. This is in some senses the high-point of Johannine Christology. It is not an aberrant text. It is, indeed, entirely consonant with all else that John has to say to us about Jesus. The exclusiveness is of its essence and can be removed from the Gospel only at the cost of destroying the coherence of the whole work.

GENERAL REVELATION[18]

The Grounds for a Salvific General Revelation

We return once more to the observation made by John Hick that for the majority of people in the world their religion is the religion into which they happened to be born. We have observed that there are still enormous numbers of people today, as there have been throughout history, who have not overtly heard of the Christian Good News. But is there not biblical support for the view that there is some more general revelation available to all, irrespective of the special revelation through Scripture and the incarnation?

Two New Testament passages may be appealed to as at least giving some measure of support to the idea of general revelation. The first, in John 1, suggests an intellectual enlightening, a direct illumination from God to the individual mind, enabling the individual to know God. The second, in Romans 1, states that God's nature is displayed in creation, and displayed quite clearly. The implication, then, is that with the mind illuminated by God it is possible for anyone to perceive God, to understand his nature, through an awareness of his creation.

We consider firstly the statement in John's prologue: 'The true light that gives light to every man was coming into the world' (John 1.9). The sentence here is by no means easy to translate. The NIV margin offers 'This was the true light that gives light to every man who comes into the world.' There is, however, general agreement that it was the Logos light that came into the world to 'give light' to everyone. Calvin, following Augustine, interprets this to mean that everyone is illuminated, everyone has some measure of light, no one is wholly in the dark: 'There is no man, therefore, whom some perception of the eternal light does not reach.'[19]

Here Calvin is arguably led astray by his preference for verse by verse exposition. Luther is obviously perplexed by what he perceives to be the germ of an undesirable universalism. He begins by restating John's proposition: 'With the exception of the Son of God, who was with the Father from the beginning and through whom all have light and life, there is no light. Whatever men are enlightened on earth are enlightened through this only light and not otherwise.'[20] He then disposes of the implied generalization by appealing to common usage which employs 'does' in the sense of 'should do'. The Logos light *should* illuminate everyone, and *could* illuminate everyone, and the fact that it does not do so is no fault of the Logos.

If we move to consider the views of modern commentators, we find C. K. Barrett (in a minority of one) denying that the statement in the prologue implies any kind of universal enlightenment at all. For Barrett, 'the light shines upon every man for judgement, to reveal what he is', and he suggests of the relevant words: 'Render, therefore, ". . . which shines upon every man" (whether he sees it or not).'[21]

Schnackenburg has an advantage over most other commentators in that he is aware of the fact that meaning is to be found not in the word, or even in the sentence, but in the larger units of discourse. In his comments on the text he makes frequent and careful reference to the cotext at this point.

In fact it is not possible satisfactorily to exegete 1.9 other than through an understanding of the entire Logos hymn. The relevant text is given in full:

> [1] In the beginning was the Word,
>   and the Word was with God, and the Word was God.
> [2] He was in the beginning with God;
> [3] all things were made through him.
>   and without him was not anything made that was made.
> [4] In him was life, and the life was the *light* of men.
> [5] The *light* shines in the darkness,
>   and the darkness has not overcome it . . .
> [9] The true *light* that *enlightens* every man
>   was coming into the world.
> [10] He was in the world, and the world was made through him,
>   yet the world knew him not.
> [11] He came to his own home,
>   and his own people received him not.
> [12] But to all who received him, who believed in his name,
>   he gave power to become children of God;
> [13] who were born, not of blood nor of the will of the
>   flesh
>   nor of the will of man,
>   but of God.

(John 1.1–5, 9–13, RSV)

Schnackenburg at once connects 1.9 to 1.4: 'In him was life, and the life was the light of men.' Setting aside the meaning of the Logos hymn in its assumed original setting in Hellenistic Judaism, Schnackenburg sees the Christian hymn as insisting that

> the Logos has a transcendent power of illumination which comes from his godhead (v. 1c) and which can and must be displayed in every man who desires to reach his goal. How far this came about in fact, how far men allowed themselves to be illumined and guided by this divine light of life – this is something of which the verse speaks as little as v. 4; *the subject is reserved for the next strophe (vv. 10–11).*[22]

62

He is, surely, correct in suggesting that procedurally we would be wrong if we were to attempt to discern the meaning of 1.9 other than as part of the meaning of the introductory pericope, 1.1-14. The hymn, if hymn we may call it, begins by consciously evoking the creation poem in the first chapter of Genesis, but as consciously transfers the theme of the creation of life to the theme of the re-creation of life, to the process of being born 'not of natural descent, nor of human decision or a husband's will, but born of God' (v. 13). And the point of this climax to the poem is man's refusal of the light unreservedly offered to him: 'He was in the world, and though the world was made through him, the world did not recognise him. He came to that which was his own, but his own did not receive him' (vv. 10-11).

However, we cannot end our understanding of the passage with the entirely negative judgement of verses 10-11. The assumed generalization, that *all* the world knew him not, or that *all* of his own people received him not, is softened by verse 12: '. . . to all who received him . . .' Taken along with its cotext, then, it seems that John is here positing a general *Logos* illumination affecting everyone, but not an irresistible illumination. But neither is it an ineffective illumination. Again it is tempting to assume that salvation, the new birth, is entirely a matter of the divine activity, on the basis of verse 13: 'who were born, not of blood nor of the will of the flesh nor of the will of man, but of God' (RSV). But there is a human contribution: some 'received him' (v. 12), and 'believed in his name', recognizing a human responsibility; and to such God gave authority (*exousia*) to become his children, recognizing the divine enabling.

In its context it is clear that John's statement of a universal enlightening is applied to the situation when the Logos came into the world. To the question 'How was it that some received him?', John gives a clear answer: through that same universal but not irresistible illumination. But as C. H. Dodd has pointed out, the ministry of the incarnate Logos parallels that of the eternal Logos:

> The life of Jesus therefore *is* the history of the Logos, as incarnate, and this must be, upon the stage of limited time, the same thing as the history of the Logos in perpetual relations with man and the world. Thus not only verses 11-13, but the whole passage from

verse 4, is *at once* an account of the relations of the Logos with the world, *and* an account of the ministry of Jesus Christ, which in every essential particular reproduces those relations.²³

It does not therefore appear to be illegitimate to take it that the same universal illumination might have the same consequence of a divided response, a response lacking universality, when considered in relation to the more general revelation of God in creation. And to this we must now turn.

We consider the teaching of Paul in his systematic exposition of his gospel in Romans. The immediately relevant statement appears in Romans 1.20. It is certainly significant that the statement follows on immediately from a statement about 'the wrath of God . . . revealed from heaven against all the godlessness and wickedness of men who suppress the truth' (v. 18). Paul continues: ' . . . since what may be known about God is plain to them, because God has made it plain to them. For since the creation of the world God's invisible qualities – his eternal power and divine nature – have been clearly seen, being understood from what has been made . . .' (vv. 19–20).

Emil Brunner felt compelled to recognize that this passage (and others), does teach natural revelation, but insisted that this revelation was not salvific. He made appeal to the 'Nature Psalms', and especially to Psalm 19, to Romans 1.18ff., Romans 2.14ff., Romans 1.28–32, John 1.4–9, Acts 14.17, and Acts 17.26–7. He summarizes this aspect of his teaching by saying defiantly. 'The fact that the Holy Scriptures teach the revelation of God in his works of creation needs no proof.'²⁴ On the other hand, he guards himself against a natural theology by insisting, 'The revelation of God in the Creation . . . does not guarantee that man, for his part, will make right use of this knowledge. As a rule, indeed, man usually does the opposite, owing to his sinful blindness, and the perversion of his will.'²⁵ But we note that even here Brunner is careful to leave open the possibility that some *might* make right use of their knowledge of God: 'man *usually* does the opposite'. The fact is that anyone who has any broad experience of humanity, and especially those who have experienced humanity outside of the so-called 'sophisticated' Western hemisphere, will have encountered people who *have* perceived God in his creation, and have *not* used that perception perversely.

Barth comments in some detail on the Romans passage, firstly in his 'Doctrine of the Word of God', and secondly in his 'Doctrine of God'.[26] It is not always and everywhere clear that Barth was able to maintain a stark and total denial of a divine self-revelation in creation, although undoubtedly that *was* his position, perhaps nowhere more forcefully stated than in his Doctrine of God: 'The logic of the matter demands that, even if we only lend our little finger to natural theology, there necessarily follows the denial of the revelation of God in Jesus Christ.'[27]

Barth also deals with this matter in his commentary on Romans.[28] The commentary at this point is remarkable for its use of paradox ('We know that God is He whom we do not know, and that our ignorance is precisely the problem and the source of our knowledge'[29]) and of rhetoric ('The clear, honest eyes of the poet in the book of Job and of the Preacher Solomon had long ago rediscovered, mirrored in the world of appearance, the archetypal, unobservable, undiscoverable Majesty of God'[30]). Concealed behind the rhetoric is the plain fact that God *was* known to Job, was revealed to Job, *existentially*, in the experience of suffering, in the context of perplexity, and that although Job was given to understand that the ultimate mystery of God's purpose, and a comprehension of God's power, were beyond him, *God himself came to Job.* Which makes Barth's confident assertion of the essential 'unknowableness' of God perplexing: 'And what is clearly seen to be indisputable reality is the invisibility of God, which is precisely and in strict agreement with the gospel of the resurrection – His everlasting power and divinity. And what does this mean but that we can know nothing of God . . .?'[31] The drama of Job in the Old Testament and the passage which Barth is wrestling with from the New Testament both testify to the fact that God may be known through existential encounter.

But Barth does help us in a somewhat different direction. Barth always and everywhere sees that any law given to the Jew and any creation-revelation allowed to the Gentile leads equally and inevitably to condemnation. Any distinction between Jew and Gentile is done away in the crucifixion of Christ: subsequent to that,[32] all fall under condemnation, ' . . . they are all drawn into the responsibility and accountability which formerly only Israel had experienced . . . The very revelation of the righteousness of God is also the revelation of the wrath of God against all ungodliness and unrighteousness . . . of men . . .'[33]

In understanding Romans 1, we again insist on the interpretation of each verse in the context of the whole. And again it is clear that verse 20 is inextricably linked both to the preceding adumbration of the wrath of God (*ta gar aorata autou*) and to the consequential phrase '. . . so that men are without any excuse'.

What clearly *is* being said here is that God's self-revelation in creation is not of itself salvific. Indeed, if it were of itself salvific we would be in conflict with the very clear perception of salvation which sees it as stemming from the grace of God.

In the larger context of Romans, Romans 1 is to be seen as a chapter devoted primarily to the task of stripping the Gentile world of any hope it might have of making its own way to God. Romans 2 performs the same office for the Jews. And this paves the way for the lament of Romans 3, a pastiche of Old Testament texts expressing the universal lostness of mankind, and, in due course, it also paves the way for the universal offering of a single way of salvation in Romans 4: the way of divinely granted faith.

But this does *not* leave that vast majority of humanity which has the general revelation of God's deity in nature but not the specific revelation of God in the incarnate Logos *both* without excuse for its sin *and* without recourse for that sin. Firstly, it is important to note that this section of Romans is concerned with the *condemnation* of the world, and not its *salvation*. Leon Morris comments of the intention of Paul at this point: 'He is not facing the question whether there was enough in the revelation for them to be saved. That is quite a different question, and we should not torture Paul's words into giving an answer to a question he is not facing.'[34]

What Paul undoubtedly conveys is the reality of a universal falling short, a universal failure to respond appropriately to whatever revelation has been given. Later on he will deal with the way of salvation in so far as it affects all those who hear the Good News concerning Jesus, whether Jews (especially in Romans 9—11) or Gentiles (especially in Romans 5—8). But nowhere in these central chapters of the letter does he consider the question of those who do not hear that Good News.

We cannot, therefore, answer the question of the *salvific* value of God's self-revelation in creation (coupled with the universal Logos illumination) from Romans. However, Paul *does* confront the problem in just one speech recorded in Acts 17:

> [24] The God who made the world and everything in it, being Lord of heaven and earth, does not live in shrines made by man, [25] nor is he served by human hands, as though he needed anything, since he himself gives to all men life and breath and everything. [26] And he made from one every nation of men to live on all the face of the earth, having determined allotted periods and the boundaries of their habitation.[27] *that they should seek God, in the hope that they might feel after him and find him.*
>
> (Acts 17.24–7, RSV)

This important passage serves on the one hand to make clear the rejection of human religion, characterized by the determination to make God no more than a super-human. He is given a better house, he is provided with better food, but for all that he is merely man writ large. On the other hand the passage serves to show that creation is so ordered that in creation we may encounter God, and even find him.

Granted that this is the record of a genuine address, it is at once clear that Paul's *kairos* (v. 26) could not possibly refer to the Christian idea of the *parousia*, a referent entirely missing from the presupposition pool of his audience, but refers to the seasons, proof of God's wisdom in creation in that the world is divinely ordered for human existence.[35] And the reference to 'the boundaries of their habitation' is to the gracious provision by God of parts of the world appropriate to the support of human life. Thus there is presented to any observer evidence of design and Designer, a God who is concerned to design his universe with the needs of humanity in mind.[36]

We are, then, in the same subject area as Romans 1: evidence of the nature of God in creation.

But here Paul moves on to ask the question *not* posed in Romans: What was the purpose of that revelation? The answer is '. . . that they should seek God, in the hope that they might feel after him *and find him*'. Jacques Dupont expresses it very clearly:

> The Areopagus address assigns a dual purpose to the creation of man: to populate the earth (v. 26) and 'to seek God' (v. 27a). To

state that man has been made so as to seek God already supposes that this search could lead to discovery, and thus that man is radically capable of finding God.[37]

There is a certain hesitancy evident in the words of Paul: there is a hope that 'perhaps' people might reach out and find God. But again, reference to the context makes that hesitancy entirely appropriate: whatever might be the expectation or experience elsewhere, in the sophisticated metropolis of Athens the people had *not* found God. They had, instead, created gods. But the thrust of Paul's statement is clear: God's purpose in revealing himself in creation *was* salvific: some, at least, would find God. And in finding God they might expect to encounter, also, his grace.

The Historic Conservative Position on General Revelation

The view of the salvific efficacy of general revelation as presented here is firmly rejected by some conservative writers even where the problems posed by the insistence on salvation solely in terms of an individual response to the received proclamation of Christ are recognized. We take two writers, both, significantly, from the same mission, J. Oswald Sanders[38] and Dick Dowsett.[39]

To the observation that it would appear to be unfair to condemn people to hell because they have failed to take advantage of a salvation of which they have never heard, both writers respond by insisting that this is not the case: '. . . the unevangelized do not die because they are unevangelized but because of their sin'.[40] But this merely pushes back the argument one further step. The unevangelized are condemned because of their sin, but since they have not heard of Christ they have no remedy for it, and, indeed, no adequate understanding of it. Their condemnation is *still* because they have not been evangelized.

Oddly enough, Oswald Sanders almost states as much, in a brief quotation from R. E. Speer:

> 'Men are in this plight,' writes Dr. R. E. Speer, 'not because they are unevangelized, but because they are men. Sin is the destroyer of the soul and the destruction of the knowledge of God which is life. And it is not the failure to have heard the gospel which makes men sinners. *The Gospel would save them if they heard and accepted it,* but it is not the ignorance or rejection of the gospel which destroys them: it is the knowledge of sin.'[41]

The exclusivist position is not restricted to active missionaries. It is also to be found among the theologians. Thus Harold Lindsell, formerly editor of the prestigious evangelical theological journal *Christianity Today*, in his definitive missiology, *An Evangelical Theology of Missions*,[42] concluded the chapter on 'The Inadequacy of the Non-Christian Religions' with an uncompromising affirmation: 'God does not reveal Himself redemptively through other means than those presently indicated in the Word of God: i.e. through His children's missionary activity to a lost world.'[43]

Lindsell considers the apparent problem raised by this doctrine for the justice of God, and responds, perhaps defiantly, 'We need simply to admit that God IS just in whatever He does. In all cases His justice is operative despite any appearance to the contrary.'[44]

This is an approach which is familiar to Islam through its doctrine of *mukhalafa*, 'otherness', which essentially serves to forbid our saying anything meaningful about God at all. Any humanly devised word used of Allah necessarily takes on a new dimension of meaning *because* it is used of Allah. So that in Islam, God can be made responsible for every catastrophe, every famine, and the question of reconciling that action to his justice does not arise. No action can be unjust because it is the action of an omnipotent Allah: what Allah does *is* just, by definition. But that is not the Christian understanding. God reveals himself to us meaningfully through a written word and through an incarnate Word, and human language does not cease to carry its normal meaning merely because of the irruption of the divine into it. Lindsell is right to perceive the injustice inherent in his scheme, but it cannot be spirited away by the simple declaration that it is *not* unjust.

Sir Norman Anderson, formerly Professor of Oriental Law in the University of London, and Director of the Institute of Advanced Legal Studies, wrote *Christianity and Comparative Religion* in 1970, and then a completely rewritten version in 1984.[45] The new version is *Christianity and World Religions*, and has a significant sub-title, *The Challenge of Pluralism*. In an addendum to chapter 5, 'No Other Name?', he comments on Dowsett's book:

> It is true that I should not always express myself in precisely Dick Dowsett's terms, but there is only one major point on which I feel

bound to differ from him: namely, that I cannot believe that *all* those who have never heard the gospel are inevitably lost.[46]

It is certainly significant that Sir Norman Anderson, who (along with John Stott) has long been perceived by evangelical Christians as a spokesman for orthodoxy, should reject this particular dogma, and do so unequivocally. It is also significant that even the ultra-conservative Charles Hodge felt compelled to admit (against his own systematic theology):

> We know from the Bible itself . . . 'in every nation he that feareth him and worketh righteousness is accepted with him' (Acts X.34, 35). No one doubts that it is in the power of God to call whom He pleases among the heathen and to reveal to them enough truth to secure their salvation.[47]

But this would appear to concede the case for salvation apart from any overt knowledge of the Christian Good News.

CONDITIONAL IMMORTALITY

In the Christian understanding the great dichotomy is between the created and the Creator, and this is well expressed by the recognition that it is only the Creator who *has* immortality (cf. 1 Tim. 6.16, God, *ho monos echōn athanasian*).

This statement draws attention to an important distinction in New Testament teaching which becomes blurred in the contemporary formulation of a doctrine of immortality. In the sense of *athanasia*, 'death-less', it is only the redeemed who are 'immortal', who are delivered from the two deaths (the first a physical dying; the second a subsequent, 'second death', (Rev. 20.6, 14–15).

But this must be distinguished from a second aspect of 'immortality', the unending existence of the soul once it has been brought into existence by God. We must at once dismiss the confusing importation of Greek philosophical notions here, which draw a sharp distinction between body and soul, characterizing the first as material and evil, and the second as spiritual and good. Such categories are not appropriate to biblical theology. On the contrary, as Alan Richardson neatly expresses it, the soul of man is correlative to a body and will be united with a body after the general resurrection of the dead.[48]

In the Platonic world-view, the soul, a spiritual entity, was trapped in the body, a physical entity, and was denied authentic life by the limitations imposed on it by the body. Death is then the liberation of the spirit, and far from being a tragedy becomes a good. As Oscar Cullmann has so clearly described it, Socrates then becomes the perfect example of the way to die a Platonic death, a serene, untroubled death.[49]

For the Christian the situation is very different. True enough, the *sting* of death is removed (1 Cor. 15.54–7), but it is still an enemy (1 Cor. 15.26). Furthermore, the human spirit is precisely *not* released from being tied to a body: rather it yearns to be reunited with its (glorified) body (2 Cor. 5.1–4).[50] But since a biblical view is of a personality consisting of body and soul-spirit, it is not clear that we can speak of the body experiencing death while the spirit-soul does not. It is clear that the shock-waves of the first death are felt by the *person*, and not merely by the body which in some sense 'belongs to' the person. In that sense, at least, the soul is not 'immortal', 'death-less'.

Just as the word 'immortal' has a certain ambiguity about it, so the term 'conditional immortality' also is ambiguous. Thus M. J. Harris uses it so as to highlight the aspect of 'death-less' as it relates to the believer but not to the unbeliever.[51] The *person* is seen to have an eternal existence, but the *unbelieving person* is not 'immortal', in that he does experience the second death, he is not 'death-less'. Immortality is then the gift of God consequent upon the resurrection experience, and humanity has only conditional immortality.

As we have seen, the vast majority of those who lived in time past, and even the majority of those who are alive today, have never heard the Christian Good News. If immortality is an inherent property of the human soul, and if that soul must, after death, experience either heaven or hell, and if the experience of heaven is only for those who have overtly heard of and responded to Jesus Christ, Son of God, Saviour, then these myriads are presumably destined for an eternal hell. Conditional immortality, however, rejects the idea of the soul being necessarily immortal, and supposes that some, at least, of the myriads might simply not transcend death . . .

71

ANNIHILATION

Related to the notion of conditional immortality is the view that although all pass through death and all face the last judgement, the outcome of that judgement is on the one hand eternal life or on the other hand actual destruction. It is argued that as in our experience fire serves primarily to destroy (and only in a secondary way to cause the pain of being burned), so the lake of fire of Revelation 20.15 indicates actually the annihilation of those hurled into it.

Now quite clearly the imagery of Revelation *is* imagery. This is clear from the description of 'death and Hades', *ho thanatos kai ho haidēs*, being thrown into the lake (Rev. 20.14). It is scarcely possible to interpret this particular imagery as signifying anything other than the *end* of death and Hades. Here the lake of fire does appear to carry with it the notion of destruction, annihilation; and if this is so in respect of death and Hades, it is clearly arguable that it is so, also, in respect of all others 'cast into' it.

We are then confronted with two distinct scenarios. In the first we are presented with an eternally continuing dichotomy, with the redeemed eternally enjoying God in conscious bliss, and the rest enduring an equally eternal experience of pain and suffering in hell. At least one problem arises with this scenario. As John Stott comments:

> . . . the eternal existence of the impenitent in hell would be hard to reconcile with the promises of God's final victory over evil, or with the apparently universalistic texts which speak of Christ drawing all men to himself (John 12:32), and of God uniting all things under Christ's headship (Ephesians 1:10).[52]

The second scenario is less complex: the impenitent are annihilated, the created world is dismissed, death and 'Hades' are no more, and God rules through Christ over a totally obedient people who enjoy him for ever. The problem here is that this attractive view does not appear to be reconcilable with those biblical passages which describe the outcome of the judgement.[53]

Firstly, Mark 9.48 describes hell as a place where the worm does not die and the fire is not quenched: the theory of annihilation suggests the opposite. Secondly, in the story of Lazarus and 'Dives' in Luke 16.19–31 the rich man continues in pain in the flames, and is clearly not annihilated. To appeal to an intermediate state between death and the final judgement, and to build on the story a doctrine of punishment *before* judgement seems to me to do violence to the very nature of the story. The story is not intended to set out a systematic thanatology, but it does treat seriously of hell, the fire being experienced by the rich man, and of heaven, 'Abraham's bosom', being experienced by Lazarus. Thirdly, Revelation 20.10 makes reference to those who have been cast into the lake of fire being tormented 'day and night for ever and ever', and it really will not do to dismiss this statement on the grounds that this is so stated only once.[54]

And fourthly, there is the very real difficulty that the eternal enjoyment of the redeemed is paralleled with the suffering of the lost: '. . . they will go away to eternal punishment, but the righteous to eternal life', *eis kolasin aiōnion . . . eis zōēn aiōnion* (Matt. 25.46). It is true that the destinies of the two groups are here being contrasted, so that in their subsequent experiences 'the more unlike they are, the better',[55] but in one matter the experiences do seem to be parallel: each is endless.

The fact is that however much we may shrink away from this, the most startling and horrific of biblical doctrines, the doctrine of an eternal hell, that doctrine cannot easily be eliminated from Scripture. The doctrine is not particularly adumbrated by Paul; on the contrary, as C. S. Lewis commented in his Introduction to J. B. Phillips' *Letters to Young Churches,*

> A most astonishing misconception has long dominated the modern mind on the subject of St Paul. It is to this effect: that Jesus preached a kindly and simple religion (found in the gospels) and that St Paul afterwards corrupted it into a cruel and complicated religion (found in the epistles). This is really quite untenable. All the most terrifying texts came from the mouth of our Lord.[56]

The real horror of the hell concept is that of its endlessness. The God of a hell-containing universe is characterized by David Edwards as 'the Eternal Torturer',[57] and, as Edwards implies, some Christian writers come close in their thinking about hell to that of the Qur'an, where Muhammad speaks of God creating new bodies to be burned whenever an existing body has been sufficiently tortured.[58]

There is an attitude towards hell which is not uncommon among evangelicals, an attitude which seems positively to rejoice in conjuring up lurid details of the expected sufferings of the impenitent there. John Stott, responding to David Edwards, comments: 'I want to repudiate with all the vehemence of which I am capable the glibness, what almost appears to be the glee, the *Schadenfreude*, with which some Evangelicals speak about hell. It is a horrible sickness of mind or spirit.'[59]

That the doctrine of an eternal hell is there in Scripture is beyond dispute. That the imagery is just that, imagery, is similarly beyond dispute. What it is that corresponds to that imagery we simply do not know. It is perfectly clear that the use of the imagery by Jesus himself must be taken as the most solemn warning to all who treat the life here, and even more the life to come, frivolously.

And finally it must be said that the emotive element in the discussion of an *eternal* hell is misplaced. We cannot import time into eternity. We are quite wrong to visualize people with physical bodies and nerves and emotions appropriate to the *present* world cowering in the *future* world in a furnace, while demons tend the fires, and going on enduring the fire 'day after day'. The resurrection body is a spiritual body (although in some essential way related to the present physical body, 1 Cor. 15.42–4), and in the resurrection life there is no time. Of course we cannot – and the prophets and apostles could not, and even Jesus could not – speak about eternity other than in terms analogous to the terms we apply to time. But in a post-Einsteinian world it is remarkable that Christians continue to debate theology in terms appropriate to the state of knowledge of the fifth century, pre-Boethius, as though we did not know the difference between time and eternity. In an eternity there can be no 'day after day'.

6 *Ten Theses* [1]

The formulation of the ten theses is in some sense a response to Hans Küng's comment on the questions traditionally asked by 'older missionaries' on the issue of the uniqueness of Christianity: 'If the conservatives in the Church are not always right with their answers, they are, however, very often right with their questions.'[2] This is very fair comment, but it underlines the reluctance of conservatives to express their answers to the questions properly raised by an exclusivist missiology.[3] The following ten theses represent an attempt to state succinctly a biblical position.

THE BASIS OF CONDEMNATION

Our first thesis is: *To any reasonable person it would appear to be unjust to condemn people to an eternal hell for failing to avail themselves of a medicine of which they have never heard and, moreover, of which they could not have heard.* That they have never heard of Jesus the Messiah is due not to a failure on their part, as if they were to seek *him*, but to a failure on the part of the Church, which is commanded to seek *them*.

The vast majority of the people born into this world have not experienced God's self-revelation through either Old Covenant or New. They have not known the law, as an indication of the will of God, nor as a guardian to lead them to Christ. They have not received messengers of the Church, announcing Good News. What they have had has been the threefold witness of conscience, the witness of God's self-revelation in creation, and the witness of some more or less defective religion. Each of these may make its contribution to an awareness of God, but none of them can give an overt knowledge of Christ. A soteriology which insists on the necessity of such an overt knowledge must necessarily condemn all these myriads to an eternal separation from God.

THE TOTAL SUFFICIENCY OF CHRIST'S ATONEMENT

The second thesis is: *The Passion – the death, resurrection, and ascension of Christ – provides sufficient covering for all sin, of all peoples, of all nations and throughout history.* The passion is clearly the focus of salvation history. The Good News is designated by Paul in his definitive summary (1 Cor. 15.3–4) as historical event, not as theological speculation. The Good News is that 'Christ died for our sins according to the Scriptures, that he was buried, that he was raised on the third day according to the Scriptures, and that he appeared . . .'

The centrality of the passion to the entire life of the Church is attested by baptism and Eucharist, each of these sacraments being related directly to the passion events. The Church then offers to the world its own life, a lively sacrifice, not as some supplement to the passion, but so as to make that passion known to the world as alone being a sufficient answer to the world's experience of *dukkha*. If the passion is efficacious for one it is similarly efficacious for all. No other Way needs to be found, no other Way can be found.

There is no attempt here to develop a particular theology of the passion in terms of satisfaction or redemption. The fact is that Christ died for our sins, and 'He is the atoning sacrifice for our sins, *and not only for ours but also for the sins of the whole world*' (1 John 2.2). How that should be is not our concern at this point.

THE CONTRIBUTION OF GENERAL REVELATION

We have already considered the combined evidence of Romans 1.18–32, Acts 17.22–34 and John 1.9 as indicative of some measure of general revelation. The Romans passage provides us with a concise statement of what has been revealed in creation, '[God's] invisible nature . . . his eternal power and deity' (Rom. 1.20, RSV), but is set in a discourse devoted at that particular point precisely *not* to the theme of salvation, but to the theme of condemnation. The Acts passage, however, makes reference to the same self-revelation of God in creation, through the obvious *design* of the world to be fitted to human habitation, and the cycle of the seasons, which guarantee the provision of human needs. And here we *are* given a clear statement of the salvific purpose of God: this self-revelation in creation *was* intended so that humanity 'should seek God, in the hope that they might feel after him and find him' (Acts 17.27, RSV).

It has been suggested above that Barth's denial of natural revelation fails to do justice to the relevant parts of Romans 1. Barth is concerned to guard his focus on the divine grace. And it may well be that, as always when we bring a systematic theology to Scripture for confirmation, the Scripture at certain points is not as compliant to the system as Barth would wish, and has to be restated appropriately.

However, it is not necessary to guard the doctrine of salvation through grace by a process of denying God's self-revelation in creation. As a consequence of an existential encounter with God through his creation, as a result of discovering his eternal power and deity, humanity is at the same time brought face to face with its own sinfulness and powerlessness, and may then acknowledge the justice of God in condemning every human religious activity, *and so be flung back on God's grace.*

Thus our third thesis is: *There is a divine self-revelation in creation which is not of itself salvific, but which may lead to the abandoning of human religious effort and to a flight to the mercy and grace of God.*

THE UNREDEEMED

Thesis four states: *Those who, in the spirit of Romans 1.21–3, refuse God's self-revelation in creation, and worship the created rather than the Creator, rightly incur the wrath of God.*

This thesis may well be expanded to include those who refuse God's self-revelation through the proclamation of the Good News about Jesus the Christ. But the fourth thesis has nothing at all to say about the position of those who, for whatever reason, are not aware of God's self-revelation in creation, and are never brought to the point of hearing the proclamation of the Good News. The teeming thousands in the shanties of Bombay and Calcutta, the starving children of the Horn of Africa, are unlikely to be able to see God in the utter meaninglessness of their existence. These who have never known anything but poverty, hunger, danger, disease, oppression . . . and the inevitability of a miserable and lonely death, these may never encounter the God of general revelation at all. And it is suggested that of these, as of the millions of infants who die prematurely, the Bible has very little to say beyond the assurance that the God of all the earth will act with justice and with mercy, he will do what is right (Gen. 18.25, in the context of an anticipated divine act of physical judgement).[4]

But the stark exclusiveness of a salvation that is offered only to those who are of the privileged few who overtly hear the proclamation of the Good News would appear to be not a biblical exclusiveness.[5]

THE REDEEMED

There are people who earnestly seek after God, seek to do what is right, even acting contrary to the religion into which they were born, so as to pursue the truth, although the truth that is in Christ has never been preached to them. Of such people Paul comments:

> When Gentiles who have not the law do by nature what the law requires, they are a law to themselves, even though they do not have the law. They show that what the law requires is written on their hearts, while their conscience also bears witness and their conflicting thoughts accuse *or perhaps excuse them* on that day when, according to my gospel, God judges the secrets of men by Christ Jesus (Rom. 2.14–16, RSV).

The fifth thesis states: *Those who have never heard the Christian Good News overtly preached, but who perceive God's eternal power and deity in his creation and seek after him in faith may, by the grace of God, be saved through the passion of that only Saviour of whom, through no fault of their own, they have not heard.*

It is instructive here to note that J. Oswald Sanders is aware of numerous examples of individuals receiving some direct revelation from God which prepared them for the coming of the Good News and predisposed them towards receiving it.[6] But he does not seem to be aware of the many poignant cases of such individuals who received just such a revelation, who abandoned their inherited religious system, who proclaimed such good news as they had perceived, *but who died before any witness to the Christian Good*

News came. In Ethiopia there was the man named Esa who, in the 1920s, called on the Gamo people to abandon the worship of their Spirit of Evil, and to worship God. When the missionaries finally reached Gamo a decade later they found the people prepared for them, but Esa had died.[7] It would be strange if they should be saved but their teacher lost . . .

It should, perhaps, be added at this point that the example of Cornelius, often referred to as indicating a way of salvation outside of either the Old or the New Covenant, is potentially misleading. He is designated 'a righteous and God-fearing man', one who was 'respected by all the Jewish people' (Acts 10.22); but if Peter's *apologia* in Acts 11 is to be relied upon, it was through the message brought by Peter that he was to be saved (v. 14). It may be argued that he has already been designated as 'righteous', *dikaios*, but the word itself has a wide domain of meaning in the Greek-speaking world, and need convey no more than that Cornelius was a man of the highest integrity.[8] Cornelius was a man who was seeking God, and it was through Peter's proclamation that he was found. Thus Cornelius is a good biblical illustration of the many examples referred to by Sanders of those who were prepared for the confrontation with the Good News by some preceding experience.

THE ROLE OF RELIGION

The Bible itself appears to be consistently opposed to religions. This would suggest that Küng's 'ordinary' way of salvation, through that religion into which an individual is born, is an unbiblical way, and that Rahner's proposal that a religion is itself salvific up to the point of its existential confrontation with Christianity[9] cannot be sustained.

This generally negative view of religions is confirmed by direct acquaintance with them. That humanity is incurably religious is undoubted, but it is our own determination to construct a religion without revelation that not infrequently blinds us to the revelation. As Barth so neatly expressed it, '. . . religion is unbelief. It is a concern, indeed we must say that it is the one great concern, of godless man.'[10] In Barth's sense, then, we distinguish between religion and revelation, we allow for a Christian 'religion' which is as man-made as all other religions, but deny any salvific efficacy to any religion.

The sixth thesis therefore states: *An individual may be saved in a religion or outside of a religion, but cannot be saved by a religion.*

SALVATION ONLY THROUGH CHRIST

There is clear biblical statement that salvation comes to us solely through Christ. The seminal reference is John 14.6, 'No-one comes to the Father except through me.' What this logion does affirm is that in so far as anyone approaches God, that approach is made possible by Christ. There is no other way. What the saying does *not* do is to define the prerequisites of the approach.

Since the logion is given without qualification, it must apply not only to us today, but also to all who lived under the Old Covenant. Indeed the central thesis of Hebrews is that the Old Covenant was of itself unable to deal with sin: 'The former regulation is set aside because it was weak and useless (for the law made nothing perfect), and a better hope is introduced, by which we draw near to God' (Heb. 7.18).[11] The basis of salvation under both covenants, then, was the coupling of the grace of the saving God with the grace-given faith of saved humanity through the work of Christ. The actual nature of the commitment to God was specific to each covenant. Under the Old Covenant there was no overt knowledge of Christ, but there was still a grace-given faith in God.

Obviously we are today, chronologically, not under the Old Covenant but under the New Covenant; that is to say, everywhere in the world it is equally true that the incarnation and the passion and the resurrection are past events. And yet in many parts of the world, and in the experience of myriads of people, the fact of the incarnation is as unknown as it was under the Old Covenant. What is required of such people is *not* the religious response, such as would have had its parallel in Canaanite religion, in the Ba'alim, in Bel and Nebo and Dagon, but the response of faith in the God of Creation, whose eternal power and divine nature was evident to them. The response, perhaps, of a Rahab, a prostitute (?), who was able to acknowledge God as 'God in heaven above and on the earth below' (Josh. 2.11).

Thesis seven is: *Salvation comes to us exclusively through*

*Christ, but an overt knowledge of Christ or of the work of Christ
was not a condition of salvation under the Old Covenant and is not
a condition of salvation under the New Covenant.*

THE ILLUMINATION OF THE LOGOS

It is clear that we are unable of ourselves to find God: the human
endeavour seems always to lead to the construction of a god made
in accordance with our own wishes. There is no common content
to the myriads of gods to be found named and described in the
world's religions. Each one reflects the particular insights of peoples
separated from one another in time and space, rather than any
genuine apprehension of the One Infinite.

This must not be interpreted to mean that all religions are at
every point wrong in their perceptions of God. There are genuine
insights, but they are so mixed with misperceptions that they
provide us with no reliable guide to the nature of God.

But we are not left without recourse. John 1.9 is our assurance
that there is such a thing as a true light, and that this one true light
gives light to each one of us. In the grace of God the true light
shines upon us all. It is precisely there that the question of greater
and lesser culpability must be introduced. There are those who,
because of their favourable conditions, because of their experience
of the good things of life, all given by God's grace, might be the
more expected to give thanks to God, might be expected to respond
the more readily to the Logos illumination. There are others who
from their birth have known little other than deprivation. Deprived
of parental love, deprived of health, deprived of education, eking
out a precarious existence in the context of fighting or famine,
they might be expected to respond very rarely to the light of God
shining fitfully into their lives. In fact we cannot predict who will
respond to the universally given light. It may well be that the
experience of *dukkha* in its most extreme form in fact impels us to
cry out to God for grace, out of an awareness that grace is to be
found nowhere else.

Thesis eight states: *God's eternal power and divine nature are
revealed in creation, and the human apprehension of that power
and nature is made possible only through the illumination from the
Logos, which shines upon everyone born into the world.*

THE VALIDITY OF CHRISTIAN MISSION

It has often been argued that if the general revelation of God's eternal nature and power are available to all in creation, and if that revelation is potentially salvific, then the whole motive for mission is at once removed. Even if that were true (and it is not), it could be no argument for denying a salvific general revelation if there were biblical grounds for affirming it. Certainly it would be inconsistent for the evangelical Christian to deny it.

The validity of the Christian mission is not to be found in a doctrine of the appalling fate of the millions who must inevitably perish unless we take the Good News to them. Nor is it to be found particularly in the terms of the Great Commission: it is striking that this is not made the foundation of mission for the New Testament Church. Of course the commission, the command *is* there, and *should* be obeyed. Paul expresses his own sense of responsibility and privilege very clearly:

> Therefore, if any one is in Christ, he is a new creation; the old has passed away, behold, the new has come. All this is from God, who through Christ reconciled us to himself and gave us the ministry of reconciliation; that is, in Christ God was reconciling the world to himself, not counting their trespasses against them, and entrusting to us the message of reconciliation. So we are ambassadors for Christ, God making his appeal through us (2 Cor. 5.17-20, RSV).

Paul's point is not so much that of a potential escape from a future hell, but the possibility of a new creation, of the end of a long period of estrangement from God, of the resolution of *dukkha*, Life *can* make sense!

Thus thesis nine states: *The Christian mission is valid because only in an overt knowledge of the Good News about Jesus Christ can we hope to live a truly human and meaningful life now, looking forward with confidence, beyond death, to the consummation of that purpose for which we were created.*

Those who are able to perceive God's eternal nature and power in creation do not thereby have that illumination, that understanding, which comes with the proclaimed Good News. The apparent meaninglessness of life remains, for them, an unresolved mystery. In some sense they share the partial sight of those who lived under the Old Covenant, lacking the full day that dawns only when Christ is really known.

Christian mission, then, confronts humanity as those who, in accordance with John 1.9 have some measure of Logos enlightenment, and who, in the spirit of Romans 1.20, have revelation already available to them in creation. Some of those we confront with the Good News might, indeed, be brought from one level of faith to another, from one experience of the grace of God to a deeper one. Others will be brought from darkness to light. Still others may determine to remain in darkness.

THE ROLE OF HUMAN LANGUAGE AND LOGIC

It is true that human language is at best imprecise. Human logic is often flawed, and the human thought process fragile. But the very process of redemption makes it possible for God's people by the Holy Spirit to use language responsibly and to think clearly. If this were not so then the writings of our theologians and the exhortations of our preachers and the ministry of mission itself would all be futile.

Thesis ten states: *Any solution to the problem posed by the continuing existence of vast numbers of those who through no fault of their own have never heard the Good News about Jesus Christ must be formulated so as to take into account the total character of God as revealed in the totality of Scripture: his grace, mercy, patience, justice, holiness, righteousness, love. And such a solution will not, then, outrage common sense and our common ideas of justice. The Lord of all the earth does what is right.*

PART TWO

Mission as Response to the Apparent Meaninglessness of Life

7 The Mission Theology of Matthew

INTRODUCTION

Part Two is concerned with a preliminary and tentative exegesis of those parts of the New Testament which appear to contribute to a comprehensive Christian response to the problem posed by the apparent meaninglessness of life.

The response is formulated in terms of mission. This involves an understanding of *the Church* which is given the mission, in terms of the people towards whom mission is directed, and therefore necessarily of an understanding of *the human predicament*. In turn this requires an understanding of *the content of the mission*: the nature of the words to be spoken, and of the praxis by which the words are to be validated.

It has been traditional to categorize the mission of the Church in terms of selected texts, among which Acts 1.8 and Matthew 28.16–20 have been the most important. Here we shall examine not merely Matthew 28.16–20, but the whole of Matthew's Gospel as representing a mission discourse, and then we shall turn to the other related themes indicated above.

THE STRUCTURE OF THE GOSPEL

The Gospel of Matthew has as its primary theme the proclamation of the Kingdom of God. There are fifty references to the Kingdom, the Kingdom of God, or the Kingdom of Heaven, in Matthew[1] and the Good News itself is overtly labelled 'this gospel of the kingdom', *touto to euangelion tēs basileias*, in 24.14. However it has reached its present form, the discourse as it now exists exhibits strong coherence and clear development. In terms of discourse analysis the *peak*[2] of the Gospel is undoubtedly the so-called Great Commission of 28.16–20.[3] David Bauer expresses the climactic nature of this passage in linguistic terms:

The fourth major structural relationship binding the Gospel of Matthew together is that of climax, found at 28.16–20. Here Jesus appears to his disciples as the exalted and resurrected Christ, who commissions them to make disciples of all nations. Moreover, the promise of Jesus to be 'with us' (28.20) serves with 1.23 to bracket the Gospel, thus indicating inclusio.[4]

Matthew has structured his writing as an entelechy of the Gospel, in which the restricted concept of the Kingdom, inseparable from its necessarily Jewish origin, unfolds into the vision of a boundless, world-embracing Kingdom from which many Jews are excluded but into which the Gentiles stream.[5] Jesus *was* a Jew, as were his first followers, and his ministry *was* firstly to the Jew. In that sense we are to understand Matthew 10.1–42. But it is (significantly?[6]) on an unnamed mountain that the greater vision and the more inclusive commission of 28.16–20 is given to the disciples.

That Matthew has carefully structured his Gospel is agreed by all commentators. The actual details of the structuring attract less unanimity. However, there are clear transition markers at various points within the Gospel which move the discourse from one episode to the next. The Gospel, then, presents the classical structure of discourse:

1. *Title.* The opening verse of the Gospel establishes genre: we are to read of an individual of a significant and Jewish background.

2. *Stage.* The staging of the total discourse, the introduction of the theme. This is effected in two parts, first through the genealogy (1.1–17) and the birth narrative (1.18—2.23), which firmly establishes the discourse in its Jewish context, and unambiguously presents to the reader a historical narrative focusing on the person of Jesus, and then through the second Stage (separated from the first part by some thirty years), the introduction of the forerunner, John, and of the central figure, Jesus, at the starting-point of his activity.

But stage does more than this: it also introduces five[7] of the topics which become part of the thematic net: the topic of conflict-about-Jesus; the topic of prophecy-fulfilment; the topic of a heaven-to-earth dialogue mediated through Jesus; the topic of the Kingdom of God, proclaimed first by John (3.2) and then by Jesus (4.17); and the topic of the disorder of human existence, of inexplicable suffering, of the non-correspondence between an individual's spiritual integrity and that individual's experiences (the sudden and, to those immediately involved, inexplicable murder of the children at Bethlehem. The imprisonment of John).[8] The five topics are clearly interrelated, thus giving strength to the thematic net and raising the level of discourse coherence.

3. *Episodes.* The discourse is carried forward through a series of related pericopae which are there to explicate further those elements which constitute the thematic net. The structure is essentially linear (unlike the structure of John's Gospel, which is cyclic), advancing steadily towards the ultimate revelation of the King of the Kingdom as a crucified, and then as an ascended, King who commissions his followers to the task of mission.

The pericopae may readily be identified by the clear transition markers used by Matthew. These usually have the effect of moving Jesus from one place to another: 'he went up on a mountainside' (5.1); 'When he came down from the mountainside' (8.1); 'Jesus went through the cornfields' (12.1); 'he withdrew by boat' (14.13). There are also chronological transition markers, often little more than literary devices, with no particular reference to real time (unlike some of John's markers and many of Luke's): 'After Jesus had finished instructing' (11.1); 'At that time' (12.1). But note the appearance of some precise and significant chronological markers of transition, as in 17.1, 'After six days'. These transition markers may be used objectively to identify the constituents of the Gospel, and a more subjective use may be made of them if the constituents are grouped or assigned relative significance.

4. *Peak.* Prominence is given to the events of the passion by the sheer amount of space accorded to it. Jesus arrives in Jerusalem in 21.1, the account of the crucifixion and burial concludes at the end of chapter 27,[9] and the resurrection events occupy 28.1–15. But while these events constitute a peak of sorts, the common characteristics of peaking are missing. The description of the unnatural darkness, the cry of dereliction, the actual death of Jesus, the eerie opening of the tombs, the confession of the centurion, any of these could have been utilized as the peak, but none is. There is no concise 'wrap-up' to the story, neither a concentration of nor a dispersing of the actors in the events; indeed, the two Marys are left sitting near the tomb of Jesus, and

the narrative continues. In fact not one of the three principal markers of peaking identified by R. E. Longacre[10] is here.

The peak is, however, in the last part of chapter 28. There is the removal of the eleven disciples to an unnamed mountain in Galilee, and the appearance of the resurrected Jesus to them. There is the act of the commissioning of the disciples . . . and the discourse ends abruptly and with great artistry with reference to the *synteleias tou aiōnos*. The commissioning of the disciples is not a post-peak episode, but the peak, and the normal 'wrap-up' or conclusion of the discourse is simply telescoped into the peak.

The discourse structure[11] may be indicated as follows, although other analyses are possible, depending on the weight given to the various transition markers available in the text (the transition markers used in the analysis of the episodes are indicated in italics):

1 Stage: 1.1−4.25
    Part One: The genealogy and birth narrative (1.1−2.23)
    Part Two: John the forerunner and Jesus the King (3.1−4.25)
2 Pre-Peak Episodes: 5.1−28.15
    (5.1, 'he went up on a mountainside and sat down')
    Episode 1 (5.1−7.29) − Explicating the Kingdom: The Sermon on the Mount
    (8.1, 'When he came down from the mountainside')
    Episode 2 (8.1−9.34) − Demonstrating the Power of the Kingdom
    (9.35, 'Jesus went through all the towns and villages')
    Episode 3 (9.35−10.42) − Inaugurating the Mission to the Jews
    (11.1, 'After Jesus had finished instructing his twelve disciples')
    Episode 4 (11.1-30) − Teaching and Preaching
    (12.1, 'At that time Jesus went through the cornfields')
    Episode 5 (12.1-50) − The Absolute Demands of the Kingdom
    (13.1, 'That same day Jesus went out of the house and sat by the lake')
    Episode 6 (13.1−20.34) − Parables and Signs of the Kingdom
    (21.1, 'As they approached Jerusalem')
    Episode 7 (21.1−28.15) − The Redemptive Foundation of the Kingdom
    (28.16, 'Then the eleven disciples went to Galilee')
3 Peak and Closure (28.16-20) − The Commissioning of the Apostles

MATTHEW'S EMPHASIS ON THE HUMAN DISORDER

Jesus is first presented through the *dukkha* of the extended birth narrative, in which the life of the infant is threatened. Joseph and Mary take him to safety in Egypt, but the consequence is the appalling and, to those involved, utterly meaningless horror of the massacre at Bethlehem. It is easy to exaggerate the event: it is unlikely that more than a dozen or so[12] children were killed, but for the parents of those few the sense of desolation, of meaninglessness, must have been almost intolerable.

It has been suggested that the story itself is a mere fabrication by Matthew as a commentary on Jeremiah 31.15. If we dismiss the visit of the wise men as pious legend, then inevitably the various consequences of their visit may likewise be dismissed. But there is no objective reason for doing so. The execution of the children would entirely accord with what we know of Herod's character. The absence of any contemporary record to confirm the biblical account is not unexpected: it was a minor event in an entirely insignificant town of a remote Roman colony.[13]

But the event introduces the theme of disordered human existence, and this theme is at once reinforced by the introduction of John the Baptist, a prophetic figure familiar from the Old Testament scriptures, a figure pitched against the rulers, against the exploiters, a new Isaiah, a fresh Jeremiah. One who will share the *dukkha* experience of many another prophet (Matt. 23.29-39). This experience of undeserved and apparently meaningless imprisonment and death will be recorded in due course, but simple reference to John at this point is sufficient for the purposes of the author, since these details (although not necessarily their *significance*) are in the presupposition pool of the readers.

The Beatitudes contribute further to an understanding of the human disorder. The natural perception of the structures of society is reversed by Jesus: it is the humble who will possess the earth, the poor and the persecuted who possess the Kingdom. And this is so because we have wrongly evaluated the present existence. Treasure amassed on earth is vulnerable, transitory, deceitful: it is treasure in heaven that is alone of significance. The balance sheet is not to be struck just yet!

But Jesus does not merely *talk*: although he is clear about the ultimate significance of the life beyond, that does not blind him to human need now. In a limited sense (in some ways parallel to what the Church might accomplish today), Jesus resolves the disorder – leprosy is cured, the blind see, the dead are raised, the mourner rejoices:

> Great crowds came to him, bringing the lame, the blind, the crippled, the mute and many others, and laid them at his feet; and he healed them. The people were amazed when they saw the mute speaking, the crippled made well, the lame walking and the blind seeing. And they praised the God of Israel (15.30–1).

Nor is the theme of human disorder missing from the parables of Jesus. Matthew records the parable of the two debtors (18.23–35), the one forgiven by the king, but who then abused and handed over to imprisonment the other, a fellow servant who owed him a comparatively trivial amount. The crushing experience of indebtedness must have been a commonplace occurrence for poor people forced to borrow at often extortionate rates of interest,[14] and the *dukkha* element is heightened, although believably heightened, by the oppressive action of the first debtor. But again the disorder in the parable is reduced by reference to the inescapable judgement by the King, and Jesus' listeners would have had no difficulty in interpreting the eschatological implications of the parable.

Finally, the space given by Matthew to the events associated with the passion makes it possible for the event to be seen as it was: the ultimate quality of *dukkha*, of the human disorder, but an event in which God himself enters into the common human experience. The baselessness of the accusations brought against Jesus is made clear: Pilate knows that the motive for the arrest is envy (27.18); his wife in a dream becomes convinced of the innocence of Jesus and conveys the information to her husband, the judge (27.19). The extraordinary fact of the release of Barabbas, the convicted insurrectionist, rather than of the guiltless Jesus, is recorded. And the painful details of the crucifixion of Jesus and the unfeeling mockery of the religious leaders are added.

Matthew's Gospel must have been an illuminating document for those who first read it, giving rise to strong feelings of identification with the thrust of it from the poor, and to internal conflict, feelings of guilt, outrage, perhaps, from the powerful. And it becomes clear that the resolution of *dukkha* will come from one who embraced it, but who also commissions his people to begin to resolve it.

THE FIRST AND LIMITED COMMISSION [15]

The Lesser Commission of the Disciples (9.36–10.42)

The first dispatching of the twelve, and the detailed explanations that accompanied the commissioning, are preceded in Matthew by a sequence of confrontations with human need, involving twelve individuals and several references to crowds:

8.2 A man with leprosy
8.6 A centurion's servant
8.14 Peter's mother-in-law
(8.16 'many who were demon-possessed')
8.28 Two demon-possessed men
9.2 A Paralytic
9.9 Matthew
(9.10 'many tax collectors and "sinners"')
9.18 The daughter of a synagogue ruler
9.20 A woman with a haemorrhage
9.27 Two blind men
9.32 A man who was demon-possessed

This sequence then leads into a generalizing paragraph in which Jesus is pictured among the people, and is touched with compassion by their condition.[16] It is primarily the ordinary people who are in mind: the uninfluential, the powerless, those whose condition is summarized as 'harassed and helpless' (9.36). It is they who can properly be characterized as 'sheep without a shepherd' (9.36).

This phrase is not unimportant. The whole thrust of the Jewish scriptures was one of concern for these sheep, and with the need to provide shepherds for them. But tragically the appointed shepherds lacked compassion, lacked motivation to be shepherds for these sheep. And when Jesus demonstrates his power to help, the response of the Pharisees, the appointed shepherds, is (in 9.34, immediately preceding the mission commission), to dismiss what Jesus has done as the work of the Second Kingdom. This then clears the way for the appointment of new shepherds, and marks a transition of power, from the power of the learned Pharisees to the dominically provided authority of the apostles. As we shall see below, pp. 104–7, the lostness and disorder of the human condition is repeatedly pictured in Scripture in pastoral terms.

The mission of the disciples is here immediately associated with the tragedies of human life, its inescapable *dukkha*. It is one thing for a Teacher to come proclaiming a new ethic, but another for that same Teacher to come down from his mountain and actually deal with *dukkha*. The Good News is demonstrated *both* in word *and* praxeologically: a dead child is brought to life, a distressed woman has her haemorrhage cured, the blind see, the demon-possessed are released.

Importantly, the commissioning of the disciples parallels the ministry they have just witnessed. There is the praxeological ministry: 'Heal the sick, raise the dead, cleanse those who have leprosy, drive out demons' (10.7). There is a proclamation ministry: 'As you go, preach this message: "The kingdom of heaven is near"' (10.7).

The mission is a limited mission. It illustrates the one undoubted priority of the Christian mission: mission to the Jew first.[17] And at this point of Matthew's discourse there can only be a limited mission paralleling the limited mission of Jesus himself. But Jesus here does what he has told his disciples to pray the Father to do (9.38), to *ekballein*, 'thrust out', labourers.

The Limited Commission of Jesus (15.21–8)

The temporarily limited nature of the mission of Jesus is made explicit in 15.21–8,[18] and the incident is very instructive. A Canaanite woman, a Gentile, asks for help. The disciples of Jesus (mindful of his limiting commission already given?) urge Jesus to send her away. His reply to the woman suggests unequivocal refusal: 'I was sent only to the lost sheep of Israel' (15.24). And yet when she persists in faith Jesus grants her request. The incident is important in two ways: it indicates that Jesus' ministry was only *generally* limited to the Jewish people, and it indicates the enormous danger of taking even the statements attributed to Jesus in some literal, grammatical, formal, way. What he said, analysed formally,

94

could only have meant a refusal. The discourse meaning, however, was only a conditional negative.

So, then, during his brief ministry in Galilee and Judaea, Jesus ministered principally, but not exclusively, to the Jews. But the new wine could not be confined to the old wineskin: inevitably it overflowed to the thirsty peoples who thronged around the one who gave it, and it overflowed beyond ethnic boundaries.

MATTHEW'S GREAT COMMISSION (28.16–20)[19]

As we have indicated above (pp. 87–90) Matthew has intentionally climaxed his record of the life of Jesus with the commissioning of the disciples for mission. This is the high-point of Matthew's Gospel, as 20.31 is the high-point of John's Gospel. The writing is highly condensed, readily memorized, and demonstrates an impressive theological profundity. These five verses explain why the labour of producing the twenty-eight chapters of the Gospel is justified.

[16] Then the eleven disciples went to Galilee, to the mountain where Jesus had told them to go. [17] When they saw him, they worshipped him; but some doubted. [18] Then Jesus came to them and said, 'All authority in heaven and on earth has been given to me. [19] Therefore go and make disciples of all nations, baptising them in the name of the Father and of the Son and of the Holy Spirit, [20] and teaching them to obey everything I have commanded you. And surely I am with you always, to the very end of the age.'

This brief pericope simply bristles with difficulties of every kind: theological, chronological and linguistic. As a foundation for Christian mission it has a certain importance, although it is notable that this commissioning is not adduced by Paul, for example, as the rationale for his mission outreach.

Structurally, there is certainly some significance to be given to the emphatic and repeated use of 'all', *pas*, in these verses.[20] What we have is an unqualified claim to authority which is to be set over against the mainly localized or ethnic claims of the Jews or the Athenians or the Corinthians for their gods. The followers of Jesus are commissioned by a God whose claims are to be pressed not for political reasons, as was the case with Rome, nor for economic reasons, as was the case at Ephesus, but because *exousia* is to be found in him and nowhere else.

In 28.10 Jesus instructs the women returning from the empty tomb that the disciples are to be ordered to Galilee, where he will appear to them. The actual confrontation is set on a mountain, although the mountain is not identified. It is possible that we are intended by the author to associate this mountain experience with that in chapter five – for the Sermon on the Mount the disciples came to Jesus (*proselthan*), and for the commissioning Jesus comes to the disciples (*proselthōn*) – but the association, if there is one, is no more than hinted at.

The narrative is presented in a clear sequence, and suggests that this appearance of Jesus is not a sudden appearance, but that he comes to them naturally, walking up the mountain pathways. Initially they see him, and tentatively identify him, [21] and it would appear that while some were at once convinced that this was the risen Lord, and worshipped, others were unsure.[22] And it was following this initial period of doubt that Jesus came close enough to them so that all doubt concerning his identity could be resolved.

It has long been agreed that the words of Jesus fall into three parts, a statement, a command, and a promise; but the laboured attempts to relate this observation to Old Testament theophanies and to some formal underlying structure, a *Gattung*,[23] represent misplaced ingenuity.

The Statement

This deals with the authority of Jesus: *all* authority, *pasa exousia*, has been given to him (28.18). This must mean that as the glorified, obedient Servant of the Lord, something has been accorded to him by the Father which was not his before. His action at the cross, the atonement that he made, the ransom that he paid, has brought about a new situation in salvation history.

There is in this pericope a significant reference to the focal role in Matthew of the Daniel 7 vision. In that vision 'one like a son of man' came to the 'Ancient of Days' and was given authority, glory and sovereign power (Dan. 7.13–14). In Matthew 26.64 that same vision, proclaimed by Jesus to his accusers, is used as the climax[24] of the trial scene. Here we have an allusion to the Daniel vision, sufficient to enable us to recognize the profound significance of what has now happened. Matthew has no account of the ascension (unlike Luke, Acts 1.9, and possibly Mark, Mark 16.19): the allusion to Daniel would have been enough for the readers for whom Matthew was writing.

The new *exousia* given to Jesus represents a new power that arises out of the salvific action of Jesus at the cross. The task of setting creation free has been decisively initiated, the cosmic conflict has been finally resolved, and a new authority, therefore, is given to Jesus. It is a cosmic authority: all power, in heaven and on earth. Thus the foundation has been laid for dealing with the problem of *dukkha*, a problem that exists as a consequence of a 'fall' of cosmic significance, the resolution of which demands a cosmic *exousia*.

The Command

The participle *poreuthentes*, 'go', marks a transition from the preliminary statement, to the threefold command to the disciples, that they are to make disciples, baptize them, and to instruct them, *mathēteusate panta ta ethnē*.

The three participles here are all in some sense subordinated to the imperitival *matheteusate*. As Donald Carson points out, the participles necessarily take on an imperatival force,[25] so that the apostles are commissioned with a specific centrifugal mission, which is now stripped of its earlier limitation to mission to the Jews.

The tendency of translators here to translate *mathēteusate* as a phrase, 'make disciples', has encouraged exegetes then to deal with the text in two discrete parts: expounding the meaning of 'making disciples' first, and then discussing the meaning of *panta ta ethnē* as a separate process. This then allows the idea of the *mathētos*, which appears elsewhere in Matthew as applied generally to the followers of Jesus, to be applied to the missionary task. In fact the commission requires the apostles to disciple all the nations. Matthew uses an aorist imperative: 'you (pl.)-disciple'. It is not a question of drawing disciples *out of* all the nations, but is a command to disciple the peoples of the world. The phrase *panta ta ethnē* is not to be understood woodenly, as producing some disciples at least from every nation known to us. Nor is it intended to indicate an end to the mission to the Jews and the beginning of mission to the Gentiles. The phrase *panta ta ethnē* is intended to be all-inclusive: nations everywhere are to be discipled. There are no longer geographical limitations placed on the mission of the disciples, such as had clearly existed in the three years of Jesus' ministry. The identical phrase occurs in

> Matthew 24.9, 'you will be hated by all nations'
> 24.14, 'this Gospel . . . will be preached . . . as a testimony to all nations'
> and 25.32, 'All the nations will be gathered before him',

in each case meaning all peoples, Jews and Gentiles. There is no reason for importing a more limited meaning, 'to all the (non-Jewish) nations', simply on the strength of the use of *ethnē*, taken to have only the Gentile nations as its referent.[26]

But we may once again see the importance of understanding Matthew not in terms of a collection of proof texts, or even of a collection of more or less related stories, but in terms of a carefully structured discourse. For in tracing the genealogy of Jesus to its origin in Abraham, Matthew was necessarily directing the attention of his readers to the original calling of Abraham, to the missiological blessing directed through Abraham to *panta ta ethnē* (Matt. 1.1–2): 'Matthew's Gospel is now, in its final verses, returning to the theme introduced in the very first verse . . . that the blessings promised to Abraham and through him to all peoples on earth (Gen. 12.3) are now to be fulfilled in Jesus the Messiah.'[27]

The command to the disciples continues through reference to baptizing and teaching those who are discipled, again using participles which necessarily take on an imperatival force from the imperative form of *mathēteusate*.[28] Clearly neither the teaching nor the baptizing are of themselves salvific, but they are both an integral part of the discipling process: proclamation is to be followed by faith and repentance, to be followed in turn by baptism and instruction. Baptism into the name (*eis to onoma*) implies a new relationship with God, a relationship which involves reconciliation, but which also implies some sense of subjection to the triune God. There is no need here to assume that Jesus was giving the disciples a baptismal *formula* to be used at all subsequent baptisms, an assumption which then gives rise to conflict with the rather consistent use of a monadic formula in Acts. The important point is that reconciliation with God is effected through incorporation into Christ, and there can be no other way. This point the first Christians perceived very clearly, and it was reflected in their baptismal practice: converts were baptized into the name of Jesus.

The Promise

Matthew's Gospel has consistently presented mission as a conflict mission, as mission in which opposition and division are to be the normal experience. There have been few 'comfortable words' about mission. It is for this reason that the Gospel concludes with a twofold assurance: Jesus is to be with his people *pasas tēs hēmeras*, 'all the days', and until *tēs sunteleias tou aiōnos*, 'the end of the age'. In the short term Jesus is to be with his messengers (in so far as they are engaged in obeying his commission?) each and every day. They will never for one moment be left to depend on their own *exousia*. In the long term the Church is to know that this will always be the case, until the final *parousia*, which will climax the age.

8 The Human Disorder

A VIEW FROM PSALM 8

We turn now from the examination of *dukkha* and the various conflicting attempts to explain and resolve *dukkha* by the world's religions to a consideration of human nature, that situation which is a particular concern of Christian mission.

Life, as we perceive it, has two apparent boundaries, birth and death. We are not able objectively to pursue our investigations into human existence beyond those two boundaries. Theoretically, there is nothing to hinder our speculating on what might lie beyond, and to attempt to correlate our speculations with such evidence as we might adduce as bearing on the subject. This evidence would certainly include the fact of human mortality: the ultimate and apparently inevitable corruption of the body. It would also include the facts regarding conception, and the phenomenon of memory: its apparent limitations and such examples as we have of 'memories' of events which lie theoretically beyond the existence span of the one who, none the less 'remembers'.[1] We would take into account our potentiality for greatness, and the contrasting realities of human wickedness. And this would cause us to consider the significance of the very possibility of our identifying a category 'wicked'.

In any assessment of humanity we must take into account our undoubted achievements technologically: the buildings we have erected, the machines we have constructed, our ability to manipulate our environment, our brash exploitation of the rest of creation, animal, mineral, vegetable. We would also take into account the undoubted failures of humanity: wars, murders, attempts at mass genocide, the ongoing class warfare that gave rise to the theories of Karl Marx, the religions which some would see as responsible for more human misery than any other single factor.[2] The long table of contemporary religious conflicts may be allowed to provide a foreground for a history of similar religious conflicts of which the Crusades present not the least discreditable.

And so we ask: What of humanity? The answer is to be given in terms of the fundamental questions, 'Who am I?', and 'Who are you?', and 'What is this world in which we must somehow live together?'

The Bible offers a stylized history of mankind, from creation in Genesis to the consummation in Revelation, with the incarnation marking the one crucial division of history acknowledged there. Of history as we traditionally recognize it there is little sign. Great events known to us from other civilizations and other histories are passed over in silence, while the apparently trivial events in the life of an apparently trivial desert people are recorded with desperate solemnity. The history that we have is a new kind of history: the history of the relationship between God and his people. In the same way the Gospels which figure so prominently in the second part of the Bible represent a new literary genre. They are not biographies of Jesus, nor are they theological treatises, but they treat of the Kingdom of God and of the salvation of man through the activities of one whom the Church eventually categorized uniquely as utterly human and yet utterly divine.

The Bible describes humanity as humanity really is. There is little attempt at idealizing the characters whose exploits are recorded. David is both a murderer and an adulterer, and these sins of God's chosen king go down in the book. Solomon asks wisdom from God, receives it, and then enforces slave labour on his peoples and vastly outdoes his father in lechery: and all goes down in the book. So again we ask: What of humanity? Psalm 8 offers a response to the question:

> O Lord, our Lord,
>> how majestic is thy name in all the earth!
>
> Thou whose glory above the heavens is chanted
>> by the mouth of babes and infants,
> thou hast founded a bulwark because of thy foes,
>> to still the enemy and the avenger.
>
> When I look at thy heavens, the work of thy fingers,
>> the moon and the stars which thou hast established;
> what is man that thou art mindful of him,
>> and the son of man that thou dost care for him?

> Yet thou hast made him little less than God,
>> and dost crown him with glory and honour.
> Thou hast given him dominion over the work of thy hands;
>> thou hast put all things under his feet,
> all sheep and oxen,
>> and also the beasts of the field,
> the birds of the air, and the fish of the sea,
>> whatever passes along the paths of the sea.
>
> O Lord, our Lord,
>> how majestic is thy name in all the earth!

(Ps. 8, RSV)

The psalm is referred to by Jesus in Matthew 21.16 to justify the uproar in the temple caused by the rejoicing of the children at his arrival there, and Paul takes up verse six in 1 Corinthians 15.27 in an important christological passage, and again in Ephesians 1.22 with the same import. Best remembered is the use made of Psalm 8 by the writer to the Hebrews, who makes Jesus the archetypical fulfilment of the psalm (Heb. 2.5–9) possibly aided in this endeavour by the appearance of the designation 'son of man' at verse 4.

However, despite this use of the psalm by New Testament writers, it clearly refers primarily to humanity at large: *this* is how God intended the order of creation to be. Significantly, the psalm which treats of the greatness of humanity is saved from the worship of man by its twinned opening and closing verses: 'O Lord, our Lord, how majestic is thy name in all the earth!' The psalmist is no worshipper of humanity, nor even of nature: 'Behind the glorious splendour of the brilliant sky his mind's eye envisages him who has created that splendour. It is for him, for the divine Creator, that his song is intended.'[3]

It is the centre section of the psalm which gives us the polarity which characterizes and informs everything that the Bible has to say to us about humanity. There are the heavens, the stars, all created by God, all so vast, so remote . . . and in all this vast creation, what is man? And yet. We look around us and ask ourselves the same question, but with a very different tone: 'What is man!' And in fine here is the heart of the human problem. We are created with gifts and graces and skills and potentialities which leave almost nothing beyond our grasp. And so we are tempted to reach out, but without God. The ultimate sin is pride, and pride can only come when there is something to be proud of. And we *have* something to be proud of. So enters pride, and sin, and God's world suffers accordingly.

As Emil Brunner points out, the world's religions all recognize the reality of futility, of the apparent meaninglessness of life, the impossibility even of behaving as rational individuals. But the explanations of this human predicament, this inner contradiction, are unsatisfactory:

> Some maintain that the contradiction springs from the dual character of our nature, that is, the fact that we are both body and mind; or it is supposed to be due to our fatal entanglement with earthly-cosmic existence, or it is a tragic Fate, due to the will of supernatural forces . . . In all these 'explanations' the attempt is made to derive evil from a kind of fate, and thus to relieve man of responsibility for his existence.[4]

But the opposite error is also found. The reality of *dukkha* is explained in entirely moral terms: evil flows from the freely exercised will of humanity. But there is then no explanation offered for the fact of the lack of concord between the will and the deed. What is needed is a reconciliation of the two conflicting theories, a perception of the human responsibility and of the human impotence, the Macquarrie polarity of responsibility and impotence,[5] which should then send us not to created man for rescue, but to the Creator.

A DOCTRINE OF LOSTNESS

Introduction

The biblical picture of humanity is that of dependence on God. We are created, not spontaneously generated, and that fact establishes our dependence. Genesis begins slowly, deliberately: 'In the beginning God . . .' Not man. It is God who brings humanity into existence, and from that beginning his very breath depends on God: 'Turn away from man in whose nostrils is breath, for of what account is he?' (Isa. 2.22, RSV), 'Stop trusting in man, who has but a breath in his nostrils' (NIV). And that is all he has: one breath, and no guarantee of another unless it come from the grace of God.

But if we are all pictured as dependent, the biblical picture is also of our being separated from God. Uniformly, we can see God seeking us, uninvited, even unwelcomed.[6] It is God who chooses Abraham, not Abraham who travels to Canaan in search of God. It is God who chooses Moses to deliver his people, not Moses whose compassion is first stirred by the plight of his people. God chooses Jeremiah, who discounts his calling. God chooses Paul when he is persecuting the Church. Always and everywhere it is God who seeks a lost humanity. There is no Muhammad, here, retiring to a cave in search of God. No Gautama, sitting beneath his tree and seeking for enlightenment.

As Isaiah so boldly puts it:

> I was ready to be sought by those who did not ask for me;
>   I was ready to be found by those who did not seek me.
> I said, 'Here am I, here am I,'
>   to a nation that did not call on my name.
> I spread out my hands all the day
>   to a rebellious people . . .

(Isa. 65.1–2, RSV)

And if this was true of the chosen people of God, the descendants of Abraham, it was even more true of the surrounding nations, of those who, lacking revelation, and failing to profit from God's self-revelation in creation, fashioned their own gods, formulated their own creeds. Against this determined religiosity of a humanity that was aware of its own potential, of its own power, God set his face.

There are, then, two characteristics of humanity: humanity is lost, and needs to be found; humanity is estranged, and needs to be reconciled. These two needs must be supplied by God. *That* is the scenario for the salvific purposes of God.

Lost: The Pastoral Illustration (Luke 15)

To a pastoral people it would be natural to compare God's people to a flock of sheep, and to identify Yahweh as the Shepherd of the flock. The analogy is one of high correspondence: it is fruitful of legitimate and meaningful extension.[7]

In Ezekiel 34 we have the most extended of the Old Testament applications of the shepherding imagery. The picture is consistent: Yahweh has appointed shepherds over what none the less remains his own flock. On the part of these shepherds there is a responsibility to carry out their duties, while their reward is from God: remaining in the imagery, it is that they should be clothed from the sheep's wool and be fed from their meat. (The parallel imagery of the New Testament is relevant here: it is entirely appropriate for Christian ministers to receive, in return for their labours, material recompense from those to whom they minister (1 Cor. 9, esp. v. 11).) But the right to benefit from the flock is conditional upon the fulfilment of the duty. Three consequences flow from the failure of the 'shepherds': the right of the shepherds to their wages is terminated, the flock is left unshepherded, and God himself steps in to assume the responsibility of Shepherd of Israel. It is worth noting here that the full range of duties for the shepherd includes a search ministry: 'The weak you have not strengthened, the sick you have not healed, the crippled you have not bound up, the strayed you have not brought back, the lost you have not sought . . .' (Ezek. 34.4, RSV). It is important here to note the consequences for the flock: they are scattered, become a prey, become food for the wild beasts. Although the application is reasonably apparent, it is yet worth stating. The shepherds are the political leaders of Judah. As Eichrodt puts it:

> Ezekiel thus supplies the final climax of the protest against the political leaders of Israel which his predecessors had raised repeatedly. The mismanagement for which the ruling classes in Judah were responsible had, especially at this point in the closing days of the kingdom, increased to a terrifying extent . . .[8]

For our present purposes it is sufficient to note that the likening of the people of God to a flock of sheep is admitted to be appropriate, that people *need* a shepherd, and without someone to care for them their situation is desperate.

Jeremiah 23 employs similar language to that of the later Ezekiel, but the passage must be understood as summarizing in a poetic form the long historical section which expresses strong criticism of the last kings of Judah. It is *they* who are in mind, they who were intended to be shepherds to the people, but in fact *they* whose conduct has led to the exile.[9]

Isaiah 53.6 may be allowed to provide a bridge to the New Testament, since 1 Peter 2.23–5 builds on it. In the context of undeserved suffering, Peter comments at length on the relationship between the shepherd role of God's people and the experience of suffering:

> For to this you have been called, because Christ also suffered for you, leaving you an example, that you should follow in his steps. He committed no sin; no guile was found on his lips. When he was reviled, he did not revile in return; when he suffered, he did not threaten; but he trusted to him who judges justly. He himself bore our sins in his body on the tree, that we might die to sin and live to righteousness. By his wounds you have been healed. For you were straying like sheep, but have now returned to the Shepherd and Guardian of your souls. (1 Pet. 2.21-5, RSV)[10]

Luke 15,[11] with its three illustrations of lostness, places the parable of the lost sheep at the beginning, presumably because the imagery would have been immediately familiar to the readers, although the story of the 'prodigal son', with the father figure humbly waiting in the background until the eventual return of the younger son, has the greater emotional impact, a more complex structure, and it has a more profound purpose.

The Luke 15 discourse[12] is provided with an important contextual setting which is later determinative of the *meaning* of the story of the *two* sons. The discourse begins with that contextual setting in 15.1, but it is only the first act of the discourse which closes at 15.32; the discourse moves from a concern to show the lostness of all humanity to a sustained concern with the deleterious effect of Pharisaism on the human personality, and this concern carries forward into Luke 20, closing with the judgement of verse 47.

The audience is presented as two disparate groups: 'the tax collectors and "sinners"', who had come to hear Jesus, and 'the Pharisees and the teachers of the law [the scribes]', who criticized this association of a prophet with 'sinners'. The story of the prodigal son (15.11-32) falls into two parts, the first centring on the younger son, and the second on the elder. The first of the brothers, to be identified with the tax collectors and sinners, has no doubt at all about his sin and the need for repentance and restoration from the far off country. The second, to be identified with the Pharisees and scribes,[13] has not physically strayed from the father's house, has not openly rebelled against the father's rule, and so is quite unaware of the need for any repentance or any restoration. But the motivation of the elder, the motivation of the religious, is revealed as no more than stern and grudging duty, not filial affection. The obviously enstranged is restored; the son who is formally *not* estranged is revealed as one who utterly failed to perceive or to profit from his relationship to his father: he could have enjoyed the feasting at any time, but never had and never could, not because the resources were not there, but because his perception of his relationship to his father was faulty.

The entire story is *not* a clumsy union of two separate parables, nor even a construction from an original parable by Jesus and a redactional creation by Luke, as J. T. Sanders has suggested.[14] However, Sanders does helpfully direct attention to the effect of the introduction of the elder brother as providing a link to the succeeding section. He notes that Luke's Gospel carries the exposure of the hypocrisy of the Pharisees beyond chapter 15 (and into chapter 20, concluding with the summary statement of 20.19: 'The teachers of the law and the chief priests looked for a way to arrest him immediately, because they knew he had spoken . . . against them'). Sanders rightly observes: 'The parable of the Prodigal Son will thus have to be seen within the context of a considerable broadside levelled by Luke at the Pharisees in chapter XVf.'[15]

What Jesus has done in the parable of the two sons[16] is to show that although lostness may be demonstrated in different ways (in the hopelessness of the prodigal, in the complacency of the elder brother), estrangement from the Father is universal. But the parable confirms the thesis of Part One of this book, that religion is a human construct which serves only to conceal our need of reconciliation to God.

Thanatologically Lost

The pastoral illustration and the story of the two sons present only one aspect of the theme of human lostness. More radical is that theme which presents humanity as in some sense already dead. It may be that the theme finds its origin in the Genesis account of the fall. The man is warned that he is not to eat the fruit of the tree of the knowledge of good and evil, 'for in the day that you eat of it you shall die' (Gen. 2.17, RSV).[17] In interpreting verse 17 we note first of all that the Garden included within it the tree of life (v. 9), which would have given to man immortality (Gen. 3.22) had he eaten from *it*. And secondly we note that the consequences of the disobedience recorded in Genesis 3 culminate in the removal of man from the Garden, precisely so as to deny him access to the tree of life. It is in *this* sense that the formally stated penalty of 2.17 was carried out. Had he remained he might have taken (might have taken what he had originally been *intended* to take?) the fruit of the tree of life and so have escaped death. That possibility was taken from him, and it was taken from him *bayyōm*, in the day.[18]

In two places in the New Testament the account of the fall is used to develop on the one hand a doctrine of mortality consequent upon Adam's transgression, and on the other hand a doctrine of immortality, consequent upon the last Adam's obedience (Rom. 5.12–21; 1 Cor. 15.20–2).

In Romans 5 we have not so much a series of comparisons as a carefully crafted series of contrasts: in so many ways the last Adam (the actual phrase 'the last Adam' occurs in 1 Cor. 15.45, but not here) is unlike, marvellously surpasses, transcends, the first Adam. Death came to all because of the transgression (*parabaseōs*, v. 14) or trespass (*paraptōmati*, v. 15) or the sin (*hamartēsantos*, v. 16) of one man. On the other hand, through the free *grace* of God, and the free *gift* of that grace, and the full *obedience* of the one man Christ Jesus, justification (*dikaiōma*, v. 16) and righteousness (*dikaiōsunēs*, v. 17) and acquittal and life (*dikaiōsin zōes*, v. 18) come to all. Paul is, of course, fully aware of the fact that *effectively* they do *not* come to all, but there can be no placing of any limitation on the consequences of the obedient life of Christ and the reconciling death of Christ (v. 10).[19]

We must note in this passage the relationship stated by Paul between Adam and human sin-and-death. It is through the first man that sin entered the world, and 'death through sin' (v. 12). But there is an obvious objection to be made. Adam's sin is clear enough, disobeying the prohibition placed on him. Similarly the Mosaic law established prohibitions on humanity, prohibitions which have been more or less uniformly broken. But there is the period between Adam and Moses. In those years there was no Torah to be broken, and no prohibition such as was placed on Adam was in effect, and yet death still reigned. As C. K. Barrett comments, 'Paul notes the anomaly, but without offering a formal explanation.'[20]

There are at least two possible explanations.[21] The first is suggested by Paul's sin-vocabulary. The words employed by Paul in this passage between them define a very wide domain of meaning for the concept of sin. Clearly any word of itself occupies a domain of meaning, but the range of words used by Paul has the effect of enlarging the *hamartiosphere*, the domain of sin. Sin is more than disobedience to specific law, though it may manifest itself as that. Something new has entered through Adam's sin: 'Sin is an inward disposition of rebellion against God arising out of the exaltation of the self.'[22] Although laws and the Mosaic law have the effect of *multiplying* transgressions, we don't even need laws to produce sin. From Adam comes the spirit of truculence, of self-assertion, the will-to-be and even the will-to-be-God (Gen. 3.5), which is of itself sinful.

Thus, in a sense, the second possible explanation of the death of those who lived prior to Torah is superfluous, the explanation that somehow the consequences of Adam's sin, the sentence of death, passed upon us all because we all, in Adam, share the guilt. This idea certainly appears in IV Ezra/2 Esdras 3.7, 21–2:

> And thou didst lay upon him one commandment of thine; but he transgressed it, and immediately thou didst appoint death for him and for his descendants . . . For the first Adam, burdened with an evil heart, transgressed and was overcome, as were also all who were descended from him. Thus the disease became permanent; the law was in the people's heart along with the evil root, but what was good departed, and the evil remained.[23]

Here the two explanations of death are both present: death is introduced as a new universal, consequent upon Adam's sin, but there is also a new spirit in humanity, a new *yetzer*,[24] which leads to universal sin, which in its turn leads to death.

The 1 Corinthians passage adds little to the foregoing, except, perhaps, the actual terminology of first Adam, last Adam, first man, second man, which does appear to represent both the terminology and the theology of IV Ezra (almost contemporary) and of the Judaism into which Paul wrote. If this is so, then we should not be surprised that he does not pause to explicate the matter further: the ideas are in the presupposition pool of his readers, and to explain unnecessarily would be not only pleonastic but also irritating.

Lost and God-less (*Eph. 2*)

The third illustration of the essential lostness of humanity heightens the sense of impotence inherent in that lostness. However we may understand the sense of 'deadness' in fallen man, he is not irreligious. Indeed, as Barth saw so clearly, it is his religiosity which, paradoxically, is a prime concern of the godless: 'We begin by stating that religion is unbelief. It is a concern, indeed, we must say that it is the one great concern, of godless man . . .'[25]

The problem of religion, as perceived with some unanimity by the biblical writers, is that the merely religious lack God. In the Ba'al encounter in 1 Kings 18, Elijah is quite sure that Ba'al cannot act, because there is only one God and the equation 'Yahweh equals Ba'al' is impossible. The same attitude is evinced by Isaiah, who mocks at the absurdities of Bel and Nebo, who, when the crisis-point comes, can deliver neither their worshippers nor themselves, and are carried off captive on the backs of the oxen (Isa. 46.1–2).

With this negative judgement, Ephesians 2 concurs. Before their conversion the Christians at Ephesus were dead (Eph. 2.2, 5). The hopelessness of their lostness is spelled out in Ephesians 2.12 in a striking sequence of statements. They were

> separated from Christ
> alienated from the commonwealth of Israel
> strangers to the covenants of promise
> having no hope
> without God in the world.

As Markus Barth points out,[26] they were estranged from the external symbol of Judaism (circumcision), from the political and sociological aspects of Judaism, and so from God; for outside of his self-revelation in Judaism, where else *could* he be found? Certainly not in the religion of Ephesus.[27] Their religion left them *atheoi*, godless, whether in the sense of not, in fact, believing in God, or in the sense of being abandoned by God because of their devotion to an abomination.[28] The use of *atheoi* here is striking. It does not occur elsewhere in the New Testament, nor in the LXX , nor in the apocryphal literature. It points to the ultimate hopelessness of humanity in its lostness: even its religions serve only to constitute them godless.

Lost and Enslaved (Rom. 6—7)

The fourth characterization of the plight of humanity involves the concept of slavery. The concept is there in the teaching of Jesus; contrasting the situation of those who are *continuing* disciples of his with their situation apart from him, Jesus says: 'If you continue in my word, you are truly my disciples, and you will know the truth, and the truth will make you free . . . every one who commits sin is a slave to sin' (John 8.31-4, RSV).

Paul has a developed view of sinning as slavery, twinning it to a parallel doctrine of a slavery to obedience (Rom. 6.16). It is, of course, particularly significant that at this point in his argument in Romans Paul does not move directly from 'slavery to sin' to 'freedom', but from 'slavery to sin' to 'slavery to obedience'. He summarizes (Rom. 6.17-23):

You were once slaves of sin	You have become obedient to the teaching
You have been set free from sin	You have become slaves of righteousness
You were committed to an ever-increasing iniquity	You should now be committed to sanctification
You were free in respect of righteousness	In that freedom the inevitable end was death
You have become slaves of God	In that slavery the inevitable end is eternal life
The wages of sin is death	The free gift of God is eternal life

Paul's terminology is not entirely consistent, referring to the slavery of the disciple to *obedience* (v. 16), which then leads to *righteousness* (v. 18), and to *God* (v. 22), but the three words all belong in a single domain, what might be termed the domain of God, over against the contrasting vocabulary: sin, iniquity, impurity, death.

In Romans 7 the concept of slavery is further explicated by

111

reference to law. It is well known that in Romans 7 we have multiple referents for the term: it is the law of Moses,[29] the Torah (v. 7), a law of the proximity of sin (v. 21), a law of the mind (v. 23) (which appears to be no more than a principle of *intention*), another law, opposing the law of the mind, and a law of sin, which, in an unexplained manner, resides not in the mind but 'within my members', *en tois melesin mou* (v. 23). It is entirely clear that different 'laws' are being referred to: indeed, as C. E. B. Cranfield points out, the reference in verse 22 to 'God's law' indicates that this is intended as a contrast to the different law spoken of in verse 21.[30]

It is possible to reduce this catalogue of laws to three. Firstly, the Torah, the law of God, the Mosaic law. Secondly, a law, a principle, which is to be found in the human will, a law which cannot do other than agree with the first law, and which produces in the will a desire to observe that law. Thirdly, a law which has invaded the human personality, which overrides the will, and which is significantly identified as residing not in the mind but as invading the whole person, his *body*. The condition of slavery consists not merely in the reality of the ultimate dominance of sin over us, but also in our awareness of that dominance: the felt frustration of a will that lacks authority. See here the penetrating comments of Barth:

> The reality of religion . . . lies precisely in the utter questionableness of my EGO, confronted, as it is, by my inability to do what I would and by my ability to do what I would not. The subject of these contrasted predicates – my EGO – becomes an *X*, capable neither of life nor of death. By the law, through which I know God, I am enabled *to will to do good*: by the same law, through which I am known by God, my success in *doing evil* is clearly exposed. Thus my noblest capacity becomes my deepest perplexity; my noblest opportunity, my uttermost distress; my noblest gift, my darkest menace.[31]

Barth interprets Paul's comments as applying specifically to religion, but perhaps the words should be allowed their wider significance. Our minds cry out for justice, 'it's not fair' is the universal if naive human characterization of *dukkha*, but another law frustrates our expectation of justice, of meaningfulness, and hurls us in utter despair[32] back on a total dependence on God.

Contrary to the teachings of Islam, instruction is *not* enough. The law tells me what I should do, but even though I may agree with the law and long to do it, I cannot. Romans 7 fittingly concludes with both an expression of despair and a statement of a single hope: 'Wretched man that I am! Who will deliver me from this body of death? Thanks be to God through Jesus Christ our Lord!' (vv. 24–5, RSV).

The prominence given in Romans 7 to the first person singular pronoun raises the question whether the passage comprising verses 7–25 is to be understood as autobiographical, or whether we have a rhetorical device which is intended to reflect the wider experience of humanity. As P. J. Achtemeier has pointed out, the interpretation of the passage has been confused by a failure to set it in the wider context of the argument of Romans as a whole.[33]

At this point Paul is, in fact, concerned to elucidate the role of the Mosaic law, and to acquit the law of the accusation that it is itself an evil. Thus whether it is Paul's personal experience, or the experience of law-observing Jews as a whole, or (by extension) of anyone who attempts to be justified by observing law, the conclusion is the same: the law is good, and I know and acknowledge that the law is good, but sin is the reality which makes justification by law a delusion. Law stirs up sin even as it identifies sin, but cannot itself be made evil merely because it fulfils its true function. And its true function is *not* to produce freedom from sin and subsequent justification.

And this directs attention to the remedy for our enslavement. In the words of Jesus: '. . . the Son of man also came not to be served but to serve, and to give his life as a ransom for many' (Mark 10.45, RSV); while Peter makes the slavery-ransom *motif* even more explicit: 'You know that you were ransomed from the futile ways inherited from our fathers, not with perishable things such as silver or gold, but with the precious blood of Christ, like that of a lamb without blemish or spot' (1 Pet. 1.18–19, RSV).

It is perhaps worth noting that our redemption from the slavery to sin does take us into a new slavery, but it appears that the nature of the new slavery is different in its essence from the old. Two contrasting ideas are in the presupposition pool of the readers of Paul's letters: the idea of slavery as it existed in the Graeco-Roman world, and the idea of slavery found in the Old Testament. The

113

former left the slave with no civil rights, a chattel to be used, sold, exchanged. The latter represented the surrender of some rights in exchange for others. Thus King Ahaz sends for assistance to Tiglath-Pileser, 'I am your servant [*'ebed*] and your *son*. Come up, and rescue me . . .' (2 Kings 16.7, RSV). The very term *'ebed* is an honourable term, used of the servant of the Lord in Isaiah. The *'ebed* is no cringing slave, but he *has* submitted himself to his master. In exchange for independence, freedom of action, he has received a suzerain, a powerful superior, one who is capable of enforcing the rights which he could not himself enforce.

9 God's Response to the Human Disorder

THE CONCEPT OF RECONCILIATION (2 Cor. 5.17-20)[1]

The essential lostness of humanity is illustrated in the pastoral imagery of sheep, more profoundly in the concepts of slavery to sin (which eliminates law as a means of salvation) and of an existing deadness, and in the recognition of the failure of religion as such even to bring humanity into contact with God. This highly pessimistic view of natural religion, of religion constructed through human insight and concern, contrasts starkly with the contemporary view of John Hick, of Karl Rahner, of Vatican II, and of those ecumenists who command the more radical forms of dialogue. In effect the biblical view does throw us back on the sheer grace of God.

The whole of humanity is seen to be estranged from God. Indeed, one may go further and say that the whole of creation is seen to be estranged from God, and it is precisely this estrangement which makes it impossible for us to contrast an intelligible view of God or of our relationship to him apart from revelation. For creation itself is a paradoxical, confusing picture of beauty and ugliness, of pastoral calm and of violent storm, of beautiful design and of design that appears cruel, abhorrent: the design of stings and poisons and webs, and teeth, and serrated claws. Creation does *not* point unequivocally to a loving, gracious Creator, though his majesty, his deity, *is* to be perceived there.

What is required is *reconciliation*. The classical locus of the New Testament doctrine of reconciliation is 2 Corinthians 5.17-20 (RSV):

> ... if any one is in Christ, he is a new creation; the old has passed away, behold, the new has come. All this is from God, who through Christ reconciled us to himself and gave us the ministry of reconciliation; that is, in Christ God was reconciling the world to himself, not counting their trespasses against them, and entrusting

to us the message of reconciliation. So we are ambassadors for Christ, God making his appeal through us. We beseech you on behalf of Christ, be reconciled to God.

In understanding this passage,[2] we note that Paul assumes the existence of an enstrangement between God and man. The source of that enstrangement is identified as our trespasses, *paraptōmata* (v. 19). God is the one who is offended. We are the offenders. But it has long been noted that Paul speaks only of man being reconciled to God, with all that that implies, not of God being reconciled to man.

The verb *katallassein* occurs only six times in the New Testament, the related noun *katallagē* only four times. The passive form is *not* used with God as subject, and the active verb is *not* used with God as object.[3] As I. H. Marshall comments: 'This in itself strongly suggests that it is God who takes the initiative in the act of reconciling.'[4] In fact we may identify a clear sequence in the process of reconciliation:

1. The condition of estrangement, produced by sin.
2. The act of divine grace in sending Christ, who dies and in so doing makes reconciliation a possibility: '. . . we were reconciled to God by the death of his Son' (Rom. 5.10, RSV). This stage is of enormous significance: although it is *we* who are in the wrong, it is *he*, God, who takes the initiative in dealing with our sins. And the reason for this act of grace is, as suggested above, our total inability to take the initiative ourselves.
3. The ministry of reconciliation, of making the changed situation known, is then given to those who have been reconciled, God choosing to make his appeal through us to the world.
4. But although it is clear that the door to reconciliation is opened freely, sovereignly, by God, this does not mean that the world is left passively to wait for the reconcilation to be effected. The process can only be completed when we respond to the offer of reconciliation: 'We beseech you on behalf of Christ, be reconciled to God' (2 Cor. 5.20, RSV).

What we must now consider is the manner in which this reconciliation is to be realized. The initiative has been taken by God; but there is still the human response to the divine initiative.

ELENCTICS[5] AND PERSUASION

Elenctics

The Christian approach to the peoples of the world is not merely *irenic*, as though we were in search of some means of peaceful coexistence with otherwise hostile powers. Nor is the Christian approach *polemical*, as though we were concerned to destroy those hostile, or at least contrary, powers. The Christian approach is *elenctic* in the fullest sense, an approach that seeks to expose error because it is error, because it leads to the impoverishment of life and because it is hostile to God. It is an approach which is directed at people, not at systems, in the hope that people will be led to recognize their error. And the expectation of elenctic is that once error is exposed, and once people recognize their error, they will repent of it, turn from it, and will receive the truth. In all of this there is an assumption that there is only one kind of truth, and that religious or philosophical systems cannot be reconciled to one another. If one is correct, then another must be incorrect. And it is assumed that it is better to be correct than to be incorrect. Truth is important. Even charity is less important than truth.

The word 'elenctics' derives formally from the Greek verb *elenchein*, which occurs eighteen times in the New Testament. In nine of those occurrences the verb is collocationally related to sin.[6] In Matthew 18.15 Jesus says, 'If your brother sins against you, go and tell [*elenchon*] him his fault', and the hope is that he will listen, and put things right. In Luke 3.19 we read of Herod being 'reproved', *elenchomenos*, for his relationship with Herodias and various other unspecified 'evil things'. In John 3.20 John comments, 'every one who does evil hates the light, and does not come to the light, lest his deeds should be exposed [*elenchthē(i)*]'. In John 8.46, Jesus asks: 'Which of you *convicts* me of sin?' In 1 Timothy 5.20 Paul advises Timothy: 'As for those who persist in sin, *rebuke* them in the presence of all . . .' In 2 Peter 2.15–16 there is reference to Balaam, who was '*rebuked* for his own transgression'. James comments: '. . . if you show partiality, you commit sin, and are *convicted* by the law as transgressors' (Jas. 2.9). And in a remarkable passage Jude comments on Enoch's words, 'Behold, the Lord came with his holy myriads, to execute judgment on all, and to *convict* all the ungodly of all their deeds of ungodliness which they have committed in such an ungodly way' (vv. 14–15). The use of the verb in 1 Corinthians 14.24–5 is particularly helpful:

> . . . if all prophesy, and an unbeliever or outsider enters, he is *convicted* by all, he is called to account by all, the secrets of his heart are disclosed; and so, falling on his face, he will worship God and declare that God is really among you.

Here we have the full range of elenctic activity: the proclamation of truth, the recognition of that truth by an unbeliever, the revelation of the contrary beliefs of the unbeliever, and his submission to God.

The RSV makes use of eight words to translate the verb *elenchein*: 'reveal', 'reprove', 'convince', 'confute', 'punish',[7] 'expose', 'rebuke', 'convict'. These words map out the domain of meaning of the verb. As F. Büchsel in TDNT comments, 'The word does not only mean to blame or to reprove, nor to convince, in the sense of proof, nor to reveal or expose, but "to set right", namely to point away from sin to repentance.'[8] Thus a biblical *elenchus* is: 'a confrontation with error in which error is exposed for what it is, the one guilty of error is rebuked and compelled to admit his error, and, hopefully, is led to repentance.'

We have thus far omitted the important usage of the verb at John 16.8. We have here one of the five Paraclete passages in John's writings. Four of these occur in the Gospel (14.16; 14.25–6; 15.26–7; 16.7–11), and one in 1 John 2.1. The word has a range of meanings spelled out in the five passages here identified. It is probably right to identify the meaning in John 16.7–11 and in 1 John 2.1 as forensic. In the Gospel the Holy Spirit is the Paraclete, the counsel for the prosecution of the unbeliever. In 1 John 2.1 Jesus is the Paraclete, the counsel for the defence of the believer. The Holy Spirit as Paraclete-prosecutor convicts an unwilling and defiant humanity of the reality of its need of reconciliation. Humanity will find a myriad alternative religious ways to circumvent the grace of God. It is for us to recognize the apparent meaninglessness of life, it is for us to confront the Creator in his creation and to acknowledge his divine power and his deity, it is for us to be confronted by the proclamation of the Good News; but it is for the Spirit to convince us that we cannot find ourselves. And yet it is still *we* who are convinced. The Paraclete-elenctic *is* effectual, but it is not irresistibly imposed. John Macquarrie puts it clearly: 'Man's natural awareness of sin is heightened and intensified by the Spirit, so that it is "noticed" in a new way and understood in greater depth; but it is certainly not imposed upon man from the outside.'[9]

The significance of the giving of the Paraclete is the ultimate helplessness of humanity in the face of its own lostness. We cannot find our way back to the Shepherd from whom we have strayed; we cannot escape from the slavery into which we have fallen; we cannot look for help to the religions in which we have put our trust; we cannot adequately identify sin or recognize righteousness. As William Temple put it:

> The Comforter will bring evidence to prove the world wrong in certain respects . . . the three matters most important to man's life, sin, righteousness and judgement . . .
> . . . The world has to learn that its very conception of these things is all wrong. If it tries to avoid sin or to seek righteousness, it does not avoid or seek the right things; if it fears or prepares for judgement, it does not fear or prepare for the right thing.[10]

Persuasion

Although it is clear that biblical elenctics result from the operation of the Spirit, that the Holy Spirit is the proper subject of the verb *elenchein* where it is applied to the sinner, this must not be allowed to lead us into the view that the Church is exempted from any responsibility for the elenctic process beyond the preaching of a sermon, or the unchurched from the responsibility to be convicted by it. On the contrary, the New Testament accounts of the activities of Paul, in particular, show us an active engagement, an expectant engagement, a persuasive engagement, with unbelievers. The confrontation event is to be entered into positively on both sides, not passively.

There is a *paraklēsis* involved. In Acts 2.40 we read of Peter, who 'testified with many other words and *exhorted* them [*parakalein*], saying, "Save yourselves from this crooked generation."' Perhaps more typically, Luke uses the verb *peithō* to describe Paul's proclamation:

119

'. . . many Jews and devout converts to Judaism followed Paul and Barnabas, who spoke to them and *urged* them to continue in the grace of God' (Acts 13.43),
'And Paul went in, as was his custom, and for three weeks he argued with them from the scriptures, explaining and proving that it was necessary for the Christ to suffer and to rise from the dead . . . And some of them were *persuaded*, and joined Paul and Silas' (Acts 17.2–4),
'And he argued in the synagogue every sabbath, and *persuaded* Jews and Greeks' (Acts 18.4),
'And he entered the synagogue and for three months spoke boldly, arguing and *pleading* about the kingdom of God' (Acts 19.8).

And we note that this aspect of argument and persuasion was recognized by Paul's opponents: 'And you see and hear that not only at Ephesus but almost throughout all Asia this Paul has *persuaded* and turned away a considerable company of people, saying that gods made with hands are not gods' (Acts 19.26).

In the same vein Herod Agrippa recognizes the forcefulness of Paul's argument: 'Do you think that in such a short time you can *persuade* me to be a Christian?' (Acts 26.28, NIV).

And finally, in Rome itself, Paul is still engaged in that same forceful process of persuasion: 'And he expounded the matter to them from morning till evening, testifying to the kingdom of God and trying to *convince* them about Jesus' (Acts 28.23).

It appears plain that the New Testament holds in a steady tension the polarities of a Holy Spirit *elenctic* and the enthusiastic and even combative *proclamation* of reconciliation which, as Paul saw, has been committed to God's people. There are, of course, no grounds for making this particular combination the exclusive means of salvation. God may see fit to exercise his salvific prerogative through the Word alone (and even through the proclamation of those who have little enthusiasm for the Word), or again through his self-revelation in creation. But Paul's example suggests that the sovereignty of the Spirit allied to the enthusiastic advocacy of Christ's cause by his people is what God expects.

10 *Christianity and Judaism* [1]

A TENSION IDENTIFIED

We have already made passing reference to the Old Testament antecedents of the New Testament missiological concern. We must now turn to a more careful consideration of the element of novelty introduced into salvation history by the appearance of the Church over against the continuing existence of Judaism.

The letter to the Romans is of itself a profound testimony to the recognition by Paul of an apparent enigma: the Jew. In the first two chapters of the letter Paul is making clear the common failure of both Gentile and Jew. The question must then be faced, 'What advantage, then, is there in being a Jew, or what value is there in circumcision?' (Rom. 3.1). The second question is, most probably, no more than an alternative expression of the first: circumcision was particularly perceived as the distinguishing feature of the Jewish male. The question is dealt with both in Romans 3 and 4, and, later, in Romans 9—11. Far from being peripheral to the theme of Romans, the question of the role of Jewry is central to it. [2]

Part of the answer to Paul's earlier question appears in Romans 9.4. Of the Jews Paul comments: 'They are Israelites, and to them belong the sonship, the glory, the covenants, the giving of the law, the worship, and the promises; to them belong the patriarchs, and of their race, according to the flesh, is the Christ' (RSV).

At 9.32 we have an explanation of an admitted change. The privileged position of the Jew is ended because the position was misunderstood. The law was never intended as an end in itself, nor even as a means in itself: the intention of the law was to inculcate in the hearer a thirst for righteousness (9.30), a thirst which the law could foster but not satisfy. Indeed the law was to destroy all hope of attaining righteousness by human effort, since a careful investigation of the demands of the law would always show them to be beyond our attainment. The law should then close the way of human endeavour and turn humanity to faith, a faith that would look to God to do what humanity could not. And this was the step that Judaism would not and will not take: 'Israel who pursued the righteousness which is based on law did not succeed in fulfilling that law . . . because they did not pursue it through faith, but as if it were based on works' (9.31–2, RSV).

However, Paul is still anxious to rescue something from the débâcle, and this he does through the Old Testament doctrine of the remnant. Elijah thought that he was alone in worshipping God when all Israel appeared to have gone after the Ba'alim, but he was mistaken: 'So too at the present time there is a remnant, chosen by grace' (11.5, RSV).

THE CONCEPT OF TWO COVENANTS (Jer. 31)

The New Testament concept of two covenants almost certainly has its origins in Jeremiah 31.31–4: 'Behold, the days are coming, says the Lord, when I will make a new covenant with the house of Israel and the house of Judah, not like the covenant which I made with their fathers . . .' (Jer. 31.31–2, RSV).

This is the only place in the Old Testament where a *hedāshāh*, 'new', covenant is anticipated. In Deuteronomy 30.1–10 the situation of apostasy described by Jeremiah is anticipated, and the Deuteronomist actually refers to a circumcision of the heart, but he does not make mention of a new *berit*, covenant. Unlike the Deuteronomist, Jeremiah does not elaborate on the consequences of this new act of grace on the part of God. We are not told what the socio-political implications of a 'circumcised heart' might be.

There are sharply contrasting assessments of the words of Jeremiah. R. P. Carroll identifies them as representing 'a minor and prosaic hope for the future'.[3] John Bright takes a totally different view: 'Although the passage may not preserve the prophet's *ipissima verba*, it represents what might well be considered the high point of his theology. It is certainly one of the profoundest and most moving passages in the entire Bible.'[4]

Carroll is critical of those commentators who have made the connection between Jeremiah's words and the New Covenant in Christ, but in fact concludes his discussion of the passage: 'In the restoration of the nation the deity will act to create the kind of society which previous generations failed so miserably to achieve.'[5]

This prophetic word from Jeremiah *is* either minor, prosaic, bland, unthinking, unreal, *or* its fulfilment is to be seen in Christ and in his New Covenant. The decision between the two is to be made from a consideration of the prophecy as a whole, not merely by reference to any single *logion*, however emotively powerful that *logion* may be. But when the prophecy as a whole is considered, it becomes clear that Jeremiah 31 and its reference to a new covenant cannot be dismissed as an isolated aberration.

As with Isaiah and Ezekiel, so also with Jeremiah the idea of covenant provides part of the thematic net[6] which gives the discourse its coherence. There is repeated reference to the (broken) covenant, linked to an implied new covenant, for example so early as in Jeremiah 3.15-17, but also in Jeremiah 11.14 and 22. There is reference to the Torah-based covenant with Zedekiah in Jeremiah 34.[7] But even more importantly, the peak of the entire prophecy is reached in Jeremiah 50, with the prophetic proclamation of the downfall of Babylon and the conclusion of a (new) covenant with Yahweh:

> In those days and in that time, says the Lord, the people of Israel and the people of Judah shall come together, weeping as they come; and they shall seek the Lord their God. They shall ask the way to Zion, with faces turned toward it, saying, 'Come, let is join ourselves to the Lord in *an everlasting covenant which will never be forgotten.*' (Jer. 50.4-5, RSV).

And it must also be said that the theme of Jeremiah is not to be detected merely by the counting of the occurrences of some key word. The covenant theme, a past broken covenant and a new and everlasting covenant, runs through Jeremiah 4—6, although the word *berit* occurs not at all.

The designation 'old covenant' occurs only at 2 Corinthians 3.14. Speaking of the Jewish people and referring back to the 'veil' which Moses used to conceal from his people the fading glow from his encounter with God, Paul writes: 'to this day, when they read the old covenant, that same veil remains unlifted, because only through Christ is it taken away' (RSV).

The designation of a 'new [*kainē*] covenant' appears in 1 Corinthians 11.25, significantly associated with the Eucharist: 'This cup is the new covenant in my blood . . .' Gordon Fee states flatly that this language 'is an allusion to Exod.24:8, where blood, designated by this exact term, was sprinkled over the people to ratify the covenant'.[8] Fee goes on to connect this new covenant with the Jeremiah prophecy. What is entirely clear is that in this verse we have both a break between the Old Covenant (ratified by a symbolic sprinkling with animal blood)[9] and the New Covenant (ratified by the blood of Christ); and we have a sense of continuity with the Old Covenant, in that in some sense sacrifice is at the heart of each, and each through sacrifice establishes a relationship to God.

It is worth noting here that the New Covenant is mediated by God, it is initiated by God, it is a covenant of grace just as was the original Mosaic covenant. So then God himself is 'the mediator of a new covenant, that those who are called may receive the promised eternal inheritance – now that he has died as a ransom to set them free . . .' (Heb. 9.15). This in turn has its effect on God's people: God has 'made us competent as ministers of a new covenant – not of the letter but of the Spirit' (2 Cor. 3.6).

The two covenants are contrasted in Paul's allegory in Galatians 4.21–31, the Sinai covenant 'bearing children for Hagar', who is 'Mount Sinai in Arabia', and the second covenant is Sarah, who is 'the Jerusalem from above'. The stark contrast drawn here between the two covenants conforms generally to the view of Hebrews, where Jesus is the surety of 'a *better* covenant' (Heb. 7.22; 8.6).

Covenant: diathēkē *and* berit

In classical Greek *diathēkē* commonly refers to a will, and this idea is present in Hebrews 9.16 and Galatians 3.15. However, in the LXX *diathēkē* is regularly used as the equivalent of the Hebrew *berit*, 'covenant'. It is from the LXX in general that most New Testament usages of *diathēkē* take their meaning.

The Sinai covenant was never perceived as a covenant entered into equally by two parties.[10] While humanity has no claim on God, the converse is not true: as Creator, Yahweh has unqualified rights over against humanity. The covenant is then seen as an act of grace: God committing himself to a relationship and to principles of reward and punishment without any sense of either relationship or principles being required of him. This essential one-sidedness of the Old Testament covenant is held constantly before the people by their leaders:

For you are a people holy to the Lord your God. The Lord your God has chosen you out of all the peoples on the face of the earth to be his people, his treasured possession.

The Lord did not set his affection on you and choose you because you were more numerous than other peoples, for you were the fewest of all peoples. But it was because the Lord loved you and kept the oath he swore to your forefathers . . . (Deut.7.6–8)

But this one-sidedness is not to be attributed to a parallel between Bible-covenant and Near Eastern vassal-treaty. G. Mendenhall's proposal[11] is suggestive, but fails to convince of its applicability to the grace element of the Old Testament covenant. The covenants of the Old Testament are of at least two types,[12] the Abrahamic type, which is promissory and unconditional, and the Mosaic type, which is related to Torah and is conditional. And yet each is essentially a grace-covenant. So, then, when Yahweh promises of David,

I will establish the throne of his kingdom for ever. I will be his father, and he shall be my son. When he commits iniquity, I will chasten him with the rod of men, with the stripes of the sons of men; but I will not take my steadfast love [*hesed*] from him (2 Sam. 7. 13–15, RSV),

the last phrase is equivalent to saying 'I will not take my *berit* [covenant] from him': *hesed* is synonymous here with *berit*.[13] The New Covenant has the same essential characteristic as the Old: it is a covenant of grace, a covenant given through Christ, but totally undeserved by lost humanity.

The Two Covenants: A Question of Continuity

The essential sense of continuity between the two Testaments is guaranteed by Christ, 'born of woman, born under the law' (Gal. 4.4, RSV). He is himself the principal link between the continuing people of God. But he is also the essential link between the two collections of books which together comprise the Christian Scriptures. It is not a matter of attempting to construct some link between Christianity and Judaism: the writings of the New Testament, whether Gospel or Epistle or Apocalypse, are simply unintelligible without their Old Testament textual forebears.

This is more than a matter of Old Testament prophecy fulfilled in the New Testament. The theology of the New Testament writers is in constant dialogue with the Old Testament: it is not a new theology, but a fulfilled theology. The doctrine of a triune God may eventually emerge, but the Christian can still stand with the Jew and proclaim without mental reservation 'The Lord our God is One'!

And there is an important Pauline teleology: 'Christ is the end [*telos*] of the law so that there may be righteousness for everyone who believes' (Rom. 10.4). This central Pauline doctrine is concisely discussed by C. E. B. Cranfield, who recognizes three possible interpretations of *telos*: as fulfilment, as goal, as termination. He rejects the third and settles in favour of the second: 'For Christ is the goal of the law, and it follows that a status of righteousness is available to everyone who believes.'[14] With respect, it seems to me that the summary statement remains unclear. The metaphor 'goal' is unhelpful, and the use of the word 'believes' without any statement of the content or object of belief vague, leaving the statement open to interpretation in a number of ways.

If we direct attention on the 'goal' metaphor, we may ask what was the purpose of the Mosaic law (for certainly Cranfield is right in insisting that the law in this verse must be the Mosaic law). Various answers may be given, each one contributing something to our understanding of biblical nomism. The law was given to provide Israel with a guide to what was required by God. Through the law came a knowledge of sin: without law there could be no certain knowledge of right and wrong. Moreover, the law brought about an awareness of the ultimate frailty of the human will. Not that we could *never* obey the law of God, but that complete obedience to it was always beyond our reach. Thus the law was intended also to lead us into an awareness that righteousness never could be attained by obedience to it. If righteousness was to be attained at all, it must come some other way.

That other way was Christ, who was born subject to the law, who was able to perceive its ultimate and absolute demands, who submitted himself to it, who did not break it, and who in the full observance of it demonstrated for the first time what the goal of the law was, what kind of person it was intended to produce. The law was intended to produce people of a particular kind. *That* was its goal. In *that* sense Jesus is the goal of the law. Those who continue to seek righteousness by an obedience to Torah remain unrighteous. Those who abandon that search, and by faith *receive* righteousness from God *because of what Christ has done in fulfilling the law*, they are the justified.

Explicitly, a mere zeal for God is *not* enough. A mere determination to obey Torah is not enough. Zeal allied to ignorance leads only to bigotry. Obedience to Torah apart from faith in God who justifies in *grace* is unprofitable. The new covenant in Christ is *not* independent of the old, for the old had as its goal the new man, the archetypal man, the last Adam, who would obey as the first Adam did not.

But we must note that there is a genuine hiatus introduced by the New Covenant. Firstly, the existence of a territorially located and physically related people is replaced by a transcendental community, born *not* of the will of man, but of the Spirit, and spread throughout the world. Its *politeuma*, citizenship, is in heaven (Phil. 3.20).

Secondly, the symbol of incorporation into the community is changed. There is no obvious connection between circumcision and baptism. Baptism looks back to the priestly lustration, and, unlike circumcision, is appropriate to all in the new community, men and women.

Thirdly, the central festival of Judaism, Passover, is transformed, so that an annual pilgrimage to Jerusalem, with a sacrificial lamb, becomes an occasional supper, with two symbols only, bread and wine. Fourthly, sacrifice ends.[15] And fifthly, the consequences of faithfulness change dramatically. Under the Old Covenant there was a statistical, macroscopic, relationship between the faithfulness of the people and the prosperity of the nation. Under the New Covenant it is entirely possible that faithfulness will bring opposition and persecution and the loss of everything. The prosperity of the Kingdom is assured, but it is the transcendent Kingdom, not the terrestrial Church, that prospers.

THE TWO COVENANTS: A RADICAL DISTINCTION?

We must now consider the question of the new condition of humanity under the New Covenant. In traditional evangelical circles this new condition has sometimes been represented as though the eschatological expectation was a present reality. It is surely dangerous to make claims beyond those made by Scripture, and these claims themselves may be checked against our experience.

In the New Testament we have as realistic a view of the people of God as we have in the Old Testament. We have the account of the deception practised by Ananias and Sapphira (Acts 5.1–11). We have the fragmented church at Corinth, where the behaviour of the rich disappointed the high expectations of the poor (1 Cor. 11.22). We have the letter of James, which must be seen as being addressed to a body of Christians who were guilty of just that kind of discrimination which is so vividly described in James 2. We have the unedifying public disagreement between Peter and Paul at Antioch (Gal. 2.11), and the no less painful personal disagreement between Paul and Barnabas over John Mark's behaviour (Acts 15.39). The designation *hagioi* may freely be used of believers, but it does not suppose perfection in them.

Romans 7 advances Paul's theology of salvation from the earlier consideration of human condemnation to the later practical consideration of just how the new life in Christ should be worked out. Here we are dealing with Paul's teaching on the theory underpinning that new life.

Much discussion has centred on the question whether Paul's words in verses 21–4 are autobiographical or not, and on whether they represent unregenerate experience or the experience of the converted. In expounding these verses at Britain's Keswick Convention in successive years, Dr Graham Scroggie (at one time a lecturer at Spurgeon's Theological College) took the one view, and Dr Ernest Kevan (Principal of London Bible College) took the opposite view.

Examination of Romans 7 shows that at verse 7 a transition occurs, signalled by the replacement of the first person plural by the first person singular. The question is then, Who is this *egō* of whom Paul writes? There are at least six possibilities:

1. Paul himself before his conversion;
2. Paul himself before and after his conversion;
3. 'Adam', mankind as encapsulated in 'Adam';

4. Humanity in general;
5. The Jewish people in general;
6. Israel, in its encounter with the Mosaic law.

These possibilities are not entirely mutually exclusive: Paul was himself a Jew who prided himself on his submission to the law; Israel is part of humanity. Further, it must be said that although W. G. Kümmel has attempted to make the *egō* a rhetorical device,[16] and this has gained widespread acceptance, it is not possible completely to rid the word of its obvious autobiographical reference.

Donald Guthrie suggests that verse 9, 'Once I was alive apart from law' must point back to the Adamic situation.[17] However, there must have been a time when the law first came to Paul,[18] and it is a little uncomfortable to move from the equation *nomos* equals Mosaic law, in verses 7–8, to the equation *nomos* equals the prohibition to Adam, in verse 9. It is, of course, tempting to import 1 Corinthians 15.22, 'as in Adam all die', at this point, but Adam is named in Romans only in 5.12–21, and it is surely significant that Paul does *not* explicitly reintroduce that theme in the context of Romans 7.

What Paul is saying here is both autobiographical and gnomic. Paul does clearly look back to his experience as a Jew, under the law, and as such his comments relate to all other Jews under the law. But he writes also as a Christian, who is not free from law, but who now stands under 'the law of God' (7.25). The understanding of the last part of Romans 7 must be determined by the *ara oun*, 'So then', of verse 25, which looks back to the resolution of the problem in the immediately preceding sentence. 'Thanks be to God – through Jesus Christ our Lord!'

The 'So then' is unexpected. 'I myself in my mind am a slave to God's law, but in the sinful nature a slave to the law of sin.' This represents a true analysis of the mixed intentions of the believer. The conflict is not ended, and this is confirmed by the experience of the Christian. But Paul is not finished (as so often, the chapter division here is intrusive), and he goes on to explicate the fundamental difference between the two covenants: 'through Christ Jesus the law of the Spirit of life set me free from the law of sin and death' (8.2). Not that the law of sin and death lets go lightly. It will continually attempt to reimpose itself on the believer. But the inevitability, the irresistibility, of that law is ended.

And all of this is part of the 'Now but not yet' of the process of redemption. Later in Romans 8 (vv. 18-25) Paul considers the 'not yet', both as it relates to creation in general, and as it relates to the individual believer . . . 'we ourselves, who have the firstfruits [*aparchēn*] of the Spirit, groan inwardly *as we wait eagerly for our adoption as sons, the redemption of our bodies'* (8.23).

Our situation, as Paul expresses it here, is an in-between situation. We are further on than those who were under the Old Covenant, since the law of sin and death has its power over the Christian broken. But we are not so far on as we shall ultimately be when our bodies are redeemed. Until that time the conflict *in our bodies* continues, the as yet unredeemed material *sōma-sarx* warring against the redeemed *pneuma* (spirit). And that spirit gains its enabling from the Holy Spirit, whose presence is the one essential characteristic of the life of the people of God.

But this is a far cry from perfectionism. We may still, with the flesh, serve the old ways. But we may now, by the Spirit, serve God. The conflict continues.

THE SOURCE OF *AKRASIA*

We may now briefly consider the question of the source of the admitted inability, sometimes, under certain conditions, of the Christian to do what he knows to be right.

In Galatians 5.16-26 the reason for unchristian conduct in the life of the Christian is quite clear: Paul confirms what we have already identified in Romans 7, that even for the Christian it is still true that the desires of the flesh are against the Spirit (Gal. 5.17). But if we revert to Romans 7, we may take a further analytical step: Paul observes that he delights after the law so far as his will is concerned, but follows the desires of the flesh in practice (Rom. 7.18-19). Sometimes. This, again, is entirely consonant with Christian experience. A. Van Den Beld suggests[19] that we must distinguish between the Christian's long-term goals, broad ethical principles, informed by the Spirit, and the powerful short-term 'wants' (for they are not 'needs') which repeatedly impose themselves through the flesh. It is here that the Christian differs from others. The Christian understands death. He is aware of, and rightly fears, judgement. He is aware of Christ's action on his behalf. He knows of the availability of the Spirit. He has new values, ambitions which are quite different from those of other peoples. And it is on such premises that his behaviour is *generally* structured. But this entirely Christian world-view is modified by self-interest, Van Den Beld's short-term 'wants', so that, practically-speaking, Christian conduct consists of a series of compromises.

What is more, I have deliberately idealized the situation. The Christian is more or less able to understand death, to fear judgement, and so on. It is the extent to which he takes these matters into his faith-obedience that determines his day-to-day decisions in his flesh. And the measure of faith-obedience is continuously variable.

At this point we anticipate the later and more detailed consideration of liberation theology, and refer in passing to the concept of humanity evinced there (see pp. 246–8). Liberation theology starts from the supposition that theology has its focus in the exodus. This becomes the exegetical key which alone opens up an understanding of the text of the Bible. In conformity with this priority, the search for the origin of sin has tended to move from Genesis 3 to Genesis 4, from the ontological to the sociological.

Adam is seen in Genesis 3 as having been given a role to play in which he is subject to and subordinate to God. His sin is (rightly) seen as a refusal of that role, and the determination to become as God (Gen. 3.5) then characterizes, at least in some focal way, sin in humanity. But this ontological understanding of sin does not suit the needs of liberation theology. It is in the following chapter, in which Cain destroys Abel, that the societal aspect of sin becomes apparent. J. Miranda presents this view forcibly in *Marx and the Bible*.[20] Adam, as an individual, is dismissed, and becomes representative man, and so the concrete disobedience of Genesis 3 is somewhat vaguely redistributed in history, while Cain is the first concrete man, and human history begins with Genesis 4.1–11. '"Listen to the sound of your brother's blood, crying out to me from the earth," (Gen. 4.10) is the essential presentation of the God who intervenes in this history.'[21] The centre of the hamartiosphere is thus identified as relational, societal, sociological sin. The restoration process is similarly seen by Gustavo Gutierrez primarily in sociological terms: 'to know, that is to say, to love Yahweh, is to do justice to the poor and oppressed'.[22] To quote Gutierrez again: 'A spirituality of liberation will center on a conversion to the neighbour, the oppressed person, the exploited social class, the despised race, the dominated country . . .Conversion means a radical transformation of ourselves; it means thinking, feeling, and living as Christ.'[23]

But this is not the biblical view at all. To be converted is to be the object of the redemptive work of Christ in the Spirit. That conversion will eventuate in certain kinds of activities, sadly only marginally those proposed by Gutierrez. The fact is that here the liberation theologians suffer from their enthusiasms: 'This is how we would wish it to be, and so this is how it *is.*' Our admittedly brief study of the biblical evidence suggests that both the Old Testament and the New Testament are more restrained. Conversion *should* mean our thinking, feeling, and living, as Christ did; and if we are converted then in some measure it *will* mean that. But if conversion *is* that, then we are entirely without hope.

11 The Church

THE ONE CHURCH

The term 'humanity' includes within it the term 'Church'. Christians are part of humanity. The Church relates to humanity in two different ways: part of humanity belongs also to the Church, and the Church has a decided biblical relationship to that part of humanity which lies outside the Church. As we have seen already, the Church consists of those who have *been* reconciled, and the Church then turns to those who have *not been* reconciled and implores, in Christ's place, '*Be* reconciled!'

There is but one Church. The confident first-century affirmations of Ephesians 4 echo hollowly in the ears of the twentieth-century Christian: 'There is one body and one Spirit – just as you were called to one hope when you were called – one Lord, one faith, one baptism; one God and Father of all, who is over all and through all and in all' (Eph. 4.4–6).

Protestant, Catholic and Orthodox, fundamentalist, conservative, liberal, whatever those terms may mean, must all wrestle with the reality of this rather obvious proposition: there is only one body, the Church. One is either part of it or one is not. And if one is part of the body, then one ought consequently to be concerned for the welfare of the whole of the rest of the body.

But further, the observation of the oneness of the body ought to lead the Christian to a certain humility about his part of the body. Most divisions within the Christian communion *think* that they have their doctrine right. This necessarily leads to the conclusion that others have theirs wrong. But it is rare for any denomination seriously to suppose that it, alone, has the whole package of its theology correctly wrapped and exhaustively explicated. We are usually prepared to admit that we might be wrong on some issues. A little reflection, however, shows us that we don't know just where the mistake lies. Presumably if we did know, then we would correct the error. But we don't, and so we can't. This should then lead us on further to recognize that there ought to be a certain caution in our criticism of the theologies of other parts of the body. Since we don't know the locus of our own errors, we cannot be sure of the locus of the errors of others.

Our discussions and disagreements with others who belong to the one body should always be tempered by those somewhat sobering facts. As Karl Barth, writing of the Church, commented: ' . . . it is the same reality which we see differently'.[1]

DEFINING 'CHURCH'

It has proved tempting to find in the etymology of *ekklēsia* a definition of the New Testament idea of 'church'. The Church has become 'the community of the called-out'. Thus Barth comments: 'The Church is a summoning forth of God's people, the community of men of faith, created through Christ on the foundation of the covenant between God and man, awakened by the Holy Spirit.'[2]

There certainly is a biblical doctrine of calling, but this is not to be derived from the etymology of *ekklēsia*, nor can the etymology of the word be allowed to substitute for an examination of the actual usage of the term in the New Testament.[3]

Biblically the word is used about one hundred times in the LXX, usually as the equivalent of Hebrew *qahal*. In Acts 9.31 it is used of the whole Church, and in Acts 11.22 of the church in Jerusalem. In Acts 19.32, 39, 41 it is used of the secular gathering at Ephesus, and of the city council. In Matthew 18.17 it is used of the juridical gathering of the people of God. It is the term used to refer to any coherent body of Christians, a local congregation, the Christians of a single city, or all Christians everywhere, perceived as the family of God.

And while it is not permissible to define the Church in terms of 'called out people' on etymological grounds, nevertheless it is absolutely permissible to distinguish between those who *are* part of the body, and those who are not. There is Church and there is not-Church. The term itself necessarily implies a certain exclusivism.

But this exclusivism has positive value. To refer to Barth again, he says: 'The true community of Jesus Christ is . . . the fellowship in which it is given to one to know the world as it is.'[4] There is a missiological dimension to the exclusiveness of the Church: from within the Church we look out upon the world and we are able to understand the world. The frustrations of its political leaders are entirely explicable. The apparent intractability of creation is entirely understandable. The perverseness of the human character is predictable. The helplessness of law to produce order is inevitable. But this is true only of that perspective which is gained from incorporation into the Church.

The Church is often defined in terms of its apostolicity. This concept, however, must not be understood in any merely mechanical way, as though the ability to establish some formal chain of apostolic succession will serve to constitute the present Church 'apostolic'. The Church is apostolic only when it functions praxeologically in an apostolic manner:

> Everything the Church does must be directed . . . towards fulfilling its apostolic mission to the outside world. To be itself the Church must follow the apostles in continually recognizing and demonstrating that it has been sent out into the world . . . This makes it clear that apostolicity, like unity, holiness and catholicity, is not a static attribute of the Church. Like them it is an historical dimension which has constantly to be fulfilled anew in history.[5]

It is the fundamental weakness of the Church in Europe that although in its many privileged forms (Anglican, Roman Catholic, Lutheran, Reformed, Orthodox) it may lay claim to a kind of apostolicity eschewed by others (Baptist, Pentecostal, the House Churches, the Salvation Army, the Christian Brethren), it tends uniformly to be inward-looking and so, in Küng's terms, not apostolic after all. In an excess of humility the mainline Churches have largely abandoned mission to the world in favour of a bland dialogue with the world. To the extent to which that is true, those Churches are no longer truly apostolic.

CHURCH AND STRUCTURE

The search for a unique authoritative structure for the Church in the pages of the New Testament is both vain and misplaced. Just as Israel survived as a nation precisely because there was no one political structure essential to her survival, so the Church survives through the centuries and across cultural boundaries because there is no one structure which must alone be designated 'biblical'. As T. C. Vriesen expresses it:

> Israel, which was doomed to destruction as a people . . . could keep on functioning as a religious community. That it did survive in this sense is due to the preaching of the prophets who, by predicting the downfall of the state, and the destruction of the national existence as being the will of God, made Israel preserve its communion with God.[6]

In a parallel manner the Church survives even though its local structures may be destroyed, as has been true of the Church in Russia, in China, in Ethiopia. The Church survives even amidst a plethora of apparently contradictory forms: the Salvation Army with neither baptism nor communion,[7] the papal system of Roman Catholicism, the Plymouth Brethren and their autonomous assemblies, the Lutheran Churches, the Baptist Churches, the Kimbanguist Church of Central Africa. Each (absurdly?) claiming to be more biblical than the others, and each bringing humanity into the ultimately important point of incorporation into the one body.

The Church has been defined in terms of catholicity and of apostolicity. The ultimate exclusivism of the Roman Catholic Church has, since Vatican II, been left behind us. The reality of one body over which none of us has any proprietorial rights is now commonly acknowledged.

It is not an apostolic genealogy that constitutes an apostolic Church, but apostolic behaviour; specifically it is behaviour that is missiologically apostolic. And this is so because mission is in essence the Church's struggle to resolve the apparent meaninglessness of life, through its proclamation of Good News, and through its compassionate ministry of sharing its resources, and through its programme of confronting all oppressive powers, secular and spiritual, in the power of the Spirit and in the name of Christ.

THE CHURCH AND THE SPIRIT (John 20.19–23)

There are at least three occasions on which the Holy Spirit is 'given' in the New Testament. These are in Acts 19.1–6, where Paul is confronted by 'believers' who had received only the baptism of John; Acts 2.1–4, the Pentecost experience; and John 20.22, where Jesus meets with the ten, breathes (on them), and says to them: 'Receive [*labete*] the Holy Spirit.'

It is clear that John intends us to think of a genuine investment of the Holy Spirit. The view that John merely signalled a symbolic giving of the Spirit, not actualized until Pentecost, was condemned by the Fifth Ecumenical Council, Constantinople, in AD 553. Examination of the cotext at this point shows that the insufflation is missiologically orientated:[8]

> Jesus said to them again, 'Peace be with you. As the Father has sent me, even so I send you.' And when he had said this, he breathed on them, and said to them, 'Receive the Holy Spirit. If you forgive the sins of any, they are forgiven; if you retain the sins of any, they are retained.' (John 20.21–3, RSV)

Bultmann comments on the relationship between the elenctic spirit in John 16.8 and the insufflation: 'If in 16:8–11 the task of the Spirit was described as an *elenchein*, so here correspondingly the bestowal of the Spirit is accompanied by the giving of authority to the disciples.'[9]

The repeated '*shalom*' is followed by a repetition of words recorded by John in the prayer of Jesus at John 17.18. These words provide a missionary commission: the disciples, now, are to take up the mission of Jesus; and as they will shortly hear, it is to be a greatly enlarged mission, from Jerusalem to Judea and Samaria, and on to the ends of the earth. But next Jesus exhales, *enephusesēn*, an important *hapāx*, in fact paralleled by the LXX at Genesis 2.7: 'the Lord God formed man of dust from the ground, and *breathed* into his nostrils the breath of life' (RSV). C. K. Barrett comments: 'That John intended to depict an event of significance parallel to that of the first creation of man cannot be doubted; this was the beginning of the new creation.'[10] If we must ask the question, 'Where does the Church begin?', the answer must be 'Here, in the insufflation'. The elenctic Spirit is now given to the apostles.

When Jesus says to the ten, 'Receive the Holy Spirit', it is as an accompaniment to the insufflation, the breathing, the new act of creation. The Spirit is given to them as the guarantee of what is to come, the *aparchēn*, firstfruits, (Rom. 8.23), the *arrabōn*, down-payment (2 Cor. 1.22). This is not mere symbolism: it is a genuine giving of the Spirit who is to be with the apostles in the weeks *before* Pentecost.

But what was the significance of the giving of the Spirit here? Koehler sees this Johannine pericope as reflecting John's polemic against the pneumatology of Acts, consciously correcting Luke at this point.[11] Calvin thought that the Spirit was only partially given: 'The Spirit was given to the Apostles on this occasion in such a manner, that they were only sprinkled by his grace, but were not filled with full power ... When the Spirit appeared on them in tongues of fire, they were entirely renewed.[12]

The significance of the giving of the Spirit in John can perhaps only be discerned by noting what the apostles did do and what they did not do in the period between the insufflation and Pentecost. There is, as M. M. B. Turner has pointed out,[13] a marked absence of Paraclete-activity. They do not appear to understand the Kingdom purposes of Christ now any more than they did previously (Acts 1.6). They are not being led by the Paraclete into a fresh understanding of truth (John 14.26). The number of disciples does not markedly increase (Acts 1.15 refers to a mere one hundred and twenty). There appears to be no Spirit elenctic, despite Jesus' words: 'If you forgive the sins of any, they are forgiven' (John 20.23, RSV). They are prepared to take the responsibility of filling the vacancy left by Judas, and Matthias is elected.[14] The Spirit preserves the Church, which has now begun; but the Church awaits Pentecost, *not* for the first bestowing of the Spirit, *but* for the inauguration of mission.

THE CALLING OF THE PEOPLE OF GOD

The Concept of Calling

It is the elenctic activity of the Holy Spirit in an individual that leads him to a true *metanoia*, repentance, a change of mind, a renewal of mind, that cannot be self-induced. It is, indeed, this elenctic activity of the Spirit that constitutes any individual a believer. It is not a question of the perception of a table of theological truths (though this may come in time). Nor is it a question of baptism (although this, too, may come in time). Apart from the elenctic activity of the Spirit, these other matters are simply irrelevant.

We are led, then, to the recognition of a certain independence of salvific activity in the Godhead. There is a chosen people? Then there must also be a not-chosen people. There are those who are called? Then there must also be those who are not-called. We are required to take seriously the words used by Jesus to his disciples: 'You did not choose me, but I chose you . . .' (John 15.16), and the enigmatic words of Matthew 22.14, 'For many are invited, but few are chosen.' Ephesians 1 spells out the relevant propositions: '. . . he chose us in him before the creation of the world' (v. 4); 'In love he predestined [*proorisas*] us to be adopted as his sons' (v. 5); '. . . we who first hoped in Christ have been destined [*prooristhentes*] and appointed to live for the praise of his glory' (v. 12, RSV).

Clearly this thinking is no more than an extension of that already plainly present in the Old Testament. There are the unelect: the Egyptians and the Babylonians, the Syrians and the Canaanites, from whom the land is unceremoniously taken, to be given to the elect. There is Isaac and there is Ishmael, there is Jacob and there is Esau. And the moral problem posed by these observations is recognized by Paul in Romans 9.6–33.[15] Paul does appear to be content with a recognition of the sheer grace of God in having mercy on anyone at all, without seriously engaging the question of the morality of reprobation. There is a certain arbitrariness about a God who rightly sees that all deserve nothing but retribution, but who inexplicably determines on mercy for one group but not for another.

But there is a further problem, posed by the universal salvific will of God. This is probably expressed most clearly in 1 Timothy 2.3–4, 'God our Saviour, who desires all men to be saved and to come to the knowledge of the truth' (RSV); but the same idea appears in Ezekiel: '. . . get yourselves a new heart and a new spirit! Why will you die, O house of Israel? For I have no pleasure in the death of any one, says the Lord God; so turn, and live' (Ezek. 18.31–2, RSV). But how may one turn if that turning is contrary to the calling of Yahweh?

Neither Augustine, in his classic formulation of the doctrine of election, nor Calvin, who elaborated it, succeeded in resolving the problem. What is noteworthy is that Paul's Ephesian doctrine of predestination is centred on Christ. As Barth has pointed out,[16] the doctrine of election must be worked out biblically and christologically, and not merely from the perspectives of historical theology or of philosophy. Ephesians 1.4 in fact becomes the cornerstone of Barth's thinking on the subject. He insists: 'Our thesis is that God's eternal will is the election of Jesus Christ',[17] but then that our election, in accordance with Ephesians 1.4, is 'in him', *en autō(i)*. But the 'him' is both the electing God and the eternally elected man Christ Jesus. The observation is important: 'God' is beyond our knowing, and if it is 'God' who elects, then we must simply stop discussing the matter which is beyond our reach. But Jesus, 'the same', *houtos* (John 1.2), the same God, we may know. In *him* we may believe. And of *his* election we need have no doubt at all.

This scheme then completes a symmetrical understanding of the passion of Christ. I am crucified with Christ. I have risen to new life in Christ. I am seated with Christ in heavenly places. And this all follows because I have been *elected* in Christ, and not apart from him.

Barth, then, understands the process of election in a most radical form. Christ was elected, chosen, before time, before the foundation of the earth, before there was any fall to demand atonement. None of this is to be seen as contingent, all is elective. The determination to create included within it the determination to elect Christ, and with him those who would put their trust in him.

But we may go much further than this. Christ is the *houtos* of John 1.2, he is God, but he is also man, fully man, paradoxically and graciously fully man in that he takes on himself all the sins of all humanity. No sin is left out. No individual is overlooked. Somehow, and it is not my purpose here to identify any one of several suggestive paradigms from Scripture as the one 'how' that explains it, somehow Christ bears all sin and atones for all sin in an act which was never contingent, but eternally determined. Thus in Christ we are all potentially elected. There is no reason for any individual to remain unreconciled to God. And yet it is open to any to refuse the election.

There is much that is helpful in Barth's scheme. A crux text,

Ephesians 1.4, is interpreted in agreement with its obvious meaning. The passion is clearly delivered from any sense of contingency. The unique sufficiency of the death and resurrection of Christ is made clear. Humanity is then confronted with an endlessly recurring choice of accepting or rejecting the divine revelation offered either in the proclamation of the Good News or in the general revelation of the eternal nature and power of God in creation. There is no sense in which the unevangelized are in a better condition in their ignorance than they would be should the Good News be preached to them. It is given to every person to respond to the grace-election that includes the universal Logos illumination, so that there is a positive affirmation of the Creator-God revealed in creation or of the God and Father of our Lord Jesus Christ, encountered through proclamation.

Rejection of the Logos illumination and of the divine self-revelation leads inevitably to the only alternative to the *grace* of God, that is the *wrath* of God. The wrath of God *is* an active wrath, and not merely a passive consequence of falling out of the hand of God. But it is an active wrath that is consequent upon the wilful rejection of the electing grace of God. To quote Barth again, 'A "rejected" man is one who isolates himself from God by resisting his election as it has taken place in Jesus Christ. God is for him; but he is against God. God receives him; but he withdraws himself from God.'[18] And, we might add, God shines upon his mind, offering him understanding of the divine revelation, but it is always open to him to choose, rather, the darkness.

The calling of God is, then, related to the election of Jesus Christ, and to the call to follow him. This calling represents both privilege: incorporation into the family of God, and responsibility: among other things, the responsibility to beseech all humanity, 'Be reconciled!'

Calling and Mission

We have already considered the relationship between the two covenants, noting points of continuity and points of discontinuity. We have noted particularly the new role of the Spirit under the New Covenant. We turn now to a distinctive feature of the New Covenant Church: its calling to centrifugal mission, contrasting with the generally centripetal mission under the Old Covenant.

The Centripetal Mission of the Old Covenant

It is clear from the promise made to Abraham that his calling was intended to represent a *berakah*, blessing, for all nations. But in general the role of Israel was essentially passive. Israel chose to practise a *presence* mission. From the practical and sociological point of view this is entirely understandable. In the late twentieth century we are accustomed to the swirl of world travellers from every part and to every part. Individuals may today move with some freedom from continent to continent. Although in Old Testament times there were, indeed, movements of entire peoples, sometimes as a matter of imperialistic policy, the movement of individuals from one culture to another must have been exceptional.

It is not difficult to locate passages from the Old Testament which indicate some contact between God's people and the surrounding nations.

1. Jonah is sent to Nineveh, the last capital of Assyria, calling the people to repentance, and Lesslie Newbigin has seen in this a foreshadowing of the world mission of the Church.[19] But there is no evidence from any source of any lasting effect of the mission, nor any suggestion that it was anything but exceptional.

2. Abraham intercedes on behalf of the cities of the plain, Sodom and Gomorrah, with some passion, but with no effect.

3. Ruth is brought into the messianic genealogy, her Moabite ancestry notwithstanding (Matt. 1.5), and Rahab of Jericho becomes an example of faith (Jas. 2.25; Heb. 11.31; and, probably, Matt. 1.5).

4. Melchizedek, king of Salem (Jerusalem?) is designated 'priest of God Most High' (Gen. 14.18), and, in an action whose significance is recognized and developed in Hebrews 5, receives gifts from Abraham. His very name 'King-of-righteousness', or 'Righteous-king' has an obvious theological significance, although he was, presumably, a Canaanite king with no lineal connection with Abraham.

5. Solomon's prayer at the dedication of the temple exemplifies Israel's expectations of the surrounding nations:

> Likewise when a foreigner, who is not of thy people Israel, comes from a far country for the sake of thy great name, and thy mighty

hand, and thy outstretched arm, when he comes and prays toward this house, hear thou from heaven thy dwelling place, and do according to all for which the foreigner calls to thee; in order that all the peoples of the earth may know thy name and fear thee. (2 Chron. 6.32-3, RSV)

Here it is Yahweh who is made responsible for the conversion of the nations, who in turn are responsible for taking the initiative in *coming* to Jerusalem, to the temple. They must come; Yahweh must answer; but Israel has no apparent responsibility beyond being *there* and offering an example of a redeemed community.

6. The law does, of course, take note of the possibility of other peoples coming to live with the chosen people. Leviticus 19.33-4 establishes the principle: 'When a stranger sojourns with you in your land, you shall not do him wrong. The stranger who sojourns with you shall be to you as the native among you, and you shall love him as yourself; for you were strangers in the land of Egypt' (RSV).

Numbers 15.14-16 appears to take this slightly further, requiring the stranger to do 'as you do . . . One law and one ordinance shall be for you and for the stranger who sojourns with you' (RSV), although this advance is probably to be seen as a differentiation between the temporary visitor and the permanent settler, rather than as an advance in the requirements expected of all strangers.

7. Amos 9.7 represents an important footnote to simplistic statements relating to Israel's election. The election is conditional, not absolute, and Yahweh's activity is not restricted to what he does for Israel:

> 'Are not you Israelites
>   the same to me as the Cushites?'
>   declares the Lord
> 'Did I not bring Israel up from Egypt,
>   the Philistines from Caphtor
>   and the Arameans from Kir?
>
> 'Surely the eyes of the Sovereign Lord
>   are on the sinful kingdom.
> I will destroy it
>   from the face of the earth . . .'
>   declares the Lord. (Amos 9.7-8)

comparison of Israel and Cush is certainly a startling one, but would have been more so to the contemporaries of Amos: the Cushites' proverbial dark skins made them obviously different: but 'Not so!' says Yahweh. 'But surely we *are* different: can we not look back to the exodus as the great indicator of our uniqueness?' But 'Not so!' is the response from Yahweh: the great migrations of the Philistines and the Syrians (of which, perhaps surprisingly, the prophet is well aware)[20] were also part of Yahweh's activities. But is it not the case that Yahweh has his eye upon Israel? 'That is true!' responds Yahweh, but it is not quite as Israel supposes: that eye perceives Israel's sin and prepares judgement. Israel, in fact, is not quite the unique nation that she conceives herself to be, is not the unique recipient of God's attention.

In fact we have to conclude that Israel's isolation from her neighbours, her failure to fulfil the Abrahamic *berit* and to be a blessing to the nations, her pride in her privilege, is a major reason for the withdrawal of that privilege. Israel has been unable to withstand the lust for power that in some sense came with the granting of the land. As Walter Brueggemann expresses it: 'The land, source of life, has within it seductive power. It invites Israel to enter life apart from covenant, to reduce covenant place, with all its demands and possibilities, to serene space apart from history, without contingency, without demand, without mystery.'[21]

The land is not meant for the proud and the confident. To quote Brueggemann again, 'The land is precisely for those and only for those who sense their precariousness and act in their vulnerability.'[22] Paul, of course, uses a similar argument in Romans 11.7–12.

The expectations of the Abrahamic covenant, that in Abraham all the nations of the earth should be blessed, were not realized. But that they were intended to be taken seriously is suggested by the repetition of the goal in Isaiah 49.6; the Servant of the Lord is to be 'a light for the Gentiles, that you may bring my salvation to the ends of the earth'.

This had not been done. The prophet was uncertain that Israel ever would do it. As G. B. Caird so strikingly expressed it:

It is as though he had published an advertisement. 'Wanted, a servant of the Lord', accompanied by a job description. He was undoubtedly aware that many famous men, such as Moses and Jeremiah, had sat for the composite portrait he was drawing. What he could not know was that in the end there would be only one applicant for the post.[23]

It is to the calling of that one applicant that we now turn.

Jesus and Centrifugal Mission

As with Old Testament Israel, so with the ministry of Jesus, centrifugal mission, mission beyond the boundaries of Israel, is exceptional. It is a commonplace in missiology to make reference to Jesus' unqualified statement in Matthew 15.24, 'I was sent only to the lost sheep of Israel.' But in fact the statement is shown by its cotext to be conditioned. Jesus has been approached by 'a Canaanite woman' from the region of Tyre and Sidon, to which, exceptionally, Jesus had gone. She asks for help for her daughter, but Jesus refuses to respond. And when he is pressed by his own disciples to make some kind of response, it is in the strongly negative words already noted. However, the woman refuses to be discouraged: 'The woman came and knelt before him. "Lord, help me!" she said.' But he is again negative: 'It is not right to take the children's bread and toss it to their dogs.'

It is difficult to know how we are to understand this apparently gratuitous insult. F. W. Beare calls it 'incredible insolence'.[24] But the text does not bear this out. The woman does not appear to be insulted: instead she continues the encounter, still hoping for the help she needs. If only we knew *how* Jesus might have said those words. Indeed if only we knew exactly *what* Jesus said. The Greek uses a diminutive, *kynarios*, which presumably points to the Aramaic *gūra'*, 'puppy',[25] and the woman's own reference to dogs picking up scraps from beneath the table shows that they are domestic animals, not mere street pariahs.

But the point of the anecdote is that Jesus' own apparently unqualified statement of an exclusive mission to Israel notwithstanding, and despite the clear indication that the woman is not from Israel,[26] still she is given what she wants: her daughter was healed.

Thus we would be wrong to follow slavishly a traditional understanding of an entirely exclusive ministry of Jesus. There was an inevitable primary mission to Israel, but even in the pre-passion period of the life of Jesus the universal salvific task of the Servant of the Lord was not overlooked.

In keeping with the priority of the mission to Israel, Jesus is found in Gentile company only occasionally. In Luke 7.1–10 he encounters the Roman centurion from Capernaum, and his words of commendation of the faith of the centurion parallel similar words of approval spoken of the Canaanite woman. The case of the Samaritan woman of John 4 is somewhat different, in that the Samaritans were at least part-Jewish, but the highly significant Nazareth synagogue discourse by Jesus in Luke 4.16–21 is a different matter. Once again it seems that Jesus deliberately gives cause for offence, by referring to the faith of the non-Jewish world and the gracious acts of God there, in contrast to the faithlessness of Israel.

The worldwide concern expressed in John 3.15 may confidently be attributed to Jesus, but the following and better-known assertion, 'God so loved the world', is almost certainly to be understood as John's comment (the Nicodemus pericope proper then ending at 3.15).[27]

THE GENIUS OF THE CHURCH: HOSTILITY ENDED

The Jerusalem Church

The characteristics of the New Covenant community are worked out theoretically in the epistles and historically in Acts, and in such parts of the epistles as are descriptive of the Church. The earliest description historically is that in Acts 2.44–7. The continuing relationship to the temple is expressed,[28] and there is particular stress on the *koinōnia* of the first believers. They were together, they had all things in common, they sold their possessions to relieve poverty, they broke bread in their homes, clearly a technical term for the later Eucharist.[29] Acts 4 develops the theme of community: the believers were of one heart and soul, they had everything in common, and there were no needy persons among them because of the practice of total commonality.

That is not to say that they became in the modern sense of the term a community, abandoning the normal family units. The very fact that they broke bread 'in their homes', *kat'oikon* (2.46), makes this clear. Nor did they pool and then redistribute their wealth: as need arose it was met. This was *not* an early experiment in communism, but it was an early and abiding experience of Christian commonality.[30] Nor are we to assume that this experience of commonality soon ended. On the contrary, the concept of commonality in the Church expanded with the growth of the Church. When there was general poverty in the entire Mediterranean basin, and the church at Jerusalem suffered the greatest deprivation,[31] it was felt to be entirely appropriate for the other churches to share their adequacy.[32]

The eclectic nature of the Christian congregations gave rise to opportunities for developing a new, cross-cultural commonality, but inevitably also gave rise to tension. As A. J. Malherbe comments of the church at Corinth: 'The Christian community, which included people from quite different social strata, might be expected to have particular problems with social integration.'[33]

The Church at Corinth

From 1 Corinthians 1.26 it is clear that the congregation was drawn from across the various levels of the social strata. Indeed, Paul is merely reminding them that the Corinthian church is a microcosm of the surrounding society. There were wise people, powerful people and even noble people in the church, but they were a minority as they were a minority in the world outside. Within the church such differentia become unimportant. All-important is the calling, the *klēsis*, of God, and the choosing, the *eklegein*, of God, emphasized by the deliberate repetition of the verb: 'What is foolish in the world God *chose*' (the fronting of the object of God's choice is emphatic), 'and the weak in the world God *chose* . . . and the low and despised in the world God *chose*' (1 Cor. 1.27–8). And as a result even those who were rich found themselves in the midst of the chosen poor, and the community together were forced to the realization that they had but one thing to be proud of: God's choosing (1 Cor. 1.31).

The present discussion is of some importance to us in that it relates to the 'Homogeneous Unit Church' notions of some proponents of Church Growth ideas. These ideas go back to Donald McGavran's foundational work *The Bridges of God*,[34] and are worked out in his later writings and those of his followers.[35]

McGavran began from the problem posed by the process of the conversion of individuals who on the one hand had to leave their own cultures and on the other hand had to be incorporated into what was, generally, an unfamiliar culture, among people whose whole way of life was different from their own. McGavran's answer was the multiplication of homogeneous unit churches.

Admittedly McGavran and others following his lead have been quite right sociologically in observing the general instability of non-homogeneous groups of people. Commonality in culture clearly does serve to facilitate stressless community. It is also clear that the early Church experienced the problems of non-homogeneity. The church at Corinth is our example.

As we have seen, its members came from all strata of society. The result was disagreement within the church on almost every level. There was disagreement on leadership, disagreement on doctrine, disagreement on diet, disagreement on dress, and even disagreement at the eucharistic meal. It is fairly clear from 1 Corinthians 11 that the Eucharist was taken in the context of a shared meal. Inevitably the contributions brought by the individual members of the congregation varied enormously: some brought meat and wine, others contributed only bread. The early experience of such selfless community must have been euphoric: the poorer members of the congregation, in particular, must have taken great pride in this new 'guild' which contrasted so significantly with the trade guilds of Corinth.[36]

Tragically, their euphoria was short-lived. The common meal continued, but the pooling of resources did not: '. . . each one goes ahead with his own meal, and one is hungry and another is drunk' (1 Cor. 11.21, RSV). It is undoubtedly true that this problem, and others, too, would not have arisen in a homogeneous church, a church where all were rich or all were poor. The solutions offered by Paul, however, require the working out of the fundamental principle of community across cultural barriers. There is no suggestion of a division of the church according to social strata or any other sociological features.

Gordon Fee neatly summarizes the thrust of Paul's perceptions:

. . .the apostle does not eliminate the social distinctions as such: The wealthy still have their own houses in which to eat their private meals (vv. 22, 34). What he will not let them do is to bring such distinctions to the common meal of believers, where Christ had made them all one, signified by their all eating of the one loaf . . . By carrying over into these meals a number of 'privileged status' aspects of both private and religious meals, the rich were in effect destroying the church as one body in Christ.[37]

A Theological Statement on Unity: Ephesians

In chapter two of his Ephesian letter, Paul lays the foundation for his later appeal to his readers that they should lead the kind of life appropriate to their status in Christ. Negatively, he pictures the former condition of his Gentile readers: separated from Christ, alienated from the commonwealth of Israel, strangers to the covenants of promise, having no hope, and without God in the world. Positively he points to a new unity which has been brought about through the cross (2.16), depicted in the metaphor of the one body.

For the Jew, therefore, the most fundamental and unquestioned of all assumptions about humanity is at a stroke dismissed. There is neither Jew nor Gentile. The consequence for the Gentile world is, then, the reversal of all that was spelled out in verse 12: the Gentiles are no longer strangers and sojourners, the two typical terms used to describe Gentiles living among Jews for a shorter or longer time, but fellow citizens, members of the household of God, built on the foundation of apostles and prophets. Where before they were *atheoi*, they are now living stones in a holy temple which is the very dwelling-place of God.

The metaphor is highly productive. God inhabits the temple. The apostles and prophets are its foundation, Jews and Gentiles are its stones, and Jesus himself is the cornerstone, a figure which directs attention back to Isaiah 28.16: 'Behold, I am laying in Zion for a foundation a stone, a tested stone, a precious cornerstone, of a sure foundation . . .' (RSV).

The prophecy is now interpreted: the stones of this new temple come not from Jerusalem alone, but from all over the inhabited world. Confidence in the new building rests in the cornerstone, Jesus. The wider prophecy is being fulfilled in this freshly conceived temple: '. . . by men of strange lips and with an alien tongue the Lord will speak to this people' (Isa. 28.11, RSV).

It is this doctrine of the community of the New Covenant that makes the very concept of a deliberately constructed homogeneous worshipping congregation not merely unbiblical but actually counter-biblical. If the claims of Ephesians 2 are unfounded, then it appears that the consequences of the gospel are almost entirely deferred to the *parousia*. And yet there is an urgent need today, in all parts of the world, and precisely because of the growing mobility of society, for a formula that will enable people to relate peacefully across cultural barriers. In Christ it can be done. Samuel Escobar comments:

> In some societies and nations there is a desperate need for healing in the area of interracial relationships. In those cases, the Christian church might be the only place where the miracle of encounter, acceptance, and coexistence can happen because the redemptive power of Christ acts. To perpetuate segregation for the sake of numerical growth, arguing that segregated churches grow faster, is yielding to the sinfulness of society, refusing to show a new and unique way of life. It is an example of reducing the gospel to make it more palatable.[38]

The doctrine of the community of the New Covenant also brings into question some of the assumptions of black theology and of liberation theology. It must be stated here that any dogma placing God 'on the side of' one group rather than another group, for the poor and against the rich, for the black and against the white, runs counter to the doctrine of the one community transcending all such barriers. As Lesslie Newbigin, with his usual sensitivity, asks: '. . . the heart of the matter is exposed when we ask what happens at the Eucharist. Can the oppressor and the oppressed share together in the Eucharist? The theologians of liberation, if I understand rightly, say no.'[39]

Newbigin goes on to remind us of the experienced reality that we are all of us to some extent both oppressors and oppressed: 'We are all so made that we are conscious of the oppression of others and unconscious of the ways in which we oppress.'[40] If the oppressor may not come until he has ended his oppression to the satisfaction of the oppressed, then we must exclude also all other categories of sinners until they have become saints, at least so far as we understand the character of saints. But it is not so. The genius of the Christian Church lies precisely in the universal invitation: 'Come to me, *all* who labour and are heavy laden' (Matt. 11.28, RSV). Of *course* the oppression must be dealt with . . . as must the other sins of which we are all guilty. But the fellowship of the Church cannot wait for the establishing of the universal Kingdom of God, nor can it arbitrarily construct its own exclusive mini-kingdom.

12 The Church Growth Movement

INTRODUCTION

A Christian world-view has already been briefly indicated on pp. 25–35 above. It is a complex view, and recognizes both the tangible and the intangible, the material world and the spiritual world. The individual is created purposefully by God, so created as to respond to communion both at the level of the human and at the level of the divine. But a 'fall' of cosmic proportions has produced the human condition of essential helplessness.

Within the two apparent boundaries of birth and death it is impossible to make sense of life in this 'fallen' world. Beyond those boundaries stands a God who has decisively intervened in the world through the incarnation so as to resolve the human inability, partially now, totally at the ultimate judgement of all things.

Humanity is a spiritual creation, infinite in one direction only, (while God is infinite with respect to both past and future). In comparison with eternity, the human existence is marked by its appalling brevity. And it is for that reason that there is an ultimate priority about the resolution of the first area of meaninglessness, the first dimension of *dukkha*. The first task of the Church is to call all humanity to reconciliation with God. It is from the Church that, in principle, the answer to meaninglessness should be given, and it is within the Church that, in principle, individuals should begin to discover the resolution of the human disorder.

The Church Growth movement, therefore, was not mistaken in recalling the Church to an awareness of this priority. The Western world has rightly shown a concern for the *dukkha* suffering of the peoples of the world in so far as that suffering was a material suffering. The Church has tended to identify with that concern, but it has been in danger of losing its vision of eternity and the opportunity, in that dimension of the human experience, of a further, and more profound resolution of meaninglessness.

The Church Growth movement has provided a major challenge to the churches with respect to the spiritual dimension of *dukkha*, but the movement has tended to lose a biblical balance in its preoccupation with growing *churches*, to the comparative neglect of the true focus of the ministry of the Church: introducing people to God.

As we consider the question of the role of the Church in resolving apparent meaninglessness through its proclamation of reconciliation to God, we do so through a critique of the Church Growth movement.

HISTORY OF THE CHURCH GROWTH MOVEMENT[1]

Donald McGavran's seminal work *The Bridges of God*[2] was published by the World Dominion Press in 1955. He and those who have followed him have spent the years since developing and refining his ideas, and responding to the many criticisms which were not slow in coming. In 1968 a complete issue of the *International Review of Missions* was devoted to a critique of Church Growth thinking. Many of the articles were disappointing, too often displaying prejudice and a woeful ignorance of what McGavran was actually saying.

McGavran's base was a criticism of a mission methodology based on an expatriate mission 'compound' into which converts were steadily drawn, so that they were turned from bridges across which God might walk into the world, into islands, isolated from their own communities. Converts became teachers in mission schools, 'dressers', nurses with a rudimentary medical training, in mission hospitals, gardeners and cooks in missionary homes, because the fact of conversion commonly meant the rejection of the convert by the community. He could get no work in the community and the missionary felt obliged to find employment for him.

McGavran saw that at least part of the problem lay in the one-by-one discipling methods of the missionaries. One individual converted from a family. One individual from a village. In many societies it is almost impossible for one individual to survive without the support of the community. In most of Africa the welfare of the village is seen to depend on the commitment of the whole community to what has been identified as a safe way of life. There is a right way to build a house, a right way to plough a field, a right way to celebrate a birth, and these right ways are all

153

religious ways. To do anything in a different way threatens the safety of the community.

McGavran developed the idea of a people movement: the concept of entire villages moving into Christianity together and so being able to support one another in the difficult first years of change. He had the example of Lydia and her household (Acts 16.14–15) to point to, and more relevant still Acts 9.35, '. . . all the residents of Lydda and Sharon . . . turned to the Lord' (RSV). He carefully disowned the idea of mass conversions, of the mass movement: 'The term "mass movement" should never be used. It obscures and distorts what is really going on.'[3] He insisted that 'large numbers are achieved only by the conversion of a series of small groups over a period of years'.[4]

As the ideas of Church Growth have developed, so a very large number of so-called 'principles' has been recognized. Peter Wagner, one of the principal proponents of McGavran's ideas, makes reference to sixty-seven such principles ascribed to McGavran, fifty-one principles ascribed to himself, and a total of 146 principles so far proposed.[5]

BASIC PRINCIPLES

From the intimidating list of principles proposed, the following have probably commanded rather general agreement.

The Priority of Numerical Church Growth

According to Church Growth thinking, numerical church growth ought to be a primary concern of any church. Admittedly, there will be times when it will only be one of several concerns, but McGavran would say that any church that is not seeing converts added to its membership should be concerned to find out why this is not happening.

This first principle reflects McGavran's recognition that missionary societies in the 1950s had simply lost their way. Their programmes had a built-in self-destruct element to them. The missionaries preached, planted churches, and then settled down to pastor their congregations: evangelism halted. But as the congregations matured they developed their own leadership, and frequently rebuffed the missionaries and their ways. The missionaries moved on to Bible teaching, and when the converts were able to teach in the Bible schools the missionaries opened seminaries. But eventually the churches were able to handle theological teaching at the seminary level also, and again the missionaries found themselves unemployed. When famine hit the Third World then a new work appeared for the missionaries: relief and rehabilitation, and development.

Indeed there were missions where the missionary did everything but evangelize. A startling example has been documented by Vincent J. Donovan in his *Christianity Rediscovered.*[6] The missionaries of the society to which he belonged in Kenya had done everything except to evangelize. Donovan determined on a radical new plan:

> From now on, I would not go in their kraals to sleep, nor would I drink their milk. I would no longer ask for their children for our schools. I wanted no land for mission buildings. I wanted nothing from them. Nor should they expect anything from me. I brought them no gifts, no sweets for the children, no tobacco for the elders, no beads for the women – no medicine for their sick. I had come only to talk about God.[7]

Donovan explained this new programme to a Masai elder named Ndangoya. He had a single question to ask: 'If that is why you came here, why did you wait so long to tell us about this?'[8]

Since evangelism clearly had a low priority for the missionary, the churches founded by the missionary similarly tended to develop a low priority for mission. Pastoral care was important. Choirs were important. Bible study was important. But evangelism was not.

Why was it, then, that the mission churches did not simply wither away? McGavran recognized that often churches were actually growing, but through what he eventually designated 'biological church growth'. One member of a family was converted, and then his extended family was gradually brought in. But there was no significant outreach into the unevangelized society. When in the early 1970s Church Growth thinking was transferred from missionary work to the North American churches,[9] it was realized that some churches were growing through transfer: simply drawing in converts from other congregations.

The model was systematized. There was 'biological church

growth', and there was 'transfer growth' (some forms of which were boldly labelled 'parasitic growth', one church deliberately feeding off another). There was 'evangelism growth'. Churches were everywhere challenged to examine what was happening to them in the matter of growth. Were they growing at all? If not, then why not? If they were, then how were they growing? Was there any real evidence of evangelism growth?

The model found a place for other types of growth: 'discipleship growth', a measure of the maturing process among the believers (see Col. 1.28), and 'extension growth', the process of actually planting new churches.

Concentration on Responsive Groups

A second principle recognized what had long been known intuitively: that in any location and at any point in history certain groups of people become particularly responsive to the Christian message, or particularly unresponsive to it. McGavran suggested that the Church should overtly attempt to identify responsive groups and should then concentrate its evangelism on them.

Once again he was aware of possible misunderstanding: the danger of being seen to suggest that unresponsive groups such as Muslims should be denied access to the Good News. He might have had Acts 13.46 on his side had he chosen to take that line: 'It was necessary that the word of God should be spoken first to you. Since you thrust it from you . . . behold, we turn to the Gentiles' (RSV).

In fact McGavran did not take that position, recognizing the probability that God would continue to call his messengers to the resistant and unresponsive peoples of the world. However, he did insist that where responsive groups existed it would be absurd for the Church not to take note of the fact, and to develop an appropriate strategy.

Recognition of 'People Movements'

Traditional evangelism in Western society has uncritically accepted the individualism of our sociology, to the neglect of its group dimension. Conversion has been perceived primarily (if not exclusively) as an individual response to proclamation. This concentration on the conversion of the individual inevitably leads to the isolation of the individual from the community, an isolation which might be tolerable in the Western world (granted the provision of some measure of church-community support), but which is not tolerable in the closely structured societies of most of the world.

As we have seen, the manner in which a house is built, in which ploughing is begun, in which a baby is born, in which the dead are buried in such societies is *not* a matter for the individuals immediately concerned, and for them only. It is a matter for the entire community. It is *their* security that is involved. Past experience, over many generations, has shown that *this* is the safe, the acceptable, procedure. Of new ways there can be no such guarantee. But the failure of one member of the community to follow tradition is perceived to be a threat to all.

Conversely, it is apparent that a whole group may safely make even radical changes, by consultation, by consensus, thereby providing all members of the group with support in the process of change. This thesis had been presented by Bishop J. W. Pickett in *Church Growth and Group Conversion* in 1936,[10] a book which included pioneering contributions from Donald McGavran.

We have referred above to Vincent Donovan's approach to the Masai, his singleminded commitment to talk about God. The consequence of Donovan's initiative were far-reaching and unexpected. After months of 'talking about God', individual communities decided *as communities* that they wished to move together into the new faith: the community leaders could declare 'for all this community that we have reached the step in our lives where we can say, "We believe."'[11] And there was the opposite decision, as communities, that they had now heard enough of the religion, and wished to hear no more.

Removing unnecessary cultural barriers

It has become a commonplace in missiology to criticize the importation into the Christian proclamation of elements that were not only culture bound, and not only incongruous, but that proved to be an actual hindrance to the indigenization of Christianity.

Some of the standard mission histories hint at the absurdities. The misplaced determination of the Ruanda missionaries that their church should have a steeple: 'The erection of the steeple . . . was a major operation . . . I remember the thrill with which we watched the steeple, teetering to one side or the other as directions were shouted . . .'[12] The strange notions of theology: the same writer records the determination of the Ruanda missionaries to found their mission on 'Bible, Protestant and Keswick lines'.[13] And missionary Joe Church's encounter with an old friend 'standing in the road in a Trinity blazer, surrounded by a crowd of smart little schoolboys'.[14]

Fortunately there were some, even then, who could ask, as did Dr Church, 'How much of the traditional English Christmas should be introduced . . . how far should the full Anglican Liturgy be introduced' to the young African church?[15] In Ethiopia the Lutheran churches proposed to the Conference of Ethiopian Evangelical Churches a united church based on Scripture *and* on Luther's *Catechism*.[16] It is scarcely surprising that the project reduced eventually to a united Lutheran Church, with the other churches withdrawing from the discussions.

The Church Growth principle relates to church music and liturgy, to church buildings and the structuring of the clergy, liturgical dress, clerical titles, and to theological issues such as Sunday observance, baptism, dispensationalism, the authority of traditional credal statements, the Eucharist, the status of polygamists, the significance of circumcision, fasting, head-coverings, feminism, and a host of such topics. It is the case that many of the movements begun by missionaries have been so loaded down with imported irrelevancies, and are correspondingly so light on such cultural relevancies as the power encounter, demonology, exorcism, that they have been unable so to reform themselves as to become indigenous even where that is a theoretical possibility.

The Kimbanguist Church, spread across a dozen countries in Africa, represents an example of a reaction against such irrelevancy, a reaction which, because its praxis was in such stark contrast to the traditional Churches, has almost always attracted hostility from missionaries.

The Church of Jesus Christ on Earth Through the Prophet Simon Kimbangu[17] is a product of the African prophetic movement of the early twentieth century, a movement whose main focus was the emergence of a free Africa. Here we have an example not of a church to which independence was given, when the structures were already securely in place, but of a church which was always independent, and which was, therefore, from its very origin, largely free of cultural irrelevancies.

Simon Kimbangu (1889–1951) in 1921 announced his calling to serve God, and publicized the first healing through his ministry at what was to become the holy spring at Nkamba in the Congo. It is difficult to imagine the colonial era in which he lived: the Belgian authorities accused him of fomenting revolt, arrested him, and in 1922 he was sentenced to death. The sentence was commuted to imprisonment, and he remained in prison until his death nearly thirty years later, in 1951. Despite a continual stream of deportations of heads of families of Kimbanguists to remote parts of the Congo, the movement grew with astonishing rapidity. In 1959 the Kimbanguist Church was legitimized, and since then has become a member of the World Council of Churches, some indication of its relative orthodoxy.

But it is clearly African in its origin, in its music, in the songs which are first 'caught' from the Spirit and then authenticated by the Church's leadership, but particularly in its emphasis on healing, so vital in a society where medical care is available only for the few.[18] Its dynamic growth to a membership of some four million in 1975 has continued, and is marked by huge additions from the 'mission' churches which on the whole have failed to meet the specific needs of Africans.

The Use of Secular Disciplines in Planned Evangelism

The Church Growth movement has encouraged churches to make use of sociological surveys, of statistical investigation, of contemporary insights into communication theory, of historical studies, and of anthropology in the development of missiology. Through its insistence on precision of language, this has not infrequently led to the identification of genuine trends in church growth, often in sharp contradistinction to pious hopes. In the area of finance, the recognition of the effect of inflation has sometimes meant that for the first time Christian organizations have become aware of a real decline in financial support, even in the context of increased annual receipts. Such bland terms as 'blessing' have been dismissed with a demand for numbers, for precision in the definition of what such a word might mean.

Allied to an insistence on the importance of actually discipling people into the Church, rather than merely bringing them to some form of 'decision', this concern for statistics has led to a reappraisal of the effectiveness of mass evangelism. It appeared that in some cases there was a serious imbalance between statistics regarding 'decisions' at the crusades, and the numbers of those incorporated into congregations.

Statistics certainly show that immediately following the Billy Graham Harringay Crusade in 1954 there was a significant rise in a graph which otherwise showed steadily declining numbers of baptisms in the English Baptist churches,[19] and this is reflected in the corresponding graph showing declining membership in the same denomination.[20] In fact it appears that there were some 4,500 baptisms in the Baptist churches which might be attributable to the Crusade. How this might be reflected in other denominations would be much more difficult to determine.

The 1954 Crusade did have the effect of bringing significant numbers of people into the Church. However the Crusade did not succeed in reversing the steady falling away in Baptist church membership. By 1960 the rate of decline was precisely what it had been before the Crusade. There is no reason to suppose that it was otherwise in other denominations.

However, in his survey of the results of the 1983–4 Mission to London, Peter Brierley reports that 13,359 persons 'committed themselves to Christ' in the two phases of the mission. Of these 3,740 were under fourteen years of age. If all those adults who made this commitment and who lived in London actually joined a church, this would add a total of *two* adults to the average church congregation. What has not so far been done is to determine whether or not even that modest expectation has been realized.[21] To refer again to the Baptist Union statistics, they indicate at least a bottoming out in a long process of decline in membership that stretches back to 1911:

1911	267,289
1982	153,159
1983–4 Mission to London	
1984	156,580
1986	157,699

But it cannot be assumed that the long period of decline is ended for English Baptists, and certainly much more needs to be done in statistical analysis before an answer can be found to the question of the effectiveness of mass evangelism as measured by increases in church membership and attendance.

THE BRIDGES OF GOD

The phrase 'Bridges of God' recalls both McGavran's original book on Church Growth and the operation in the Second World War aimed at securing a succession of bridges across which a significant advance by the Allied armies might have been made across Europe. In the event, ambition over-reached itself and the goal was not reached. It is possible for us so to be carried away by our enthusiasm that we forget the limitations placed on Church Growth thinking by McGavran himself, and attempt to cross or construct unlawful bridges.

The Bridges of God was published in 1955, and the intervening years have been spent in working out the implications of that book, and its literary descendants. In those years Church Growth thinking developed from what was primarily a missions model, to a model relevant to the North American Church, to a model relevant to the wider church scene. We have been concerned to develop bridges, following McGavran's original and fruitful imagery. But we must be cautious: the imagery quickly sets us thinking in terms of the approach roads to the bridge, the signposting of the bridge, the foundations upon which the bridge is built, the width of the bridge, and so on. In fact to a fascinating but merely diversionary encounter with allegory, to the neglect of the fundamental issue: Where does the bridge lead? For McGavran the bridge was one across which God might come to us. At the present time in Europe it would generally be calamitous if all that was on the other side of the bridge was the local church.

CRITICISMS OF CHURCH GROWTH THEORY

Criticisms of Dr McGavran's ideas have not been slow in coming. As noted earlier, in 1968 the *International Review of Missions* devoted an issue to the subject of Church Growth. J. G. Davies, then of Birmingham University, tabled four criticisms:

1. To define the goal of mission as *church* growth is to indulge in an artificial narrowing of the concept of the Kingdom of God. But of course no one was saying that growing churches is all that we are required to promote. Of course God's rule elsewhere is also a concern to God's people.

Still, there is legitimate criticism here: much Church Growth writing has concentrated on the phenomenon of growing congregations, first of all of 'large' churches, and now of 'mega' churches. John Vaughan has published case studies of the world's twenty largest churches, and edited a periodical publication updating his register of these mega-churches.[23] The methods employed in growing such churches are carefully tabulated, but the question of the validity of such churches in terms of a truly biblical ecclesiology rather than a pragmatic sociology is simply not asked. To see the Church of Jesus Christ grow is one thing. To ensure the numerical increase of a particular local congregation is quite another. The former is the work of the Spirit and brings glory to God. The latter may do little more than bring notoriety to the pastor.

2. To think in terms of church growth is to plan for survival. Not so; McGavran has consistently reminded us that there can be no certain outcome to our endeavour to plant churches. But in any event there is no need for us to plan for survival: it is no mere jingoism to assert that the Church is already here and there, in time and eternity, and it cannot do other than survive.

But again there is a measure of truth in the complaint: the sharing of the Good News must be because it *is* good news, and out of compassion for those who do not have it, and in obedience to Christ, but not as an answer to dwindling congregations or to financial insufficiency. And this in turn raises the fundamental question: Does the average churchgoer actually recognize 'good news' in his understanding of Christianity? Is Christianity actually perceived to be relevant to the admitted *dukkha* experience of the people by whom the Christian is always surrounded?

Church Growth may be embraced rather for the sake of the church than for the sake of those being invited in to the church: a larger church becomes some kind of survival insurance for its members.

3. The strategy of deliberately planned church growth is a limitation of the free activity of the Holy Spirit. This represents no more than an affirmation of what McGavran has always said: no methodology can serve to circumvent the sovereign Spirit.

4. To place church growth at the centre of Christian concern is illegitimate, because God's concern is the world, not the Church. This is sheer obfuscation. God's concern is to gather his world into his Church.

FOUR AFFIRMATIONS

In 1974 Orlando Costas published *The Church and its Mission*,[24] which devoted three chapters to the ideas of Church Growth. Costas took the trouble to attempt to understand McGavran, and he identified one major issue which concerned him: McGavran's concentration on the Church. This provides the first of four points to make in reaffirming what McGavran has himself repeatedly said, but what has been as repeatedly forgotten.

God is the Focus of Theology

Costas complained that Church Growth had an ecclesiology but little else. Like Davies he wanted to see the Kingdom of God placed in the focus, not the Church. Walter Hollenweger had even quoted, with approval, the comment that McGavran was misreading Luke 12.31 as 'Seek ye first Church Growth.'[25]

The fact is that we have seen a renewed interest in the central New Testament theme of the Kingdom of God, possibly culminating in George Beasley-Murray's book, *Jesus and the Kingdom of God*.[26] The debate has tended to centre on the relationship between the Church and the Kingdom. John Macquarrie identified the relationship in the very appropriate term *entelechy*, the Kingdom is the entelechy of the Church, the 'perfect unfolding of the potentialities that are already manifesting themselves in the church'.[27]

But it must be said that however important the Kingdom may be, the King is more important still. The focus of our thinking is neither the Church nor the Kingdom, but God himself. He is on the other side of the bridge; it is he whom I wish to encounter. To quote the *International Review of Missions* again, 'The centre of the Church is the person of Jesus Christ . . . The Church is His people, His disciples, His friends, gathered round him because He has called them. They hear His word and see Him acting.'[28]

But is this the case? Do they see God acting, or do they see ministers acting? To see God acting is not merely entertaining and exciting, but it may also be frightening. In Acts 2 we are allowed a glimpse of the early Church:

> All the believers were together and had everything in common. Selling their possessions and goods, they gave to anyone as he had need. Every day they continued to meet together in the temple courts. They broke bread in their homes and ate together with glad and sincere hearts, praising God and enjoying the favour of all the people. And the Lord added to their number daily those who were being saved. (Acts 2.44–7)

But Acts 5 reminds us of the other aspect of the activity of God: 'Great fear seized the whole church and all who heard about these events' (v. 11); 'No-one else dared join them, even though they were highly regarded by the people' (v. 13).

We affirm that *God* is the focus of theology. If Church Growth ideas lead only to the proliferation of 'churches', without people having a radical and liberating, and even frightening, encounter with God, then those ideas are to that extent unbiblical.

The Sovereign and Unpredictable Spirit

In the 1950s it was possible to say that the doctrine of the Holy Spirit was the great neglected doctrine of the Church. In the 1980s it might be more true to say that it is the great *exploited* doctrine of the Church. Throughout the short life of the Church Growth movement it has been a constant criticism that it represents an attempt to circumvent the work of the Spirit.

It is the Holy Spirit who convicts and converts. The technical term for this process of conviction and conversion is *elenctics*, which we have already examined on pp. 117–19 above. The Holy Spirit is the unique source of conviction. But he is also the unpredictable Spirit. Jesus told us 'The *pneuma* blows wherever it pleases. You hear its sound, but you cannot tell where it comes from or where it is going' (John 3.8). Thus we cannot say what the outcome of any particular proclamation of the Good News by any particular individual may be. This is both exciting and disturbing. If the Spirit is free, then the limitations placed by sociologists and sociolinguists, and by communication theory on effective communication, may be entirely mistaken.

In other words, ideas of homogeneity may be wrong not only in so far as they relate to the Church, but also as they relate to evangelism. Sociologically it may be true that people communicate best with people from a similar social background. But granted the general unpredictability of the Spirit, is he equally unpredictable in matters of conviction and conversion across these apparent barriers? Are we right in supposing that the Spirit is somehow limited by group dynamics, by the dynamics of class distinctions?

Perhaps I may be allowed a personal testimony at this point. As a missionary in Ethiopia I formed innumerable friendships across vast cultural barriers, and in even the most remote parts of that country saw people coming to Christ in large numbers through the witness of expatriates as well as through the witness of the national believers. In the United Kingdom I think of Vi, an older lady, living on a council estate, who came to some meetings we organized in the local school. She bought herself a Bible. She announced her commitment to Christ. She led her husband to Christ just a few months before he died of the cancer from which he had suffered for years. I conducted the funeral service. Vi was astonished: she had never been to a funeral service like that before. And now, with her fear of death, that 'last enemy', astonishingly set at rest, she announced to her friends and family, 'Peter's going to do me when I die'!

Nor is it only across social classes that the free Spirit builds bridges: across the barriers of age, also, the bridges are built, in defiance of our communications theories. Older people communicate powerfully with younger, younger with older, because it is the Spirit who communicates.

The sovereignty and the liberty of the Spirit is well illustrated from the trinitarian passage of 1 Corinthians 2.1–5:

> When I came to you, brothers, I did not come with eloquence or superior wisdom as I proclaimed to you the testimony about God. For I resolved to know nothing while I was with you except Jesus Christ and him crucified. I came to you in weakness and fear, and

with much trembling. My message and my preaching were not with wise and persuasive words, but with a demonstration of the Spirit's power, so that your faith might not rest on men's wisdom, but on God's power.

And Paul assesses the relative significance of evangelists in the process of the elenctic confrontation:

> What, after all, is Apollos? And what is Paul? Only servants, through whom you came to believe – as the Lord assigned to each his task. I planted the seed, Apollos watered it, but God made it grow. So neither he who plants nor he who waters is anything, but only God, who makes things grow. (1 Cor. 3.5–7)

The Need to Develop a Canonical Understanding of Scripture

To say that the Bible ought to control our thinking in the sphere of Church Growth is to say nothing at all, for the fact is that not only orthodox teaching but, arguably, even more so unorthodox teaching, seeks its authority in the Bible. What we are talking about here is a responsible, a correct, understanding of the Bible.

Paul Ricoeur, the philosopher-theologian, has given us what might be termed a spiral model for representing the exegetical task.[29] The spiral begins with event: the crucifixion, shall we say. Time passes, and eventually a written record of the event is produced, and event becomes word. Again time passes, and the exegete approaches the word in order to understand the event. But with the passing of time there has inevitably been an increasing possibility of polysemy arising out of the text. We are, today, separated from the events of the Bible by centuries in time, by many miles in distance, and by vast differences in culture.

So we have event, word, and the contemporary confrontation with the word. We seek always to regain the event, although we have only the intermediate word. With the greatest reluctance I have been forced to recognize that we can only perceive the event correctly if we are prepared to work very hard. We are confronted with an ancient text from a culture which has long since passed away, formalized in languages which are no longer extant. To attain an adequate perception of these sacred texts is *not* easy, and no *translation* will ever make it possible for the casual reader to grasp the profound truths they contain.

166

The meaning of the original event as it was perceived by the gospel writers, and the significance of the event for us today, will be recovered through an understanding of the teaching of the Pharisees, of the status of the Sanhedrin, of the contemporary concept of blasphemy, of the situation of Pontius Pilate at that particular point in history, of the details of the Passover celebrations, of the doctrine of the Trinity, and of many other matters besides. In other words, I now realize, as I did not thirty years ago, that the responsible and accurate interpretation of Scripture is not, in fact, in the hands of the ploughman, and that even the best of translations of the Bible will not make that possible. Rene Padilla reminds us:

> The ordinary Christian usually assumes that in his Bible reading he can get along quite well without hermeneutics. He approaches the Bible as if it had been written by only one human and in historical circumstances much like his own. He believes he has direct access to the message revealed in Scripture, and he even distrusts any effort that may be made to understand the message in the light of its original historical context.[30]

In particular, in attempting to understand the message of the Bible it is absolutely essential to bridge across the cultural and linguistic gap that separates us. Regretfully, ordinary people do not have the materials from which to build the bridge. It is true that having the tools does not necessarily lead to the right bridges being built. On the contrary, the theological departments of our universities seem perversely determined to produce graduates with the right tools but with their faith in tatters. It may at times be better to lack the technical tools and to retain a sure faith, for faith will always enable the faithful to identify serious error. But to have faith and exegetical tools is best, and those who are so equipped may save their churches from unbiblical and yet plausible theologies.

We are urgently in need of a comprehensive biblical theology which integrates missiology, and in particular church growth, into a whole, a whole which does justice not merely to a select basket of texts, but to the whole canon of Scripture. We need to replace a merely *textual* theology by a genuinely *canonical* theology. We have a good German Church Growth theology in the book by Fritz and Christian Schwarz, *Theologie des Gemeinde-aufbaus*,[31] but we still await a work which integrates Church Growth with the rest of theology, notably with soteriology, pneumatology, ecclesiology, and the doctrine of God.

The importance of such an endeavour may be seen in the lengthy and sometimes acrimonious debate about the so-called homogeneous unit. It has been argued frequently, on both sides of the Atlantic, that this concept reflects good sociology but poor theology. The subject is discussed in some detail by Peter Wagner in *Our Kind of People*.[32] In Alfred Schutz's formulation, a homogeneous unit of society is one recognized by the self-perception of its members. According to Schutz the 'acceptance of a common system of relevances leads the members of the group to a homogeneous self-typification'.[33] That is to say, the members of the group differentiate between a clear 'us' and an equally clear 'them', with a corresponding view of 'our' ('right') way of doing things and 'their' ('wrong') way of doing things. The homogeneous unit church was proposed as a response to this potentially divisive notion of a 'right' way and a 'wrong' way of being a church. But however sociologically plausible this might be, the concept of a homogeneous unit church is clearly unbiblical.

Rene Padilla summarized the case against homogeneous unit churches in the *International Bulletin of Missionary Research*, [34] and two years later in his *Leading your Church to Growth* Peter Wagner removed the concept from the list of Church Growth principles, recognizing it as no more than a sociological observation.[35]

On Dispensing with Barriers

What I label Church Growth's 'Principle Three' follows on from an early observation by Dr McGavran, that people prefer to make their commitment to Christ without crossing cultural barriers. My own formulation of the principle is: 'In making their commitment to Christ, people should not be required to cross unnecessary cultural barriers.' As it stands this principle would seem to me unexceptionable. However, it is not difficult to move from that principle to the assumption that removing unnecessary cultural barriers makes grace irresistible. Conversely, it becomes only too easy to assume that the existence of high barriers makes the operation of grace impossible.

First of all we must note that in coming to Christ we have all had to cross cultural barriers. In Christianity there is an ultimate and unavoidable scandal. This *skandalon* is the cross, but it is much more than that. It is the scandal of God incarnate. It is the scandal of a Trinity who will not be reduced to an uncomplicated monad. It is the scandal of the Son of God who is born among the poor and identifies himself with them and not with the respectably religious of his day. It is the scandal of a gospel which turns us all into beggars, suppliants, which, in a word, has as its starting-point the removal of our self-sufficiency.

Secondly, we note that even the highest barriers cannot serve to keep God the Holy Spirit out. In China the Marxist regime toiled for thirty years to destroy religion. David Edwards, in his remarkable book *The Futures of Christianity*, comments of the Church in China: '. . . although it had been without open churches, full-time ministers, public meetings, literature or even Bibles in adequate supply, it had grown.'[36]

On the other hand we might consider with some dismay the favourable conditions for belief that exist in Western Europe, with abundant churches, a superabundance of ministers in some denominations (British Baptists are the most obvious example), an embarrassing number of readily available Bible translations, a total lack of persecution, an affluent society, an array of Bible Schools and Colleges and University Departments of Theology, radio and TV which still transmit religious materials, a flood of Christian literature, and a plethora of conferences.[37] There is no real price to be paid for becoming a Christian.

Christianity has become a swinging cult. Church is sometimes a religious rock-concert, sometimes a sacred operatic performance, sometimes a substitute magic show. Even so the millions stay outside. We have fallen into the trap against which Dietrich Bonhoeffer warned us: we offer cheap grace. 'Cheap grace is the preaching of forgiveness without requiring repentance, baptism without church discipline, communion without confession . . . cheap grace is grace without discipleship, grace without the cross, grace without Jesus Christ, living and incarnate.'[38]

13 The Church in Europe

INTRODUCTION

There is general agreement that the Church in Europe is in a poor state of health. It is not difficult to find statistics to support that contention: for example, it is said that some 1.8 million people leave the Church in Europe each year.[1] This appears to mean that according to some system of counting church members or church attendance there is a net decline each year of 1.8 million. According to Adrian Hastings, 'between 1960 and 1985 the Church of England as a going concern was effectively reduced to not much more than half its previous size'.[2]

However, this at once directs attention to a problem unique to Europe: the existence in very large numbers of nominal Christians, people who are assumed by the Church to be Christians, or who assume themselves to be Christians, without conforming to the biblical norms for Christianity. The figure of 1.8 million people leaving the Church each year is, therefore, very difficult to interpret. It is not clear whether these people merely represent a shake-out of pseudo-Christians, leaving behind the committed believers, or whether they represent the committed believers abandoning a pseudo-church, or a mixture of both groups. The question is not an academic one. The fact remains that large numbers of people abandon the Church in Europe annually. Even if we accept a figure of 300 million as representing the total nominal membership of the European churches, it is clear that such an enormous defection cannot long be sustained without seriously undermining the effectiveness of the Church's outreach.

Nor must we be lulled into a false sense of security by the developments within the House Church movement,[3] or the proliferation of conferences which attract thousands of people. These features of contemporary life are, in fact, the visible evidence of the malaise within the Churches, an unheard protest against the general irrelevance of what passes for the Church in contemporary Europe.

In a vivid characterization made as far back as 1974, Jan van

Capelleveen referred to the attitude of the younger generation about the Churches, 'They speak warmly about them, like one speaks about his own grandmother who spends her last days in a room full of portraits of the past. It is wonderful to visit her for just a short time; it would be impossible to live with her.'[4]

HISTORY

Perhaps the greatest burden borne by the Church in Europe is its history. It is precisely its history which gives the Church in Europe its tired and outdated form, and the structures which have developed over the centuries which seem to make it all but impossible to introduce the radical reforms called for. Four aspects of that history may be noted.

The Ecumenical Councils

It was the Councils (particularly of Ephesus and Chalcedon) which identified heresy and codified orthodoxy, leaving us with creeds which expressed the agreed doctrines of the Church, particularly in the area of Christology. However, the credal statements are today in good measure irrelevant in what they affirm and inadequate in their scope. Not that the creeds do not deal with potentially vital issues, nor that those issues are settled beyond dispute. But the non-professional Christians have learned to repeat them without understanding them,[5] and many professional Christians have learned to repeat them without believing in them.

There are new issues confronting the Church today, of which the classical creeds necessarily say nothing. Oppression, racism, poverty, abortion, euthanasia, Aids, homosexuality and so on are inevitably missing. This is no fault of those creeds: rather it is the fault of the Church which has been content to allow the creeds to remain unchanged, petrified witnesses to arguments long past. The creeds lack bite: we have learned to affirm them without any challenge to contemporary secular values.

The Reformation

It could be argued that the Reformation gave shape to the Church in Europe, a shape which was to continue essentially unchanged for four hundred years. The Lutheran and Reformed Churches of

Germany, Switzerland and Scandinavia, the Anglican Church, and the Roman Catholic Church still virtually monopolize Christian resources in Europe.

And yet in spite of the very Reformation terminology that is traditionally used to describe European church history, it would not be difficult to argue that the Churches remained with the task of reformation barely begun. Clericism remains, the dichotomy between clergy and laity is still firmly in place, and the magical element within the liturgies has not been exorcized.

In his Foreword to Leonard Verduin's *The Reformers and their Stepchildren*, H. L. Ellison comments of the Anabaptists of the sixteenth century: 'It is an error to call them reformers, for it was a new beginning they wanted . . . Until recently their history has been known to us mainly through the vilifications of their opponents, both Roman Catholic and Protestant.'[6]

In 1981 came the invaluable work on the Anabaptists by Walter Klaassen, *Anabaptism, Neither Catholic nor Protestant*.[7] Franklin Littell of Temple University, in the Foreword to Klaassen's book, confirms Ellison's assessment of the Anabaptists:

> The Anabaptists were condemned and defamed by spokesmen of the sixteenth century establishments because they refused to support the power systems then emerging . . . Today we can see that the Anabaptists/Mennonite testimonies were very important for both church and state. While much of the teaching of the Roman Catholic and Protestant theologians of the sixteenth century is today unreal and irrelevant, what the Anabaptists taught about mutual aid, peace, discipline, religious liberty, lay witness, etc. is as fresh and important as it was fifteen generations ago.[8]

Not a few Christians in Europe would agree that there is an urgent need for a new and radical reformation of the Church.

The World Wars

Two world wars have left their mark not only on Europe in general, but on the Church in particular. The clergy of both sides in both wars blessed the weapons and lent a religious gloss to the policies of the politicians. Padres earned a confusing reputation: for extraordinary devotion and heroism (one of the Chavasse twins[9] actually winning two Victoria Crosses, Britain's highest award for bravery), and for being 'wet'. Some saw through the intentions of the politicians very quickly, and refused to be used. Others were pliable under the flattery of officer status, privilege, badges of rank, medal ribbons and apparent influence. The British Commander, Montgomery, explicitly employed his padres as part of his resources: the troops were to be urged on as crusaders, and lacklustre padres who could not produce the necessary rhetoric were soon dismissed by him.[10]

However, during the war the combatants on both sides had time to think, and even to become philosophers of life. Their padres were often unable to give intelligible answers to the questions they were asked, and there was no other authority who could give such answers. There was a widespread abandoning of religion after the First World War and continuing through and beyond the second, and it was abandoned because it was seen to be irrelevant and unbelievable.

The Rise of Marxism

Karl Marx was a German who spent much of his life studying social conditions in England, and whose theories were put into practice first in Russia and then in Eastern Europe.[11] Marxism made its appeal primarily to the working classes, although there were some intellectuals, too, who were attracted to it. Its later development, Marxism-Leninism, provides the primary division within Europe, between East and West, and the Church has a totally different image in these two contrasting Europes. If in the West Christianity appears irrelevant, in the East it is perceived by believer and unbeliever alike as representing the major challenge to materialism, offering a new and powerful alternative dynamic.

It simply cannot be denied that under persecution Christianity has shown a power to survive, and more than survive, to outlive and outlove the strengths of Marxism, a power it has not demonstrated under the threat of affluence in the West.

THE FIVE EUROPES

Although the United Nations recognizes four Europes, a division into five zones[12] has more to commend it, broadly linking areas having common cultural and linguistic features. The five are:

Mission and Meaninglessness

Nordic: Norway, Sweden, Denmark, Finland, Iceland

The high percentage of the population nominally associated with the Lutheran Church in these areas is characteristic: Norway and Denmark 92%, Finland 93% and Sweden an astonishing 96%, astonishing primarily because it is freely admitted that in fact at most 5% of the population actually attend any church more than once a year.[13] The Pentecostal churches, with a membership of just over 100,000, have been growing rather steadily over the past decade, and there are several with attendances of more than a thousand.

Norwegian Lutherans have developed a unique but potentially confusing dual system, with evangelical Prayer Houses (or 'Mission Halls') operating alongside the official Lutheran churches.

Germanic: Germany, Austria, Switzerland

Although there are clear cultural ties between these countries, there is no common pattern of church life. Switzerland is the richest country in Europe. Its population of some 6.5 million is diluted by almost a million foreigners. Almost one half of the population is notionally Protestant, and 96% of them would associate with the Reformed Churches. Austria provides a striking footnote to the history of the Reformation: in the decades after the Reformation the country was 80% Protestant, but is today 83% Catholic.

The Church in Germany is a major employer of labour, with an estimated quarter of a million employees. But it is typical of the Lutheran Church in Germany that the majority of these owe only a nominal allegiance to Lutheranism. The Church Growth movement will almost certainly have a major role to play in the coming years; *Arbeitsgemeinschaft für Gemeindeaufbau*, AGGA, based in Giengen, was already leading parties of German pastors on visits to growing churches around the world in the early 1980s.

Western: The United Kingdom, the Republic of Ireland, the Netherlands

Again, despite some measure of cultural affinity between the three members of this group, church life in each is very different. Holland has three dominant churches: the Roman Catholic; the Netherlands Reformed Church, the NHK; and the Reformed

Churches in the Netherlands, the *Gereformeerd*, or GKN Church. This last has remained plateaud at about 9% of the population in membership, but with a steadily declining pattern of attendance. The general mobility of the Dutch peoples makes leaving the Church relatively simple: on arrival at the new location the head of the household registers at the City Hall but denies church membership.[14]

The Roman Catholic Church in Holland faces a massive decline in clergy: from 1970 to 1981 a decrease from 3,433 to 2,285, a decrease of 33%. This reflects a profound defection from actual belief: only 54% of Catholics indicated a belief in Christ as Son of God, compared with 70% of the Reformed, and 94% of the *Gereformeerd*.[15]

In the UK in 1988 the principal Churches continued to show declines in attendance of the order of 1% to 2%, although it is possible that the Salvation Army and the Baptist Churches in England (but not in the UK as a whole), were growing slightly.[16] The House Church movement has grown so that in membership it probably equals the Christian Brethren, but the movement is splintered, with some twenty-one separate groups.

Indeed this splintering is typical of the Churches in Europe in general and of the UK church scene in particular: although there are fewer members and fewer churches, there are *more* denominations than ever before.

Perhaps the most valuable commentary on the Church of England is *The Church in Crisis*, by Charles Moore, A. N. Wilson and Gavin Stamp,[17] the title of which speaks volumes. Of all its crises, there is perhaps no one more poignant than that confronting its theological colleges, which have been radically criticized steadily over the past two decades for their general irrelevance, without evoking anything other than cosmetic changes in training practices.[18]

Latin: Belgium, Luxembourg, France, Spain, Portugal, Italy, Greece, Malta

In this grouping the theme must again be that of fragmentation. It may be that we have simply a manifestation of the individuality of the Latin character, but it is a fact that in these countries it is exceedingly difficult to obtain anything in the way of an overview of the Church. In France all of the Protestant groups together constitute less than 2% of the Christian community,[19] and yet there are some sixty such groups! And it is estimated that 32,000 towns and villages have no gospel witness. By contrast, it has been estimated that there are one hundred mediums to each Christian worker in France.[20]

Eastern: Albania, Bulgaria, Czechoslovakia, Hungary, Poland, Romania, Yugoslavia

This division is probably the most significant of all those associated with European Christianity. The problems of the West are not those of the East. What is of enormous importance, however, is the clear evidence that the Church has outlasted doctrinaire Marxism in Russia and China, and the changed policies of those nations so far as religion is concerned must now inevitably be worked out in the European satellites. In this respect Hungary has led the way. In June 1988 the Hungarian Communist Party not only dethroned the veteran party leader Janos Kadar, but appointed as President a non-communist intellectual, Professor Bruno Straub. It is significant that this movement actually preceded the Moscow Communist Party Conference, anticipating the new liberalizing policies of Russia, where since Mr Gorbachev came to power some 300 religious communities had been officially recognized. Poland, too, profited from Gorbachev's policies, the strength of Roman Catholicism in the country running strictly parallel with the growing political influence of the Solidarity movement through the late 1980s.

SIX PROBLEMS FOR THE EUROPEAN CHURCHES

A number of problems for the Church in Europe have already been noted above. Six are selected for further consideration.

The Problem of the State Church

A state church is here taken to be any Church that is given particular and unique recognition by the State over against other Churches. In the European setting the designation would apply, for example, to the Anglican Church in England, the Lutheran Church in Germany or Norway, to the Reformed Church in some of the Cantons of Switzerland, the Roman Catholic Church in Spain or Italy, and the Orthodox Church in Greece.

In attempting to make generalizing statements about state churches there will inevitably be a certain blurring of distinctions between these churches, distinctions which arise out of the particular relationships which exist between any one state church and the respective State. However, it would seem better to make such generalizing statements rather than extend this section into a detailed consideration of each Church-state dyad.

Four characteristics of State Churches

The first characteristic of the state church is that of ease of entry into the church community. In each case this is through infant baptism. There is no necessity that this practice should lead to ease of access, but historically it has done so. It is, of course, open to clergy to refuse indiscriminate baptism, and some have done so. The vast majority have not.

The process of formal admission to the local Christian community is then forwarded by some second step, confirmation or the first communion or both. The second step is not by any means taken by all who underwent the initial rite of baptism: in the Anglican Church in 1979 (the last year for which such statistics were published) statistics showed a difference of some eighteen million between the baptized and the confirmed. The second step is commonly taken between the ages of twelve and sixteen.

However, there is a further discrepancy between the numbers who have taken the second step in identifying with their local congregation and those who are later on found with some degree of regularity attending that church. To quote the UK Anglican statistics again, in 1979 there were some 26.8 million baptized, and some 8.7 million confirmed, but the average number of communicants was a mere 0.7 million.[21] It is very difficult to know how the lapsed envisaged themselves, and even more difficult to know how those who are entirely outside the Church viewed them. In Norway, a theoretical 97.6% of the population belong to the Lutheran Church, but a mere 3% actually attend the weekly services in the state churches (and probably some 10% of the population attend a weekly service in some church). Indeed, a comparison often quoted is that proportionately more Russians attend church than do British.[22]

There is another aspect to this issue: it is easy to get into the state church, but it is extraordinarily difficult to get out. And the consequences of getting out may be serious. In Germany there has been a negative reaction to the church tax, and while on the one hand opting out of the Lutheran Church ends the unwanted taxation, on the other hand it frees the state church from the responsibility for burying the exile. And unlike the United Kingdom, cremation has not, it appears, commended itself in Germany. One response to the impasse has been for a husband to opt out of the church, and so be free of the church tax, but for the wife to remain in, and so ensure for her family a church funeral. This particular rite of passage retains an importance for the marginally religious which has largely faded from baptism.

Thus the church member *may* find a way to leave the state church, but it is certainly troublesome. On the other hand it is almost unheard of for a state church actually to discipline its members, still less to expel any. The result is a church membership that displays a bewildering kaleidoscope of morals, often unrelated to biblical patterns of behaviour.

Related to the above is a second feature of the state church: a responsibility for certain social services, marriage and burial in particular. To these may usually be added baptism-naming. These ministries, usually recognized by the Churches as sacraments, become in some sense part of the duty the state church owes to the community in return for its privileged position. The church building offers a fine setting for a wedding, and the community expects to make use of it: taking in its stride the necessity of making formal and serious vows which it often has neither the will nor the spiritual resources to keep. And again, a church may serve a large parish of elderly persons, and have a small congregation and only a small staff, so that the priest in charge might spend a significant part of each week simply conducting funeral services.

Thirdly, the state churches must submit to some measure of state involvement in church affairs.[23] As with the Anglican Church, this may even include the anomaly of having bishops appointed by the Prime Minister and the Queen (as temporal head of the Church), although, of course, on the recommendation of the

Church's own hierarchy.[24] And revision of the liturgy or statutes of the Church may well be subject to government approval. The General Synod of the Church of England distinguishes between two types of legislation brought before it. The first is concerned with Canon Law, and a Canon does not affect the law of England. The second is termed a Measure, and affects both the practice of the Church of England and the law of England. It therefore requires the approval of Parliament.[25] In several countries the State acts on behalf of the Church in collecting the church tax. The obverse is the provision for leaders of a state church to play some more or less direct role in government. In the Anglican Church a quota of bishops is provided for in the House of Lords, and the Bishop of London and the Archbishops of Canterbury and York are Privy Councillors.

It is interesting to note that from within a state church it is only too easy to identify the problems faced by other state-related Churches, and yet to fail to identify parallel problems to be dealt with by one's own Church. Thus Peter Hall, writing in *Hope for the Church of England*,[26] identifies the problem posed for some Lutheran Churches by the existence of a national tax (p. 41), but quite fails to see the insensitivity displayed when he refers to the Church of England as *the* 'National' Church (p. 36).

Fourthly, there is always a strong hierarchical structure in the state church, leading to firm centralized control and little autonomy for the local congregation, which, for example, may have no meaningful part to play in the appointment of their own clergy. There is a further aspect to this issue, in that the local congregation is usually freed from the responsibility for the salaries of the clergy; this may initially appear to be a positive feature of the system, but it does often result in the congregation's refusal to accept financial responsibility for other aspects of the church's activities: for secretarial and administrative assistance, for audio-visual equipment, for literature to be used in outreach. Imaginative and progressive clergy may find themselves immobilized by a lack of financial resourcing.

Problems Related to the Existence of State Churches

1. Perhaps the most important problem is that of the blurring of identity so far as the Christian community is concerned. There is

179

no clear distinction between Christian and non-Christian. The apparent identity 'Christian means "Church Member"' loses its denotative power.[27] The very important consequence here is that the observer is quite unable to determine whether the Church is able to resolve the problem of the human condition or not. Some church members appear to have resources which others do not have, but since those resources of patience and faith and grace are not uniformly distributed through the members of the Church, it is logically impossible to claim that they result from membership.

2. It is common to find that the training of the clergy is only marginally in the hands of the Church, and even then only in the hands of the church hierarchy. As in Germany, the secular universities may have a monopoly in training ministers, with the lecturers selected in the main for their academic gifts rather than for their spiritual insights or pastoral experience. This in turn leads to disillusionment in the pews: the sermons may, occasionally, sparkle with academic brilliance, but fail to feed the sheep.

And there may well be no alternative route for potential clergy to take. Evangelical theological colleges are marginalized and their graduates (degree-less, and therefore excluded from the pulpits of the State Churches) have no possibility of contributing to the Churches of which they might well be members. The universities are notorious for their refusal or inability to up-date their syllabuses. Such vital topics as liberation theology, Church Growth, contextualization, universalism, Islam, human communications, hermeneutics, linguistics, sociology, psychology, pastoral theology, evangelism, counselling, are only occasionally found in the courses taught in state universities in Europe. A great deal has been written and said on the subject of clergy training, but so far virtually no move has been made towards a comprehensive solution.[28]

What is needed here is a curriculum *from below*,[29] to replace the curriculum which is imposed *from above*, by academics whose interests are necessarily different from those of the missiologically orientated Christian. What is needed is a persuasion elenctic rather than simple dialogue, a positive missiology rather than a comparison of truth claims.

3. Again, partly because of its status as an adjunct of the state, the Church may become a major employer of labour, so that clergy

are turned into administrators, and become involved in industrial disputes. In West Germany the Church is the second largest employer of labour, in Britain the Anglican Church is one of the most powerful of landlords.

4. And there is a further dimension to the problem: if the 'state church' is accorded certain privileges, this necessarily means that other Churches are disadvantaged by not having those privileges. In other words, the essential unity of the body of Christ is brought into question. As Mark Santer admits, speaking from within the established Church:

> The worst thing about the special status of the Church of England is the corruption of spirit which it encourages. We collude, implicitly, with the notion that 'Anglican' equals 'really English', thereby reducing our fellow-Christians to the status of inferior citizens. We may not feel it; they do.[30]

The Problem of Nominalism

This is clearly related to the first issue: the existence of a state church, and the formalized mode of entry into some state churches, inevitably leads to nominalism. The high proportion of nominal Christianity in Europe has no parallel anywhere else in the world. But what is now needed is a rediscovery of what it is to be a Christian. The answer to this vital question could be expected to come from one of the following:

1. From Western orthodox evangelicals. But so often we find ourselves the prisoners of our own histories, unable actually to discern from Scripture (and apart from the cultural and historical accretions inevitable in Churches with a long history) the true nature of what it is to be a follower of Jesus.

2. From missionaries to Europe from the 'Third'[31] World. Third World Christians are almost invariably disillusioned when they actually encounter European Christianity: to them, as to their colleagues living in Eastern Europe, Christianity is holistic, it makes its demands on every part of the life of the disciple. The lifestyle of most Christians in Europe, that is to say of the nominal membership of the churches, seems to demonstrate little of that wholehearted and holistic and joyful commitment to be found in many other parts of the world. Certainly it is true that many

European Christians have been perplexed to discover a more *satisfying* lifestyle among Christians with only marginal material resources, than is generally to be observed in the so-called developed nations.

3. From Eastern Europe, where it has become clear that Christianity must have relevant comment to make on virtually every subject: on criminal law, on oppression, on bribery, on divorce, on free Trade Unions, and so on. The Christianity of Eastern Europe is *not* irrelevant, and it will be interesting to see how the Churches emerge to play a major role in Eastern European society as the Gorbachev reforms, and in particular the tolerance of the Church, work through the satellite countries.

The Problem of Materialism

The world of Islam has criticized Western society in general for being irreligious, materialistic, humanistic, and without community.[32] In measure these accusations must also be seen as directed against the Church in Europe. Our Christianity, other than on Sunday, is almost invisible, where the Muslim is almost ostentatious in his display of his religion. And we *are* materialistic: the contemporary success of prosperity theology, open in the teaching of Kenneth Copeland and T. L. Osborne, implicit in the ministry of Reinhard Boncke, and proclaimed to large congregations in London and Stockholm, bears witness to the success of the surrounding culture in penetrating the Church.[33]

There is a need, here, for theological reflection: not so as to produce a theology of suffering for the sake of suffering, but so as properly to understand the extent to which the Christian is to expect to share in the ills of the world, and the extent to which his faith delivers him from them. Material, physical and spiritual prosperity are currently being offered in many Churches, a guaranteed return for faith. Tragically, many are abandoning their faith because the reality fails to match the theory.

The Problem of Fragmentation

This problem is particularly associated with France, Spain and Portugal, Italy, and Greece. In each of these countries a multitude of small groups is at work, but there are no leaders strong enough to claim the support of the whole. Missionaries sent in to France from America and Britain often operate in splendid isolation from existing churches. Johan Lukasse speaks of missionaries being as it were 'parachuted' into Europe, often quite unaware of existing mission activity, and unwilling even to seek help in language study.[34]

The inevitable consequences of these activities is frustration for the missionary, who retires from Europe after only a few years, leaving behind at best an embattled and leaderless congregation, at worst no enduring evidence of his labours. Here particular attention is drawn to David Edwards' very important book *The Futures of Christianity*,[35] especially chapter 6, 'In Secular Europe'. Europe's malaise is so great that we cannot expect to be taken seriously when our energies are dissipated in attacking one another. And yet there must be limits to formal associations where doctrine varies so violently. As Paul commented ruefully 'there must be factions . . . in order that those who are genuine . . . may be recognized' (1 Cor. 11.19, RSV).[36]

The Problem of Pluralism

Two quite distinct problems must be recognized here: the problem posed by the macro-presence of Islam in Europe, and the problem of the more general phenomenon of Eastern mysticism appearing actually *within* Christianity. On the former problem a vigorous debate has been taking place for half a century, and the relevant literature is abundant.[37]

However, it may well be that the second is the greater problem, since Islam is, at least, clearly *external* to Christianity.[38] In an important new book, *New Religious Movements and the Churches*, Allan Brockway and Paul Rajashekar deal with the multitude of New Religious Movements, and demonstrate a common origin in Eastern mysticism, especially Hinduism and Buddhism.[39] But the significance of these movements is that they occur *within* Christianity, and represent a new option, Christianity *plus*. New techniques are offered which relate directly to the contemporary demand for so-called 'counselling'. These techniques in turn build on theories of the nature of humanity which are highly speculative, subjective, and unrelated to any biblical doctrine of the human

183

personality. There is much to be done by evangelical theologians in developing that biblical doctrine so as to protect believers from the sheer manipulation of many contemporary counsellors.

The Problem of the Occult World

We have noted the growth of the occult influence in France, but there is no doubt that there has been a growth throughout Europe. There appears to be a new strategy on the part of the Second Kingdom, a strategy of open challenge to Christianity.

The new developments are an indication of a fresh interest among the peoples of Europe in the world beyond this world, in existence after death. Many of the leaders in the occult world are women, and I. M. Lewis has hinted at the possibility that where women are excluded from the mainstream of spiritual leadership in a society it is very likely that there will be a compensating leadership in, say, spiritism.[40] This could direct attention to the current discussions on the ordination of women, and to the need for a biblical reappraisal of ordination. Michael Green was surely wrong when he said: 'When we talk of the Christian ministry today, we instinctively think of a man ordained to the "ministry" of Word and Sacraments: you either are a minister, or you are not. The New Testament knows nothing of any such distinction.'[41] There is a clear biblical doctrine of laying on hands as a sign of separation for specific ministry, but there is less clarity in the evangelical understanding of it.

In the matter of the occult, however, we need an understanding of the limitations of the power of the Second Kingdom, and we also need a doctrine to express the measure in which the Church has authority to withstand that power. The current practice of 'binding' that power (and even of 'releasing' the Spirit) raises many questions which demand biblical and not merely pragmatic and existential answers.

14 *The Church: The Reality*

THE CHURCH

In Chapters 11–13 we have looked in some detail at the nature of the Church as it appears through a number of New Testament analogies. It is, however, exceedingly difficult for us truly to see the biblical picture, because of the historical grid which is inevitably interposed between the modern reader and the New Testament.

THE IDEAL OF CHURCH, AND THE REALITY

Both the Old Testament *qahal* and the New Testament *ekklēsia* are presented *both* in idealized terms *and* with realism. We are made aware of what the people of God *should* be, but there is no concerted attempt to conceal the contrasting reality. The scandal involving Ananias and Sapphira (a piece of deception which, outside of the early Church, would have been unremarkable) is fully documented in Acts 5. The unity of the Church is excitingly expressed in Ephesians 2, but we have both the Acts 6 conflict between Hellenists and Hebrews and the rich-poor conflict at Corinth (1 Cor. 11) also recorded.

On the one hand, the Spirit is given to the apostles in a spectacular Pentecost event, and on the other hand we have undignified conflict between Peter and Paul (Gal. 2), and between Paul and Barnabas (Acts 15). Paul's loss of temper, though admittedly under extreme provocation (Acts 23.1–5), is there, too. And for those who are prepared to work at the evidence concerning the progress of the relationship between Paul and the church at Corinth through the process of letters, personal visits and emissaries in both directions, it is quite clear that the apostles of the first century had no easier time than the bishops of the twentieth.

If some churches were generous, others were remiss of mind: the church at Philippi sent financial support to Paul, the other churches did not (Phil. 4.15). And if today some missionaries of the Church are scandalously under-supported, Paul himself had to admit that he had often been without food (2 Cor. 11.27).

A PARTICULAR PROBLEM: THE MINISTRY

Again, we have been made uncomfortably aware of the inappropriate pride of office of some prelates through the cutting language of Martin Luther or John Calvin,[1] but 1 Corinthians 1.10ff., makes us aware of a similar problem in the early days of the Church, and suggests that it is not impossible that much of the pretentiousness of the church leadership is actually a response to the demands of their would-be followers.

And there is an ongoing problem with the Church's ministry. In one of his less well-known books, John Robinson comments of the ministry:

> In the New Testament the whole people of God is called to the priesthood – the priesthood of Christ. It is called to share his priesthood to the world, mediating his atoning and reconciling work. In that priesthood every baptized member has a share. Within the Body there are, and were from the beginning, men ordained on its behalf to exercise, in the name of both its head and its members, the functions which belong to it as a whole. But this ordained ministry, which is priestly because the whole ministry of the Church is priestly, is in the strict sense representative, not vicarious. The priesthood does in the name of the Body what, essentially, the whole Body is doing: it is not doing for the rest of its members what only it can do – except in so far as by ordination the Church as a whole deliberately reserves certain of its functions to certain authorized persons.[2]

There is here a reaching after the truth from within the limiting confines of a misconception. When the writer refers to 'this ordained ministry', he is making an enormous and unjustified leap between the 'ordained ministry' of the New Testament period, and the 'ordained ministry' of the Church today. The two are quite simply incommensurate with one another. To attach the same label to each is the most elementary linguistic and philosophical blunder. And, of course, it simply is not the case that 'the Church as a whole' has agreed to reserve certain of its functions to particular individuals. The Church has, in fact, *received* an unreformed ecclesiology. As a result, in Europe today the ministry probably constitutes the highest barrier to the believableness of the Church.

And this of itself may well lead us to a new evaluation of the results of statistical surveys purporting to show a steady erosion of faith in Europe. That there is a steady erosion of belief in the Church is undoubted. That there is an actual loss of faith is quite another matter. For the concerns of the Church are not the concerns of the people. The people are concerned with *dukkha*. The people know that between the apparent boundaries of birth and death life does not make sense. The task of religion, of any religion, is to show that it does make sense. But to this fundamental question the issues of the ordination of women, of the Real Presence, of Sunday observance, of the inerrancy of Scripture, are irrelevant. To the real questions of life – the questions provided with quasi-answers by the Preacher (Eccles. 3.19–20!) – to these questions the Church appears to have no answers and no competence or concern to provide answers.

Stephen Neill comments on the significance of statistics on Anglican baptisms and confirmations (between 1960 and 1970, baptisms approximately halved, and confirmations dropped by more than a half), and on Methodist membership (in 1933 the membership was nearly 770,000, by 1960 it had declined by almost 100,000, and in the next ten years by another 100,000): 'Believers whistle to keep up their courage by asserting that what the churches have lost in numbers they have gained in sincerity . . . But is this the whole picture?'[3]

Neill goes on to point out that in a university context 60.4% of the students questioned professed a belief in God, and nearly 40% claimed to have a fairly regular habit of prayer. The tragedy in all of this is that people in general recognize the need of God, of *God*, to complete their world-view, to explain the apparent meaninglessness of life, but not a need of *religion*, or at any rate of religion as they see it practised in the mainline Churches.

The Church envisaged in the New Testament is a radical new community, within which the meaninglessness of life is marvellously resolved. The contemporary reality, and especially the European reality, is vastly different: an institution, locked into its past, preoccupied with arcane irrelevancies, yet perennially confronted by a hurting, helpless world, its fundamental questions unanswered and its meaninglessness unresolved.

15 A Theology of the Poor

Although it is true that we all experience the apparent meaninglessness of life, it is the unimportant, the poor, the powerless who experience it most profoundly. Both Old and New Testaments express a profound concern for 'the poor', and we turn now to the task of outlining a biblical theology of the poor. We begin with the complex analysis offered in Psalm 37.

THE OLD TESTAMENT[1]

Psalm 37: A Complex Analysis

Psalm 37 is an alphabetical acrostic, so written that for each letter there is what amounts to a complete proverb. Thus it is to be compared as to its origins, contents and purpose with the wisdom literature in general and with the Proverbs of Solomon in particular. The ascription *le-Dawid* is valuable: traditionally it has been taken to indicate the authorship, but the preposition is ambiguous, and the psalm could be one of many composed for the use of David in the role allowed to him in the temple ministry.[2] However, there is no particular reason for rejecting Davidic authorship: it is certainly the work of an older person (v. 25), and is intended for the instruction of the less experienced. David, certainly in the later period of his life, would have been in a good position to reflect on his own experience of the apparent success of the wicked and the undeniable hardships of many of the righteous.

We begin from Psalm 37 since it was a statement made in this psalm which, many years ago, sent this author on the search for an understanding of the apparent meaninglessness of life. The psalmist comments (v. 25):

> I was young and now I am old,
> yet I have never seen the righteous forsaken
> or their children begging bread.

But that has not been my experience. In Ethiopia one of the two areas to be hit by famine was a predominantly Christian area, where I lived for several years. When the famine came they, like the Muslims in the north, died, and so did their children.

And so the first neat, tidy resolution of *dukkha*, produced by a generalization of David's personal comment, was abandoned. It is simply not true that life makes complete sense, even to the people of God, between the two apparent boundaries of birth and death. That accidents pass them by. That their children are spared deformity, disease, early death. It is not true that Christians in business will prosper, and that the godless will fail. There are situations where the children of the people of God beg for bread.

But a second formulation also failed: that the psalmist's words were true under the Old Covenant, but no longer true in the same sense under the New Covenant. Reading the Old Testament, and especially the Proverbs, made it clear that even under the Old Covenant the poor were oppressed, and their righteousness did not protect them from the depredations of the powerful.

A third model steadily emerged, a model that appeared generally to do justice *both* to the evidence of the whole Bible *and* to common experience. The model related to two collocations of words and to the two ways open to every individual, the way of the righteous and the way of the unrighteous.

The way of the righteous is characterized by a clear lexical collocation: trust, doing good, righteousness, justice, patience, hope, meekness, generosity, faithfulness, wisdom, peace. Such Hebrew concepts as *tōv*, *tzedaqah*, *mishpat*, *shalōm*, *hokmah*, recur as themes in the psalm. On the other hand, we have the collocation of evil, wrong, wicked, perish, ruthless, anger, wrath, and such actions as carrying out wicked schemes, plotting against the righteous, lying in wait against the righteous, drawing the sword to bring down the poor. The picture is clear, a picture of conflict between two groups, the righteous and the unrighteous. In that conflict it is not immediately apparent that the unrighteous come off second best. But to the ageing and experienced psalmist the short term is unimportant. It is the long term that counts: and it is above all that boundary of death that counts. Towards that boundary every individual advances, and as he does so, so the significance of the material diminishes, and the significance of the spiritual values of righteousness, and especially of peace, *shalōm*, becomes apparent. The time comes when the wicked are no more to be found, and the righteous enjoy *shalōm*.[3]

More precisely, it is the righteous who 'inherit the land', a recurrent promise in the psalm (vv. 9, 11, 22, 29, 34). However, the psalm is decisively *not* a simplistic promise of material wealth. It is concerned with the land, the land promised to Abraham's descendants, and the question is not one of individual prosperity or the individual's ownership of land, but the question of the vindication of the righteousness of God. The very character of God is threatened if the unrighteous inherit the land. Peter Craigie expresses it clearly:

> In the short run the wicked seem to prosper, whereas the righteous very often seem to suffer at their hands. But it is the longer run that counts, and in the long run the only true satisfaction is to be found in the righteousness which is the hallmark of the one who lives in relationship with the living God . . . it is a question of determining the God-given purpose in human life and then living in accord with it; that is the essence of life and the essence of morality.[4]

The outcome of the moral life of the people of God, of their submission to the law of God, is that they inherit the land. Not for themselves, but as Yahweh's husbandry.[5] In the long run this is how it will be.

If this is the *meaning* of Psalm 37, the contemporary *significance* is not difficult to perceive. The praxis of the people of God is to be in accord with the same collocation of words as characterizes the walk of the righteous in the psalm: peace, righteousness, justice (and *not* plotting, scheming, defrauding). The outcome of such a life is, in material terms, uncertain: the people of God may find themselves oppressed precisely because of their righteousness, precisely because the plotting and scheming common to the unredeemed world is simply not an option for them. (As Paul once graphically expressed it, 'we are weak in him' (2 Cor. 13.4).) But the result of such a life is the rule of God, not in the generally godless nation, but among the people of God who live in the way of God. The problem of the apparent meaninglessness of life is to be resolved (in so far as it can be resolved in the present mode of existence) by a refusal of God's people to act as oppressors, or even to countenance oppression by others, and by the recognition by those same people of God that in the long run – that long run that looks beyond this life – all will be well with the righteous.

But all this is a far cry from that pietist theodicy that sees virtue in a passive enduring of meaninglessness, as though that meaninglessness were somehow the will of God . . .

The Contribution of Torah

Law is given to Israel both as an indication of the moral character of Yahweh and as a means of curbing the powers of the oppressors. It has a vertical and it has a horizontal dimension. It is, therefore, the guardian of the poor and powerless against the rich and powerful, but it reflects the *mishpat* of Yahweh.

We have already encountered the ongoing problem of borrowing and indebtedness. Pragmatically, it must be said that for the materially poor indebtedness is a calamity that is always to be feared, for once a poor person is in debt it becomes increasingly difficult with the passing of time for the debt to be paid off. Even if the debt repayments are reasonable, and it is unlikely that they will be, the poor person may be unable to do more than repay the interest on the loan, or the servicing charge on the loan, and this in turn becomes an addition to the family outgoings, thus reducing still further the chance of clearing the debt.

Deuteronomy confronts this and other problems of the poor with a comprehensive (if idealistic) range of legislation which represents to Israel the right way for the people of God to live. As J. A. Baker expresses it:

> Deuteronomy is God's authentic statement of his relationship with Israel, revealed through the prophetic ministry of Moses to be both a means of grace enabling the Israelites to stay within that relationship, and also a prediction working life or death for them according as they do this or not.[6]

Deuteronomy deals with the complex problem firstly by forbidding the charging of interest on a loan made to a fellow Israelite. Of course in a situation of zero inflation such a prohibition makes good sense, which it does not in any inflationary context. But the prohibition does not apply to the non-Israelite: 'You shall not lend upon interest to your brother, interest on money, interest on victuals, interest on anything that is lent for interest. To a foreigner you may lend upon interest, but to your brother you shall not lend upon interest . . . (Deut. 23.19–20, RSV).[7]

The same section of the law further restrains the rich from compounding the miseries of the indebted: a millstone may not be 'pawned', taken in pledge (Deut. 24.6),[8] and the house of the debtor may not be entered for the purpose of reclaiming a loan (Deut. 24.10–11). A man's cloak, if taken in pledge, is to be returned at the end of the day, since it provided also the poor man's blanket (Deut. 24.12–13). If a widow has nothing to pledge but some personal garment, that garment must not be taken: the implication is that the widow's need is to be supplied without requiring any pledge at all (Deut. 24.17). The same chapter provides for gleaning rights for the poor, for grain, olive and grape harvests.

And there is the injunction not to withhold the wages of a day-labourer (Deut. 24.14–15), which is convincingly linked to Job 31.38–40 (where it is the land that cries out against its abuse rather than the labourer on the land), as well as to the more obvious James 5.4, by A. van Selms.[9] To these and other provisions of the Deuteronomic statement of Torah there is added the gift of a sabbath, a 'ceasing'.

The complex system of sabbath ceasing set out in the law may never, in all its ramifications, have been operative, but the system does demonstrate a concern to deal practically with perceived dangers to the poor of what developed into a quasi-capitalistic system. The legislation appears in Leviticus 25: a seventh-year 'ceasing', during which the land itself is allowed to lie fallow, is buttressed by a fiftieth year sabbath,[10] the purpose of which is to lift the burdens from the backs of the impoverished, to restore the land to the landless, to recognize, as we have already seen, that it was Yahweh who owned the land. Martin Noth comments on Leviticus 25.23: 'A very remarkable concluding sentence (v. 23) brings together and expresses the principle behind the jubilee-year regulations. It shows that the land was in general and in principle not to be sold, because it was Yahweh's property, which men might not dispose of as of private property.'[11]

However idealistic and impractical this might appear, it represents legislation that takes seriously the burdens of the impoverished. There is, here, an actual entering into the feelings, the hopes and the anxieties of the poor, and there is legislation that might curb the oppressive activities of the rich and powerful, and give hope to the poor and powerless. The human experience of *dukkha* needs some such legislation, legislation that *feels*. Emilio Castro refers to the Jubilee as ' . . . that moment once in every fifty years when the land was redistributed and when every family, every tribe had the chance of a new beginning. It was not justice based on merit, but pure grace, a redistribution of land to create a new beginning in history.'[12]

The effect of the legislation would be to provide the poor with 'a light at the end of the tunnel'. There was always, in the future (and not in the too distant future), the assurance that the burden of debt would be lifted. And for the rich there was the constant reminder that the wealth that had been amassed, and the fields that had been added on to other fields, were not ultimately a possession at all.

There is within us all a fatal flaw, a blemish, that makes legislation necessary to bring about what sheer humanity ought to bring about were it not so flawed. The Scripture is remarkably balanced: it presents us *both* with the ought *and* with such laws and their associated penalties as should at least give cause for pause to the inherent rapacity of fallen human nature. We have a presentation of how we ought to live. But there is no out-of-this-world naive optimism here: with calm judgement the Scripture recognizes the reality of oppression, and legislates against it.

As Baker expresses it:

> The web of suffering and injustice is the result of defects in the human psyche which are not to be cured by removing the symptoms of them, but which will persist and take other forms when one lot of effects has been relieved . . . The inequities and hardships of life and the inward distortions and corruptions are alike both aspects of what has gone wrong with us.[13]

However, although the intention of the Jubilee legislation was to ensure the eventual lifting of the burdens of the impoverished, it seems that there was sufficient power in the hands of the wealthy to frustrate the expectation of the human spirit and the legislation of the law. The jubilee trumpet never sounded.

It was Jesus who resurrected the jubilee provision and brought it from the level of the theoretical to the level of the practical in the life of just one Person. The sermon in the synagogue (Luke 4.16–21) is no less significant than the Sermon on the Mount. It is programmatic for Luke's account of the Good News, as the preaching of John the Baptist is for Matthew's account. The task of Jesus is seen to be nothing less than to do what the religious leaders of contemporary Judaism had not done: to proclaim the acceptable year of the Lord (Luke 4.19). Jesus could not end all of the sufferings of the oppressed peoples of his day, he could not cancel the debt of everyone who had borrowed from the rich. But he could do something. Matthew was one tax collector who came into the forgiving family of God. Little Zacchaeus restored what he had wrongly extorted. And all over Palestine there were families who rejoiced because a child was alive who had been dead, because a blind man could see, because a cripple could walk. And the religious and the rich began to tremble over a Man who had reminded them of divine law.

To the question of the significance of this jubilee legislation for us, today, the answer is clear. On the one hand it is true that the Church should be anxious to see Matthew and Zacchaeus in their modern forms brought to faith in Jesus Christ. We should look to see presidents and prime ministers and judges and managing directors and newspaper tycoons brought to faith in Jesus Christ, to have their lives, their priorities, changed from inside. But the very fact that Torah provided formal legislation to enforce social justice makes it clear that this inner transformation will never be enough. The Church must involve itself in promoting legislation for a more just society. It must be our concern to support legislation that will shield the poor effectively in our generation, as the jubilee legislation was intended to shield the poor of the past. They are wrong who take evangelism as being the sole means of bringing effective change to the world. But they are also wrong who suppose that social action is the only worthwhile praxis. Jubilee reminds us that we need both.

The Teaching of Proverbs[14]

The biblical book of Proverbs consists of eight distinct collections of wisdom sayings, each collection identified by its own title:

The proverbs of Solomon son of David, king of Israel (1.1—9.18)

The proverbs of Solomon (10.1—22.16)

Sayings of the wise[15] (22.17—24.22)

Further sayings of the wise (24.23-34)

More proverbs of Solomon (25.1—29.27)

Sayings of Agur (30.1-33)

Sayings of King Lemuel (31.1-9)

The wife of noble character (31.10-31)

There is some disagreement about the origins of the individual sayings. On the one hand, much of the wisdom of the proverbs is rough-hewn, generalizing, even inconsistent. On the other hand, some of it is carefully crafted and poetic. R. N. Whybray is quite sure that the material originates with the educated: '. . . most of the sayings in Proverbs are literary creations whose authors had a high degree of education'.[16]

But our own experience of proverbs is of a universally recognized linguistic genre with its origins firmly among the ordinary people. Although we could envisage Whybray's people with a high degree of education *collecting* the proverbs, it is very much more difficult to conceive of their sitting down actually to *create* them. In fact William McKane produces a neat and believable schema:

> When it is remembered that this literature emerged from popular wisdom and arrived gradually at the form in which it is known to us today, the influence of poetry is a reasonable postulate. Because the literature grew out of popular wisdom and was not originally poetry, something of the prosaic still attaches to its form and content . . . The Old Testament wisdom literature has popular origins and takes on literary characteristics when the collectors of individual sayings come on the scene . . . These collections have altered and expanded the sayings greatly, but it is not to be supposed that the sayings themselves stem from individual authors; they have a popular or folk origin.[17]

On this view the book of Proverbs results from the reflection of ordinary people on the complexities, the absurdities and the realities of life. There is little accompanying commentary, and no attempt to relate the proverbs to the salvation history of the people of

Israel. Nor is there any attempt, even by the editors, to reconcile apparently conflicting proverbs. The conflicts in the proverbs are apparent only: their resolution lies in the correct identification of the appropriate *Sitz im Leben* for each.[18]

Proverbs offers what appears at times to be a capitalistic and élitist model of society, perhaps best illustrated by the criticism of the 'slothful man'. He does not plough in season, and that explains his lack of success (20.4). His hands refuse to work, although his mind is set on gain: but he won't gain because he won't work (21.25-6). He stays inside his house with some more or less specious excuse: anything to avoid getting out into the fields (22.13). He won't weed his fields. He won't repair his fences, and that is the source of his poverty (24.30-4). He is in bed, yawning, stretching, when everyone else is at work (26.14), and yet is wonderfully convinced of his own wisdom (26.16). The inference is clear enough: the poor are poor because they won't work.

But Proverbs recognizes that that is not the whole story. 'A poor man's field may produce abundant food, but injustice sweeps it away' (13.23). Hard work is *not* enough. Poverty is *not* always due to laziness. In fact a very complex picture emerges. Poverty may come because a man is lazy, because a man is a sinner, or because a man is sinned against. Wealth and prosperity may come because a man is a hard worker, because he is righteous, or precisely because he is not righteous, and exploits the people of God. There are dishonest scales (11.1), lying tongues (11.9), ruthless men, who profit from their ruthlessness (11.16). The clever financier stores his grain until the price rises, and the poor hate him for it (11.26).

But through it all there runs a single clear conviction: it is right to do what is right. There is One who ultimately judges us all, and he ultimately restores the balance. 'The faithless will be fully repaid for their ways' (14.14); 'He who oppresses the poor shows contempt for their Maker' (14.31); 'The Lord detests the way of the wicked' (15.9); 'Death and Destruction lie open before the Lord – how much more the hearts of men!' (15.11). The answer to the confusion of life, to the human disorder, lies in the existence of God. Take him out, and life *is* meaningless. But he is the one certainty in a life characterized by uncertainty.

Proverbs is *not* a superficial prosperity theology. It is thoroughly based in the human experience, an experience of *dukkha* that is as relevant today as it was then. And the proverbs agree with our earlier thesis: within the two apparent boundaries of human existence, birth and death, life does not make sense. But break down those barriers and allow eternity in, and the possibility of significance is restored.

The Role of the Prophets[19]

Particular stress has long been laid on the ethical role of the prophets of the eighth century. However, it is clear that Israel's prophets always represented a caution to the authorities and their incipient tendency to adopt the oppressive governmental models by which they were always surrounded: 'The visible peculiarity of Israel includes an additional component in the apparatus of her governance, namely, the prophet. It is the prophet who stood vis-à-vis the king to assert continually dimensions of governance and land management which kings prefer to disregard.'[20]

Little is known of the social stratum from which the prophets came. Of Elijah's origins we know little beyond the fact that he came from Gilead. Much has been made by some writers of his access to the king (1 Kings 17.1), but such free access was quite typical of the day, and tells us nothing of Elijah's social class. Elisha came from a rural setting (1 Kings 19.19). Isaiah might have come from a priestly family, and that might explain his presence in the temple (Isa. 6), but it is precarious to use a vision to support such a proposition. Jeremiah certainly came from a priestly family (Jer. 1.1), but Amos, equally certainly, was a shepherd from rural Tekoa (Amos 1.1).

There is something to be said for differentiating between these individual prophets and the sons of the prophets (the *bene ha-nebi'im*, who appear to have been disciples attached to an individual prophet) and the groups of prophets characterized by a kind of infectious ecstasy.[21] It is the acts of the first group that are the prime concern of the court chroniclers, and it is their words which are preserved from an oral tradition and incorporated as Scripture.

These prophets functioned primarily, but not exclusively, as a brake on political leadership. Nathan deals with David's multiple crimes of murder and lechery (2 Sam. 12). Elijah confronts Ahab over the murder of Naboth (1 Kings 21). But the prophets also found themselves opposed to the people as a whole: '. . . it is quite evident that the Old Testament reports situations of conflict between prophets and kings, and later between prophets and all Israel.[22]

This situation of conflict arose out of the very core of the prophetic theology: the demand for *mishpat*, 'justice' in its widest possible sense.[23] Micah begins with this as the first requirement of Yahweh:

> He has showed you, O man, what is good,
> And what does the Lord require of you?
> To act justly [to do *mishpat*] and to love mercy
> and to walk humbly with your God. (Mic. 6.8)

The demand for *mishpat* is laid on the whole of society, representing in some measure the horizontal component of that *tzedaqah*, righteousness, which is the vertical, Godward, component. The prophet is the herald of *mishpat* as he is of *tzedaqah*.

And here, again, the contemporary significance is clear. The continuing significance of prophecy is apparent in the New Testament, but the particular discussion of prophecy in 1 Corinthians 12—14 was dealing with a specific abuse of prophecy, and must not be taken to represent all that the prophet is and does. That view of the prophet must be augmented from what we know of prophecy under the Old Covenant: the New Covenant prophet is not less than but more than the Old Covenant prophet. There is a need today for the element of passion for *mishpat* among the prophets, a social conscience for Church and nation. Ecstatic utterances, mystical language and visions of the future are by no means the entire content of prophecy. Nor is the social conscience sufficient of itself: it needs also the prophetic sense of a direct commissioning from God.

The Identity of the Poor

This section may usefully provide a bridge between the theology of the poor as it appears in the Old Testament and the corresponding theology of the poor in the New Testament. In each case we must ask, 'Who *are* the poor?'

A range of Hebrew words is employed to map out the domain of poverty.[24] The issue of the poor is, perhaps, most conveniently discussed from the book of Psalms,[25] since the range of meanings for the relevant words as found there appears to represent the range of meanings found elsewhere in the Old Testament.

The word *'ebyōn*[26] usually denotes the *economically* deprived, although in Psalms 40.17, 70.5, 86.1 and 109.22 it is preceded by a second common Hebrew term, *'ani*, and could therefore carry also the concept of humility which is undoubtedly there in *'ani*.[27] Included in the domain we also have the words *rash* and *dal*.[28] The complex question of the relationship between these and other Hebrew terms in the domain is convincingly dealt with by Steven Croft in *The Identity of the Individual in the Psalms*.[29] As Croft points out in what is almost a throw-away aside, 'The psalms are not written in code, they are written in the Hebrew language';[30] that is to say there can be no one-to-one correspondence between the linguistic sign and that which is signified by it. Each word has a domain of meaning, and the particular meaning of a particular occurrence of any word is determined by the context within which it occurs and the cotext which surrounds the particular occurrence.

In the Psalms it is the two words *'ebyōn* and *'ani* which dominate the poverty teaching. The *'ebyōn* are contrasted with the rich in Psalm 49.2. It is they who are protected by Yahweh (Pss. 69.33; 72.4; 12; 109.31; 140.12). The connection between the poor and righteousness is suggested by the parallelism of Psalm 37.14:

> The wicked draw the sword
> and bend the bow
> to bring down the poor and needy,
> to slay those whose ways are upright.

Again it is Yahweh who delivers the *'ani* (Pss. 34.6; 35.10; 72.2). They are oppressed by the powerful (Pss. 10.2, 9; 14.6; 109.16). Psalm 40.17 is *le-Dawid*, and suggests that the important, the powerful, the rich, might even so hope to gain the help of Yahweh provided that they take on the character of the *'ani*:

> . . . I am poor and needy;
> may the Lord think of me.
> You are my help and deliverer;
> O my God, do not delay.

The word *'ebyōn* occurs four times in Psalm 72, a psalm which is designated *li-Shelomoh*, 'to' or 'of' or 'for' Solomon, and is an idealization of the monarchy. One of the duties of the king is that as Yahweh's representative he should do what Yahweh does – protect the poor:

> He will defend the afflicted [*'ani*] among the people
> and save the children of the needy [*'ebyōn*];
> he will crush the oppressor . . . (v. 4)
> . . . he will deliver the needy [*'ebyōn*] who cry out,
> the afflicted [*'ani*] who have no-one to help.
> He will take pity on the weak [*dal*] and the needy [*'ebyōn*]
> and save the needy [*'ebyōn*] from death.
> He will rescue them from oppression and violence,
> for precious is their blood in his sight. (vv. 12–14).

If we may now generalize on the question of the teaching of the Psalms on the question of poverty, we may say that we have a spiralling process in which the action of the economically and socially deprived, insignificant, powerless[31] individual who responds by confessing that powerlessness, and thus is cast on the grace and mercy of God, is reflected back upon the nation as a whole and on the king as representing both the nation and, in some sense, Yahweh himself.

That is to say, it is quite clear that the rich tend to that pride which encourages them to stand without God. The poor and the powerless cannot think to do so. The poor can hope for the grace of God to be shown to them; the rich cannot, unless they can exhibit the same spirit of submission to and dependence on Yahweh as is found in the poor.

The linguistic domain of poverty, then, is employed in the Psalms both literally and metaphorically, in what amounts to a chiastic structuring. The economically poor are, generally, the spiritually rich. The economically rich are, generally, the spiritually poor. What the psalmist looks for is spiritual riches for the whole people of God, which, however, does *not* necessitate the material impoverishment of the whole people of God. To be spiritually rich it is not necessary to be materially poor, but material poverty and powerlessness encourage the all-important spirit of dependence on God.

For our present purposes, however, our identification of the poor as those who are materially, sociologically and politically deprived, and who consequently look in a spirit of humility to

Yahweh for his protection and vindication, leads us to recognize that the plight of the poor as it is depicted in the Psalms is precisely this multiple disability exploited by the unfeeling rich and powerful. The *significance* of this analysis of the situation of the poor is that, properly, they should be able to look to God through his Church for their defence. But too often the Church is at best careless of the plight of the poor, at worst it is an integral part of the exploiting structure.[32]

And, with some hesitation, one is tempted to conclude that the leaders of the Church, at every level, from parish to palace, in all the magnificence of their multitudinous titles, should, like the kings of Israel, have a primary concern to protect the poor, the powerless, the minorities. However, it is not clear that many ministers have given thought to this aspect of their sacred calling.

THE NEW TESTAMENT[33]

Words Used for the Poor in the New Testament
The word most commonly used to designate the poor is *ptōchos*. As with the corresponding vocabulary of the Old Testament, so here the meaning of material deprivation leads on to the use of the word to signify the exploited, the powerless, the unimportant, the insignificant, and in turn to the idea of humility. Matthew 19.21 contrasts the rich and the *ptōchoi*: the former are to give to the latter. In Mark 12.41–4 the widow's entire estate consists of a couple of coins, and she is *ptōchos*. Similarly the collection being made for the *ptōchoi* of Jerusalem (Rom. 15.25–7) was explicitly a *material* return for the *spiritual* riches which had originated in Jerusalem.

James 2.2–4 offers the example of an assembly of God's people into which come both a rich man and a *ptōchos*. The former is given a seat, the latter is left to stand up or to sit on the floor, an indication on the one hand of the oppression of the poor, and on the other hand of the meekness and submission expected of the poor who are subjected to such discrimination. And this leads on to the remarkable principle laid down in the same chapter: 'Has not God chosen those who are poor in the eyes of the world to be rich in faith and to inherit the kingdom he promised those who love him? (v. 5).

As with the Old Testament, so here there is no general idealizing of the poor, nor, even more importantly, is there any attempt to sanctify poverty. But what is done consistently throughout the Bible is to recognize that wealth brings power, and with it that spirit of independence which is the antithesis of what is required of humanity before God. By contrast, poverty, of necessity, not as a virtue, brings submission and a spirit of dependence and need which is of the essence of the human approach to God. It is then inescapably the case that the rich find it hard to enter the Kingdom of God. Not that they must first be impoverished, but they must first become dependent.

Jesus and the Poor

It is clearly significant that Jesus chose to be born into a relatively poor family.[34] His life, in so far as it is known to us, confirms that general impression of poverty.[35] The circumstantial detail added by Luke which describes the offering of a pair of doves on the occasion of Jesus' circumcision and of Mary's ritual purification (Luke 2.22–4), an offering authorized in Leviticus 12.8 for the woman who was unable to afford to offer a lamb, is good evidence of the financial situation of the family. The life of Jesus did not demonstrate that prosperity which contemporary wisdom expected as a return for particular holiness.[36] In his years of teaching he and his immediate followers were financed by a group of prosperous women (Luke 8.1–3). At the end of a comparatively brief life he is (apparently) caught up in the religious and political intrigues of the day, denied the protection of religion, condemned to death by a judge who was convinced of his innocence, and executed as a political agitator. This simplistic recapitulation of the life of Jesus makes clear his real experience of the apparent meaninglessness of life, of the human disorder.[37]

Here it is particularly interesting to listen to the conclusion reached by an intellectual Marxist, Milan Machovec, on the significance of the teaching of Jesus:

> Jesus . . . abolishes the future as something that merely replaces the present, a wretched, lost, squandered future, a future in which the prevailing misery of human reality is met only by empty dreams. Jesus shows not how to escape from the misery of real life but how to overcome one's own moral misery . . .[38]

And in general agreement with what we have already seen as the thrust of Old Testament teachings on wealth and poverty, Machovec adds:

> Just as poverty is not glorified for its own sake, so wealth as such is not condemned . . . However much the poor and hungry are to be helped, the ideal is not simply that there should be abundant wealth and possessions for everybody; for these can so easily be accompanied by other manifestations of human weakness.[39]

Indeed this very point lies concealed in the deceptively simple words of the Magnificat (Luke 1.46–55); the words of Malcolm Muggeridge at the 1974 Lausanne International Congress on World Evangelism have stayed with me through the years:

> The splendid words of the Magnificat go on being fulfilled; the mighty are put down from their seats and the humble and meek exalted, the hungry are filled with good things and the rich sent empty away. Yes, but how soon, how very soon, the humble and meek who have been exalted become mighty, and in their turn fit to be put down! How quickly the poor who have been filled with good things become rich, thereby likewise qualifying to be sent away![40]

We have already noted the sermon in the synagogue and the jubilee motif placed by Luke at the beginning of his account of the ministry of Jesus. Matthew uses the Sermon on the Mount to explicate the main thrust of the teaching of Jesus. It begins with the enigmatic blessing on 'the poor in spirit' (Matt. 5.3), which corresponds to Luke's unqualified 'Blessed are you who are poor' (Luke 6.20). In both places it is the *ptōchoi* who are blessed. There is no good reason for supposing that we have two different sermons in the two places.[41] The terms *ptōchoi* and *ptōchoi tō(i) pneumati* are the two redactors' suggested renderings for whatever was originally said in Aramaic: and so we are back to *'ebyōn* again. With all that has been said thus far, it is quite clear that there is no conflict between the two Greek renderings. The *'ebyōn* are the materially poor, but they also are those who generally represent that spirit of submission and, above all, *dependence* which is the principal precondition of Yahweh's *berakah*.

In the teaching of Jesus, arguably the most concise and convincing pericope is that concerning the rich fool, Luke 12.13–21. The pericope is tightly structured. Stage appears in

v. 13 with the request that Jesus should adjudicate between two brothers who had inherited a piece of land. One wished to sell the land, the other did not. The response of Jesus makes it clear that what he is faced with is sheer materialism, 'Be on your guard against all kinds of greed' (v. 15). The story is then told of the rich fool, who supposed that by his riches he could so far prolong life as to make it, for the time being, unnecessary to consider eternity.[42]

The parable is bracketed by two remarkable statements, the one a negative and the other a positive: '. . . a man's life does not consist in the abundance of his possessions' (v. 15) and 'This is how it will be with anyone who stores up things for himself but is not rich towards God' (v. 21). Negatively, a worthwhile life is not ensured by material wealth. Positively, a worthwhile life results when it and its resources are placed at the disposal of God.

Among the many other aspects of the teaching of Jesus on the subject of poverty which might be dealt with here, mention must at least be made of the rationale offered by him for his comparative disregard of any legislative programme for the redistribution of wealth. Money and God are made antithetical: 'You cannot serve both God and Money' (Luke 16.13). In using the Aramaic term *mamōna* (one of the very few *ipsissima verba* of Jesus preserved for us) in this way Jesus encapsulates his own attitude to wealth. Mammon is wealth. Wealth is either given over to God, for him to use, or it stands antithetically over against God, and becomes another god, a god to be served.

Poverty and the New Testament Church

Acts 2.42–7 and 4.32–5 give a tantalizingly brief account of the way of life of the peoples of the first Jerusalem church. There has been an attempt to interpret the information as an experiment in total community of goods: 'In two places in Acts . . . the community of goods is described as an expression of the love based on Christ which the members of the community have for each other. The ideal of common ownership was also to be found in non-Christian philosophy.'[43]

It is true that individual statements in the two passages referred to give the impression of a total community of goods ('All the believers were together and had everything in common', Acts

2.44; 'No-one claimed that any of his possessions was his own, but they shared everything they had', Acts 4.32). However, it is quite clear that they did not simply move into one another's homes, and so destroy the family unit. And it is also clear that although what was there was, generally speaking, available to the community, the sale of property was an ongoing process, not a once-and-for-all group action, and that 'from time to time those who owned lands or houses sold them' (Acts 4.34). Individuals still owned property, and it was they who, like Barnabas and Ananias, decided if and when to sell up. Ananias is clearly told concerning his property: 'Didn't it belong to you before it was sold? And after it was sold, wasn't the money at your disposal?' (Acts 5.4).

However, we would be wrong to err too far in the other direction and attempt to deny the ethos of the Jerusalem church. The church at Jerusalem had resources, and those resources were to be used to eliminate (and not merely to alleviate) poverty: 'There were no needy persons among them' (Acts 4.34).

This situation did not long continue. Perhaps the most important evidence of the changed ethos of the early believers is supplied by Paul's first letter to Corinth. The church there was a thoroughly confused and divided church. As A. J. Malherbe has shown, it was a church drawn not exclusively or even primarily from the poorer classes, but from right across the social spectrum.[44] In this church the practice of the common meal had developed, but was giving rise to tensions. There were the wealthier members who could bring much to the meal, and there were others who could bring little or nothing. And eventually all pretence at a common meal was abandoned, and each ate what he had himself brought (1 Cor. 11.21).[45] In fact this meant that some did not eat at all: there were some who had nothing (1 Cor. 11.22).

The result of such appalling discrimination was the humiliation of the poor. This could have been their own feeling of humiliation as a result of their treatment by the wealthier members of the church, or it is possible that they were humiliated by having to confess to this state of affairs to fellow slaves, for whom the words of Jesus might well have offered hope of better things, but who were now necessarily disillusioned.

The situation addressed by James is little different from this. The admonition *not* to discriminate between rich and poor (Jas. 2) could only be required in a situation which demonstrated precisely that discrimination.[46]

It is a tragic commentary on fallen human nature, and a confirmation of the 'now-and-not-yet' of the process of salvation, that mere decades separated the early serious grappling with the issue of poverty and the appearance of class distinctions within the New Testament Church.

What is encouraging, however, is that neither Paul, in writing to Corinth, nor James, in his more general letter, surrenders the essential position. Discrimination is wrong. The humiliation of the poor by the rich is wrong. Within the Church of Jesus Christ there should be a sharing, a mutual concern, arising from a common devotion to the one Lord who set the example: 'though he was rich, yet for your sakes he became poor, so that you through his poverty might become rich' (2 Cor. 8.9). His material poverty has its particular and often unperceived significance: it is in embracing *that*, in accepting that God stands over against mammon, that material riches must and shall be handed over to God, that the believer enters into spiritual riches. But the Church is not to use the commonality of *spiritual* riches as a substitute for the commonality of *material* resources.

PART THREE

Alternative Responses to Meaninglessness: Islam, Marxism, and Liberation Theology

16 Islam: An Alternative Monotheism

INTRODUCTION

Few Muslims would perceive Christianity as a monotheism: the doctrine of the Trinity has always appeared to the Muslim as a thinly disguised tritheism. Mohamed Al-Nowaihi expresses it very clearly:

> It is true that many Muslims have mistakenly believed that Christians worship three separate Gods, and have not paid sufficient attention to the latter's protestation that their belief in the Trinity does not imply a multiplicity of Gods, that God is still one with them. But even when Muslims realize that in the Christian belief the Trinity does not conflict with God's unity, still the most tolerant and broadminded of them fear that it does in some way detract from that absolute oneness and uniqueness, and that it does smack of anthropomorphism.[1]

Although the theologies of the three disagree fundamentally, Islam, Judaism and Christianity have a theoretical commonality in their scriptures. The Jewish Bible is the Christian Old Testament to which Christianity adds the New Testament; Islam in theory recognizes both, adding the Qur'an as a specifically *Arabic* scripture.[2] But Islam understands itself as being the fulfilment of Judaism and Christianity, and claims Muhammad as the seal (*khatem*)[3] of the line of prophets which includes both Abraham and Jesus.

MUHAMMAD

Muhammad was born at Mecca, an important city which had developed as part of a gradual process of urbanization among the Arab peoples. The Quraish were the dominant tribe: he was born into the Hashimite clan of the Quraish. His grandfather Abd Al-Muttalib was Custodian of the Ka'ba, a cube-shaped building housing the hundreds of idols worshipped at the time. His father was Abdullah, the name ('Servant of Allah') a reminder that Muhammad did not create the name Allah, but found it already, attached to the Creator God of the Arab pantheon. Abdullah died before Muhammad was born, his mother died when he was six. He was first put out to a foster-mother, the normal practice at the time, but was later brought up by his grandfather. It is very probable that it was his early association with the Ka'ba that caused him later on to retain it, and its Black Stone,[4] as the focus of Islam when much else of traditional Arab religion was swept away.

Traditionally, it was at the age of forty that Muhammad first claimed to have received revelations from God through the angel Gabriel, and these claims were made throughout the remainder of his life. He presented himself as a Warner, in particular warning the people of Mecca of the hell that was awaiting the idolater. His message aroused intense opposition, primarily among the wealthy, who saw the abolition of traditional religion as an attack also on trade, and so on their prosperity.

Persecution followed, and in AD 615 the first *hijra*, 'withdrawal', took place, when some eighty-three men and eighteen women took refuge across the Red Sea in Ethiopia, which had been Christianized in the fourth century.[5] Some of these embryonic Muslims embraced Christianity; one of them, Ubayd-Ullah, later returned to his home country and is recorded as saying to Muhammad's Companions, 'Our eyes are opened but yours veiled.'[6]

It was during the absence of these first emigrants that the incident celebrated in Salman Rushdie's book *The Satanic Verses* occurred.[7] It is now quite impossible to determine precisely what happened. The most reasonable explanation is that to ease the pressure on his followers Muhammad offered a limited recognition of the patron goddesses of Mecca. In the process of reciting the opening words of Sura 53, 'The Star', he said:

> Have you considered El-Lat and El-Uzza
> and Manat the third, the other?

He appeared then to continue the Sura:

> These are the Exalted Ones
> Upon whose intercession you may rely.[8]

Muslim apologists have found it extremely difficult to explain this 'compromise with idolatry' or 'lapse of Muhammad' as it has been termed. It certainly cannot be designated a Christian fabrication, since all the evidence for the event comes from Muslim sources. Ibn Ishaq suggests[9] that it was Satan who put the offending words on Muhammad's tongue.[10] The Ahmadi text and translation of the Qur'an by Malik Ghulam Farid has an extended footnote on the matter[11] which appears first to deny the event altogether, and then to explain the offending words as being an interjection from an unbelieving Meccan bystander.

There can be no doubt that the words were spoken: such a discreditable event could not have been fabricated. The result of the promise was entirely predictable: when Muhammad reached the end of his recitation and prostrated himself, everyone, his disciples as well as the uncommitted bystanders, joined him. If his intention had been to lift the persecution from his followers, he had more than attained his objective.

However, on reflection Muhammad recognized the significance of his compromise over the three Meccan goddesses, and subsequently withdrew the original words, substituting instead:

> They are naught but names yourselves have named,
> and your fathers;
> God has sent down no authority touching them.

It is these words which now stand in the Qur'an. And with the retraction of the compromising words persecution of Muhammad's followers increased, thus forcing their withdrawal to Yathrib (later *al-madina an-nabi*, 'The City of the Prophet', and then, simply, 'Medina'). This became the power base from which Muhammad operated from AD 622, the year of the *hijra* until his death only some ten years later, 8 June AD 632.

THE HISTORY OF ISLAM

The history of the Muslim world passes through a number of clearly discernible phases.

The Lifetime of Muhammad: 570–632

The period before Muhammad is known as 'The Age of Ignorance', *jahiliyya*, an ignorance which manifested itself in a debased morality, in the careless oppression of the unimportant, in the free exercise of power to the detriment of the powerless.[12]

The remarkable success of Muhammad in sweeping away that particular form of 'ignorance' and in uniting the disparate peoples of Arabia (whose only common possession had been their language) left his successors with the task of consolidating the religious unity into a viable political and economic power.

The Period of the Four Rightly Guided Caliphs: 632–80

The four caliphs, Abu Bekr, Umar, Uthman, and Ali ben Abu Talib (who had married Muhammad's daughter Fatima) welded the Arab peoples together primarily through the common adherence to Islam. The transformation from polytheism and idolatry was rapid and radical. Politically, Islam began to expand northwards into Syria and westwards along the northern coasts of Africa.

But this period also gave rise to the great schism in Islam. Ali, a blood descendant of Muhammad, and married to Muhammad's daughter, had demonstrated a powerful claim to the succession from the moment of Muhammad's death. That claim was rejected in favour of the respected but ageing Abu Bekr, Muhammad's companion on the *hijra*, and the man who led the Friday prayers in the mosque at Medina when Muhammad was ill.

Ali did eventually succeed to the caliphate, but the leadership of the Four Rightly Guided Caliphs then gave way to the Umayyad caliphate of Mu'awiya, Yazid and their successors. Ali had two sons, Al Hasan and Al Hussein, and it was this second son who gave to Islam a martyr it could well have done without, and with martydom an end to the comparative monolithic unity of Islam. After the death of his elder brother, Al Hussein was encouraged by supporters in Iraq to believe that he could take back the caliphate from the Umayyads. With a token force of his immediate supporters, he marched north to Syria to confront the army of the Umayyad caliph Yazid, expecting to be reinforced by an army from Iraq. That army did not materialize, and Hussein, grandson of the prophet, was killed in the battle of Karbala. And there was the rub: it was the grandson of the prophet who was killed by Muslim forces, his head struck off and carried ignominiously to Yazid in Damascus. The first major division thus occurred in Islam, between the 'orthodox' Sunni Muslims, and the 'schismatic' Shi'a Muslims, a division which is perpetuated by the annual re-enactment of the battle of Karbala by Shi'a Muslims.[13]

*The Rise of the Four Law Schools and the Assimilation
of the Traditions: 680-915*

This third period, also, has its significance for any understanding
of Islam today. During these two centuries Islam was steadily
formalizing its beliefs and practices. The centrality of *tawhid*, the
doctrine of the oneness of God, was never in question. But Islam
needed a clear statement of what it was to be a Muslim. Muhammad
had not been a systematic theologian, the Qur'an was not a textbook
of systematic theology. But a system could be distilled out from it,
provided that an appropriate methodology could be evolved.

The evolutionary process was a complex one, but it resulted
ultimately in the recognition of four Law Schools which all agreed
on the fundamental importance of Qur'an and tradition (*hadith*),
interpreted as necessary through *qiyas*, 'analogy', and the consensus,
ijma, of the *ulama*, the learned.

But there was a further step taken which has consistently barred
the way to progress in actually moving Islam from the seventh
century into the twentieth. The jurists insisted that they had
authoritatively completed the work of interpreting the Qur'an.
That work could not be done again. The door to *ijtihad*, engagement
with the original text, was closed:

> Radical innovations in legal or ritual matters would naturally
> threaten . . . consensus, and it was no doubt for this reason that
> after the tenth century there gradually developed the doctrine,
> sanctioned, of course, by the *ijma'* of the scholars, that the gates of
> *ijtihad* (creative interpretation of the law) had been closed . . . New
> attempts at *ijtihad* came to be condemned as *bid'a* – innovation.
> Only among the Shi'a, whose Imams were regarded as all-powerful
> in matters of religion, were the doors of *ijtihad* to remain open.[14]

But this has proved to be no minor inconvenience. The
punishment laid down in the Qur'an for theft is amputation, and
that understanding is enshrined in tenth-century law: without
ijtihad it cannot be challenged. Polygamy is allowed in the Qur'an,
and that, too, is indelibly written into Shari'a law. The right of a
husband to beat his wife is there, too, and much else that was
entirely appropriate in the seventh century but which is generally
unacceptable in the twentieth century. Modern understanding of
textual interpretation – for example, the distinction between the

meaning of a text to its first recipients and the significance of that same text for the modern reader – could provide the Muslim world with a way out of an antiquated law code. If the gateway to *ijtihad* is indeed closed, there can be no way forward. Islam, at least in its major, Sunni, constituent, is condemned for ever to look backwards.

Ibn Hanbal, the last of the great jurists, died in AD 855, but with the question of the actual identity of authoritative *hadith* tradition unanswered. Over the next thirty-five years, until the death of Ibn Maja in AD 889, this question was steadily resolved by a painstaking process of collecting, classifying, and codifying the mass of traditions in circulation. Two collections gained particular authority,[15] those of Bukhari and Muslim. Bukhari is said to have separated his four thousand *sahih*, 'reliable' traditions, from a total of more than half a million. These traditions, primarily concerning the lifestyle of Muhammad, provide the Muslim with a guide to everyday behaviour, and this is obviously vital to a religion which is essentially one of salvation through right action.

An Islamic Empire: 915–1683

Muhammad died in AD 632; only a century later Islam had expanded across North Africa, had crossed the Straits of Gibraltar, had occupied the entire Iberian peninsula, and was finally stopped at Tours. But elsewhere the advance continued, eastward into India and beyond, northwards and to the gates of Vienna, where again Islam was turned back.

The supremacy of Islam was not merely in matters military and political: in the arts, in science and in mathematics Islam was dominant. But 1683 was probably the high-water mark for Islam, and the retreat from Vienna marked the beginning of a long period of gradual but steady decline.

The Turn of the Tide: 1683–1946

There is little to be said of this period. Perhaps the most striking indicator of the decline of Muslim power is to be seen in the arrogant way in which the Middle East was carved up by the Christian democracies after the First World War, without any particular reference to the people involved. The French laid claim to Syria and ejected the Emir Feisal from Damascus. In Britain the

Arabs had at least one staunch friend, T. E. Lawrence, 'Lawrence of Arabia', but even he could do little to counter the extraordinary arrogance of Britain's Colonial Office. In the context of his reminiscences of Lawrence of Arabia, Winston Churchill recalled:

> In the spring of 1921 I was sent to the Colonial Office, to take over our business in the Middle East and bring matters into some kind of order. At that time we had recently suppressed a most dangerous and bloody rebellion in Iraq, and upwards of forty thousand troops . . . were required to keep order. In Palestine the strife between the Arabs and the Jews threatened at any moment to take the form of actual violence. The Arab chieftains, driven out of Syria . . . lurked furious in the deserts beyond the Jordan . . .
>
> I therefore convened a conference at Cairo . . . We submitted the following main proposals to the Cabinet. First we would repair the injury done to the Arabs and to the House of the Sherifs of Mecca by placing the Emir Feisal upon the throne of Iraq as King, and by entrusting the Emir Abdulla with the government of Trans-Jordania. Secondly we would remove practically all our troops from Iraq . . . All our measures were implemented, one by one.[16]

The post-World War One period marked the nadir of Arab and Muslim power, but the very perceptiveness and even (in a peculiar way) sensitivity of some of the dispositions made by the British Government were paving the way for a renewal of Muslim self-confidence.

Economic and Political Revival: 1946-78

The end of the Second World War introduced a new era in which the distribution of power was radically different. Britain and France had been bled white economically, and the colonies which had been sucked into the conflict were now demanding independence. Some forty Muslim countries achieved independence in the post-war years and set about creating new and more or less Muslim societies.

Egypt provided the example which confirmed a growing impression in the Muslim world that the Western democracies were not, after all, invincible. Colonel Nasser was determined on exercising Egyptian sovereignty over the Suez Canal; Britain and France were equally determined to maintain international control over the militarily and economically vital waterway. The war was brief, and international opinion forced an ignominious climb-down by the British Government. True enough, the Western armies were not defeated militarily, but no matter: the point was made. Egypt's sovereignty was recognized against the wishes of the invaders. Nasser became a beacon of hope to the Muslim world. The long years in which Muslim intellectuals, spearheaded, perhaps, by the anglophile Sayyid Ahmed Khan,[17] had essentially surrendered to Western ways of thinking, had attempted to produce some kind of compromise between Shari'a and Western law codes, had marketed a new reformed and liberal Islam, were coming to an end.

The Islamic world found new economic power through oil. In 1970 oil was selling at less than one dollar a barrel. In 1973, when the Organisation of Petroleum Exporting Countries was formed, eleven of the thirteen members were Muslim states. By 1980 oil was selling at thirty-four dollars a barrel. The difference to the hitherto impoverished Muslim world was, literally, revolutionary. Oil revenues made it possible for the Muslim world to invest in sophisticated military hardware from the capitalist world, or, where that failed, from the communist world. Libya might not be able to match the challenge of the United States of America, but it was well able to threaten less well-equipped neighbouring countries.

The Fundamentalist Challenge: 1979–

Ruhollah, of the town of Khomein in central Iran,[18] was born in 1902, and followed a lengthy programme of orthodox Islamic studies, first in Qur'an school and later in the holy city of Qom, where he studied theology, philosophy and mysticism. He grew up in a period when the rule of the liberally-minded Shah lacked any serious challenge. Khomeini, as he was now known, provided that challenge: he was imprisoned and then, in 1964, exiled to Turkey, and from there to Iraq.

Khomeini's opposition to the regime of the Shah was simply expressed: a Muslim people should live under Shari'a law, and it was the duty of the leadership to make that possible.[19] That the Shah did not do so was because of his subservience to the United States of America. It is quite clear that the Shah was out of touch with his people: in place of dialogue he chose the way of repression;

in place of reconciliation he chose confrontation. The opposition found its focus in Khomeini: finance flowed to him from throughout the Shi'a world, and from him to succour the growing opposition to the Shah's rule.

In 1978 the Shah could no longer tolerate Khomeini's residence in neighbouring Iraq, and he persuaded the Sunni President Saddam Hosein of Iraq to expel Khomeini, who was forced to Paris. But the exile was soon over. Throughout the towns and villages of Iran the Mullahs, the teachers, of Islam, promoted the fundamentalism of Khomeini. In 1979 the Shah was deposed and Khomeini returned, to begin a process which resulted in the total eclipse of the liberal movement in Iran and the transfer of real power to the clerics, more precisely to the Ayatollah. Here was the first revolution[20] in the Third World that did not depend for its ideology on any one of the competing developed world ideologies.

Shi'a Islam[21] differs in many ways from the mainstream Sunni movement. Leadership in Shi'a Islam was vested in a succession of blood descendants of Muhammad, until with the Twelfth Imam the line came to an end with his 'occultation', his disappearance and constitution as the 'Hidden Imam', to be revealed in due time. Meanwhile the authority of the Imam is exercised by the *fukaha*, the jurists, among whom, eventually, he became *the* jurist, the *Fakih*. Khomeini consistently taught that the Muslim should live holistically, that he should live under *Sunna*, the orthodox praxis of Qur'an and tradition, and that since only the jurists could authoritatively interpret those texts, only the jurists were qualified to lead the affairs of the nation. It has been estimated that of one thousand senior administrative posts in the country, some six hundred were given to direct descendants of Muhammad, the so-called Sayyeds; many positions of significance were filled through a blunt nepotism which put at least fifty of Khomeini's own relatives into power. The power of the clerics was, therefore, all but absolute.[22]

In a violent reaction to Iran's past, Ayatollah[23] Khomeini set about what appeared to be a sustained attempt to antagonize the rest of the world. The Soviet Union and the United States of America were the two Satans. The war with his old enemy, Saddam Hosein of Iraq, split the Arab world, and his attempt to export Iranian-style revolution to Egypt and Pakistan, to Lebanon and to Saudi Arabia, left Iran essentially isolated even within Islam.

Ayatollah Khomeini died in 1989, without having convinced any other country to follow his lead (if a return to the past can properly be called a lead) into orthodox fundamentalism. Even Pakistan, which had under the military leadership of General Zia al-Haqq come very close to Khomeini's position, retreated abruptly from it when the General was succeeded by Benazir Bhutto: a woman leading a Muslim state. Perhaps the only success Khomeini could have pointed to was the establishment of a small revolutionary movement in Beirut, a movement which had succeeded in little more than turning a once-prosperous city into ungovernable chaos.

With the death of Khomeini it is clear that Islam has been returned to the still unresolved problem of the form that Islam should take as it moves towards the twenty-first century.

ISLAM IN THE MODERN WORLD

The end of the twentieth century has seen the emergence of Islam as a new world power, but as Islam has become the focus of attention in the mass media, and as the emergent image has been given more solid form, so the verdict of the non-Muslim world has been increasingly negative. In a review of David Pryce-Jones' influential book *The Closed Circle*,[24] Conor Cruise O'Brien commented acidly:

> It remains true that Arab and Muslim society is sick, and has been sick for a long time. In the last century, the Arab thinker Jamal al-Afghani, wrote: 'Every Muslim is sick, and his only remedy is in the Koran.' Unfortunately the sickness gets worse the more the remedy is taken.[25]

But the Islamic world is far from being a monolith. Firstly, there is the obvious division between Sunni and Shi'a Islam (and the deviant or possibly heretical Ahmadiyya providing a very much smaller splinter group), with the Shi'a representing the movement towards orthodox fundamentalism. Secondly, in the larger Sunni world there is the movement for a pragmatic and limited orthodoxy, accepting the need for some measure of accommodation to twentieth-century concepts of justice and civil rights, even those rights claimed for women. But thirdly, Islam is inevitably confronted by a left-wing and even Marxist philosophy, which has produced an alternative reason for exporting violence specifically into the Western democracies.

The Orthodox Fundamentalists

The Iranian revolution represented the attempt to impose more of the Qur'an on Muslim society: there can be little doubt that the result has been an appalling denial of human rights. With the return of Khomeini to Iran there came the thousands of local and central revolutionary *komiteh*, and the quasi-legal tribunals which dispensed a kind of justice which smacked more of Stalinism than of Islam. Khomeini's view was that the insistence on open trials, defence lawyers and proper procedures was a reflection of 'the Western sickness among us',[26] and that criminals should not be tried, they should be killed.

The details given by Shaul Bakhash and by organizations such as Amnesty International make horrific reading. Amnesty noted 2,946 executions in a single year; the left-wing Mujahidin opposition listed 7,746 deaths from June 1981 to September 1983.[27] According to Bakhash, when the former Prime Minister Amir Abbas Hoveyda was to be tried his judge went to the prison where he was held, ordered all the doors locked and the telephones disconnected, tried him, sentenced him, and had him immediately executed for fear that international intervention might result in some measure of clemency being shown.[28]

However, it must be said that this appalling violence cannot of itself invalidate the wishes of the Iranian Muslims to return to what they saw as orthodoxy. Islam is essentially holistic, and it necessarily looks back to the example of Muhammad. Granted the foundation of Qur'an plus *hadith*, and granted on the Sunni hand the closed gates of *ijtihad*, and on the Shi'a hand the absolute authority of the Imam, it is difficult to resist the conclusion that much of Islam today is formal, external, and infected throughout with compromise. Fundamentalism is, in fact, a return to an orthodoxy that successive generations have found pragmatically not to work.

Mission and Meaninglessness

The fundamentalists are aware of the fact that the twentieth-century developed world is inimical to Muslim orthodoxy. The response is simply, 'So much the worse for the twentieth-century world'. Twentieth-century ideas of justice, of the criminal code, of human rights, and especially of the rights of women, are simply rejected out of hand. However, the Iran experiment has shown that it is impossible to create and maintain a fundamentalist seventh-century vacuum in a twentieth-century environment.

Anti-Western Marxish [29] Fundamentalism

There is a second major division within Islam which has not enjoyed as sharp a focus as the orthodox fundamentalists, although they, too, could be classified as fundamentalists. The members of this group are committed to the Qur'an and (to a lesser extent) to *hadith*, and they recognize that it is all but impossible to live under Shari'a law in the context of Western materialism. The answer, then, is the dismantling, even the destruction, of Western materialism. The orthodox fundamentalists have attempted to export revolution to the Muslim world; this group[30] attempts to export revolution to the non-Muslim Western world, particularly to that part of the Western world relevant to the Muslim heartlands, Europe.

The group is not Marxist: it would agree with Khomeini in seeing Marxism as one of the two contemporary Satans. But certainly the group has a strong socialistic commitment, which it claims to have identified in the Qur'an. And there is a good measure of truth in this claim. Muhammad was himself an orphan at six years of age, and the Qur'an clearly reflects his early concern for the poor, the uninfluential, the unimportant. The warnings that he sounded in the early years are most commonly directed against the exploiters of widows and orphans:

> Did He not find thee an orphan, and shelter thee?
> Did He not find thee erring, and guide thee?
> Did He not find thee needy, and suffice thee?
> As for the orphan, do not oppress him,
> and as for the beggar, scold him not . . .
>
> (Sura 93, 'The Forenoon', vv. 6–8)

. . . fear God by whom you demand one of another,
and the wombs . . .
Give the orphans their property,
and do not exchange the corrupt for the good;
and devour not their property with your property;
surely that is a great crime . . . (Sura 4, 'Women', vv. 1–3)

We created man in trouble.
What, does he think none has power over him,
saying, 'I have consumed wealth abundant'?
What, does he think none has seen him?
Have we not appointed to him two eyes, and a tongue,
and two lips,
and guided him on the two highways?
Yet he has not assaulted the steep;
and what shall teach thee what is the steep?
The freeing of a slave,
or giving of food upon a day of hunger
to an orphan near of kin
or a needy man in misery . . . (Sura 90, 'The Land', vv. 5–15)

This group is implacably opposed to the so-called Western democracies, and its members are those who are primarily responsible for the kidnapping of Western nationals in Beirut: such groups as *Hizb-Ullah*, 'The Party of God', the 'Organization of the Oppressed of the World'[31] and *Islamic Jihad*.

It is worth adding that not a few of those who adopt this stance are Marxists who have somehow come to terms with atheistic communism: As Maxime Rodinson puts it, such people

. . . have no intention of adopting the communists' fundamental atheism. How they react to this atheism, and how they find a way to excuse it, varies from case to case. They can simply refuse to believe that it exists, or they can see it, as Christians have often done, as a mere appearance beneath which lies a profound attachment to God's designs, and a profound, if distorted, apprehension of the divine.[32]

For this group the real enemy is clearly the capitalistic West rather than the communistic East.

Pragmatic Liberalism

The Muslims who fall into this third category would certainly not recognize themselves in the designation 'liberal'. Indeed it is arguable that within Islam there is no liberalism. But the confrontation with Khomeini's fundamentalism has made it quite clear that most Arab nations have settled for something less than orthodoxy. And it must be remembered that the search for orthodoxy has not been restricted to the Shi'a branch of Islam: in 1979 the Grand Mosque at Mecca was seized by an international group of some two hundred extremists protesting at the laxity of the lifestyle of the Saudi leadership.[33]

Pragmatism in Islam must be perceived as a spectrum of compromises, ranging from a modified implementation of Shari'a law to the imposition of a dual structure separating religion from state affairs, allowing for the essential setting aside of Shari'a. Perhaps surprisingly, Islam has found little difficulty in introducing practices which have clearly been innovations, *bida'*: '... the deepest transformations have been accepted almost without resistance if they have coincided with the interests of the state or of powerful strata of individuals, despite any previous theoretical reticence about the type of behaviour they implied'.[34]

Westernized Liberalism

It is unclear to what extent this movement, strong at the beginning of the century, has survived. And yet, in the long run, it may well prove Islam's one hope of survival. If the gates of *ijtihad* can again be opened, to allow for a fresh interpretation of the *significance* of the Qur'an to be produced, and if, as has been argued, Shari'a law and its distasteful punishments can be understood as taking on relevance only when the ideal Muslim society has been produced, and poverty banished,[35] and if a way can be found to recognize the dignity of women and of circumventing the *rib'a* ban on usury, then, perhaps, Islam will be able to open its windows and its gates to the world. But if not, then it does appear that the Muslim world must remain isolated, denied even those basic freedoms theoretically accorded by the Charter of the United Nations.

THE ISLAMIC WORLD-VIEW

The Muslim begins with God. Indeed this starting-point for all Muslim thinking provides also a principal criticism of the Western democracies, which are characterized as materialistic and humanistic: it is humanity, and worse still the individual, who occupies the centre of the stage in the Western world. The first of the doctrines of Islam is the doctrine of the oneness of God, undifferentiated monotheism, *tawhid*, and the first of the five pillars of Islam is the duty of reciting the confession of *tawhid*.

Allah is the Creator of the universe and its Absolute Ruler. There is no Second Kingdom to challenge his rule. Satan is not a fallen angel, leader of a cosmic revolt; and there is no universal fall of humanity, no essential disability in the human will. It is true that we are weak, but that weakness stems from our ignorance. What is needed for right living and a just society is right teaching. That teaching is to be found in the Qur'an and *hadith*. The implementation of that teaching is a possibility for every Muslim. Islam is submission to the one God, and that submission is expressed through a *sunna* lifestyle.

That this lifestyle is no less demanding even than that required by Orthodox Judaism (as illustrated in the detailed systemization of Torah by the rabbis) is readily confirmed from such writings as those of Ayatollah Khomeini.[36] The provision of detailed guidance on matters which must appear to the non-Muslim as trivial is clearly inevitable in any religion in which salvation comes through the observation of an authoritative *sunna* praxis.

The Muslim world-view is encapsulated in the single concept of submission. Islam *is* submission to Allah. In the absence of a Second Kingdom doctrine, Allah is necessarily the author of every event in human history. He must be responsible for the good that falls into an individual's life, and for the tragedies too: 'Wheresoever you may be, death will overtake you, even if you be in strongly built towers. And if some good befalls them, they say, "This is from Allah;" and if evil befalls them, they say, "This is from thee." Say, "All is from Allah".'[37]

The Muslim submits to the decrees of Allah, whatever those decrees may be. But as H. U. Weitbrecht Stanton comments in his classic *The Teaching of the Qur'an*, the doctrine of predestination is explicit if illogical.[38] The apparent illogicality of a religion which combines an absolute God (who is at the same time *al-Rahman*, the Merciful) with a judgement on the basis of human achievement is only marginally reduced by the dual concepts of *tanzih*, removal, and *mukhalafa*, difference, 'otherness' (see above, p. 69). Stanton comments: 'The idea of divine transcendence, so relentlessly developed by Muslim theology in its conception of *tanzih* = removal and *mukhalafa* = contrariety (between Allah and the creature) is expressed in the Qur'an, as to some extent in the Old Testament, by its teaching on the Throne of Allah . . .'[39]

The Muslim believes in life beyond this life: a life of bliss for the Muslim; a life of torment for the rest. The Muslim believes in a bodily resurrection and in judgement on the basis of the individual's behaviour during his lifetime. The outcome of that judgement is uncertain: the Muslim can only hope either that his lifestyle has been sufficiently in line with *sunna* to allow him into Paradise, or that the mercy of Allah, *al-Rahman*, will let him in, or, for some at least, that Muhammad or some one of Islam's many holy men will intercede so as to secure admission which would not otherwise be gained.

Muslim theology has to be produced from a deficient appreciation of the true predicament of humanity and an inadequate understanding of the Godhead. The doctrine of *tawhid* is appealing in its simplicity, but that very simplicity makes it impossible to produce a comprehensive theology that does justice either to God or to humanity.

AN ASSESSMENT

The present century has been marked by an admission that the characterization of Muhammad and of Islam by Christians in the past[40] has owed more to malice and prejudice than to knowledge. But this has then resulted in the opposite error – Islam in general and Muhammad in particular have been accorded a character which fails to match the reality: 'The denigration of him by European writers has too often been followed by a romantic idealization of his figure by other Europeans and by Muslims.'[41]

The Qur'an

There can be no doubt that the teaching of the Qur'an represented in many ways a significant advance on the ethics of Muhammad's day. New rights were given to women, and curbs placed on the grasping nature of contemporary business practices. But the Qur'an remains a product of its own day. Its bland approval of prostitution and of the supplementing of the permitted four wives by women seized in warfare cannot be conjured away.

The Qur'an is claimed to be an infallible and inspired book. If it is, then clearly neither the Old Testament nor the New Testament is, for the Qur'an contradicts both. The denial of the crucifixion of Jesus is the most glaring example of this contradiction, but the Sura 'Joseph' presents another example of the contradictory process.

The Qur'an is not free of error. It represents the attempt of a remarkable man to resolve the *dukkha* issues of his own people, but it is *his* attempt.

Muhammad

We have put behind us those interpretations of Muhammad which saw him as an illiterate camel-driver who suffered from epileptic fits. We know him to have been a man of enormous ability in the business world, a man of great political ability, a military leader of some genius. And more: in the early years in Mecca there is no reason at all to doubt his sincerity, his genuine horror of idolatry, his real concern for the oppressed.

But he suffered the immense disadvantage of not having the Judeo-Christian Scriptures available to him in Arabic. The Bible he knew only anecdotally. The unfolding history of the two Testaments he knew only as individual stories: like a string of beads, but without any chronological string to link them together, and with seductive beads from other strings mixed in with the rest. He had no way of separating biblical material from legend.

At Mecca his texts were challenged only as to their origins. At Medina they were challenged as to their accuracy. At Medina, confronted by Jews who knew the Old Testament, he had just two choices: to admit his errors or to insist on infallibility and divine revelation. He chose the latter course, and with that choice there seems to have come both a deepening conflict with the Jews and a more general decline in personal morals. The appalling massacre of the Jewish Qurayzah clan after the Battle of the Ditch; the cynical claim to revelation to allow him to marry his adopted son's wife, Zaynab; revelation again to justify the raid on the Nakhla caravan; breaking the sacred truce: these are not trivial charges.[42]

Of course, if Muhammad is judged by the moral standards of his own day then there is little in his conduct to excite comment. But if he is to be presented as the great exemplar, the perfect man, then other standards become relevant.

The Theology of Islam

The theology of Islam is clearly a partial borrowing from Christianity and Judaism, with no little contribution from Persian Zoroastrianism and a leavening of Arab traditional religion. But the mixture is unsatisfactory, since Muhammad did not adequately know any one of the religions he plundered for his teaching.

A reductionist doctrine of God is superficially attractive, but there is no particular reason for supposing that the least complex formulation of the doctrine is the right formulation. Indeed it is entirely logical to suppose that the more powerful the model is in explaining the nature of God and his relationship to creation so the more complex it will be. Muhammad's vehement rejection of a trinitarian model[43] is emotional, not theological.

The Human Disorder

Muhammad's perception of the human disorder is inadequate. There is no salvation in Islam: instead instruction is offered. Abd al-Tafahum expresses it clearly enough: 'Islam does not normally use the word "salvation", still less "regeneration".'[44] Muhammad saw the absurdity of idolatry and of polytheism, he observed the tragedy of the oppression of the powerless by the powerful, but attributed it all to ignorance.

Islam offers an alternative to Judaism: each represents a means by which an individual should respond to the admitted holiness, righteousness and justice of God. But each fails to offer any solution to the problem posed by Paul's Romans 7.13–24 experience of an inner inability to reconcile will with behaviour. So profound is the human disorder that it cannot be resolved from the inner resources of humanity. Islam offers no other resources.

The Creation of the Umma

It is often claimed that the creation of the *umma*, the creation of a genuine community out of the disparate tribes of Arabia, was one of the great accomplishments of Muhammad, and that this creation of community continues to be the great strength of Islam today.

It is doubtful if this fiction can any longer be maintained. The community that now exists in the Muslim world is a closed community which fearfully shuts out the rest of the world, a community that imposes conformity on its members. Within that community there is no open scholarship, no true freedom other than the freedom to conform. Wherever there is a Muslim majority there, eventually, is the spirit of intolerance. This has never been so clearly demonstrated as in the history of the Iranian revolution. The mass hysteria, the quasi-justice of the clerics, the arrests of dissidents, irrespective of age or sex, irrespective of the area of dissent,[45] must give the non-Muslim world cause for serious thought. But this intolerance is not restricted to Iran: it has long been true, also, of Saudi Arabia and the Yemen, of Pakistan and Malaysia, of the other protagonist in the Gulf War of the 1980s, Iraq, and of Syria.

Malise Ruthven comprehensively summarizes conditions in the Muslim world:

> ... most Muslim states are ruled by bloody and repressive dictatorships which, far from satisfying the imperative of social justice exemplified by the Prophet's career, seem to be incapable of granting even the most basic human rights to their citizens. Official murder, arbitrary imprisonment and extra-legal government in all its forms can be found in Muslim states from Morocco to Malaysia.[46]

17 Marxism:
A Political Alternative

MARX'S PHILOSOPHY

Marxism has been characterized by Leszek Kolakowski as 'the greatest fantasy of our century'.[1] Karl Marx was born in 1818 and died in 1883. The popular view of Marx as a demagogue rabble-rouser, as a mindless revolutionary, is vastly wide of the truth. He was, in fact, a brilliant student at Berlin University, and could have gone on to a career in any one of several fields. But his pathway was in good measure determined by his background. Both of his parents came not merely from Jewish families, but from rabbinical families. Herschel Marx's career was threatened by the racist and particularly anti-Jewish policies of Prussia under King Frederick Wilhelm III: Jews were banned from the professions. Herschel apparently experienced little difficulty in changing such faith as he had: he became a Christian.

The consequence for his children was a certain ambiguity; as J. H. Jackson expresses it: 'Karl Marx was thus a Jew and not a Jew, a Christian and not a Christian, a Prussian and not a Prussian.'[2] His identity was in fact worked out through his relationships with his intellectually sophisticated father and with his philosophically minded friends, particularly Friedrich Engels, whom he first met in 1844. It was through Engels that Marx was introduced at first hand to the world of industry. To quote Jackson again, 'Marx learnt precisely and in human rather than statistical terms what was the condition of the working class in England in 1844.'[3]

This exposure to the realities of life for the wage-earners of British industry was meticulously detailed by Marx, and eventually appeared as part of his major work *Capital*.[4] He referred to the health of the potters of North Staffordshire, quoting the official and unofficial reports of senior medical practitioners: 'The potters as a class, both men and women, represent a degenerated population, both physically and morally. They are, as a rule, stunted in growth, ill-shaped, and frequently ill-formed in the chest; they become prematurely old, and are certainly short-lived . . .'[5]

He gave a remarkable and detailed account of the working day of the London journeyman baker which is of real value for reconstructing the sociology of the time.[6] He knew of the incredible working hours forced on labourers by their employers: fourteen, eighteen, twenty hours, with the inevitable consequence of accidents produced through sheer exhaustion.[7] He had details of children aged from nine to twelve working an eighteen-hour day for three days of the week, and fifteen-hour shifts for the remainder of the week.[8]

This was the raw material from which Marx worked. His self-imposed task was twofold: to discover how these conditions developed, and to determine how the situation should be remedied. This dual thrust is fundamental to Marx's thinking: there could be no hope of a successful end to the intolerable situation of the working class without a correct analysis of the causes which gave rise to those conditions. Conversely, there could be no justification for the analysis of the situation other than the determination to change it.

Marx's analysis rather quickly focused on what was to become the keystone of his entire philosophy: the class struggle. He perceived three stages in European society. In the sixteenth and seventeenth centuries trade guilds emerged with the intention of protecting the middle-class entrepreneurs from the aristocracy who saw them as a threat to their power. The guilds were highly successful in countering the manoeuvres of the aristocrats, who moved to introduce heavy taxation on factories as a disincentive to the new industries.

Paradoxically, this created a power-vacuum: the power of the aristocrats was broken, but was at once taken up by the bourgeoisie, who then used that power to exploit the wage-earners of the factories. Even this elementary analysis sufficed to show that society was in a state of flux, was a dynamic and not a static phenomenon. Marx believed that he could anticipate a third stage, in which the proletarian wage-earners would do to their employers what the employers had done to the aristocrats.

Marx had absorbed the philosophy of Hegel during his years in Berlin. Hegel had convinced Marx that behind the apparent randomness of history there were not merely principles but actual laws of change to be formulated. For Hegel there was a dialectical process, a process of interaction, of the interaction of opposites, which could be invoked to explain change. Society at any point in time presented a thesis, a situation, a philosophy, which inevitably created its antithesis, an opposition. And out of the opposition emerged a new synthesis, which in its turn became the thesis for the dialectic to engage once more.

This model captivated Marx, and it remained the theoretical focus of his subsequent thinking. At the same time Marx contributed to the dialectic a radical materialism. Hegel had been an idealist, Marx was not. Hegel perceived his dialectic as operating in the world of ideas, of theories. Marx accepted the concept of a dialectic with gratitude but rejected the idealism with scorn. Hegel was stood on his head; in Marx's view only so could any value be gained from his theories. The dialectic was materialistic, not idealistic. The dialogue was between social classes, not between rival thinkers. The two classes which engaged his attention were the bourgeoisie, those who owned the means of production, and the proletariat, the daily-wage earners, who of necessity sold their labour to the bourgeoisie. Interestingly neither Marx nor Lenin had any understanding of the peasantry, of the farm-labourers: to Marx rural life was idiocy.[9] It was between these two classes that the dialectic was to operate, and the outcome was certain since it represented science, law. The expectation was of the isolation and elimination of the bourgeoisie, and the eventual establishment of a classless society which would at last offer stability since with the abolition of the class system there would be no further material on which the dialectic could operate.

This, in essence, represents the Marxist understanding of the human disorder. Humanity results from the process of evolution. Its progress has not, however, been a matter of mere chance: dialectical materialism explains the progress that has been made. The present stage is characterized by a disorder which is the result of the class struggle. That disorder may be resolved by abolishing the classes, by moving into the classless society.

There is, for obvious reasons, no attempt to explain the deeper disorder involved in the conflict between the human will and human behaviour. Nor is there any attempt to deal with the cosmic aspects of the human disorder: the major environmental catastrophes, the personal tragedies of malformed babies, of disease, of earthquake and typhoon and drought and flood.

And there is no evidence, either, of that evolutionary process or revolution which would eliminate class distinctions, end class struggle, and resolve the human disorder. Indeed, the 1989 uprising of students in various parts of China and the savage repression of that uprising by the army demonstrated very clearly the failure of the Chinese system to accomplish either the one or the other.

MARX AND RELIGION

Marx did not, in fact, have a great deal to say about religion. It did not particularly interest him, except that it clearly represented one way of dealing with the miseries of the working classes. As he saw it, religion was part of the oppressive machinery of the bourgeoisie. By promising the workers an indefinitely postponed paradise in return for patient endurance, the priests kept the toiling masses submissive.

Marx had a profound contempt for religion as he perceived it in industrial Britain in the nineteenth century. This contempt comes through repeatedly in the pages of *Capital*. In Section Five, 'The Struggle for a Normal Working Day', his horror at the plight of the ordinary working man trapped in an unending round of labour broken solely by a minimal allowance of time for sleep is apparent:

> Time for education, for intellectual development, for the fulfilling of social functions and for social intercourse, for the free-play of his bodily and mental activity, even the rest time of Sunday (and that in a country of Sabbatarians!) – moonshine! But in its blind unrestrainable passion, its were-wolf hunger for surplus-labour, capital oversteps not only the moral, but even the merely physical maximum bounds of the working day. It usurps the time for growth, development, and healthy maintenance of the body. It steals the time required for the consumption of fresh air and sunlight. It higgles [sic.] over a meal-time, incorporating it where possible with the process of production itself, so that food is given to the labourer as to a mere means of production, as coal is supplied to the boiler, grease and oil to the machinery.[10]

In a footnote he comments:

> In England even now occasionally in rural districts a labourer is condemned to imprisonment for desecrating the Sabbath, by working in his front garden. The same labourer is punished for breach of contract if he remains away from his metal, paper, or glass works on the Sunday, even if it be from a religious whim. The orthodox Parliament will hear nothing of sabbath-breaking if it occurs in the process of expanding capital . . . These 'holy ones,' . . . show their Christianity by the humility with which they bear the overwork, the privations, and the hunger of others.[11]

In all of this Marx's deep anger and his implacable hostility to those powers which dehumanized the working classes is apparent. His was no mere theoretical concern: he portrays *people*, and his concern is with people who appear to have no protector. In biblical terms, he sees them as sheep without a shepherd. At the same time the corrupt state of the Church is such that he cannot bring himself to see any hope of a shepherd for the sheep there. He alone is the good shepherd.

It is worth noting here that Marx always began from society, and developed his analyses and his remedies on the basis of that analysis. It was not his theory which informed his understanding of society, but society which dictated the theory. Of course this inevitably means that Marxist theory, which informs most models of liberation theology, implies an existential hermeneutic in which any authoritative text is subordinated to its contemporary context.

Marx understood why religion appealed to the people, and he saw that religion, although an illusion, pointed beyond itself to a reality:

> Religious suffering is the expression of real suffering and at the same time the protest against real suffering. Religion is the sigh of the oppressed creature, the heart of a heartless world, as it is the spirit of spiritless conditions. It is the opium of the people.
>
> The abolition of religion as the people's illusory happiness is the demand for their real happiness. The demand to abandon illusions about their condition is a demand to abandon a condition which requires illusions. The criticism of religion is thus, in embryo, a criticism of the vale of tears whose halo is religion.[12]

Thus Marx does not merely dismiss religion: he seeks to understand it and the part it plays in making life tolerable for the daily-wage earner. Later on, Lenin turned on those of his followers who thought only in terms of the violent overthrow of religion: religion must be opposed, it must be consigned to oblivion, but that must be done not through idealistic explanation but through a materialistic explanation. Lenin's own paper 'The Attitude of the Workers' Party to Religion' is quite explicit:

> Marxism is materialism. As such, it is as relentlessly hostile to religion as was the materialism of . . . Feuerbach . . . We must combat religion – that is the ABC of all materialism, and consequently of Marxism. But Marxism is not a materialism which has stopped at the ABC. Marxism goes further. It says: We must know how to combat religion, and in order to do so we must explain the source of faith and religion among the masses in a materialist way.[13]

The same passage explains the origin of religion: 'The deepest root of religion today is the socially downtrodden condition of the working masses and their apparently complete helplessness in face of the blind forces of capitalism . . .'[14]

The masses were to be delivered from the clutches of religion by changing the condition which gave rise to the need for religion, not by any violent attack on the Church. Lenin quoted Engels, who had bitterly attacked communists in London who had 'declared war' on religion: 'Engels called their vociferous proclamation of war on religion a piece of stupidity, and stated that such a declaration of war was the best way to revive interest in religion and to prevent it from really dying out.'[15]

Neither Marxism nor its later development Marxism-Leninism has been able to maintain a consistent answer to the question of how religion was to be eliminated. There has been a tendency for Marxism to respond more violently to Christianity than to other religions, and to approach Islam with greater subtlety. Islam demands much more careful handling in the twentieth century, since it is more holistic than Christianity, in particular in that Islam represents a strong political force.

It must further be recognized that Christianity in Russia before the First World War, and in Western Europe generally in the nineteenth century, may readily be perceived as part of the oppressive machinery of government. In Russia the Orthodox Church was hopelessly compromised by its relationship with the

Czarist rulers, while the British and German and Dutch missionaries were seen by many as being part of the machinery of colonialism. Geoffrey Moorhouse has graphically pictured this unsavoury aspect of nineteenth-century missionary endeavour in *The Missionaries*, where he details the use of Royal Navy gunboats in West Africa to further the work of the missionaries.[16]

There is a further reason why Marxism opposes religion: it is itself a religion. Political systems do not normally offer a holistic view of human existence, but Marxism does. It does not only explain the how, it also deals with the why of existence. It is wedded to the concept of evolution, both biological and moral, and through its scientific materialism offers an eschatological dimension to politics. The *eschaton* is not yet, but can be brought in by Marxism, so that in some sense society will be perfected. What is more, Marxism is opposed to long-term syncretism. In the short term an alliance with Islam, as in Somalia, is tolerable, but solely as a means to an end, the displacement of one religion by another.

And finally Marxism is necessarily opposed to Christianity because where the community envisaged in the New Testament actually comes into existence it represents a challenge to the fundamental Marxist dogma of the class struggle. Entirely contrary to what the American school of Church Growth thinking has proposed, the local congregation is a community within which rich and poor, black and white, men and women, old and young are to find a commonality in Christ. The New Testament precisely does *not* propose homogeneous churches, churches within which the congregations have a high level of commonality, excluding others from their fellowship. Instead it proposes a grand breaking down of all sociological barriers.[17] Where Christianity *as religion* confirms class division, as is commonly the case with the state or national churches, Marxism may well find it possible to come to some kind of agreement with it, allowing for its continuation under Marxist scrutiny. But where Christianity *as an eschatological community* exists, Marxism finds its fundamental theoretical basis under threat and responds with some form of persecution.

In its confrontation with militant Christianity Marxism has failed to evolve a methodology which would produce the desired result, the disappearance of religion. The persecution of the Church in China led Western observers to believe that Christianity was all but extinct there. In 1980 the *World Christian Encyclopedia* estimated a mere 1.8 million Christians in a population of some 800 million. In 1985 David Barrett wrote: 'Since then, serious estimates of the size of China's burgeoning house-church movement have mushroomed first to 15 million, then to 50 million, then to 75 million, and now to 98 million.'[18]

The problem of the relationship between Christianity and the Marxist State has been illustrated in terms of the petrol engine. Persecution is like the compression stroke: the explosive mixture in the Church is expelled violently into the community where, far from flickering out, it has a tendency to set the community ablaze. On the other hand, when persecution is relaxed and the churches legitimized, the induction stroke, the new believers are drawn into the churches, where they can be nurtured, energized, and eventually exploded again. The gathered Church can be easily monitored, but it can also disciple and train its members and so enjoy discipleship growth. The scattered Church lacks the formal teaching but can no longer be monitored and enjoys evangelism growth. Either way, the Church offers to Marxist society an alternative lifestyle which is demonstrably a *good* lifestyle, even allowing for the effects of persecution.[19]

A HISTORICAL SURVEY

It is useful to trace Marxism back into the eighteenth century, to the birth of Hegel in 1770, to the American Declaration of Independence in 1776 ('. . . all men are created equal . . . endowed . . . with certain inalienable rights . . .'), but much more significantly to the French Revolution in 1789. As R. Struik comments: 'The French Revolution is one of the most dramatic events in history. It swept away all feudal encumbrances impeding the development of capitalism and bourgeois society . . . the fruits were eventually harvested by the bourgeoisie.'[20]

The rest of Europe trembled at the thought of that same violent revolution being repeated elsewhere. And it was into this context that Marx was born in 1818. His meeting with Engels in 1844 has already been noted, and is in some sense the starting-point of classical Marxism. The *Communist Manifesto*, the foundation document of communism, authored by Marx and Engels, appeared a mere four years after their first meeting, and *Capital* in 1867.

In its first decades Marxism was seen as a movement of the masses, as in that sense a *democratic* movement. The will of the people was paramount, and precisely because it was the will of the masses Marx had the expectation that it would triumph. But he was disappointed: in the event the revolutions in France and Austria and Germany in 1848 were anti-climactic, the new day did not dawn, the working classes were not set free.

Lenin was born Vladimir Ilyich Ulyanov in 1870. Marx died in exile in London in 1883. When Lenin was only seventeen his elder brother was accused of being implicated in a plot to assassinate the Tsar and was executed, a family tragedy that clearly marked the whole of Lenin's life. By 1893 Lenin had already begun his life as a revolutionary, staking a claim to fill the power vacuum left by Marx.

The initial period of the development of the ideas of Marx and Engels was brought to a close by the First World War. The war demonstrated a fallacy in Marx's thinking: the masses, the workers, did not simply abandon their nationalities so as to function across those barriers as one working-class democracy. Instead the working classes of England and France filled the trenches and faced the working classes of Germany. The dream of working-class solidarity evaporated. But the confusion produced by the war provided the opportunity for which Lenin was looking: the October Revolution in Russia in 1917 put Lenin into near-absolute power. He had just seven years to exercise that power.

In this situation Lenin was forced into making radical changes in Marx's theories. Power was transferred pragmatically from the people to the Party. Membership in the Party was limited. The Party became a highly disciplined centralized body, totally obedient to Lenin. Democracy disappeared. The Party ruled on behalf of the people. As Lenin realized at the end of his life, he had been instrumental in recreating most of the worst aspects of Czarist rule.

Lenin died in January 1924. Although communism looks to Marx as its founder, communism today looks far more to Lenin as the man who first applied Marx's principles to a modern state. It was Lenin who designed the model for Marxist rule which has been adopted by later revolutionary leaders across the world. However, it was Stalin, more than any other individual, who hammered out the implications of Marxism-Leninism and who enslaved the Russian peoples under the new chains of an absolutism which even the Czars had not known.

Stalin was born in 1879 in Georgia. He was no intellectual, rising from total obscurity to absolute power through a policy of unremitting ferocity. By the age of thirty-three he was already on the Bolshevik Central Committee, and was rescued from exile in Siberia only through the October Revolution. By 1922 he was General Secretary of the Communist Party, and when Lenin died two years later he was in a position to organize the successive defeat of each of his rivals for power. By 1929 supreme power was his.

Lenin's concept of a totally loyal and unquestioning Party entirely suited Stalin. Opposition to his ideas was crushed. He was soon surrounded by men who were as unforgiving, as unbending, as unswerving in their loyalty to Marxism-Leninism, as he was himself. Marxist dogma informed all he did. Industrialization and collectivization were the pillars of his economic policy, and all who resisted were destroyed. Class struggle was to be seen on every hand. When the peasants (the 'idiocy' of rural life appears again) resisted collectivization he announced a policy of extermination.

The period from 1934 to 1939 has no parallel in Russian history, and perhaps no parallel either in the history of any other great nation. Stalin's potential and actual rivals were eliminated in an extended blood-bath, rendered the more obscene by the readiness of those accused to confess their guilt: 'Millions were arrested, hundreds of thousands executed . . . the climate of atrocity brought about a kind of universal paranoia.'[21]

Among those leaders arrested and executed in 1938 was Bukharin, reinstated by Gorbachev in 1987. The Bolsheviks who had swept Stalin into power disappeared in a welter of blood. Industry heaved its way through the carnage to some kind of progress: 'It did so by methods of mass coercion and complete or partial enslavement, which had as side-effects the ruin of the nation's culture and the perpetuation of a police regime. In these ways Soviet industrialization was probably the most wasteful process of its kind in history.'[22]

Marxism imposed its demands everywhere. Dmitri Shostakovich

was required to write his symphonies in line with proletarian ideology. The poetry of Boris Pasternak was suppressed. The absurdities of Lysenko in the field of genetics became official dogma. Lysenko's theories were beautifully materialistic. Through manipulation of the environment plants acquired new tolerances, new characteristics, and, quite contrary to the facts, Lysenko insisted that these acquired characteristics could be passed on to successive generations of the plants.

For a quarter of a century Stalin wielded absolute power. That power saw Russia through the Second World War with its incredible demands on the Russian peoples, but the collapse of the tyrannical empire followed almost immediately upon the death of Stalin in 1953. The head of Stalin's secret police, Beria, was shot before the year was out. Nikita Khrushchev denounced Stalinism in February 1956, and this was taken in the Eastern European satellite states as an invitation to reform. In October Hungary was in revolt, but the revolt was crushed by Soviet troops sent in to reinforce those already there. The former Prime Minister, Imre Nagy, was executed.

There was something of a lull until the 'Prague Spring' of 1968. Alexander Dubček was elected First Secretary of the Czech Communist Party on 5 January, and Eastern Europe had its first encounter with *Glasnost*. The problems of the inhuman face of communism were for the first time debated openly. The rest of the Warsaw Pact countries watched, waited, and eventually acted. Armed units from Russia, Poland, Hungary, Bulgaria and the German Democratic Republic invaded Czechoslovakia, and the year ended not in a flowering of freedom but in the renewed and bitter frosts of totalitarian Marxism. Dubček was steadily stripped of his posts and marginalized. But the hour produced its hero: in January 1969 the young student Jan Palach publicly set himself on fire in a last and desperate gesture of an implacable opposition to the oppressive power of the Marxists.

The lights would not gleam again for Eastern Europe and its Russian masters until Gorbachev's reforms almost twenty years later.[23] But then the results were dramatic. In Poland the formerly banned Solidarity independent trade union was legitimized, and swept the polls in the election that followed. In Hungary, in an extraordinary act of confession of political oppression and injustice, the body of the former Premier Imre Nagy was exhumed from its unnamed grave and given honoured burial in the presence of vast crowds of people. In November 1989, in a single shattering week, the Berlin Wall was breached, free passage between East and West Germany was sanctioned, Todor Zhivkov, for thirty-five years the master of Bulgaria, was forced to resign, and vast demonstrations in Prague brought democratization to Czechoslovakia. On Christmas Day, the hated Ceausescus, Nicolae and Elena, were shot by a firing squad at the climax of two weeks of bloody fighting in Romania. The great Marxist experiment has proved to be a horrendous failure. Kolakowski was right: it has been 'the greatest fantasy of our century' (above, p. 228).

Inevitably the events in the Eastern Bloc countries had an impact on communism in the rest of Europe. The violence, the cynical overruling of the wishes of theoretically independent nations, perhaps above all the television pictures of the helpless rage of the citizens of Hungary and then of Czechoslovakia and Romania, forced communist parties in France and Germany and Britain to rethink their position. Euro-Communism emerged as an attempt to distance the parties from the Russian violence. The violence had effectively ensured that communism would not attract even the mass support of the workers, who now knew that in fact it was precisely in communist-ruled countries that the workers had the fewest rights. Communism must now move from confrontation to co-operation. Communists would seek to develop a power-sharing base with socialism, a base from which it might then prove possible to gain absolute power. New cover organizations appeared, including the Militant Tendency in the United Kingdom. Communists infiltrated the trade unions at every level. Local government became a target, even the churches, where idealism could be exploited. Euro-Communism no longer talked of barricades in the streets, phraseology which was dangerously evocative of Hungary and Dubček, but of the democratic process.

And yet despite this new direction taken by European communism, there was no outright condemnation of the crushing of the uprisings in Hungary and Czechoslovakia and Romania and Poland and East Germany, or of the invasion of Afghanistan. There could be no such condemnation: Marxism is a science, the unfolding of history is an inevitability, not a contingency.

We must be aware of the error of supposing that behind the communism we have observed there is another communism, the *real* communism, that would give freedom. No Marxism can be constructed which is what it claims to be: historically based, scientifically precise, and predictive.

COMMUNISM IN CHINA

A Historical Overview

It was Chiang Kai-shek (1887–1975) who dragged China into the twentieth century. As a revolutionary he pitted his followers against the old regime of the warlords, entering Peking in 1928. Two years later he announced his conversion to Christianity. The next two decades were concerned firstly with the Japanese invasion and then with the growing challenge of communism. In 1949 he was forced to withdraw to Taiwan.

Chiang Kai-shek had inherited a complex mission situation characterized by the multiplicity of competing missionary societies.[24] This situation was utterly transformed by the new Marxist regime. The Chinese People's Republic was formally proclaimed under Mao Tse-tung on 1 October 1949, and religious matters placed under the authority of a newly constituted Bureau of Religious Affairs.

The ensuing years were remarkably planned to ensure at all times the maximum of uncertainty in the minds of the people. This involved a cyclic approach to publicly espoused policies, which might bear no particular relationship to the ongoing policies of Mao himself. We have, in fact, a pathway for developing Marxism which differs from that found in the Soviet model. Here the route is from Marxism to Marxism-Leninism to Maoism, this last being the result of a dialogue between Marxism-Leninism and the writings of Mao. Two features of Maoism are of importance: it is based on that peasantry which Marx had dismissed as 'idiocy', and it is based on the concept of permanent revolution.

The emphasis on the peasantry clearly relates to the reality of the Chinese situation, but gains in importance from the fact that Mao's early revolutionary experience was in those guerrilla forces of the struggles of the 1920s which consisted largely of peasants. Mao knew this class, and knew both its strengths and its weaknesses.

The peasants were firmly built into his system, and it was their core role which in some measure determined the second distinctive feature of his philosophy, the rolling revolution. Continuous revolution had two benefits for Mao: it maintained a class division within China sufficient to ensure that there could be no concerted movement against the leadership. But it also kept that leadership permanently insecure: he seemed determined to avoid that process of bourgeois transformation that had so penetrated and emasculated Marxism-Leninism in the Soviet Union.

Destabilizing movements were instituted by Mao through the Rectification Campaign of 1942, the establishing of the Chinese People's Republic in 1949, the Great Leap Forward (ostensibly aimed at decentralizing the economy), only seven years later, in 1957,[25] and less than a decade later the Cultural Revolution of 1966–9, with the Thought Propaganda Teams mobilized to reindoctrinate the academic world. A further decade brought Mao's death, and renewed uncertainty following the trial of the so-called Gang of Four (one of whom was Mao's widow) and an apparent programme of liberalization. This was again brought into question by the huge pro-democracy student demonstrations throughout China in 1989, demonstrations which were brutally suppressed: the massacre of hundreds of students in Peking's Tiananmen Square[26] was reminiscent of the worst days of Mao's destabilizing phases. The aged Deng Xiaoping and the Prime Minister Li Peng introduced a new cycle of mass arrests, public denunciations, hysteria, and executions, not only among the students, but also among the peasantry, the masses of the capital and of other major cities, who had joined in the demand for democracy.

Here again the failure of Marxism, of Marxist-Leninism and of Maoism to resolve the human disorder is unmistakable. It is quite clear that whatever the ostensible purpose of the Chinese leadership might have been, in fact it was there, like other hierarchies, to guard its own interests. The voice of the people, once the noble toiling masses, was designated the voice of hooligans, of imperialists, of counter-revolutionaries.

Religion in China

Mao Tse-tung was an original Marxist theorist. But Mao was also an empire-builder, totally unprepared to allow China to become a mere Soviet satellite on the pattern of the Eastern Europe satellites. The Sino-Soviet dispute emerged steadily through the 1960s. In 1956 Mao warmly approved the Soviet intervention in Hungary. In 1968 he roundly condemned the Soviet intervention in Czechoslovakia. In between those dates the division between the two communist superpowers had appeared, the difference had grown, and two competing Marxist states stood in confrontation.[27]

Mao was totally committed to dialectical materialism, determined on the one hand to eliminate idealism, but on the other hand to accommodate the dialectic to what he perceived to be Chinese culture. And that culture was, in the broadest sense of the word, a religious culture.

He distinguished between spontaneous religions, which might be said to arise out of the experience of *dukkha*, and what might be termed feudalistic religions, which are specific tools of the oppressing classes.[28] Spontaneous religion is the religion of the masses, resulting from their ignorance, and including a fair measure of superstition, and was to be countered, in general, by propaganda, by teaching, by the spread of Maoist ideas, but specifically not by legislation or coercion.

Feudalistic religions, however, are in a different position. They represent part of the class struggle and must be countered accordingly. A clear distinction is to be made between the freedom to worship, which applies to the spontaneous religions, and the freedom to promote counter-revolutionary activity, which is no part of Maoism.

The result of this little-understood distinction between two types of religion was that all missionaries were expelled, and the churches which they had established were closed as being examples of bourgeois exploitation of the people. The Christian Three-Self Patriotic Movement was then constituted to oversee the legalized Christian religious activities of the people. This movement was consciously and overtly anti-American.

The occasional statements of the leaders of the Three-Self Movement on religion in China were uniformly positive. In 1965 Burhan Shahidi, President of the China Islamic Association claimed: 'All Moslems in China today enjoy full religious freedom.'[29] The Chairman of the Catholic National Patriotic Association claimed, in December 1973: 'For the past ten years, the 3,000,000 Chinese Catholics, like the rest of the Chinese people, have been living a democratic, free, and increasingly happy life.'[30]

However, the fact is that in 1966 the last seminary, in Nanking, was closed, and the Cultural Revolution of 1969 brought once again the experience of persecution to the churches. The 1975 Constitution made the changed situation clear: Article 28 stated that the Chinese people should have 'the freedom to practice a religion, the freedom not to practice a religion, *and to propagate atheism*', a clear departure from the 1954 Constitution.

It was the death of Chairman Mao in the following year that initiated what appeared to be a liberalizing process. A new openness towards the rest of the world emerged. Trade barriers were dropped, trade delegations welcomed. And in all of this the Christian Church flourished. As we have seen already, estimates of the size of the Church in China escalated, and although the numbers can be estimates only, in his Annual Statistical Table on Global Mission for 1987 David Barrett could comment: 'Thirteen large cities have baptized church members numbering over ten percent of the population. House churches are now known to exist in virtually every one of China's 2010 administrative counties. A vital, evangelizing church has come into existence almost everywhere throughout the nation.'[31]

MARXISM AND THE HUMAN DISORDER

Julius Nyerere may be allowed the final comment on a dogma which has been exported from Russia into China (and from there to Tanzania), and to Cuba (and from there to Ethiopia):

> This attempt to create a new religion out of socialism is absurd. It is not scientific, and it is almost certainly not Marxist – for however combatant and quarrelsome a socialist Marx was, he never claimed to be an infallible divinity! Marx was a great thinker. He gave a brilliant analysis of the industrial capitalist society in which he lived . . . but he was not God. The years have proved him wrong in certain respects just as they have proved him right in others. Marx did not write revealed truth . . .[32]

In particular, Marx's analysis of the human condition was inadequate, and as a consequence his solution has proved to be no solution at all. The workers of the world have not united, and, indeed, show no signs of doing so. Instead there has been a process of migration between the social classes, with Marx's 'day-labourers' becoming 'upwardly mobile' and taking advantage of the concessions made to their relative powerlessness by the relatively powerful through trade unions and through shared management.

It is demonstrably the case that Marxism has failed to abolish the bourgeoisie. As Mao was quick to recognize, Marxism-Leninism in the Soviet Union succeeded only in producing a new pseudo Marxist bourgeois leadership: few could fail to recognize in Gorbachev the characteristics of the bourgeoisie.

But worse still, Marxism has evolved into one of the most absolute and repressive political systems in human history. Established, in principle, to represent the aspirations of the masses, it became successively in the Soviet Union, in Eastern Europe, in Ethiopia, and, possibly most horrifying of all in the China of 1989, a machine to deny that measure of human liberty and dignity which was taken for granted in the despised Western democracies.

But the true irony of the situation faced by world communism is the reversal of Marx's own expectation that under the relentless pressure of communisim religion would wither away. At the end of the 1980s *communism* in the Soviet Union and Eastern Europe was withering away, and *Maoism* in China was entirely discredited. By contrast, in each area the Church emerged from its severe testing immeasurably stronger than when its failings were first challenged by Karl Marx and his disciples.

Strangely, liberation theology has turned to Marxism for its analysis of society, and for its revolutionary praxis, both of which must now be considered.

18 Liberation Theology: An Alternative Christian Missiology

INTRODUCTION

Although it is convenient to write of the *theology* of liberation, it would be more accurate to recognize that in fact we are confronted with a non-homogeneous collection of *theologies*. The movement has coherence in so far as it has been primarily a Latin American movement, directed against right-wing oppression of the powerless and challenging the traditional theologies of the Churches in general and of the Roman Catholic Church in particular.

Historically, the movement looks back to the period of colonization of Latin America by Spain and Portugal, and the associated role of the Catholic Church, perceived as supportive of the colonizers.[1] This period extends from the fifteenth to the nineteenth century, when the advance to independence of Latin American countries began. In the twentieth century this process was completed, but the Church was left with no clear idea of its role. Its bishops had not, on the whole, sided with those who campaigned for independence. Once independence was attained the general inertia of the Church led to a resumption of the earlier relationship, but now with the mainly right-wing leaders of the independent countries.

A second strand in the development of liberation theology may be seen in the dominant role played by North American missionary societies in Latin America. Much as British missionaries in Africa and Asia had been perceived as part of the expansionist aspirations of Britain, so American missionaries were seen in South America as part of the economic imperialism of the United States of America. In particular, the theology of the missionaries was seen to be in good measure culturally determined rather than biblically based, and to omit issues of enormous importance to the sub-continent. Among these issues was that of the nature of the appropriate Christian response to systematic oppression. Since North American missionaries did not encounter such oppression in their own country, they had no theology of oppression to offer Latin America.

It must at once be added that although these missionaries did not *encounter* such oppression in their own country, this is not to say that such oppression did not exist there. On the contrary, the rise of black theology in North America, formalized by writers such as James Cone,[2] made it clear that the phenomenon of oppression of the powerless by the powerful, and specifically of the black by the white, was one common to the entire American continent, and would quickly become one for the United Kingdom also, where, again, most missionaries had no theology of oppression and a remarkable blindness to its existence.

The rise and the comparative decline of liberation theology may be charted by reference to the meetings of CELAM, Consejo Episcopal Latino Americano: CELAM I in 1955, CELAM II in 1968, and CELAM III in 1979.[3] The Council was set up with the task of interpreting Catholic documents to the Latin churches. The 1955 gathering saw a beginning of liberationist thinking, but the Medellín Council in 1968 witnessed something like triumphalism, with an absolute priority given to social problems, a rejection of Western-style capitalism, the embracing of socialism and a commitment to change the structures of society so as to bring some measure of power to the poor. At Puebla in 1979 the atmosphere was more cautious, the Pope had issued a warning against 'human, rational, truth' and the delegates initiated a review of the theology they had begun to create. The process of official opposition to the theology of liberation, an opposition actively furthered by Pope John Paul II,[4] has continued.

EIGHT FUNDAMENTAL PROPOSITIONS OF LIBERATION THEOLOGY[5]

1. That the institutional Church, and in particular the Catholic Church, has taken sides with the powerful against the powerless. As a result theology has served the Church, to the neglect of the needs of the powerless who are outside the Church. This in turn leads to a demand for the liberation of theology.[6]

Traditional theology is perceived as a deliberately limited exegetical exercise. Themes central to Scripture have been marginalized, and attention focused on issues which are of theoretical value, but arguably of no practical importance. Two models of the Church's leadership emerge: the North American model, where the theologians surround the Church, looking in; and the Latin American model, where the theologians surround the Church, but are looking outward.

That this can still be said despite the enormous missionary outreach of the North American Churches is quite remarkable. It can meaningfully be said, however, because in the main the perception of the North American missionaries has been of people in relation to the Church, not of people in relation to the world in which they live. Soteriology has focused on a gathering into the Church, and scarcely at all on the problem of the human predicament as a this-world phenomenon as well as an eschatological problem. It is significant that the three volumes on the Christian mission and social progress by J. S. Dennis,[7] published at the turn of the century, which surveyed the contribution of mission to resolving social evils, were entirely unknown to evangelical missionaries who constituted by far the majority of the North American missionary force. Waldron Scott's *Bring Forth Justice*[8] brought the whole question of a wider theology before the evangelical churches, but it was only published in 1980.

2. That in contrast with the institutional Church, God is decisively on the side of the powerless. This divine priority is perceived particularly in the Old Testament exodus, where God intervenes on behalf of the powerless Israelites against the oppressive power structures of Egypt, and in the incarnation of the New Testament, where God chooses not merely incarnation, but incarnational powerlessness.

3. That the domain of sin, the *hamartiosphere*, must be enlarged from that perceived by traditional theologies, to include social and sociological sin. Sin is to be perceived as humanity is to be perceived, holistically. Humanity is essentially gregarious; to be human is to form part of group existence, part of society. Sin is not merely what one individual does to another individual, nor even what one individual does to God, if, indeed, such a formulation of sin can have any meaning, but it is also what society does to

individuals, what society does to society, and even what individuals may do to society.

4. That the exodus is to be seen as paradigmatic for the understanding of the Bible, and that in using this paradigm we shall discover a firm basis for a Christian *praxis*, action, which might bring a contemporary and parallel liberation experience to society.

5. That a new epistemology is needed, an epistemology which validates any theology through the *praxis* it produces. To know a truth is to act on that truth, and to fail to act is to demonstrate a failure of knowledge. Truth must be rescued from its arid isolation in propositional theology, and must be transferred to the arena of everyday living.

6. A hermeneutic which starts from the Bible must be displaced by a new hermeneutic which starts from the world. The traditional hermeneutic can of its very nature do nothing but support tradition.[9] It is reflection on the contemporary world that must inform a biblical theology: any *prior* reference to Scripture can only lead to an irrelevant agenda for theology.

7. The traditional interpretation of the passion narrative as representing exclusively or even *primarily* vicarious atonement must be replaced by an interpretation which sees *also* the ultimate identification of God with man in the experience of undeserved and apparently meaningless suffering;[10] in fact in the experience of the oppression of the powerless God by a powerful political force.

8. That the confusion of Western theologians is in part due to their failure to recover the original *events*, the exodus, the passion, and their contenting themselves with exegeting *texts*, which are, in fact, overlaid with the theological reflections of the early Church. Following Paul Ricoeur, it is insisted that we must return to the *event* as primary.

FOUR HERMENEUTICAL PRINCIPLES[11]

Liberation theology demands that theology be approached in a new way. Examination of the principles enumerated above will quickly show that a new hermeneutic is implied, a hermeneutic which has four strands to it.

The Epistemological Base

The statement by Jose Bonino that 'Action is itself the truth' and that 'Truth is at the level of history, not in the realm of ideas'[12] focuses attention on the now-present world as the stage on which Christianity must be worked out, rather than on any supposed or expected new and better world. Any meaningful 'God-reference' must necessarily be my neighbour, not an abstract theological proposition, and any theology is assessed not by its logical coherence but by the praxis it supports.

The emphasis on praxis does, probably, originate with Karl Marx, who contrasted his own intentions with those of mere theorists: 'The philosophers have only interpreted the world: the point is to change it.'[13] Marx dismissed equally both religion and philosophy because of their inconsequential (literally) investigations into human existence. Marx required that thought should lead to belief and that belief should lead to action, but that actionless belief was a contradiction.

Of course neither Marx nor Bonino believed that in the literal sense action *is* the truth. But action betrays the truth about the actor. Praxis enables the observer to reinterpret the linguistic phrases of the one who acts. Lenin himself admitted the limitation of this subjective process of reinterpretation: 'The criterion of praxis can never, in fact, fully prove or disprove any human view.'[14]

But there is a danger in this admission – the danger that we will ignore the praxeological emphasis in the teaching of Jesus: a good tree will produce good fruit, a thornbush does not produce grapes (Matt. 7.15–23). The context in which this particular teaching is set is that of the need to differentiate between false prophets and true prophets, and it is not distorting this context to apply the principle to Christians in general and to Christian teachers in particular. Taking the argument one step further back, we may surely assume that proper exegesis of Scripture will produce appropriate behaviour, not merely appropriate and consistent theology. A theology that fails to produce action cannot be biblical theology. It may be *consistent*, but it would lack the essence of biblical theology, a validating dynamic of the Spirit.

Scripture is Secondary to Event

The linguistic theories of Paul Ricoeur are used so that the text of the Bible may be used as a source for the recovery of the all-important event.[15]

Ricoeur produced a spiral model (see also pp. 166–7 above) for what might be termed a process hermeneutic. The theory itself is relatively unobjectionable: there is necessarily a time interval between any event and the recording of that event. In that time interval, however small it may be, a process of reflection is initiated, and that process is then reflected in the ultimate text. So between the event of the exodus and the writing of the biblical account of the exodus there was a long period of time, in which Israel reflected on the event. Eventually event became a word, and at that point the text was more or less frozen.

However, although the text was frozen, time did not stand still. And with the passage of time words took on new meanings, meanings they did not have when the text was produced. There is, then, a growing *polysemy*, even with words which in the original text were unambiguous. The task of hermeneutics is, then, to get back behind the word to the event, stripping away both the polysemous interference of later centuries following the production of the word, and the reflections of Israel in the period between the event and the creation of the word.

But there is still more to Ricoeur's hermeneutics. To this process hermeneutic he adds the contribution of a recognition of the central importance of *symbol*: 'It is in the symbol that language is revealed in its strongest force'.[16] It is true that events in religious history become symbols and as symbols begin to display an autonomy that in some measure distinguishes them from the real events from which the symbols have been created. Thus exodus as a *symbol* is quite distinct from the exodus as *event* and may influence us in distinctive ways precisely because of the power of the symbol. Rubem Alves saw the need for modern man to recapture *power*, power to cope with and then to transform human existence: 'Certain symbols derive their success from their power to convoke human beings, who use them to define their situation and articulate a common project of life.'[17] This power can come through a reinterpretation of the *event* in the light of our contemporary needs.

According to liberation theology the approach to the word must take second place to a consideration of the human context. Reversing the traditional evangelical approach to Scripture, an absolute priority is given to the environment into which it is to be introduced. Thus the environment sets the agenda for any theology, and the theology will produce the symbolism which may in turn supply the power to the people to transform that environment.

On all of this two things must be said. Firstly, that it is simplistic to talk of event as preceding word. In a limited sense that is, of course, true, and it cannot be otherwise. But in the fuller sense of an inspired Word that is not true. Neither the exodus nor the exile, neither the incarnation nor the ascension, nor any other biblically recorded event, is without a prior and prophetic word. Scripture is more than post-event commentary: it is also pre-event prophecy, so that event actually occurs in fulfilment of prophecy, which may in turn be used to interpret the event. In other words, the recovery of the event does *not* depend on a critique of the post-event word, but on a total awareness of the cotext: pre-event prophecy, event history, post-event commentary.

The second thing to be said is that there is a fundamental hermeneutical principle that the contemporary *significance* of an event may only be determined out of an understanding of the *meaning* of the event in its original setting. To understand the significance of the exodus for society today we must first identify its meaning for the author of the biblical record, and by extension for the first readers of that record. It is a methodological error to begin from contemporary society, to observe its needs, and then to proceed to reconstruct the exodus event in terms of contemporary needs.

The Exodus is the Hermeneutical Key to Scripture[18]

In 1970 Rubem Alves described the exodus as 'The centre and hermeneutical principle of all biblical language'.[19] This has generally represented the viewpoint of the mainstream of liberation theology, and although caution is always needed when any theologian claims to have found *the* key to an understanding of the Bible, it is clear that on the one hand Israel perceived the exodus as the great event in their history, and on the other hand that

Christians saw the passion as the second focus of that ellipse of world history of which the exodus was the first focus.

It must be said that even Alves has not remained convinced of the central role of the exodus in interpreting Scripture. In his autobiographical contribution to *Frontiers of Theology in Latin America*, dated to 1975, Alves has moved from his earlier preoccupation with the exodus to a new interest in the captivity:

> Now, in trying to find meaning in our biographies, we find that we have been steadily beating a retreat. Our backs are to the wall, and there is no escape. The exodus of which we dreamed earlier has miscarried. Instead we now find ourselves in a situation of exile and captivity.[20]

By 1981 Alves had moved further in his preoccupation with the exile as the focus for biblical interpretation. The success of the scientific world-view, the human preoccupation with *coherence*, with *efficiency*, with teleology, usefulness, was perceived to have in effect eliminated mystery, wonder, uncertainty, and with them God had disappeared. The human race is in exile.[21]

Thus Alves has moved the focus of his thinking from Exodus to Isaiah, from Egypt to Babylon. More recently, however, there has been a tendency in liberation theology to return to the exodus paradigm as a starting-point.

In a more formal way, Enrique Dussel identifies six fundamental *categories*, which give rise to nine[22] *relations*, which then constitute the exodus paradigm.

The six categories are:

1 The dominators, the sinners, the oppressors: Egypt and the Pharaonic class (and their army? and their civil servants? and their entrepreneurs?);
2 The oppressed, the just(!), the slaves;
3 The prophet;
4 God;
5 The journey from Egypt, through the desert, and its accompanying testings;
6 The promised land.

The relations are:

1 The fact of domination, or sin;
2 The cry of the people to God;

3 The calling of God to the prophet;
4 The challenge to the oppressor;
5 The challenge to the oppressed;
6 Departure, liberation;
7 The prophetic critique of the entire people;
8 Entry into the promised land and the construction of a new system;
9 The resulting kingdom, a new community, but itself subject to failure and division.

The entire *schema* evokes a sense of unease, in spite of the confidence of its promoters, who project an aura of objectivity about it. The unease probably stems from earlier encounters with the same paradigmatic text as handled by the pietists, who allegorized the narrative so that it became the paradigm of the sanctification process. The unease is heightened when Alves, for example, identifies the same three stages in the journey perceived by the pietists: Egypt as past, the past slavery; the desert as the intermediate time, the present unsatisfactory, paradoxical, life; and Canaan as the utopian future, the experience of deliverance from sin, of 'victorious Christian living'.[23]

Following the earlier principle of liberation hermeneutics, the relevance of the exodus would be heightened if it could be shown that the world, or the Church, or the poor, on whose behalf God acts, is in an exodus situation. One might then move from the contemporary situation to the exodus so as to understand what should be done now. But while admitting that the powerless of Latin America are oppressed, it is less clear that they are in an oppression-in-Egypt situation. If we go back to the exodus text and cotext it is clear that Israel is displaced. Israel's place is Canaan, not Egypt, and Israel must be delivered from Egypt into Canaan. It is, as the later prophets perceived, in Yahweh's sovereign call to Abraham, and then in Yahweh's sovereign deliverance of Israel out of Egypt, and in Yahweh's sovereign granting of a covenant-law, that Israel is constituted. Israel is to be constituted as a nation for the task of bringing God's Servant into the world, and Israel's deliverance from Egypt appears to be part of a programme designed to demonstrate the total sovereignty of God, both in giving that task to Israel and in enabling Israel to fulfil the task. In other words, deliverance from Egypt had more to it than a response to one example of a localized oppression, which was, after all, only one of many contemporary manifestations of oppression.

If we examine the text of the exodus as formal discourse, we find two important features. The first is that the apparent plot of the discourse is frustrated. The second is that the peak of the discourse is correspondingly displaced.

The plot of the discourse is basically simple:

Jacob-Israel in Canaan;
Joseph persecuted by his brothers;
Exile to Egypt;
Persecution, and appeal to Yahweh for deliverance;
The birth of a deliverer;
The approach to Pharaoh and Pharaoh's intransigence;
Exodus;
(Triumphant return, now a mighty nation, to Canaan).

This last event does not take place. Instead we have an insertion:

The giving of the law;
Rebellion, idolatry;
Forty years of wandering;
Return of a new generation to Canaan.

and this entire event now becomes the starting-point of a long history of Yahweh's dealings with a fundamentally rebellious people. The history in fact leads to a remnant theology, with its culmination in the ultimate obedience of just one Servant of the Lord, a theology which has its clearest expression in Isaiah 40—55.

In the exodus text we have a succession of peaks and troughs. The low points are the betrayal of Joseph and the rebellion at Kadesh. The high-points are the Passover meal, the giving of the law, and the entry into Canaan. Of the three high-points the last is certainly the least significant. The edge has been taken off it by the rebellion of the people and the subsequent exile in the desert. The oppressed of Egypt are not the same as those who enter Canaan.

Any exegesis of the relevant texts must take this analysis of the discourse as a whole into account. The discourse appears to place an emphasis more on 'the glory of the Lord', his majesty, his holiness, his unapproachableness, his otherness, than on the deliverance of the people (who, indeed, are *not* delivered *to* but only *from*). A people, a nation, such as it is, *is* created, but that nation is not idealized, it does not even remain independent: rather its continued existence serves primarily to reflect the utter *otherness* of God. God is holy, the nation is not. And this emphasis is reflected in the cultic concerns of the exodus narrative. Repeatedly Israel is called out to worship Yahweh, specifically to worship 'on this mountain' (Exod. 3.12). In fact sixteen chapters of Exodus relate events covering the period of the arrival of the Israelites at Sinai, and Moses' final descent from the mountain. Throughout those chapters the emphasis remains on the holiness of God and the means provided for Israel to worship him. It is too easy for us to dismiss as irrelevant the chapters which deal with the priests and their dress, and the furniture for the tabernacle. To the redactor it was all clearly important, it did not detract from the thrust of his narrative.

And finally, as has often been pointed out, the exodus event *cannot* be used paradigmatically to encourage a violent response to oppression.[24] In the exodus it is Yahweh who responds, not Israel. It is Yahweh who delivers the people with a mighty outstretched arm. And in the New Testament polarity it is again Yahweh who acts to deliver his people, and their attempts to defend God's Servant by violent means are indignantly repudiated. It is in and through the most extreme *experiencing* of the apparent meaninglessness of life that the human disorder is resolved.

It may well be the case that in the Western tradition theologians have been unduly obsessed with one aspect of the passion to the exclusion of others, but what is clear both in the exodus and in the passion is the dependence of the oppressed on God. It is to Yahweh that they uniformly look for deliverance.

The Cross is to be Understood as more than Vicarious Atonement

The hermeneutical ideas of Ricoeur are introduced here to facilitate a reassessment of the event of the cross. According to Jon Sobrino, the event of the cross has already been overlaid by post-event assessment, so that the word ultimately produced can only be seen as a base from which event must be reconstructed. He puts it clearly:

In the various descriptions of Jesus' death in the New Testament we can already detect a trend toward mollifying [sic] the death in theological terms. In Mark's version, the most primitive and original one, his death is described in terms of tragedy . . . But in the Gospels of Luke and John we can detect efforts to soften the edges of this scandalous happening . . . In Luke's Gospel the scandalous phrase of Psalm 22 is replaced with the triumphant strains of Psalm 31 . . . The Gospel of John does not mention Psalm 22 either. There Jesus dies majestically, completely in charge of the situation right up to the very end . . . The point we want to emphasize here is that the event of Jesus' death itself begins to lose its cutting edge in the very first efforts to interpret it . . .[25]

Sobrino points to Anselm as the theologian responsible for imposing on the passion the categories of vicarious satisfaction. These, insists Sobrino, are foreign concepts:

In the background of his view are categories derived from the legal system of Germanic tribes . . . One seeks to arrive at a knowledge of the cross on the basis of some previously held conception of God, when, in fact, one should try to arrive at God on the basis of Jesus' cross.[26]

Sobrino is not alone in his criticism of Anselm's theology. Leonardo Boff agrees:

The interpretation of the death of Christ as sacrifice is one among many. The New Testament texts themselves do not allow this interpretation to be absolutized as it has been in the history of the faith within the Latin Church . . .

Has the death of Christ, considered in itself, theological relevance for us today? Yes, it has . . . The universal meaning of the life and death of Christ . . . is that he sustained the fundamental conflict of human existence to the end: he wanted to realize the absolute meaning of this world before God, in spite of hate, incomprehension, betrayal and condemnation to death.[27]

The central position of liberation theology is best summarized in Sobrino's Thesis Thirteen:

On the cross of Jesus God himself is crucified. The Father suffers the death of the Son, and takes upon himself all the pain and suffering of history. In this ultimate solidarity with humanity he reveals himself as the God of love, who opens up a hope and a future

256

through the most negative side of history. Thus Christian existence is nothing else but a process of participating in this same process whereby God loves the world, and hence is the very life of God.[28]

The Christology of the liberation theologians clearly owes a great deal to Jürgen Moltmann, and in particular to his *The Crucified God*, published in 1972.[29] The model that emerges does not exclude a soteriological Jesus, nor, indeed, an eschatological Jesus, but it does restore to Christianity a Jesus of identification. At the cross Jesus *does* share in our experience of *dukkha*, of the unfairness, the unsatisfactoriness, of life, and does so to a degree unknown to the rest of creation.

And so when we cry out to God that life is not fair we may do so in the knowledge that he understands, and in liberation terms stands beside us, beside all powerless humanity, and does so as one of us.

AN ASSESSMENT

Negatively, it must be said that the hermeneutics of liberation theology allow for such a subjectivity in handling the relevant texts as will yield the meanings and significances wished for them. The exodus narrative *is* important to an understanding of the Bible as a whole, but it is not primarily a liberation narrative. It focuses rather on the glory of God, and on the corresponding duty of his people to worship him in humble submission.

We are probably misunderstanding the liberation theologians if we suppose them to identify the materially poor as being the saints, and the materially rich as being the sinners: a more nuanced position must be held, and is probably intended by them.[30] God is decisively on the side not of any one sociological class, but of all who are oppressed. He alone *is* justice. But the criticism of the North Atlantic Church in general and of the missionaries in particular is, certainly in its wider application to world mission, seriously prejudiced. As Stephen Neill commented in a major work devoted to the whole question of the relationship between missions and colonialism, and published as far back as 1966:

> From the days of Las Casas in New Spain to the days of the Anglican Bishops in East Africa at the time of the forced labour ordinances, there has been a memorable succession of missionaries who were

not afraid to fight their own governments, and to jeopardize their own comfort and reputation for the sake of what they understood to be justice to those for whom they could speak and who could not speak for themselves.[31]

The use of organized violence by the Church cannot be justified, even if it is arguable that the use of violence by the State can be justified. The general question of the use of violence by Christians must be separated from the question of pacifism. It is *possible* to find justification for Christians, in obedience to government, engaging in war. It is similarly *possible* to think of individual Christians responding to an individual act of violence (or threatened or attempted violence, such as rape) with violence. No recreation of the event of the exodus, however, can be used to justify the New Testament Church as Church engaging in violence. Indeed, such acts of violence committed by the Church could only serve to *increase* the world's experience of *dukkha*.

However, there can be little doubt that liberation theology has drawn the attention of the Western Church to a prominent theme which runs through Scripture, and which has been neglected by many missionaries. Thus Harold Lindsell, in what might be described as a standard text for North American evangelical missionaries, *An Evangelical Theology of Missions*,[32] almost entirely omits reference to an appropriate missionary response to that injustice which the missionary would most surely encounter. The theme of God's care for the oppressed is once more on the agenda for all Christians, but it appears likely that the theme will find expression through a theology of the poor (see Chapter 15, above) rather than through any of the current expressions of liberation theology.

PART FOUR

Meaninglessness and Mission

19 Meaninglessness and Mission

INTRODUCTION

It is the common experience of humanity that between the two apparent boundaries of human existence, birth and death, life is characterized by 'unsatisfactoriness', by *dukkha*. Life appears to be without ultimate meaning. The apparently random intrusion of disease and death, the apparently inexplicable occurrence of accident, whether on the micro-scale in a largely personal experience, or on the macro-scale in an experience of a major national disaster, requires us either to accept that life is meaningless (and so to an acceptance of some ultimate form of existentialism) or to seek a reinterpretation of the human condition through religion or revelation.

Religion has been understood here as a systematic response to the fundamental questions of life, offering both answers to the questions, and so constructing a specific world-view, and a more or less systematic lifestyle appropriate to the answers and the world-view. Religions, then, serve to enable their adherents to cope with *dukkha*. The Hindu in the shanty township of Bombay will understand that his misery is the consequence of his conduct in previous existences, and must be appropriately embraced and endured if a better reincarnation is to be attained. The Muslim will recognize that there is no such thing as an accident, that all is positively willed by Allah, and that as a Muslim the appropriate response to every experience of life, and therefore the proper response to personal tragedy, is submission. In African Traditional Religion it will be understood that famine is the response of the spirit world to neglected human duty, and the *shaman* will be consulted to make possible the determination of the appropriate action to be taken to remedy the situation. In prosperity theology financial collapse will be seen as the inevitable consequence of a lack of faith in the Word of God, and specifically as a failure to entrust to God the 'seed corn' of the tithe; restoration of the tithe will probably be sufficient to bring prosperity back again.

In all of this any religion will be 'successful' in so far as its philosophy seriously grapples with, responds to, and provides explanations of the entire range of potential *dukkha* experiences encountered by its adherents, and in so far as the adherents are aware of, and are able to understand those explanations, and find the explanations convincing. Since many of the explanations of *dukkha* are generalizing explanations, it may not be possible rigorously to demonstrate either their strengths or their weaknesses. If a Hindu suffers, it is not required of Hinduism that it shows specifically for what action in which previous existence this experience is the consequence. In prosperity theology it is not required that any specific failure to honour Scripture should be identified as the cause of some current loss of prosperity, still less what specific action, in accordance with the theology, is *guaranteed* to remedy the situation.

And it must be recognized that the vast majority of humanity simply lacks either the energy or the leisure to philosophize about the meaninglessness of life. Undernourished, exploited, working long hours, plagued by a multitude of debilitating diseases, they necessarily live out their lives not merely one day at a time, but often one hour at a time. The *awareness* of *dukkha* as a problem is in a sense a luxury for the prosperous. And yet even from the outside it may be possible for us to perceive the meaninglessness of life for others who cannot see it for themselves.

Each religion, then, offers to its adherents an explanation of the apparent meaninglessness of life, constructs a world-view, and requires an appropriate lifestyle appropriate to the explanation. A religion may be ethnically restricted or it may be a missionary religion, in which case the same world-view and the same lifestyle may be offered to all. Few of the Traditional Religions (African, Indian, Chinese) have been missionary, and until the present century Hinduism could be characterized as the religion of the Indus valley or, more broadly, the religion of India.

In the case of Old Testament Israel a mid-way position was taken up, where the physical descendant of Abraham was required to submit to the full requirements of *Torah*, while something less was required of the 'stranger within the gate'. We should be careful to understand this not as an additional *burden* placed on the descendant of Abraham, but as a greater *privilege* accorded to the descendant of Abraham. In modern Orthodox Judaism two quite distinct ways of salvation are identified for the Jew and for the Gentile – the full privileges of the Torah covenant for the Jew, and the lesser privileges of the Noachic covenant for the Gentile:

> Judaism does not actively proselytise because it does not see the need to do so. 'The righteous of all nations have a share in the world to come', said the Rabbis. The Jew can say to mankind, 'You don't have to be Jewish to enter into a relationship with God; you just have to live a righteous life.' Judaism defines righteousness in terms of the seven Noachide laws and sees these as the basis of a moral and spiritual life.[1]

In general Judaism has not been a missionary religion, although Jesus' characterization of the Pharisees as those who traversed sea and land to make a single proselyte (Matt. 23.15) is a reminder that that has not always been the case. Of that time Douglas Hare comments: 'The eagerness with which proselytes were sought and the success of such efforts are attested by pagan, Jewish and Christian writers of the period.'[2]

From the first post-resurrection appearances of Jesus the Christian Church has been of its essence a missionary Church. Both Peter (with some reluctance) and Paul were committed to one gospel for both Jew and Gentile. There was salvation in Jesus and nowhere else. There was no salvation to be found in the plethora of religions on offer around the Mediterranean basin. Gods constructed by human hands were no gods at all. The Christians were confident that in Christ God had not merely *spoken* to all humanity: he had himself come among them with the ultimate authoritative response to the human condition. In the past God had spoken at various times and in various ways through the prophets. It might be argued that other religions had their prophets too. But this was different. In Christ God had come to deal with *dukkha*, to share it, to embrace the apparent meaninglessness of life, to know for himself the ultimate apparent meaninglessness represented by the apparent abandoning of the one good man to an undeserved suffering by the theoretically just and loving God. At the cross Jesus submits himself to it. That cross and the person fastened to it were the measure both of the ultimate hideousness of the human condition and of the radical salvation which would in some measure affect every aspect of the human predicament.

THE EXPERIENCE OF MEANINGLESSNESS

The actual domain of meaninglessness, of undeserved pain and suffering, of alienation, is vast, identified in some measure by the characteristic response 'It isn't fair', sometimes by an irrational desire to lash out, to cry out, even though there appears to be nothing to lash out at, no one to cry out to. And this, too, is part of the *dukkha* experience.

The first area of the domain involves the physical aspects of life, and particularly includes the experience of illness, disease, and ultimately involves the anticipation of death, the experience of death, or coping with all the concomitants of the death of another. It involves bereavement, loneliness, the frustration of hopes, the pain of being unable to share in or bear or alleviate another's suffering. Paul Sangster unforgettably records the words of his father, the Methodist preacher W. E. Sangster, when Paul was desperately ill in hospital: 'I can't help you. Why can't I help you? Son, I'd go to hell for you if it would help . . .'[3]

There is the apparent meaninglessness of mental illness, so often misunderstood and misrepresented and even feared by others. And there is the fearful experience of possession,[4] an experience to be carefully distinguished from normal mental illness, caused not by some disease or physical damage, but by a destructive invasion from the Second Kingdom. The New Testament is careful to distinguish between the two types of disease. Jesus is stated to have given his followers 'power and authority to drive out all demons *and* to cure diseases' (Luke 9.1), and Luke also records of Jesus that 'all those who had any that were sick with various diseases brought them to him; and he laid his hands on every one of them and healed them. And demons also came out of many . . .' (Luke 4.40, RSV).

In Matthew 10 there is a significant saying attributed to Jesus in which four categories of the healing activity are indicated; the twelve are commanded: 'Heal the sick, raise the dead, cleanse those who have leprosy, drive out demons' (Matt. 10.8). As Michael Green puts it: '. . . although Satan is the great wrecker of human wholeness . . . the Bible writers decline to attribute all illness to direct satanic activity. They distinguish between "healing" and "casting out demons" . . . Demons are expelled; diseases are healed. The two are not the same . . .'[5]

After a long period of time in which anthropologists generally have shown a lofty, if superficial, contempt for such a primitive concept as 'possession' it is salutary to find I. M. Lewis of the London School of Economics surveying the subject and then commenting: 'Spirit-possession thus occupies a central position in comparative religion and theology, in religious phenomenology, in the sociology of religion, and in psychology.'[6]

Both voluntary and involuntary experiences of possession have in the past contributed to the *dukkha* frustration, and both experiences continue to do so today.

But this by no means exhausts the domain of *dukkha*. There is the meaninglessness of the accident: the personal tragedy or the major disaster. The car accident in which a drunk driver loses control of the vehicle and smashes into another vehicle, killing, maiming, paralysing, destroying. The earthquake, the tidal wave, the typhoon, in which personal tragedy is blended sometimes with thousands of others, all equally apparently meaningless.

But still the domain is not complete. We must add in the experience of discrimination, discrimination against a person's colour, or dialect, or physical appearance, or race, or religion, or sex. The realization that had I been precisely the same real person, but with a slightly different mix of external attributes – a different skin or accent, a more attractive body – then I might have had opportunities which are now closed to me. If only I were not a Jew. If only I were not black. If only I were not a woman. If only I were not old. If only I had not contracted polio. The reality is that I am what I am, and society rejects me because of what I am. And I was never asked if this was how I wanted to be.

There is the peculiar paradox of loneliness when surrounded by related people. When everything that is said appears to be addressed to people who have normal human relationships, relationships which are somehow denied to me. The denial of a basic premise of human existence, that to be human is to be gregarious.

Nor may we forget the human predicament which is the focus of Paul's thinking in Romans 7, the experience of willing what is right but lacking the power to act accordingly, or rejecting wrong action but continuing in it. The predicament may arise simply out of the normal context of human behaviour, but may be aggravated by drug dependency, alcoholism or some other physical disorder.

The domain of meaninglessness also includes the wider experience of discrimination and oppression, political and societal oppression. The mere initialling of the United Nations Charter, the inclusion of the appropriate wording in a nation's official Constitution, is no measure at all of the actual experience of the citizens of that nation. Ethiopia's Marxist rulers included freedom of religion in the Constitution, but that did not prevent their closing down some 1,600 churches of the 2,700 churches belonging to the Kale Heywet ('Word of Life') churches, and a further one thousand churches belonging to the Makane Yesus (Lutheran) fellowship in the 1980s. The Muslim world has yet to face up to its appalling record of religious intolerance[7] and discrimination, continuing long after the Christian Churches have repented of a similarly misguided intolerance. In the pre-Gorbachev Soviet Union it has been standard practice to treat Christian leaders as political dissidents and to consign them to mental hospitals. In Latin America, in the Argentine and elsewhere, huge numbers of people have simply disappeared under the oppression of right-wing dictatorships. In Haiti there was widespread intimidation under François Duvalier, of whom David Barrett comments that 'he exercised progressive control over the Catholic Church through intimidation and violence',[8] to which one can only add that the intimidation and violence were typical of the regime and by no means restricted to the churches.

And finally there is that meaninglessness which arises out of belonging to the powerless masses. These are the people who, to varying degrees, make no plans for tomorrow, because there are no resources which would make *choice* a possibility. Today I collect firewood, and I shall collect firewood tomorrow. Today I am in debt, and I shall be in debt tomorrow. The manifestos of the politicians do not speak to me because I can offer nothing to the politicians. The arms sellers will go on selling weapons which destroy the town in which I live, and I have no voice which can ever be heard above the sound of violence.

MEANINGLESSNESS AND MISSION

The Christian Mission

It is into this domain that the Church is to speak and within this domain that the Church is to act. Not to speak only, nor to act dumbly, but in a holistic response to the human condition to seek to understand theologically, to explain believably, and to act so as to end the *dukkha* experience, or at least to offer the hope of an end to it.

The Christian mission is biblically understood as the people of God speaking and acting on behalf of God to explain and to resolve the apparent meaninglessness of life wherever that meaninglessness appears and however it is experienced.

There can be no question of an absolute prioritization of 'spiritual mission' over 'social action'.[9] These two do not represent a unique pair of poles in the Christian praxis, but sectors of a spectrum of action all of which is properly 'mission'. But mission is not talk. Mission is not powerlessness. In mission the Church through its members brings into the situation of meaninglessness the power and authority of the Kingdom of God, not yet the full power and authority of that Kingdom (the power of the Second Kingdom is not yet put down), but still a new power and authority external to us but potentially operative in us to give to us and to all who will have it a resolution of the human predicament, of *dukkha*.

Four Aspects of Meaninglessness

The Christian mission speaks into and acts to deal with the human experience of meaninglessness. Its ability to deal with this *dukkha* is in some measure related to John Macquarrie's polarities of the human existence (see pp. 7–10 above). Some aspects of *dukkha* are more readily dealt with than others. But the Christian mission has something to say and some action to take in respect of each and every occasion of meaninglessness.

The Ultimate Meaning of Life

If it is true that between the two apparent boundaries of human existence life does not appear to make sense, then sense can come only where one or other or both of the boundaries can be transcended. Hinduism abolishes both. Christianity abolishes just one. There was a time when I was not, but now that I am there will not be a time when I shall not be.[10]

The Christian agrees that life cannot be neatly and logically explained, its accidents rationalized, its agonies interpreted, its unfairnesses unravelled, within time. This world is not the way it was meant to be, and it is not the way that it one day will be. Humanity is more than flesh and blood. I am not a finger, nor an eye, nor a heart, nor even a brain, nor any combination of these. My inner turmoil, my desire for purpose, my bliss in the occasional experience of God, my desolation when I am left alone with my intolerable burdens, these all testify to my origins: I am made for God. And as God is just, so I long for justice and tremble when I fail to find it. It is not to be found here. I am made for God, created with eternity in my heart. And it is that very fact which makes me cry out against injustice.

The good news is that there is justice. That somehow, at the end, the God of all the earth will himself be justified, our clamouring tongues will be silenced, our limited understanding will be amplified, and we will see what we cannot see now, that life, after all, was just. Death does not close the account; it merely invites the Auditor to prepare the Statement of Accounts.

But the good news is also, inevitably, bad news. If all humanity is to be submitted to a final audit, and if the justice I have demanded is to be given to me . . . then, knowing myself, I can have nothing but fear of the outcome. True enough, I have longed to do right, but I have done wrong. I have known the wrong, and have tried to escape it, but in the event I have not escaped. In this universal condition of humanity there is good news: we can be reconciled to God, our failures can be forgiven, in some inexplicable way because of the passion of Christ. Even where I am utterly unable to put right what I have done wrong, although my debt may be immeasurable, Christ, somehow, in sheer grace, deals with it, freely, fully. He may, indeed, give me the grace and the strength to put wrongs right. He may require that I do so. But I can genuinely be set free from a tormenting past. I may have abused my children, abandoned my wife, exploited my workers, cheated my employers, but there is nothing in my past that the mercy of God cannot touch.

And I may be at the end of my life, but there is no need of time in which to do what I have not done through the years. Forgiveness and reconciliation can be taken now, and the life that opens up ahead, what the Bible refers to as eternal life, the life of eternity, can be mine.

The question of the inadequacy of the human will must also be addressed. It is clear from experience, and reasonably clear from Scripture, that God forgives but also gives. He gives to his people an inner awareness of what is right and wrong (a renewed conscience informed by the Holy Spirit), an authoritative Word, the Bible (which is of *timeless* authority, but which, for this very reason, requires most careful interpretation), a community, the Church, whose leaders have a responsibility as 'shepherds' to care for the respective communities, but all of this necessarily constrained by the extent to which God's people submit themselves to him.

As we have suggested above (pp. 127–30), the Christian *experience* is part of the 'now but not yet' of redemption and reconciliation, and we may know more of it or less of it according to the measure of maturity, of *holiness*, we have reached and we wish to reach. And this is a holiness, a *not-ordinariness*, of a lifestyle that represents praxeological deviance arising out of cognitive deviance, thought-processes which stand in radical contrast to those obtaining in contemporary society.

The *dukkha* Experience of Disease and Death

Here, also, we are confronted with the now-and-not-yet of the Christian Good News. But it must at once be recognized that there are those who deny the now-and-not-yet, who insist that the Christian can experience here and now *all* of the consequences of the bringing in of the Kingdom of God. One of the more radical is Ray McCauley,[11] a South Africa-based exponent of prosperity theology, who stated in an interview, 'There is suffering in the Christian life but I don't believe it includes sickness, financial or spiritual need – we've been redeemed from that.'[12]

In the same interview he was asked, 'Do you teach that it is always God's will to heal sick Christians?' and responded:

Yes. Galatians 3:13 tells us that Jesus has redeemed us from the curse of the law – and that includes poverty and sickness. I don't accept that it is God's will for some to be healed, while others are not . . . I don't believe that believers have to die of cancer – they can die of old age![13]

Firstly, it must be said that 'old age' is a chronology, not a cause of death. In old age people die of disease or from trauma, but the calendar cannot kill. Secondly, the fact is that Christians do die of cancer, and other diseases. McCauley explains this by reference to the Bible: 'There are about 37 reasons in the scriptures why people are not healed, including strife, unforgiveness, not discerning the Lord's body; unbelief is only one of them.'[14]

Those who pursue this particular teaching are not always consistent. Colin Urquhart, an Anglican minister, on the one hand insists 'God has promised to do what we believe. In His generosity He is likely to do much more, but He has pledged Himself, as our covenant God, to do whatever we believe He will do.' On the other hand he adds, 'That does not mean that we can dictate to God *how* He is to answer, or even *when* the answer is to come. It does mean that, as His new covenant children, we can afford to be specific and clear about what we ask . . .'[15] However, it is not at all clear why this caveat is needed: what can be more specific and clear than time itself?

The great danger of this particular means of resolving the *dukkha* experience of suffering is that since not everyone who is prayed for is healed[16] and explanation for the failure has to be found, and it is always found as some moral or spiritual failure in those involved. With thirty-seven biblical explanations available, and granted the relative poverty of our Christian commitment, there can be no difficulty in locating one, or several, contributing factors. And this places an intolerable load of guilt on those whose faith is in some way found to be lacking.

Joni Eareckson contributes to Henry Frost's *Miraculous Healing* a Foreword which expresses with great poignancy the feelings of the unhealed. She describes her morning routine:

. . . if it's a Sunday morning there's often a TV preacher on . . . Sometimes there's a healing service on, and I will watch it as I am being exercised, dressed, made up, and lifted into my wheelchair. It's rather paradoxical, to be sitting there, handicapped, and unable to care for myself, listening to the sermon and watching people hobble onstage with crutches and walk off without them.[17]

Joni Eareckson has not been healed. Presumably McCauley would invoke one of the thirty-seven reasons to explain the fact. But it would be difficult to produce a similar rationalization for George Whitefield and Charles Haddon Spurgeon, both of whom died before they were sixty, or for William Branham, one of the early prophets of prosperity theology, who died at the age of fifty-six and who was in debt for the last nine years of his life, or for Catherine Booth and David Watson, both of whom died not of old age but of cancer.

Although it is not our purpose to deal with prosperity theology in any detail, it may be said that the theology represents a failure in the doctrine of Scripture, in the doctrine of God, and in the doctrine of the Church. In the matter of Scripture, there is a failure to grasp the implications of the two covenants. The terminology appropriate to the first is unthinkingly transferred to the second (on the two covenants see pp. 122–30 above). In the matter of the doctrine of God, there is an unthinking adoption of a naive theology in which God is, in popularist terms, omnipotent. That would be good Muslim theology, but it is not a biblical theology. The power of the Second Kingdom is not ended until that point in history signalled by the second part of Revelation 20. In the matter of the Church, we note the distinction between the Old Testament people of God, with a defined territory, a specific capital city, a human king with a limited life-span and rule, with wars to fight and crime to combat, and the New Testament people of God spread through all space and time, whose citizenship is in heaven, whose capital is the Jerusalem of heaven, whose King is the Eternal. The prosperity of the one kingdom was visible here on earth, the prosperity of the other is laid up in heaven. The hard fact is that faithfulness to God does not necessarily lead to prosperity either for the individual or, more generally, for the Church. It will certainly lead to there being treasure in heaven; the treasure on earth is less certain.

On the positive side, it is certainly true that healing takes place in response to prayer and without recourse to medicine or surgery. The key to this understanding of prayer for healing is rightly identified by John Wimber: 'A secret to healing prayer is that it comes from God having already touched our spirits; it is agreement with God about his will.'[18] This is the precise opposite of McCauley's doctrine, that God must do what we agree he *should* do. It is not a question of my fulfilling a set of conditions which then give me the right to dictate to God. My task is the less onerous (but actually *possible*) task of discerning the will of God. Not that this is easy. My humanity predisposes me to wish for a particular outcome: the healing of my wife, the provision of this house, an end to my unemployment. Most of us have yet to learn that in the Kingdom of God all the normal priorities are reversed. It is safer to lose one's life than to preserve it. It is dangerous to be wealthy. The unimportant are on centre-stage. And at the end of it all the ultimately important relationships are utterly astonishing. The last are first, the first are last. The beggars are at the banquet.

And this is the Christian response to the *dukkha* of illness and death. That God may well heal miraculously. Of course it may be so. But that in our illness we are sharing in the common experience of peoples everywhere, and at that cost we are earning the right to say to the peoples around us that we understand. Just as God understands because he, too, once came among us and experienced not merely death, but death on the cross.

And, we must add, death is not the end, but the beginning. In C. S. Lewis' unforgettable expression, term is ended, the holidays have begun. In more orthodox terms Paul writes: 'Now we know that if the earthly tent we live in is destroyed, we have a building from God, an eternal house in heaven, not built by human hands' (2 Cor. 5.1). The tent in which we live does age. The ropes fray, the tentpoles crack, the canvas splits (or note the corresponding imagery of Eccles. 12!). The storm rages and the tent blows down. But the occupant is not left naked, without a home: out of the tent and into the building from God. Death is not the worst thing that can happen to us.

The Experience of Political and Economic Oppression

The Church cannot return to a world-view which relates solely to the so-called spiritual aspects of human existence without losing its biblical authenticity. The Good News must relate to the whole world and so it must relate to those political and economic powers which so often become quasi-religious powers, arrogating to themselves oppressive and possessive activities which ought not to belong to any human construct.

The Christian world-view is that the powers (and no attempt is made, here, to differentiate between political and economic powers since very little scrutiny is required to convince us that the two are radically interdependent) should exist to maintain justice, and that in so far as they serve to reward the righteous and to punish the wrongdoer they are worthy of the support of every Christian. This is the perceived meaning of Romans 13.1-7.

The passage gives no support to the thesis that the Christian is obliged to submit to any and every government however constituted. The type of government envisaged by Paul here is perfectly clear: 'rulers hold no terror for those who do right' (v. 3). That is not always the case. Here, for Paul the relevant authority is just and so we are to 'do what is right and he will commend you' (v. 3). By contrast, however, there are authorities, powers, whose response to goodness is the reverse of this. For Paul the authority is there acting on God's behalf 'to bring punishment on the wrongdoer' (v. 4). By contrast, however, the government may work together with the wrongdoer to their mutual benefit. In such societies the rubric of verse 1, 'Everyone must submit himself to the governing authorities', is inapplicable.

The question must then be asked: In an oppressive and unjust society, what is the duty first of the believer and then of the Church? First stands the duty of identification with the oppressed, and its concomitant is to stand against the oppressive powers. The Good News is Good News when we all abandon all specious pleas about expediency and do what is right because it is right and without any reference to the consequences of doing what is right. Too few missionaries have been expelled for speaking out against political and economic oppression. Too few missionary societies have been closed down because of their refusal to play along with the double-talk of oppressive regimes. We have purchased the right to continue to be Christ's witnesses at the cost of the believableness of our testimony.

But secondly, we oppose the powers with our weakness, not with a Christian gloss on unredeemed violence. In a highly poignant phrase Paul once commented 'we are weak in him' (2 Cor. 13.4).[19]

To the oppressive power of Rome Jesus opposed his weakness, accepted crucifixion, embraced the apparent meaninglessness of oppression on top of oppression. But it was precisely that double oppression that eventually produced a Church which outlived and outloved the Roman power.[20] We oppose the powers with our weakness. The liberation theologians are wrong. The mixture of Marxist sociology and Christian theology is a mixture of iron and clay. For Paul the treasure of the Good News is in clay pots, *en ostrakinois skeuesin* (2 Cor. 4.7), but precisely not in iron cauldrons. We do not respond to violence with violence, and no hermeneutical principle can be found to extract that meaning either from the exodus or from its New Testament pole, the passion. We disobey unjust laws. But we submit to the consequences of our disobedience.

And this I can say out of my experience in Ethiopia.[21] There the Church was tempted, even encouraged, to take up the struggle against the self-imposed Marxist regime. There was every good reason to do so. The land of the peasants was nationalized. The shops were closed down, the churches destroyed, Christian leaders imprisoned, Christian gatherings banned, the importing of the Bible halted. Discrimination was naked. A ruinous war was being fought in the north, and tens of thousands of the young men of the country were marched away to a meaningless death in it. It was a war that neither Eritrea nor Ethiopia could hope to win. Famine marched through the land: not just in the north, but north, south, east and west. There was tribal discrimination: as under Haile Sellassie, so now under President Mengistu the élite prospered, the rest merely existed. And there was a resistance movement to be supported. Red Terror and White Terror invaded the streets of Addis Ababa until eventually sheer exhaustion brought the nightly horrors to an end.

The Kale Heywet Church did not oppose the Marxists in that way. Their philosophy was simple, even simplistic. All governments would be corrupt. The Church should expect to be persecuted in proportion to her faithfulness to God. And so the Church suffered. Over the years thousands went to prison, many died there, some simply disappeared. And the nation discovered that there was this unusual people among them who were endlessly patient, always ready to forgive, always willing to help. Out of their poverty they gave even beyond their ability (cf. 2 Cor. 8.2), the ultimate paradox. And although their church buildings were closed, the Church grew because people found within the community of the Church what they could not locate in Marxism. This is the way of faith. It is not obvious how it might lead to the end of Ethiopia's years of *dukkha*. But it is a way chosen by a Third World Church informed by Scripture, not a way imposed on the Third World by their North Atlantic oppressors. The suffering Church of Ethiopia stands very close to its origins in the passion of Christ.

In contrast there is the alternative praxis of the liberation theologians, but the theology is flawed and so is the praxis it supports. The liberation theologians are wrong. Despite the identification with the poor, it is not the spirit of Christ that breathes, for example, through *The Road to Damascus*,[22] the 1989 document issued by consciously Third World liberationists from El Salvador, Guatemala, Korea, Namibia, Nicaragua, the Philippines and South Africa. This gives the impression of a self-righteous and judgemental group of churchmen, yet one more Christian sect of one-and-onlies, sowing division and even hatred in the Church. The work of missionaries is denigrated ('In the case of Korea, European missionaries came without colonisation. It was only later that we discovered that this God and this Jesus had been formed in the image and likeness of European kings, emperors and conquerors').[23] Right-wing Christianity is denounced in favour of left-wing Christianity ('Right-wing Christianity is the conscious or unconscious legitimation of idolatry . . . [it] replaces Christian responsibility and trust in God with submission to the yoke of slavery').[24] What is presented here is a parody of conservative Christianity, but it is a parody that exudes a spirit of divisiveness, of schism, and even of hatred. Oddly, the left-wing theology of liberation is reminiscent of the far right-wing theology of Ian Paisley in his opposition to the Roman Catholic Church in Northern Ireland. Neither takes Scripture with sufficient seriousness. For both the political imperatives obscure an unpalatable Scripture.

The answer to violence is not more violence. The answer to hatred is not to hate. The Church has acknowledged its partial Bible-blindness, but there is room for the liberation theologians to share in the humility they demand of the rest of us, and to submit in turn not to an already discredited Marxist philosophy, but to the profounder wisdom of Scripture.

The Experience of Natural Disaster

Here again it is vital that the moral problems posed by natural disasters should be accurately identified. In many such disasters there is a major component of human irresponsibility. I have argued elsewhere[25] that the naive analysis of the repeated famines in Ethiopia, which places the blame on a God who 'turned off the tap', denied rain, must be replaced by an analysis which takes into account the gross political and economic mismanagement of the country involved. Even if there is less rain than in the past (and it is not clear that this is the case), the mass destruction of ground-cover due to decades of war precisely in the principal famine region must be at least partially responsible. If there are no crops, then at least some account must be taken of the wholesale conscription of young men and women into the armies on both sides of the battle-front so that the farms are without labourers. If there is no money to pay for the needed infrastructure of roads, there must be some significance in the fact that Ethiopia has the largest standing army in black Africa, and spends rather more than 60% of its gross national product on weapons despite being, now, under Marxism, the poorest nation in the world.[26]

We have referred on p. 6 to the Aberfan disaster, in which a slag heap collapsed into the village below it, killing more than a hundred little children. But local people knew that the heap was dangerous, and had drawn the attention of the authorities to the danger. It was not merely a matter of God deciding to give the slag heap a push, of God organizing a calamity. In California everyone is aware of the fact that a major earthquake is bound to occur in the not too distant future, and yet Los Angeles continues to be thronged by millions who may one day be asking why God allowed a major catastrophe to happen to *their* city.[27]

The meaninglessness of catastrophe does present a bewildering spectrum, ranging from those events clearly caused by willed human activity, as in bombing incidents, to those in which there appears to be no human contribution to the catastrophe at all, as in the birth of a malformed baby or in the destructive power of a typhoon. What must be admitted is that life is made possible by the regularity and reliability of the laws which govern creation. The processes of photosynthesis or of oxidation, the principles of chemical combination, the rates of decay of radioactive elements, the cycle of precipitation, are all now to some extent understood, and our environment can be to some extent manipulated and ordered by our awareness of the laws and principles. Take that order away and life would become impossible. If miracle was the norm, we would be unable to take even the least breath or a single step with any certainty of the outcome. But this very regularity carries a penalty. Fire burns, and will burn a child's hand as well as it will burn a log. The laws of gravity will govern an aircraft in its flight, or will tumble a slag heap into the valley below it. Radioactivity may cure or kill.

There are laws which govern economics, too. Resources devoted to one project cannot also be devoted to a different project. Fallen human nature enters into the equation: unless the civil and criminal law work to prevent it, fallen human nature will exploit the masses with little or no regard to the misery produced. And since governments cannot long survive without a firm economic base, it is only too normal to find power-hungry governments *of all political persuasions* forming unholy alliances with profit-hungry industry to the detriment of their peoples.

In all of this the Church has a choice to make. On the one hand to become part of the exploiting alliances and so to share in their power and profit, or on the other hand to stand with God on the side of the oppressed, poor, middle-class, or rich, whoever they may be. On the one side is Establishment. On the other side is not merely Disestablishment but possibly disinheritance, the loss of a power base from which to operate. Except that the loss of a human power base is the necessary and sufficient condition for access to the power of God.

It is in that power that the Church may confront all unholy alliances with the reality of their exploiting methodologies, exposing hypocrisy, making clear the mishandling of resources, demanding justice not for herself but for others. But more: the Church will demonstrate through its creation of a genuine community, a task which must be a priority for the coming decades, its readiness to share its good things so that there may be no needy among us, just as there should be no needy in the world.

Postscript

To be a missionary, today, is not merely to belong to a missionary society, nor is it merely to cross high cultural barriers to herald the Kingdom of God, though it might involve either of these. To be a missionary is to confront human *dukkha*. It is to *hear* the cry of the world, even the cry which sheer hunger and exhaustion and despair stifle at its birth. It is to hear that cry as God hears it, and to respond not with more books and more international conferences, but with a truly biblical praxis, a praxis which is not Marxist, nor yet capitalist, but a praxis which incarnates the will of God in an as yet unredeemed world.

The missionary will understand the *reasons* underlying the human condition: fundamentally *spiritual* reasons, but at the second level political reasons and economic reasons and religious reasons. Marx was right: it is not enough to offer a superficial solution to the human predicament. The causes of the human predicament must be identified, and only then can any meaningful resolution of that predicament be expected. But the missionary will be able, then, to move on both to explain the *why* of the human predicament and to proclaim the central imperative of the Christian Good News: Be reconciled to God. Be reconciled to one another. Come into the community which is the Church.

But more: even where that reconciliation is refused, the missionary, the Church, will none the less still insist on sharing what it has in *koinōnia* among the believers and in *philanthrōpia* towards all, in confronting the oppressive powers of the Second Kingdom, and in rebuking the political and economic powers often directed by it. Mission will always be a power confrontation which includes those signs of the presence of the Kingdom so confidently announced in the New Testament. Mission is more than the multiplying of missionaries or even of churches. It is rather the confrontation of the human condition, of human meaninglessness, and in the name of God so resolving it that God's Kingdom comes. The Kingdom is the entelechy of the Church. The mission of the Church is to be that entelechous flower out of which the perfect will come.

Notes

1 THE APPARENT MEANINGLESSNESS OF LIFE

1 Harold S. Kushner, *When bad things happen to good people* (London: Pan Books, 1982).
2 ibid., p. 10.
3 See Edward England, *The Mountain that Moved* (London: Hodder & Stoughton, 1967).
4 John Macquarrie, *Principles of Christian Theology* (London: SCM Press, 1966), pp. 59f.
5 Trevor Ling, *A History of Religion East and West* (London: Macmillan, 1968), p. 86.
6 David Cook, 'Existentialism', in Sinclair B. Ferguson and David F. Wright (eds.), *New Dictionary of Theology* (Leicester and Downers Grove, IL: Inter-Varsity Press, 1988), p. 224.
7 Macquarrie, *Principles of Christian Theology*, pp. 56–9.
8 F. G. Bailey, 'The Peasant View of the Bad Life', *Advancement of Science* (December 1966), pp. 399–409.
9 *Newsweek*, 6 July 1987, pp. 20–1.
10 Raymond E. Brown, *The Gospel According to John, I–XII*, Anchor Bible (New York: Doubleday; London: Geoffrey Chapman, 1966), p. 208.
11 Rudolf Schnackenburg, *The Gospel According to St John*, vol. 2 (London: Burns & Oates, 1980), p. 240.
12 For fuller details, see I. H. Marshall, *The Gospel of Luke*, New International Greek Testament Commentary (Exeter: Paternoster Press, 1978), p. 553. See also J. Fitzmyer, *The Gospel According to Luke X–XXIV*, Anchor Bible (New York: Doubleday, 1985), pp. 1003–9.
13 See Fitzmyer, *The Gospel According to Luke X–XXIV*, p. 1007.
14 See, for example, Kenneth Copeland, *The Laws of Prosperity* (Fort Worth: Kenneth Copeland Publications, 1974), p. 88, for a rather typical example, and *per contra*, Jacques Ellul, *Money and Power* (Basingstoke: Marshall Pickering, 1986), translated from the 1954 *L'homme et l'argent*.
15 Jean-Paul Sartre, *Existentialism and Humanism* (London: Methuen, 1948), p. 33. The book has passed through numerous reprints.

2 RELIGIONS IN CONFLICT

1 For a more irenic approach, see Michael Barnes SJ, *Religions in Conversation* (London: SPCK, 1989).
2 See particularly E. J. Sharpe, *Understanding Religion* (London: Duckworth, 1983), chapter 3, for examples of definitions and sources of some of the definitions quoted here.

3 Sharpe, *Understanding Religion*, p. 37.
4 ibid., p. 39.
5 It is important to recognize the centrality of this question, particularly in the West today. See Martin Ballard's gentle but well-informed introduction to the issue in *Who am I?* (London: Hutchinson, 1971).
6 *Nostra aetate*, in A. Flannery (ed.), *Vatican Council II: The Conciliar and Post-Conciliar Documents* (Leominster: Fowler-Wright Books, 1975), p. 738.
7 See the article *Yezer Ha-Ra'*, in *The Jewish Encyclopedia* (New York: Ktav, 1901).
8 John Hick, *The Second Christianity* (London: SCM Press, 1983), p. 86. The book was first published by Macmillan in 1968 as *Christianity at the Centre*, but the new title was justified by the important addition of Section IV, 'Christianity and Other Religions'.
9 See, for example, Karl Popper, *The Open Society and its Enemies*, vol. 2 (London: Routledge & Kegan Paul, 1966), especially chapter 13, 'Marx's Sociological Determinism'.
10 J. H. Jackson, *Men and Their Times: Marx, Proudhon and European Socialism* (London: English Universities Press, 1958), p. 64.
11 Mary Baker Eddy, *Science and Health with Key to the Scriptures* (Boston, 1875 and onwards), p. 7.
12 ibid., p. 47.
13 ibid., p. 48.
14 There is a beautiful presentation of *The Bhagavad Gita* (London: Faber & Faber, 1978), translated by Shri Purohit Swami, and illustrated with photographs by Curt Bruce. The extract is taken from chapter 2.
15 Edward Conze (ed. and trans.), *Buddhist Scriptures* (Harmondsworth: Penguin Books, 1959), p. 186.
16 Owen C. Thomas, *Attitudes Toward Other Religions* (London: SCM Press, 1969).
17 See Sir James Frazer, *The Golden Bough*, published in twelve volumes 1911–15, with a thirteenth volume, *Aftermath*, in 1936. He produced a single-volume abridged version, *The Golden Bough* (London: Macmillan, 1922).
18 Thomas, *Attitudes Toward Other Religions*, p. 23.
19 William Temple, *Readings in St John's Gospel: First and Second Series* (London: Macmillan, 1961).
20 ibid., pp. 270–1.
21 Karl Barth, *Church Dogmatics* I/2, section 17, 'The Revelation of God as the Abolition of Religion'.

3 THE CHRISTIAN WORLD-VIEW

1 J. Bonino, *Revolutionary Theology Comes of Age* (London: SPCK, 1975), p. 72.

2 See Peter Cotterell and Max Turner, *Linguistics and Biblical Interpretation* (London: SPCK, 1989), 2.2., pp. 53–72.

3 See above, pp. 7–10 and John Macquarrie, *Principles of Christian Theology* (London: SCM Press, 1966), pp. 56–9.

4 cf. the long-running Sino-Soviet border conflict of the 1970s.

5 Cotterell and Turner, *Linguistics and Biblical Interpretation*, chapter 3.

6 ibid., pp. 58f.

7 Obviously allowing for such features as polysemy, as in John 3.8, '*to pneuma . . . pnei*', 'the wind blows', 'the Spirit moves'.

8 Note here the first of David Steinmetz' ten theses on theology and exegesis: 'The meaning of a biblical text is not exhausted by the original intention of the author' (D. Steinmetz, 'Theology and Exegesis: Ten Theses', in Donald K. McKim (ed.), *A Guide to Contemporary Hermeneutics: Major Trends in Biblical Interpretation* (Grand Rapids, MI: Wm B. Eerdmans, 1986), p. 27). Steinmetz does not follow the convention introduced by E. D. Hirsch (see Hirsch's *The Aims of Interpretation* (Chicago: University of Chicago Press, 1976), pp. 1–13), which distinguishes between meaning and significance. He is right in pointing out in his thesis 8 that if meaning-and-significance is limited to author intention, then the Church must abandon the Old Testament to the Jews.

9 H. P. Grice, 'Logic and Conversation', in P. Cole and J. L. Morgan (eds.), *Syntax and Semantics* (New York: Academic Press, 1975).

10 F. P. Cotterell, 'The Nicodemus Conversation: A Fresh Appraisal', *Expository Times* 96.8 (1985), pp. 237–42.

11 I do not suggest that it is the presupposition *alone* which would necessarily determine the exegesis. In the case of a careful scholar that presupposition would simply contribute to the total interpretation.

12 See especially Brian Hebblethwaite, *The Ocean of Truth* (Cambridge and New York: Cambridge University Press, 1988). The book sets out to offer an alternative to Don Cupitt's interiorized religion. Lesslie Newbigin, *The Gospel in a Pluralist Society* (London: SPCK, 1989), presents the issues of truth and belief with characteristic profundity and humility. He draws attention to 'the cultural collapse which has abandoned the struggle to find truth in the welter of human experiences' (p. 161).

13 Or, in the Ahmadi understanding, that Jesus *was* crucified, but did *not* die on the cross (see, for example, Hazrat Mirza Ghulam Ahmad, *Jesus in India* (London: The London Mosque, 1978), chapter 1, or Muhammad Zafrulla Khan, *Deliverance from the Cross* (London: The London Mosque, 1978), chapter 3).

14 Rabbi Arye Forta, 'The New Christian Missions to the Jews: How Should we Respond?', *L'eylah* (April 1988), pp. 22–5.

15 Karl Jaspers, *Philosophical Faith and Revelation*, trans. E. B. Ashton (London: Collins, 1967), pp. 105–6. John Kane's *Pluralism and Truth in Religion* (Chico, CA: Scholars Press, 1981) is a critique of Jaspers's approach to pluralism of truth.

16 Jaspers, *Philosophical Faith and Revelation*, pp. 105–6.
17 See Kane, *Pluralism and Truth in Religion.*
18 ibid., p. 7.
19 Forta, 'The New Christian Missions to the Jews', p. 24.
20 Seyyed Hossein Nasr, *Islamic Life and Thought* (London: George Allen & Unwin, 1981), p. 209.

4 THE PROBLEM OF PARTICULARITY

1 See Malcolm Guthrie, *Comparative Bantu* (London: Gregg, 1964).
2 John Hick, '"Whatever Path Men Choose is Mine"', in John Hick and Brian Hebblethwaite (eds.), *Christianity and Other Religions: Selected Readings* (London: Collins Fount, 1980), p. 172.
3 See John Hick, 'The Reconstruction of Christian Belief', 'The Essence of Christianity', 'The Copernican Revolution in Theology' and 'The New Map of the Universe of Faiths', in *God and the Universe of Faiths* (London: Collins Fount, 1977); *God has Many Names* (London: Macmillan, 1980); *Problems of Religious Pluralism* (Basingstoke: Macmillan, 1985); and, with P. F. Knitter (eds.), *The Myth of Christian Uniqueness* (Maryknoll, NY: Orbis Books, 1987; London: SCM Press, 1988).
4 Gavin D'Costa, *Theology and Religious Pluralism* (Oxford: Basil Blackwell, 1986).
5 Gavin D'Costa, *John Hick's Theology of Religions* (Lanham and London: University Press of America, 1987).
6 John Hick, 'The Non-Absoluteness of Christianity', in Hick and Knitter (eds.), *The Myth of Christian Uniqueness.*
7 See Geoffrey Moorhouse, *The Missionaries* (London: Eyre Methuen, 1973), pp. 92ff. However, the notorious book of the same title by Norman Lewis, *The Missionaries* (New York: Secker & Warburg, 1988), is in quite a different category. It singles out the Summer Institute of Linguistics and the New Tribes Mission for a sustained attack which makes up for in imagination what it lacks in fact. The picture which is constructed, of these missions operating their own air forces, and acting as the extended arm of a government set on the destruction of the Indian peoples, must be one of the most impudent parodies of contemporary journalism.
8 As D'Costa, *John Hick's Theology of Religions*, pp. 115f., has pointed out.
9 Peter Cotterell and Max Turner, *Linguistics and Biblical Interpretation* (London: SPCK, 1989), p. 84: '. . . the *referent* of a word or expression in an utterance is the *thing in the world which is intentionally signified by that word or expression.*'
10 Or, more precisely, *not* given to Jesus!
11 Clearly neither Islam nor Judaism would admit that designation for Christianity.
12 D'Costa, *John Hick's Theology of Religions*, pp. 111–15.

13 Hick, 'The Non-Absoluteness of Christianity', p. 32.
14 ibid.
15 See, for example, J. N. D. Kelly, *Early Christian Doctrines* (London: A. & C. Black, ⁵1977), pp. 119–23.
16 Hick, 'The Non-Absoluteness of Christianity', pp. 32f.
17 ibid., p. 33.
18 See Michael Barnes SJ, 'Vatican II and the Values of the Religions', in *Religions in Conversation* (London: SPCK, 1989), pp. 50–1.
19 Quotations from the documents are made from A. Flannery (ed.), *Vatican II: The Conciliar and Post-Conciliar Documents* (Leominster: Fowler-Wright Books, 1975).
20 We note in passing Verkuyl's assessment of a wide sweep of contemporary Roman Catholic missiologies: 'Each of these schools has breathed deeply the air of *aggiornamento*, the attempt to modernize the Roman Catholic church, and in its approach to the religions and religious communities each is following the guidelines set down in *Nostra Aetate*,' J. Verkuyl, *Contemporary Missiology* (Grand Rapids, MI: Wm B. Eerdmans, 1978), p. 350.
21 Karl Rahner, *Theological Investigations*, vol. XIV (London: Darton, Longman & Todd, 1976), p. 284.
22 We note the passing reference to John 1.9.
23 An error here: John 1.6 stands in Flannery's text.
24 Paul Knitter, 'Roman Catholic Approaches to Other Religions: Developments and Tensions', *International Bulletin of Missionary Research* 8.2 (April 1984), pp. 50–4.
25 Gavin D'Costa, in his *Theology and Religious Pluralism*, pp. 140–9, includes a comprehensive bibliography with some twenty items from Hick.
26 The concept of the 'anonymous Christian' has been subjected to a steady process of criticism from such writers as Lesslie Newbigin, Stephen Neill, John Stott, Hans Küng, and many others. The argument is neatly and concisely summarized in Michael Barnes, *Religions in Conversation*, pp. 52–9.
27 The Council met between 1962 and 1965 at the initiative of Pope John XXIII, who died in 1963 and was succeeded by Pope Paul VI.
28 Rahner discusses the question of anonymous *Christianity*, as against the anonymous *Christian*, in his *Theological Investigations*, vol. XIV, pp. 280–1.
29 Rahner's *Theological Investigations*, vols. VI (1974), XII (1974), and XIV (1976), all contain important discussions of the concept.
30 See Karl Rahner, 'Christianity and the Non-Christian Religions', in Hick and Hebblethwaite (eds.), *Christianity and Other Religions*, pp. 52–79.
31 Rahner, *Theological Investigations*, vol. XIV, p. 283.
32 Rahner, *Theological Investigations*, vol. V (London: Darton, Longman & Todd, 1966), chapter 6, p. 116.
33 ibid., p. 118.

34 ibid., p. 119.
35 On the conflict between Judaism and Christianity, see, for example, A. R. Eckardt, *Jews and Christians: The Contemporary Meeting* (Bloomington: Indiana University Press, 1986), and David Berger (ed.), *History and Hate: The Dimensions of Anti-Semitism* (London: Jewish Publication Society, 1986).
36 Rahner, *Theological Investigations*, vol. V, chapter 6, p. 121.
37 ibid.
38 ibid., p. 122.
39 ibid., p. 123.
40 Rahner, 'Christianity and the Non-Christian Religions', p. 76.
41 Rahner, *Theological Investigations*, vol. V, chapter 6, p. 131.
42 It is the fashion to pretend that this is not so, but following proper hermeneutical procedures it is entirely clear that the *meaning* of the relevant Qur'anic passages on life in Paradise is a sensuous meaning. No attempt to determine *significance* for today can succeed unless it begins from Muhammad's intended meaning.
43 For example, in John 16.8, the starting-point of elenctics, but particularly in the doctrinal statements of such passages as Romans 5—8.
44 Karl Rahner, *The Spirit in the Church* (London: Burns & Oates, 1979), p. 19.
45 'A sinner does not "decide" for Christ; the sinner "flies" to Christ in utter helplessness and despair . . . No man truly comes to Christ unless he flees to Him as his only refuge and hope,' Martyn Lloyd-Jones, *Preaching and Preachers* (London: Hodder & Stoughton, 1971), pp. 279f.
46 Although we would find it very much more difficult to adopt some of the other models which Rahner adds in the passage quoted. These appear to descend to such a level of generality that it would be possible to interpret almost any faintly unusual and disinterested human act into a decisive confrontation with the Spirit.
47 Rahner, *Theological Investigations*, vol. V, chapter 6, p. 131.
48 For example, David Hogan, 'The Names of God in the Urak Lawoi' Scriptures', *The Bible Translator* 35.4 (1984), p. 410, says that 'The Urak Lawoi' use the word *Lah*, an abbreviation for *Allah-ta'alah* . . . as a swear word'!
49 See particularly the series of articles in *The Bible Translator* 35.4 (1984), 36.2 (1985), 36.4 (1985) on various aspects of the problem of translating the names of God.
   Jacob A. Loewen, 'Translating the Names of God: How European Languages Have Translated Them', *The Bible Translator* 36.4 (1985), pp. 401–11, draws attention to the practice of the LXX in rendering *elohim* as referred to the gods of other nations: they become *agalmata* (Isa. 21.9), *eidolon* (Exod. 15.17) and *bdelugmata* (1 Kings 11.5).
50 Rahner, *Theological Investigations*, vol. V, chapter 6, p. 133.
51 Rahner, *Theological Investigations*, vol. XIV, chapter 17, pp. 283.
52 Lesslie Newbigin, *The Open Secret* (London: SPCK, 1978), p. 195.

53 Hans Küng, *On Being a Christian* (London: Collins, 1977), p. 99.
54 Hans Küng, 'The World Religions in God's Plan of Salvation', in H. Neuner (ed.), *Christian Revelation and World Religions* (London: Burns & Oates, 1967), p. 34. See also Flannery (ed.), *Vatican Council II*, pp. 367–9.
55 See Barth, *Church Dogmatics* I/2, section 17.
56 Küng, 'The World Religions in God's Plan of Salvation', p. 55.
57 ibid., p. 52.
58 One is tempted to say, much as Vatican II created its own, innovative, way of salvation, a way of good intentions and good works.

5 EXCLUSIVISM AND THE BIBLE

1 See R. de Vaux, *Ancient Israel: Its Life and Institutions* (London: Darton, Longman & Todd, 1961), pp. 68–79.
2 cf. Isaiah 40.18–31; 43.8–13; and especially 44.6–20.
3 If the designation 'To the Ephesians' is justified as the original ascription, then the Acts 19.23–6 allusion to their religiosity is entirely relevant to this issue. If the letter was in some sense a circular letter, then the Acts passage is still of relevance for our purposes, although not necessarily of equal relevance to all of the original readers of the letter. See Donald Guthrie, *New Testament Introduction* (Leicester: Inter-Varsity Press, ³1970), pp. 508ff.
4 Paul Knitter, *No Other Name?* (Maryknoll, NY: Orbis Books, 1985), p. 185. On Acts 4.12, see also C. K. Barrett, 'Salvation Proclaimed; XII. Acts 4.8–12', *Expository Times* 94.3 (December, 1982), pp. 68–71.
5 Peggy Starkey, 'Biblical Faith and the Challenge of Religious Pluralism', *International Review of Mission* LXXI.281 (January 1982), pp. 66–77.
6 ibid., p. 69.
7 F. F. Bruce, *The Acts of the Apostles* (Leicester: Inter-Varsity Press, 1971), pp. 120–1. Starkey appears to have misunderstood Bruce at this point, assuming that he recognized the possibility of there being other saviours, where, in fact, his point was solely concerned with the highlighting of the givenness of Jesus.
8 Starkey, 'Biblical Faith and the Challenge of Religious Pluralism', pp. 70–1.
9 Karl Popper, *The Open Society and its Enemies*, p. 260. Chapter 25, 'Has history any meaning?', is essential reading for anyone interested in the question of historicity and the supposed objectivity of the sciences.
10 Starkey, 'Biblical Faith and the Challenge of Religious Pluralism', p. 71.
11 ibid., p. 70.
12 ibid., p. 71.
13 Charles W. Forman and Gregory Baum, 'Is There a Missionary Message?', in Gerald H. Anderson and Thomas F. Stransky (eds.), *Mission Trends No. 1* (New York: Paulist Press; Grand Rapids, MI: Wm B. Eerdmans, 1974), pp. 75–86.

14 C. K. Barrett, *The Gospel According to St John* (London: SPCK, [2]1976), p. 382.

15 I. de la Potterie, *La Vérité dans Saint Jean*, vol. 2 (Rome: Biblical Institute Press, 1977), p. 939: 'He *is* the truth (14.6); but nowhere does Jesus say that the truth is *in* him' (my translation).

16 R. Schnackenburg, *The Gospel According to St John*, vol. 3 (Tunbridge Wells: Burns & Oates, 1982), p. 64.

17 J. H. Bernard, *St John*, vol. 2, International Critical Commentary (Edinburgh: T. & T. Clark, 1928), p. 537.

18 See especially Bruce A. Demarest, *General Revelation: Historical Views and Contemporary Issues* (Grand Rapids, MI: Zondervan, 1982), and Kenneth S. Kantzer, 'The Claims of Christ and Religious Pluralism', in R. E. Coleman (ed.), *Evangelism on the Cutting Edge* (New Jersey: Revell, 1986), pp. 16–28.

19 John Calvin, *The Gospel According to St John*, trans. W. Pringle (Grand Rapids: MI: Wm B. Eerdmans, 1949), p. 38.

20 *Luther's Works, vol. 22: Sermons on the Gospel of St John chapters 1–4*, ed. Jaroslav Pelikan (Saint Louis: Concordia, 1957), p. 66.

21 Barrett, *The Gospel According to St John*, on John 1.9.

22 My emphasis. The quotation comes from his *The Gospel According to St John*, vol. 1 (London: Burns & Oates, 1968), pp. 253–4.

23 C. H. Dodd, *The Interpretation of the Fourth Gospel* (Cambridge: Cambridge University Press, 1953), p. 284.

24 Emil Brunner, *Revelation and Reason* (London: SCM Press, 1947), p. 60.

25 ibid.

26 See Karl Barth, *Church Dogmatics*, volumes 1 and 2.

27 Barth, *Church Dogmatics*, II/1, 'The Doctrine of God', p. 173. See particularly Demarest, *General Revelation*, chapter 7, 'Yahweh vs. Baal: The Barthian Backlash', for a nicely balanced critique of Barth's position.

28 Karl Barth, *The Epistle to the Romans*, trans. Edwyn C. Hoskyns (London: Oxford University Press, [6]1933), pp. 45–8.

29 ibid., p. 45.

30 ibid., p. 46.

31 ibid., pp. 46–7.

32 It is interesting to note that at this point Barth comes close to Hans Küng's distinction between an ordinary way of salvation, by one's 'natural' religion, and the extraordinary way of salvation, through the Christian Good News. Karl Rahner, too, would sympathize with the idea of a point at which non-Christian religions were invalidated, but before which they were in some sense legitimate. This was not, of course, Barth's intention, but it appears to be the result of his explanation. See further on Rahner, pp. 43–51 above.

33 Barth, *Church Dogmatics* I/2, p. 304.

34 Leon Morris, *The Epistle to the Romans* (Grand Rapids, MI: Wm B. Eerdmans; Leicester: Inter-Varsity Press, 1988), p. 79.

35 See especially M. Dibelius, *Studies in the Acts of the Apostles* (London: SCM Press, 1956), pp. 32–4.
36 ibid. See also F. F. Bruce, *The Book of the Acts*, New London Commentary on the New Testament (London: Marshall, Morgan & Scott, 1968), pp. 358f.
37 Jacques Dupont, *Nouvelles études sur les Actes des Apôtres* (Paris: Editions du Cerf, 1984), p. 420.
38 J. Oswald Sanders, *What of the Unevangelized?* (London: Overseas Missionary Fellowship, 1966). The author was General Director of the OMF (formerly the China Inland Mission).
39 Dick Dowsett, *God, That's not Fair!* (Sevenoaks: Overseas Missionary Fellowship; London: Send the Light Books, 1982).
40 ibid., p. 50.
41 Sanders, *What of the Unevangelized?*, pp. 59–60.
42 Harold Lindsell, *An Evangelical Theology of Missions* (Grand Rapids, MI: Zondervan, 1970). This book is a revised version of the book by the same author, published in 1949 under the title *A Christian Philosophy of Mission*.
43 ibid., p. 113.
44 ibid., p. 111.
45 Sir Norman Anderson, *Christianity and the World Religions: The Challenge of Pluralism* (Leicester and Downers Grove: Inter-Varsity Press, 1984).
46 ibid., p. 175.
47 Charles Hodge, *Systematic Theology*, vol. 3 (London and Edinburgh: Nelson, 1878), p. 468.
48 Alan Richardson, 'Soul', in Alan Richardson (ed.), *A Dictionary of Christian Theology* (London: SCM Press, 1969), pp. 316–17.
49 Oscar Cullmann, *Immortality of the Soul or Resurrection of the Dead?* (London: Epworth, 1958), p. 20.
50 For the view that Paul is here referring to a corporate, and not an individual, 'house', the church, see Donald Guthrie, *New Testament Theology* (Leicester and Downers Grove, IL: Inter-Varsity Press, 1981), pp. 831–2. Although accepting that the corporate interpretation suits Hebrew thinking better than Greek, one notes that the 1 Corinthians 15.42–54 passage does clearly represent an individual embodying in the resurrection, and here, at least, I would have no difficulty in allowing the one (clear) passage to interpret the other (ambiguous) passage.
51 Murray J. Harris, *Raised Immortal: Resurrection and Immortality in the New Testament* (London: Marshall, Morgan & Scott, 1983), pp. 197–8.
52 David Edwards and John Stott, *Essentials* (London: Hodder & Stoughton, 1988), p. 319.
53 John Stott sets out the problem in *Essentials*, pp. 317–18.
54 ibid., p. 318.
55 ibid., p. 317.

56 C. S. Lewis, 'Introduction' to J. B. Phillips, *Letters to Young Churches* (London: Geoffrey Bles, 1947), p. ix.
57 Edwards and Stott, *Essentials*, p. 292, quoting Jonathan Edwards.
58 Sura 4.58–9, 'Surely those who disbelieve in our signs – we shall roast them at a Fire; as often as their skins are wholly burned, We shall give them in exchange other skins, that they may taste the chastisement.'
59 Edwards and Stott, *Essentials*, p. 312. It is, perhaps, not without significance that in the first draft of the *Manila Manifesto* (which came from the 1989 Congress on World Evangelization held in Manila), the section on 'Our Human Predicament' made reference to *hell*, revised in the final draft to state that humanity is 'on the broad road which leads to *destruction*' (my emphasis).

6 TEN THESES

1 These theses appeared first in an abbreviated form in Peter Cotterell, 'The Unevangelized: An Olive Branch from the Opposition', *International Review of Mission* LXXVII.305 (January 1988), pp. 131–5.
2 Hans Küng, *On Being a Christian* (London: Collins, 1977), p. 98.
3 It is not without significance that John Stott, long taken to be the spokesman for Western evangelical Christianity, was forced into grappling with some of these questions by his dialogue with David Edwards – formalized in David Edwards and John Stott, *Essentials* (London: Hodder & Stoughton, 1988) – and that this dialogue has resulted in sharp criticism of Dr Stott from within the evangelical tradition.
4 Nor do I intend to explore in any detail the related question of the destiny of aborted or miscarried foetuses, or of the point at which a foetus becomes a person. These issues are explored sensitively in Nigel M. de S. Cameron (ed.), *Embryos and Ethics: The Warnock Report in Debate* (Edinburgh: Rutherford House Books, 1987).
5 Contrary to what is stated in the *Manila Manifesto*, paragraph 3, 'The Uniqueness of Jesus Christ', which states: 'We have no warrant for saying that salvation can be found . . . apart from explicit acceptance of his [Christ's] work through faith'. Of course the *Manifesto* does not anywhere directly address itself to the question of the situation of those who have never heard the Good News: it is primarily concerned with the question of how they are to be enabled to hear.
6 J. Oswald Sanders, *What of the Unevangelized?* (London: Overseas Missionary Fellowship, 1966), pp. 66–71.
7 F. P. Cotterell, *Born at Midnight* (Chicago: Moody Press, 1973), p. 114.
8 See the article on '*dikaios*', in Gerhard Kittel (ed.), *Theological Dictionary of the New Testament*, vol. 2, trans. and ed. G. W. Bromiley (Grand Rapids, MI: Wm B. Eerdmans, 1964), pp. 182–91. It would certainly be a serious exegetical mistake to import into Luke's account the Pauline understanding of the term.

9 Following Rahner's second thesis. See pp. 121–31.
10 Karl Barth, *Church Dogmatics* I/2, pp. 299f.
11 But the verse is no more than an exemplar of the entire basis from which the writer develops his thesis of the vital importance of commitment to the *New* Covenant.

7 THE MISSION THEOLOGY OF MATTHEW

1 Which may be contrasted with John's Gospel, which has only two references to the Kingdom of God, and two further references by Jesus to 'my kingdom'.
2 On peaking, see R. E. Longacre, *The Grammar of Discourse* (London and New York: Plenum, 1983), pp. 25–38, and section 7.5.5 of Peter Cotterell and Max Turner, *Linguistics and Biblical Interpretation* (London: SPCK, 1989).
3 'There is general and widespread agreement among scholars that [Matthew] 28.16–20 was carefully crafted in accordance with the evangelist's particular theological interests in such areas as christology, ecclesiology and salvation history, and that it serves as a summary and climax of these themes as they are developed throughout the Gospel', Terence L. Donaldson, *Jesus on the Mountain: A Study in Matthean Theology*, (Sheffield: JSOT Press, 1985), p. 170.
4 David R. Bauer, *The Structure of Matthew's Gospel* (Sheffield: Almond Press, 1988), p. 109.
5 See G. R. Beasley-Murray, *Jesus and the Kingdom of God* (Exeter: Paternoster Press; Grand Rapids, MI: Wm B. Eerdmans, 1986), pp. 283ff.
6 See especially Donaldson, *Jesus on the Mountain*, for a systematic presentation of a radical view of the significance of a mountain setting in Matthew. The view has not commended itself to all scholars.
7 Donaldson, *Jesus on the Mountain*, suggests that the author builds a chain of mountains through his discourse, and it is this chain which provides it with a unifying structure.
8 The restrained statement, 'When Jesus heard that John had been put in prison' (4.12), helps to identify the presupposition pool in Matthew's mind: no more information was needed about John, because his readers already knew the details of John's imprisonment and eventual death: H. P. Grice's 'Maxim of Quantity' (see Cotterell and Turner, *Linguistics and Biblical Interpretation*, p. 261).
9 A very long chapter, of sixty-six verses, preceded by an even longer chapter of seventy-five verses.
10 Longacre, *The Grammar of Discourse*, pp. 25–38. See also Cotterell and Turner, *Linguistics and Biblical Interpretation*, 7.5.5.
11 In the sense that the transitions between the sections indicated are clear, although there are similar transitions within the various pericopae which would allow for alternative or more finely detailed analyses.

12 See D. A. Carson, 'Matthew', in Frank E. Gaebelein (ed.), *The Expositor's Bible Commentary*, vol. 8 (Grand Rapids, MI: Zondervan, 1984), p. 94.

13 R. T. France, 'Herod and the Children of Bethelehem', *Novum Testamentum* 21 (1979), pp. 98–120.

14 In my own experience in a Semitic culture, it was part of the human disorder that the rich could borrow from the banks at perhaps fifteen per cent, while the poor were driven to borrow from village money-lenders whose rates were regularly of the order of two hundred per cent per annum and more.

15 See particularly Donald Senior and Carroll Stuhlmueller, *The Biblical Foundations for Mission* (London: SCM Press, 1983), pp. 250f.

16 The chapter division here is intrusive. What the disciples are to ask the Father to do (9.38), to commission workers, the Son now does (10.5), and the Son does so as a consequence of his having himself been sent (10.40).

17 Peter Cotterell, *The Eleventh Commandment: Church and Mission Today* (Leicester: Inter-Varsity Press, 1981), 3.6.1., 'The priority of the Jew', pp. 69–70. Note especially C. E. B. Cranfield, *The Epistle to the Romans*, vol. 1, International Critical Commentary (Edinburgh: T. & T. Clark, 1975), p. 91, commenting on Romans 1.16: 'The word *te* (though its presence is simply ignored by RV, RSV, NEB and JB) is suggestive of the fundamental equality of Jew and Gentile in the face of the gospel . . . while the word *proton* indicates that within the framework of this basic equality there is a certain undeniable priority of the Jew.'

18 See also pp. 145–6 below.

19 See also Senior and Stuhlmueller, *The Biblical Foundations for Mission*, pp. 251f.

20 See particularly the extended footnote in Bruce Malina, 'Structure and Form of Matt. XXVIII.16–20', *New Testament Studies* 17 (1970–71), p. 97.

21 There is a similar uncertainty evidenced by the disciples in John's account (John 21) of the appearance of Jesus to them by the Sea of Galilee.

22 But see Carson, 'Matthew', pp. 593f., for a more detailed discussion of the doubts of 'some'.

23 cf. B. J. Hubbard, *The Matthaean Redaction of a Primitive Apostolic Commissioning* (Missoula, MT: Society of Biblical Literature and Scholars Press, 1974).

24 In linguistic terms, it is the *peak* of the trial narrative.

25 Carson, 'Matthew', p. 595.

26 Nor, indeed, is it legitimate to use the commission as justification for Church Growth 'People Movements', as though Jesus actually commissioned a 'People Movement', 'Group Conversion' mission. That conversion does take place in groups as well as individuals is undeniable, but Matthew 28.19 is not the locus of justification for it.

27 Carson, 'Matthew', p. 596.

28 But note Carson's comment ('Matthew', p. 597) on the significance of the fact that these participles *follow* the imperative.

8 THE HUMAN DISORDER

1 Perhaps the most intensively investigated case is that of Ruth Simmons, who, under hypnosis, 'remembered' detailed events from the life of Bridey Murphy, who had lived a century earlier. The case is discussed in M. Bernstein, *The Search for Bridey Murphy* (New York: Doubleday, 1956).

For further discussion of retro-cognition, see, for example, Terence Penelhum, *Survival and Disembodied Existence* (London: Routledge & Kegan Paul; New York: Humanities Press, 1970), chapter 7, '"Bodily Transfer"', pp. 79–89. See also Antony Flew's contribution to the chapter entitled 'Theology and Falsification', in Antony Flew and Alasdair MacIntyre (eds), *New Essays in Philosophical Theology* (London: SCM Press, 1955), pp. 96–9.

Metempsychosis represents an attempt to explain the phenomenon of retro-cognition by postulating the transmigration of the soul. See 'Metempsychosis', in S. G. F. Brandon (ed.), *A Dictionary of Comparative Religion* (London: Weidenfeld & Nicolson, 1970), pp. 439–40.

2 At the time of writing, the world was recovering from the spectacle of the war between two divisions of the Muslim world, Iran and Iraq. Fighting continued between two divisions of the Christian world, Catholic and Protestant in Ulster. War also proceeded apace between Marxism and Islam in Afghanistan, and between Hindu and Sikh in India, as well as between Buddhist and Hindu in Sri Lanka. In the Near East, Judaism confronted Islam in Israel and Lebanon.

3 Artur Weiser, *The Psalms*, Old Testament Library (London: SCM Press, 1962), p. 140.

4 Emil Brunner, *Man in Revolt* (London: Lutterworth, 1939), pp. 115ff.

5 See John Macquarrie, *Principles of Christian Theology* (London: SCM Press, 1966), pp. 59f., and see pp. 7–10 above.

6 'He came to that which was his own, but his own did not receive him' (John 1.11).

7 And not surprisingly the imagery is also applied in ancient Near Eastern literature to king and people, see W. Eichrodt, *Ezekiel*, Old Testament Library (London: SCM Press, 1970), pp. 469f.

8 Eichrodt, *Ezekiel*, p. 471.

9 For the interpretation of this passage, see the very full discussion in W. McKane, *Jeremiah*, International Critical Commentary (Edinburgh: T. & T. Clark, 1986), pp. 553–7.

10 cf. also 1 Peter 5.1–5 (RSV), which provides a peroration for the letter, urging the elders of the church to 'Tend the flock of God' (v. 2), and assuring them of a reward 'when the Chief Shepherd is manifested' (v. 4).

11 See the extended exegesis of the chapter in Kenneth Bailey, *Poet and Peasant* (Grand Rapids, MI: Wm B. Eerdmans, 1976), chapter 7. See also I. Howard Marshall, *The Gospel of Luke*, New International Greek Testament Commentary (Exeter: Paternoster Press, 1978), pp. 597–613.

12 It is clear that whatever the facts concerning the original locus of the three stories contained in the chapter, Luke has brought them together and

provided them with a *coherence* and a *context* which results in a discourse, and not a mere sequence of stories. See Peter Cotterell and Max Turner, *Linguistics and Biblical Interpretation*, 7.1.

13 '. . . the Pharisaic audience may perhaps approve of the story as a story, but their own attitude to returning prodigals must be clarified', Marshall, *The Gospel of Luke*, p. 611.

14 But see especially J. T. Sanders, 'Tradition and Redaction in Luke XV.11–32', *New Testament Studies* 15 (1968–69), pp. 433–8.

15 ibid., p. 438.

16 And note the similar parable of two sons in Matthew 21.28–32.

17 Some commentators, wishing to take the 'day' as literally one *yom*, have made use of Psalm 90.4, 'a thousand years . . . are like a day', and argued that since Adam died aged 930 years, he *did* die 'that day'. But that kind of interpretation represents misplaced endeavour.

18 See U. Cassuto, *A Commentary on the Book of Genesis* (Jerusalem: Magnes Press, 1961), pp. 124ff., and Claus Westermann, *Genesis 1–11* (London: SPCK, 1984), pp. 224f., who follows J. Skinner in simply assuming that God changed his mind about his threat. Skinner (*Genesis*, International Critical Commentary (Edinburgh: T. & T. Clark, ²1930), p. 67) comments: 'The simple explanation is that God, having regard to the circumstances of the temptation, changed his purpose and modified the penalty.'

19 We would, of course, miss the thrust of Paul's argument in this second section of Romans if we were to deduce that we are saved by Christ's *life*. His obedient life *is* important, but it is not the ground of our reconciliation.

20 C. K. Barrett, *The Epistle to the Romans* (London: A. & C. Black, 1957), p. 111.

21 See the long and invaluable discussion of the passage in C. E. B. Cranfield, *The Epistle to the Romans*, vol. 1, International Critical Commentary (Edinburgh: T. & T. Clark, 1975), pp. 269–95.

22 Barrett, *The Epistle to the Romans*, p. 112.

23 But notice the saying attributed to Adam:

> I died with but one sin,
> but you have committed many:
> on account of these you have died;
> not on my account. (Tanhuma B. Hukkat, 16)

24 See the careful discussion of the entire subject by A. L. Thompson, *Responsibility for Evil in the Theodicy of IV Ezra* (Missoula, MT: Scholars Press, 1977), including a very full bibliography, and see also pp. 16–17 above.

25 Karl Barth, 'The Revelation of God as the Abolition of Religion', in John Hick and Brian Hebblethwaite (eds.), *Christianity and Other Religions* (London: Collins, 1980), p. 35. See also Karl Barth, *Church Dogmatics* I/2, section 17, 'The Problem of Religion'.

26 Markus Barth, *Ephesians 1–3*, Anchor Bible (New York: Doubleday, 1974), pp. 255ff.

27 Even assuming that the *en Epheso(i)* is not original, it yet appears probable on the 'circular letter' theory that among other churches it was intended to go to Ephesus.

28 Although Markus Barth's suggestion that 'God himself had not shown that he cared for the Gentiles' (*Ephesians 1–3*, p. 260) goes far beyond what is implied by Paul's vocabulary and runs contrary to what has already been said of a universally available self-revelation by God in creation.

29 There is an extensive literature on the question of the understanding of *nomos* in Romans 7, but see D.J. Moo, 'Israel and Paul in Romans 7.7–12', *New Testament Studies* 32.1 (1986), pp. 122–35, for a summary of the arguments and a concise bibliography.

30 Cranfield, *The Epistle to the Romans*, vol. 1, p. 362.

31 Karl Barth, *The Epistle to the Romans*, trans. Edwyn Hoskins (London: Oxford University Press, [6]1933), p. 266.

32 But perhaps it should be added here that we do not deny the possibility that even unregenerate man should do 'good', in our understanding of that term. Article 10 of the Thirty-Nine Articles could be misunderstood at this point, as though it denied the possibility of doing good at all: 'The condition of man after the fall of Adam is such, that he cannot turn and prepare himself, by his own natural strength and good works, to faith . . . wherefore we have no power to do good works *pleasant and acceptable to God* . . .' (my emphasis). Until the state of estrangement is ended, until sin is dealt with, our admitted good works cannot serve to please God.

33 P. J. Achtemeier, 'Some Thing in Them Hard to Understand', *Interpretation* 38 (1984), p. 265.

9 GOD'S RESPONSE TO THE HUMAN DISORDER

1 See especially Donald Guthrie's detailed exposition of this concept in his *New Testament Theology* (Leicester: Inter-Varsity Press, 1981), pp. 486–92, and F. Büchsel's article *'dialassein'*, in Gerhard Kittel (ed.), *Theological Dictionary of the New Testament*, vol. 2, trans. and ed. G. W. Bromiley (Grand Rapids, MI: Wm B. Eerdmans, 1964).

2 See, for example, R. P. Martin, *2 Corinthians*, Word Biblical Commentary (Waco, TX: Word Books, 1986), pp. 134–59.

3 Although we note that in the Apocrypha we do have the concept of God being reconciled to man (note 2 Maccabees 1.5; 7.32–3), and it is prcisely through man doing something to remove his own transgression.

4 I. Howard Marshall, 'The meaning of Reconciliation', in R. A. Guelich (ed.), *Unity and Diversity in New Testament Theology* (Grand Rapids, MI: Wm B. Eerdmans, 1978), p. 122. See also I. Howard Marshall, *Jesus the Saviour* (London: SPCK, 1990).

5 J. H. Bavinck devotes the whole of Part Two of his *An Introduction to the Science of Missions* (Grand Rapids, MI: Baker Book House, 1960) to the subject of elenctics.

6 Unless indicated otherwise, the rest of the biblical quotations in this chapter are from the RSV.

7 The RSV translation of Hebrews 12.5–6 which renders *elenchein* by 'punish' is unfortunate. Note NEB 'corrects', NIV and GNB 'rebukes', Phillips 'reproves', all of which fairly represent the domain of meaning of the verb, which does *not* mean 'to punish'.

8 See the article on '*elenchein*', in Kittel (ed.), *Theological Dictionary of the New Testament*, vol. 2.

9 John Macquarrie, *Principles of Christian Theology* (London: SCM Press, 1966), p. 301.

10 William Temple, *Readings in St John's Gospel: First and Second Series* (London: Macmillan, 1953), pp. 270–1.

10 CHRISTIANITY AND JUDAISM

1 For a helpful, concise and sympathetic examination of the relevant issues, see particularly S. Motyer, *Israel in the Plan of God* (Leicester: Inter-Varsity Press, 1989), which focuses on the exegesis of Romans 9—11. Volume 13.4 of the *International Bulletin of Missionary Research* (October 1989) is largely devoted to the subject, and contains extracts from the crucial source documents.

2 I recall hearing, many years ago, a systematic exposition of Romans which completely omitted Romans 9—11, dismissing those chapters as 'parenthetical'. On the contrary, the biblical doctrine of salvation cannot adequately be worked out other than in the context of a proper understanding of the status of the Jew.

3 R. P. Carroll, *Jeremiah* (London: SCM Press, 1986), p. 612.

4 John Bright, *Jeremiah*, Anchor Bible (New York: Doubleday, 1965), p. 287.

5 Carroll, *Jeremiah*, p. 614.

6 Peter Cotterell and Max Turner, *Linguistics and Biblical Interpretation* (London: SPCK, 1989), p. 232.

7 Note also Yahweh's covenants with day and with night, Jeremiah 33.20f.

8 Gordon Fee, *The First Epistle to the Corinthians*, New International Commentary on the New Testament (Grand Rapids, MI: Wm B. Eerdmans, 1987), pp. 554–5.

9 The two covenants are equally covenants in *blood*: 'to Jesus, the mediator of a new covenant, and to the sprinkled blood . . .' (Heb. 12.24); 'How much worse punishment do you think will be deserved by the man who has spurned the Son of God, and profaned the blood of the covenant by which he was sanctified . . .' (Heb. 10.29, RSV).

10 On the theology of covenant, see R. E. Clements, *Old Testament Theology:*

A Fresh Approach (London: Marshall, Morgan & Scott, 1978), chapter 4.
On a massive scale, see W. Eichrodt, *Theology of the Old Testament*, vol.
1, Old Testament Library (London: SCM Press, 1961), especially chapter
2, 'The Covenant Relationship'.

11 G. E. Mendenhall, 'Covenant', in G. A. Buttrick *et al* (eds), *The Interpreter's Dictionary of the Bible*, vol. 1 (New York: Abingdon Press, 1962), pp. 714–23.

12 See also John Bright, *Covenant and Promise* (London: SCM Press, 1977), especially chapter 5, 'Jeremiah: The Prophet *Contra Mundum*', for a consideration of the relationship between prophet and people in the context of a broken covenant.

13 See M. Weinfeld, 'Covenant, Davidic', in K. Crim *et al* (eds), *The Interpreter's Dictionary of the Bible: Supplementary Volume* (Nashville: Abingdon Press, 1976), pp. 188–92.

14 C. E. B. Cranfield, *The Epistle to the Romans*, vol. 2, International Critical Commentary (Edinburgh: T. & T. Clark, 1979), p. 520.

15 Which is presumably what Hebrews 10.26 is expressing.

16 W. G. Kümmel, *Römer 7 und das Bild des Menschen im Neuen Testament: Zwei Studien* (Munich: Chr. Kaiser, 1974).

17 Guthrie, *New Testament Theology*, pp. 689f.

18 Or, indeed, to any Jew who might have been among those who read this letter or who heard it read, perhaps in the congregation at Rome. The autobiographical reference is appropriate to Paul and to such auditors (see C. K. Barrett, *The Epistle to the Romans* (London: A. & C. Black, 1957), pp. 143f.). W. Sanday and A. C. Headlam in their 1895 International Critical Commentary take the same autobiographical view of the passage (p. 180), but C. E. B. Cranfield, in the new ICC, does not.

19 A. Van Den Beld, 'Romans 7:14–25 and the Problem of *akrasia*', *Religious Studies* 21 (1985), pp. 495–515.

20 J. P. Miranda, *Marx and the Bible: A Critique of the Philosophy of Oppression* (London: SCM Press, 1977), pp. 88–92.

21 ibid., p. 92.

22 Gustavo Gutierrez, *A Theology of Liberation* (London: SCM Press, 1974), p. 194.

23 ibid.

11 THE CHURCH

1 Karl Barth, *Theology and Church* (London: SCM Press, 1962), p. 274.

2 Karl Barth, *Church Dogmatics* (Edinburgh: T. & T. Clark, 1961), IV/3, pp. 274–5.

3 See Peter Cotterell and Max Turner, *Linguistics and Biblical Interpretation* (London: SPCK, 1989), 5.1.2.

4 Barth, *Church Dogmatics*, IV/3, p. 769.

5 Hans Küng, *The Church* (London: Search Press, 1968), p. 358.

6 T. C. Vriezen, *An Outline of Old Testament Theology*, vol. 2 (Oxford: Basil Blackwell, ²1970), p. 373.

7 And although it does not officially claim to be a church, it is the only church known to most of its members.

8 But see, among others, Barnabas Lindars, 'The Composition of John XX', *New Testament Studies* 7 (1960–61), pp. 142–7; C. K. Barrett, 'The Holy Spirit in the Fourth Gospel', *Journal of Theological Studies* n.s. 1 (1950), pp. 1–15; G. Johnston, 'The Spirit-Paraclete in the Gospel of John', *Perspective* 9 (1968), pp. 29–37; A. R. C. Leaney, 'The Resurrection Narratives in John 20', *New Testament Studies* 2 (1955–56), pp. 110–14. For a beautifully concise contemporary study, see M. M. B. Turner, 'Receiving the Spirit in John's Gospel', *Vox Evangelica* XX (1977), pp. 24–42.

9 R. Bultmann, *The Gospel of John* (Oxford: Basil Blackwell, 1971), pp. 692f.

10 C. K. Barrett, *The Gospel According to St John* (London: SPCK, ²1976), ad. loc.

11 See Bultmann, *The Gospel of John*, ad. loc.

12 John Calvin, *The Gospel According to St John*, vol. 2, trans. W. Pringle (Grand Rapids, MI: Wm B. Eerdmans, 1949), p. 268.

13 Turner, 'Receiving the Spirit in John's Gospel'.

14 The action of the disciples is criticized by some who would have Paul as the twelfth apostle, and who then point to the lack of any further reference to Matthias. But of course the same criticism could also be made of seven of the apostles whose names are not mentioned in Acts or in the Epistles.

15 C. H. Dodd was deeply dissatisfied with Paul's argument at this point. His response to God's sovereignty in choosing is characterized by Dodd (*The Epistle of Paul to the Romans*, Moffatt New Testament Commentary (London: SPCK, 1932), p. 159) as 'the weakest point in the whole epistle'. But see C. K. Barrett's rejoinder in his *A Commentary on the Epistle to the Romans* (London: A. & C. Black, 1957), pp. 188f.

16 Karl Barth, *Church Dogmatics* II, 'The Doctrine of God', chapter 7, which in fact extends over five hundred pages.

17 ibid., p. 146.

18 Barth, *Church Dogmatics* II, 'The Doctrine of God', chapter 7, p. 449. Barth helpfully works his thesis out in great detail, making particular reference to the specific case of Judas.

19 Lesslie Newbigin, *The Open Secret* (London: SPCK, 1978), p. 35.

20 See J. L. Mays, *Amos*, Old Testament Library (London: SCM Press, 1969), pp. 157f.

21 Walter Brueggemann, *The Land* (London: SPCK, 1978), p. 68.

22 ibid.

23 George Caird, *The Language and Imagery of the Bible* (London: Duckworth, 1980), p. 58.

24 Quoted by R. T. France, *The Gospel According to Matthew*, Tyndale New

Testament Commentaries (Leicester: Inter-Varsity Press; Grand Rapids, MI: Wm B. Eerdmans, 1985), p. 247.

25 See R. H. Gundry, *Matthew* (Grand Rapids, MI: Wm B. Eerdmans, 1982), ad. loc.

26 The Aramaic term which would have been used by Jesus could be equally well translated Canaanite or Syro-Phoenician, but Matthew employs the former term to heighten his own redactional concern with a Gentile mission, a concern which will culminate in his record of the so-called Great Commission.

27 Jesus not infrequently referred to himself as 'Son of Man', so the indirect language of John 3.15 does not necessarily imply that it did not come from Jesus. However, the first person disappears from the pericope at 3.16, suggesting that 3.16–21 represents author's commentary.

28 Although the Jewish authorities very quickly realized that the new preaching must ultimately threaten the centrality of the temple, as their accusation of Jesus (Matthew 26.61) and of Stephen (Acts 6.14) indicates.

29 F. F. Bruce, *The Book of the Acts*, The New London Commentary on the New Testament (London: Marshall, Morgan & Scott, 1968), p. 79. Ernst Haenchen, *The Acts of the Apostles* (Oxford: Basil Blackwell, 1971), p. 191, disagrees, and suggests that the term 'breaking of bread' is a metonymic reference to a simple common meal.

30 Christopher Rowland, *Christian Origins* (London: SPCK, 1985), pp. 272f.

31 The suggestion that this poverty was, in fact, a direct result of the ill-advised experiment in communism has no evidence to support it and little to commend it. See, for example, Haenchen, *The Acts of the Apostles*, p. 233, and William Neil, *The Acts of the Apostles*, New Century Bible (London: Oliphants, 1973), p. 145.

32 And it was no more than an adequacy if we are to take Paul's comments on the Macedonian churches seriously. Their 'extreme poverty' had, apparently, overflowed 'in a wealth of liberality' (2 Cor. 8.1–5).

33 A. J. Malherbe, *Social Aspects of Early Christianity* (Baton Rouge: Louisiana State University Press, 1977), p. 77.

34 Donald McGavran, *The Bridges of God* (London: World Dominion Press, 1955).

35 Donald McGavran, *Understanding Church Growth* (Grand Rapids, MI: Wm B. Eerdmans, 1970), chapter 11; F. Gibbs, *I Believe in Church Growth* (London: Hodder & Stoughton, 1981), 5.1; R. Pointer, *How Do Churches Grow?* (London: Marshalls, 1984), Appendix 3; C. P. Wagner, *Our Kind of People: The Ethical Dimensions of Church Growth in America* (Atlanta: John Knox Press, 1979); *Explaining the Gospel in Today's World* (The Pasadena Consultation), Lausanne Occasional Paper 1 (London: Scripture Union, 1978). There is something of a retreat from the idea of promoting homogeneous unit churches in C. P. Wagner, *Leading Your Church to Growth* (London: MARC Europe and the British Church Growth Association, 1984).

36 Malherbe, *Social Aspects of Early Christianity*, pp. 84–91. See also Rowland, *Christian Origins*, section 4, chapter 4, 'Coming to Terms with the Old Age'.

37 Gordon Fee, *The First Epistle to the Corinthians*, New International Commentary on the New Testament (Grand Rapids, MI: Wm B. Eerdmans, 1987), p. 534.

38 Samuel Escobar, 'Search for Freedom, Justice, and Fulfillment', in G. H. Anderson and T. F. Stransky (eds), *Third World Theologies*, Mission Trends No. 3 (Grand Rapids, MI: Wm B. Eerdmans, 1976), p. 109.

39 Newbigin, *The Open Secret*, p. 123.

40 ibid.

12 THE CHURCH GROWTH MOVEMENT

1 There is an enormous, and largely ephemeral, literature on the subject of Church Growth. Particularly important are Donald McGavran, *Understanding Church Growth* (Grand Rapids, MI: Wm B. Eerdmans, 1970), which deals largely with the world mission model, and Eddie Gibbs, *I Believe in Church Growth* (London: Hodder & Stoughton, 1981). Wilbert Shenk (ed.), *Exploring Church Growth* (Grand Rapids, MI: Wm B. Eerdmans, 1983), is useful as a critical survey of developments in Church Growth thinking, and includes Rene Padilla's important critique of the so-called Homogeneous Unit church.

2 Donald McGavran, *The Bridges of God* (London: World Dominion Press, 1955).

3 ibid., p. 13.

4 ibid.

5 C. P. Wagner, *Leading Your Church to Growth* (London: MARC Europe and the British Church Growth Association, 1986), p. 43.

6 Vincent J. Donovan, *Christianity Rediscovered* (London: SCM Press, 1978), p. 24.

7 ibid., p. 24.

8 ibid., p. 22.

9 Writing of early 1972, Peter Wagner (*Strategies for Church Growth* (London: MARC Europe and the British Church Growth Association, (1984), p. 144) says, 'Up to this time the entire Church Growth Movement had concentrated its research and teaching on the Third World. No models for teaching it to Americans and applying it to American churches had yet been developed.'

10 J. Waskom Pickett, *Church Growth and Group Conversion* (1936), reissued in a revised form by the William Carey Library, Pasadena, in 1973.

11 Donovan, *Christianity Rediscovered*, p. 92.

12 Patricia St John, *Breath of Life* (London: Norfolk Press, 1971).

13 ibid., p. 55.

14 ibid., p. 61.

15 ibid.

16 See Olav Saeveras, *On Church-Mission Relations in Ethiopia 1944–1969* (Oslo: Lunde, 1974), III.6.

17 See, for example, Marie-Louise Martin, 'Confessing Christ in the Kimbanguist Church', *International Review of Mission* LXIV.253 (January 1975), pp. 25–9.

18 See Marie-Louise Martin, 'Kimbanguism', in David Hesselgrave (ed.), *Dynamic Religious Movements* (Grand Rapids, MI: Baker Book House, 1978), and W. MacGaffey, *Modern Kongo Prophets* (Bloomington: Indiana University Press, 1983).

19 *Signs of Hope* (London: Baptist Union, 1979), p. 15.

20 R. Currie, A. Gilbert, L. Horsley, *Churches and Church-goers* (Oxford: Oxford University Press, 1977), pp. 150–1.

21 See Peter Brierley, *Mission to London* (London: MARC Europe, 1985). In a pilot study of a single London church (undertaken by the present writer on behalf of the British Church Growth Association in 1986) it was only possible to confirm that, out of a total of sixty-three people referred to the church from the Mission, six had actually become members of that church or another. See also Peter Wagner's comments on the discrepancy between crusade 'commitments' and the growth of relevant congregations in Wagner, *Strategies for Church Growth*, pp. 140f.

22 *Baptist Union Handbook* statistics.

23 John Vaughan, *The World's Twenty Largest Churches* (Grand Rapids: Baker Book House, 1984).

24 Orlando Costas, *The Church and its Mission* (Wheaton, IL: Tyndale Press; London: Coverdale, 1974).

25 Walter J. Hollenweger, in a 'Guest Editorial', *International Review of Mission* 57 (1968), p. 272.

26 George Beasley-Murray, *Jesus and the Kingdom of God* (Grand Rapids, MI: Wm B. Eerdmans; Exeter: Paternoster Press, 1986).

27 John Macquarrie, *Principles of Christian Theology* (London: SCM Press, 1966), p. 349.

28 Marie-Louise Martin, 'Does the World Need Fantastically Growing Churches?', *International Review of Mission* 57 (1968), p. 312.

29 Paul Ricoeur, *Interpretation Theory* (Fort Worth, Texas: Christian University Press, 1974).

30 Rene Padilla, *Mission Between the Times* (Grand Rapids, MI: Wm B. Eerdmans, 1985), p. 84.

31 Fritz and Christian Schwarz, *Theologie des Gemeinde-aufbaus* (Neukirchen-Vluyn, Aussaat Verlag, 1985).

32 C. P. Wagner, *Our Kind of People: The Ethical Dimension of Church Growth in America* (Atlanta: John Knox Press, 1979), especially chapter 3, 'What is a Homogeneous Unit?'

33 ibid., p. 59.

34 C. R. Padilla, 'The Unity of the Church and the Homogeneous Unit Principle', *International Bulletin of Missionary Research* 6.1 (January 1982), pp. 23–30.

35 Peter Wagner, *Leading Your Church to Growth* (London: MARC Europe and the British Church Growth Association, 1986), p. 43.
36 David Edwards, *The Futures of Christianity* (London: Hodder & Stoughton, 1987), p. 232.
37 See David Barrett's trenchant comments in his 'Annual Statistical Table on Global Mission: 1988', *International Bulletin of Missionary Research* 12.1 (January 1988), p. 16: 'Since 1948 there has been a vast mushrooming of 5,300 significant congresses or conferences – Catholic, Protestant, Ecumenical, Evangelical, Charismatic – dealing with evangelization at national, regional, continental, or global levels . . .

'With this vast proliferation of planning . . . one would have expected the total of persons who have never heard the good news of Jesus Christ to fall . . . But this is not happening . . . Something has indeed gone wrong.'
38 Dietrich Bonhoeffer, *The Cost of Discipleship* (London: SCM Press, 1959), p. 36.

13 THE CHURCH IN EUROPE

1 Press release from the Association for the Promotion of Church Growth in Europe, now the European Church Growth Association, ECGA, January 1987.
2 Adrian Hastings, *A History of English Christianity 1920–1985* (London: Collins, 1986), p. 603.
3 In 1988 numbering some 300 congregations with a total of perhaps 40,000 adherents in the Apostolic wing (or RI group of Andrew Walker, *Restoring the Kingdom* (London: Hodder & Stoughton, ²1988) of the Restorationist movement in the UK. This might be contrasted with, say, 150,000 and more people in the mainstream Baptist churches of the UK.
4 Jan van Capelleveen, 'Western Europe in the Seventies', in J. D. Douglas (ed.), *Let the Earth Hear His Voice* (Minneapolis: World Wide Publications, 1975), pp. 151–2.
5 The credal confession awakes in the theologian important memories of the debates of the early Church, and each phrase can be mentally ticked off as it very properly excludes one heresy after another:

. . . and in one Lord Jesus Christ
the only begotten Son of God,
Begotten of His Father before all worlds.
God of God, Light of Light, Very God of Very God,
Begotten not made.
Being of one substance with the Father . . .

But these same phrases are literally meaningless to the majority of those who regularly repeat them. And people like the Bishop of Durham, the Right Reverend David Jenkins, still find it possible to repeat the phrase 'born of the virgin Mary', the public meaning of which they do not believe in, without, apparently, compromising their consciences, and this despite the apparently orthodox statements of the House of Bishops on the subject (*The Nature of Christian Belief* (London: Church House Publishing, 1986), p. 33).

6 H. L. Ellison, 'Foreword' to Leonard Verduin, *The Reformers and their Stepchildren* (Grand Rapids, MI: Wm B. Eerdmans; Exeter: Paternoster Press, 1964).

7 Walter Klaassen, *Anabaptism, Neither Catholic nor Protestant* (Ontario: Conrad Press, 1981).

8 ibid., p. v.

9 Noel Chavasse. His brother, Christopher Maude Chavasse (1884–1962), also was a chaplain, won the Military Cross, and later became an outstanding Bishop of Rochester.

10 On the whole subject of Christianity and warfare, see especially Alan Wilkinson, *Dissent or Conform?* (London: SCM Press, 1986), and on the First World War the same author's *The Church of England and the First World War* (London: SPCK, 1978). The naive and popular understanding of the role of prayer in the hour of danger is nowhere better illustrated than in the first of these two books, which records a woman's comment, 'I heard a bomb coming and I prayed to God as hard as I could to push it a bit further down the street and he did' (pp. 277f.)!

11 For a fuller treatment of Marxism, see below, Chapter 17.

12 See the MARC Europe Monograph number 11, *European Churches and Western Missions*.

13 W. Detzler, *The Changing Church in Europe* (Grand Rapids, MI: Zondervan, 1979), p. 15.

14 K. G. Pederson, 'Wearing Joseph's Coat in a Secular Society', unpublished paper circulated from Lelystad, June 1986.

15 ibid.

16 See Paul Beasley-Murray and Alan Wilkinson, *Turning the Tide* (London: Bible Society, 1981), and Peter Brierley (ed.), *Prospects for the Eighties* (London: Bible Society, 1980).

17 Charles Moore, A. N. Wilson, and Gavin Stamp, *The Church in Crisis* (London: Hodder & Stoughton, 1986).

18 See A. N. Wilson's contribution to *The Church in Crisis*, 'The Clergy'. There can rarely have been published such a comprehensive and cynical attack on Anglican theological colleges.

19 Information from Howard Foreman, Sous la Colletière, Chatillon d'Azergues, January 1987.

20 Information from Jean-Marc Lepillez, 425 rue Marcel Champion, Portes Les Valence.

21 The figure for 1986 was 716,000. The statistics were obtained from the Statistical Office of the Church of England.

22 Detzler, *The Changing Church in Europe*, p. 13.

23 See Hastings, *A History of English Christianity 1920–1985*, chapter 29, 'Church and State', pp. 417–35. The classical investigation into the

problem of Church-State relationships is probably J. N. Figgis, *Churches in the Modern State*, but since it was published in 1912 it is seriously dated. For a brief but serious examination of the issues, see Donald Reeves (ed.), *The Church and the State* (London: Hodder & Stoughton, 1984). The two contributions on disestablishment, one from a politician, Tony Benn, and the other from the then Bishop of Kensington, Mark Santer, are particularly relevant. See also the Report of the Archbishops' Commission, *Church and State* (London: Church Information Office, 1970).

24 For an explanation of the procedure followed in the appointment of bishops in the Church of England, see Paul A. Welsby, *How the Church of England Works* (London: Church Information Office, 1985), chapter X, 'Church and State'. See also Hastings, *A History of English Christianity 1920-1985*, p. 607.

25 See, for example, Part One, 'The Central Organisation', in Moore, Wilson and Stamp, *The Church in Crisis*. The title of the book is itself instructive. It is not simply *a* church, one of several, that is in crisis, but *the* Church. This is, unfortunately, a not uncommon piece of delusion, presumably resulting from meaningless statistics which show the Church of England to have an overwhelmingly large 'membership' compared with that of other groups, from the parish system which theoretically places everyone in England under the care of some parish clergyman, and from the privileged position of the Church of England and its overt share in government through its bishops.

26 Peter Hall, 'Why I Belong to the Church of England', in Gavin Reid (ed.), *Hope for the Church of England?* (Eastbourne: Kingsway, 1986).

27 See David Holloway, *The Church of England: Where is it Going?* (Eastbourne: Kingsway, 1985), especially Part Two: 'Doctrinal Arguments'.

28 See, for example, *Theological Colleges for the Future* (London: Church Information Office, 1968), the Report of a Working Party set up by the Archbishops of Canterbury and York.

29 Which is not to go all the way with Paulo Freire and his concept of *conscientization*, which is, as Edward Norman noted in his 1978 Reith Lecture, ordinary indoctrination (see Edward Norman, *Christianity and the World Order* (London: Oxford University Press, 1979), p. 55).

30 Mark Santer, 'The Freedom of the Gospel', in Reeves (ed.), *The Church and the State*, p. 117.

31 There is at least this to be said in favour of the alternative term 'Two-thirds World', that it reminds us of the numerical priority of this part of our world.

32 See the valuable article by Godfrey Jansen, 'International Islam: Moslems and the Modern World', in *The Economist*, 3 January 1981.

33 See, for example, Kenneth Copeland, *The Laws of Prosperity* (Fort Worth: Kenneth Copeland Publications, 1974), on the one hand, and Jacques Ellul, *L'homme et l'argent* (Lausanne: Presses Bibliques Universitaires, 1979), English translation, *Money and Power* (London: Marshall Pickering, 1986), on the other.

34 See Monica Hill (ed.), *How to Plant Churches* (London: MARC Europe and British Church Growth Association, 1984), p. 91.
35 David Edwards, *The Futures of Christianity* (London: Hodder & Stoughton, 1987).
36 Paul is here referring to *internal* disagreements relating to questions of crucial doctrine, rather than to the divisions based on questions of leadership which he had condemned in the earlier part of the letter.
37 See, for example, Paul Knitter, *No Other Name?* (Maryknoll, NY: Orbis Books, 1985), and Gavin D'Costa, *Theology and Religious Pluralism* (Oxford: Basil Blackwell, 1986). Both of these have valuable guides to further reading.
38 Note the important and clear statement by Seyyed Hossein Nasr, *Islamic Life and Thought* (London: George Allen & Unwin, 1981), p. 209:

> Islam does not accept the idea of incarnation or filial relationship. In its perspective Jesus . . . was a major prophet and spiritual pole of the whole Abrahamic tradition, but not a god-man or the son of God. The Qur'an does not accept that he was crucified, but states that he was taken directly to heaven. This is the one irreducible 'fact' separating Christianity from Islam, a fact which is in reality placed there providentially to prevent a mingling of the two religions.

39 Allan Brockway and Paul Rajashekar, *New Religious Movements and the Churches* (Geneva: World Council of Churches, 1987).
40 I. M. Lewis, *Religion in Context* (Cambridge: Cambridge University Press, 1986), p. 27.
41 Michael Green 'Mission and Ministry', in John Stott (ed.), *Obeying Christ in a Changing World: The Changing World*, vol. 2 (London: Collins Fountain, 1977), p. 69.

14 THE CHURCH: THE REALITY

1 cf. Calvin's 'Prefatory Address' to his *Institutes of the Christian Religion:*

> Their belly is their God, and their kitchen their religion . . . although some wallow in luxury, and others feed on slender crusts, still they all live by the same pot . . . He, accordingly, who is most anxious about his stomach, proves the fiercest champion of his faith. In short, the object on which all to a man are bent, is to keep their kingdom safe or their belly filled; not one gives the even the smallest sign of sincere zeal. (Beveridge Translation)

2 John A. T. Robinson, *On Being the Church in the World* (London: SCM Press, 1960), p. 79.
3 Stephen Neill, *Crises of Belief* (London: Hodder & Stoughton, 1984), p. 248.

15 A THEOLOGY OF THE POOR

1 See T. R. Hobbs, 'Reflections on "The Poor" and the Old Testament', *Expository Times* 100.8 (1989), pp. 291–4.

2 See Steven J. L. Croft, *The Identity of the Individual in the Psalms* (Sheffield: JSOT Press, 1987), chapter 3.

3 Surely the 'peace' of AV, NIV, and not the 'prosperity' of RSV and NEB?

4 Peter C. Craigie, *Psalms 1–50*, Word Biblical Commentary 10 (Waco, TX: Word Books, 1983), pp. 299f.

5 Note Brueggemann's comment (*The Land* (London: SPCK, 1978), p. 92): 'The land and the illusion of self-sufficiency seduce and lull people into managing their lives and their land in ways that seem beyond the terrors of history . . . The prophet . . . is to assure that the land be discerned in covenantal ways.'

6 J. A. Baker, 'Deuteronomy and World Problems', *JSOT* 29 (1984), p. 5.

7 Gerhard von Rad comments on 'the enormous height of the rates of interest in those days', suggesting rates between twenty and fifty per cent, but this would be a very conservative figure, applicable, possibly, to the professional traders who, however, are *not* the people in view in this legislation; see G. von Rad, *Deuteronomy*, Old Testament Library (London: SCM Press, 1966), p. 148.

8 'It is a law against oppression', A. D. H. Mayes, *Deuteronomy*, New Century Bible (London: Oliphants, 1979), p. 324. A more nuanced explanation is offered by C. M. Carmichael, *The Laws of Deuteronomy* (Ithaca and London: Cornell University Press, 1974), p. 211, in the interests of a unity of theme (enslaved women) that is not there.

9 A. van Selms, 'Job 31:38–40 in Ugaritic Light', *Semitics* 8 (1982), pp. 30–42.

10 See C. J. H. Wright, 'What Happened Every Seven Years in Israel?', *Evangelical Quarterly* LVI (1984), pp. 129–38 and pp. 193–201.

11 Martin Noth, *Leviticus*, Old Testament Library (London: SCM Press, 1965), p. 188.

12 Emilio Castro, *Your Kingdom Come* (Geneva: World Council of Churches, 1980), p. 31, quoted in Mortimer Arias, 'Mission and Liberation', *International Review of Mission* LXXIII.289 (January 1984), pp. 32f.

13 Baker, 'Deuteronomy and World Problems', p. 12.

14 See R. N. Whybray, 'Poverty, Wealth, and Point of View in Proverbs', *Expository Times* 100.9 (June 1989), pp. 332–6.

15 These sayings closely parallel the *Instructions of Amenemope*, an Egyptian Wisdom collection.

16 R. N. Whybray, *The Book of Proverbs*, Cambridge Bible Commentary (Cambridge: Cambridge University Press, 1972), p. 6.

17 William McKane, *Proverbs*, Old Testament Library (London: SCM Press, 1970), pp. 2–3.

18 A standard school exercise has been to assemble contemporary proverbs in mutually contradictory pairs: 'Many hands make light work' and 'Too

many cooks spoil the broth'. But even the least sophisticated child would know the appropriate time to use the one or the other. Each is true *in its context*.

19 See Gerhard von Rad, *The Message of the Prophets* (London: SCM Press, 1968), especially chapter 4, 'The Prophets' Freedom'.
20 Brueggemann, *The Land*, p. 90.
21 R. Rendtorff, *The Old Testament* (London: SCM Press, 1985), p. 112.
22 ibid., p. 113.
23 John F. A. Sawyer, *Prophecy and the Prophets of the Old Testament*, Oxford Bible Series (Oxford: Oxford University Press, 1987), p. 40.
24 See the brief discussion of these terms in Julio De Santa Ana, *Good News to the Poor* (Maryknoll, NY: Orbis Books, 1979), p. 10.
25 See S. Gillingham, 'The Poor in the Psalms', *Expository Times* 100 (October 1988), pp. 15–19.
26 The word occurs twenty-four times in the Psalms.
27 Note, for example, Psalm 35.10:

> You rescue the poor [*'ani*] from those too strong for them,
> the poor [*'ani*] and needy [*'ebyon*] from those who rob them.

The parallelism here is quite clear, and it is difficult to see that the addition of *'ebyon* adds anything to an understanding of the referent.
28 cf. John Stott, *Issues Facing Christians Today* (Basingstoke: Marshalls, 1984), p. 216, 'Who are the Poor?'
29 Croft, *The Identity of the Individual in the Psalms*, especially chapter 2, 'The Poor in the Psalms'.
30 Croft, *The Identity of the Individual in the Psalms*, p. 71.
31 J. E. Weir, 'The Poor are Powerless: A Response to R. J. Coggins', *Expository Times* 100.1 (October 1988), pp. 13–15.
32 See for example, Santa Ana, *Good News to the Poor*, and Julio de Santa Ana (ed.), *Towards a Church of the Poor* (Geneva: World Council of Churches, 1979). Michael Paget-Wilkes, *Poverty, Revolution and the Church* (Exeter: Paternoster Press, 1981) has an important chapter, 'The Church, the Elite, and Poverty in History', directly bearing on this subject.
33 See particularly John Stambaugh and David Balch, *The Social World of the First Christians* (London: SPCK, 1986), and A. J. Malherbe, *Social Aspects of Early Christianity* (Baton Rouge and London: Louisiana State University Press, 1977).
34 I am not aware that any aspect of the doctrine of the atonement actually requires that the Redeemer should be poor. If we accept the reality of incarnation then we must accept also the divine decision as to its implementation. God chose to be poor. That must be significant. It is also significant that Jesus died poor. To be born poor is no guarantee of understanding and sympathizing with the poor. Indeed, those who have escaped from poverty may prove to be the least sympathetic to the poor.
35 Kenneth Bailey's argument against the notion of a stable (in its modern sense) for the birthplace of Jesus is interesting (see K. Bailey, 'The

Manger and the Inn: The Cultural Background of Luke 2:7', *Evangelical Review of Theology* 4.2 (1980), pp. 201–17), although R. T. France's gloss on Bailey's reconstruction which turns a peasant home into 'the Palestinian equivalent of a two-bedroomed semi' is misleading (see R. T. France, *The Evidence for Jesus* (London: Hodder & Stoughton, 1986), p. 158).

36 Or, for that matter, which is promised today by the teachers of prosperity theology, such as Kenneth Copeland; see, for example, his *The Laws of Prosperity* (Fort Worth: Kenneth Copeland Publications, 1974).

37 See Gerd Theissen, *Shadow of the Galilean* (London: SCM Press, 1987); the entire book succeeds in creating imaginatively, sensitively, and in a scholarly way a three-dimensional picture of Jesus, not merely the politicized Jesus, nor the romanticized Jesus, nor even the Marxist-humanist Jesus, but certainly a *poor* Jesus (see especially pp. 67–74).

38 Milan Machovec, *A Marxist Looks at Jesus* (London: Darton, Longman & Todd, 1976), p. 89.

39 ibid., p. 97.

40 Malcolm Muggeridge, 'Living Through an Apocalypse', in J. D. Douglas (ed.), *Let the Earth Hear His Voice* (Minneapolis: World Wide Publications, 1975), p. 452.

41 See the brief discussion in I. H. Marshall, *The Gospel of Luke*, New International Greek Testament Commentary (Exeter: Paternoster Press, 1978), p. 243, and R. T. France, *Matthew*, Tyndale New Testament Commentaries (Grand Rapids, MI: Wm B. Eerdmans and Leicester: Inter-Varsity Press, 1985), p. 108. A beautifully concise summary appears in D. A. Carson, 'Matthew', in Frank E. Gaebelein (ed.), *The Expositor's Bible Commentary* 8 (Grand Rapids, MI: Zondervan, 1984), p. 125.

42 On this passage, see particularly I. H. Marshall, *The Gospel of Luke*, pp. 521–4. The crisis anticipated in the parable is clearly the *death* of the rich man, and not, as Jeremias has suggested, the *eschaton*.

43 Rainer Kampling, 'Have we not then Made a Heaven of Earth?', in L. Boff and V. Elizondo (eds), *Option for the Poor*, Concilium 187 (Edinburgh: T. & T. Clark, 1986), p. 52.

44 Malherbe, *Social Aspects of Early Christianity*, pp. 31–5.

45 ibid., pp. 81f.

46 On the whole question of wealth and power, see the classic work by Jacques Ellul, *Money and Power* (Basingstoke: Marshall Pickering, 1986), but first published in 1954 as *L'homme et l'argent*. The admonition of James 2 that the believers should *not* discriminate between rich and poor is a nice illustration of H. P. Grice's Maxim of Relevance (see Peter Cotterell and Max Turner, *Linguistics and Biblical Interpretation* (London: SPCK, 1989), p. 261).

16 ISLAM: AN ALTERNATIVE MONOTHEISM

1 Mohamed Al-Nowaihi, 'The Religion of Islam', *International Review of Mission* LXV.258 (April 1976), pp. 216–25.

2 Sura 42.5: 'We have related to thee an Arabic Qur'an'; Sura 46.11: 'Yet before it was the book of Moses for a model and a mercy; and this is a Book confirming, in Arabic tongue, to warn the evildoers . . .' However, the Qur'an contains much that is *not* Arabic: Hebrew, Syriac and Ethiopic words occur in abundance, and lend support to accusations that Muhammad received his Qur'an not by revelation but from informants (see Alfred Guillaume, *Islam* (Harmondsworth: Penguin Books, ²1956), p. 61).

3 This claim is one of the reasons for the designation of the Ahmadi movement within Islam as heretical; Ghulam Ahmad (1836–1908) allowed himself the designation *nabi*. See the defence of this position by K. Moakan, 'Seal of the Prophets', *The Review of Religions* LXXIII.9 (September 1988), pp. 19–26.

4 The Black Stone, built into one corner of the Ka'ba, remains today a focus for the *hajj*, pilgrimage to Mecca. And yet the respect paid to it has caused questioning from the earliest times. On the practice of kissing it, Umar, second in succession to Muhammad, commented: 'I well know that you are but a stone that cannot do good or harm . . . and if I had not seen that the Prophet kissed you, I would certainly never kiss you' (I. Goldziher, *Muslim Studies II* (London: George Allen & Unwin, 1971), p. 333).

5 E. Ullendorff, *The Ethiopians: An Introduction to Country and People* (London: Oxford University Press, ³1973), chapter V, 'Religion and the Church'.

6 A. Guillaume, *The Life of Muhammad* (London: Oxford University Press, 1955), p. 527. The book is a translation of Ibn Ishaq's biography of Muhammad, the earliest available to us. Ibn Ishaq explains the phrase used by Ubaid: '. . . you can't yet see clearly, the metaphor being taken from a puppy who tries to open its eyes and flutters them . . . i.e., We have opened our eyes and we see, but you have not opened your eyes to see, though you are trying to do so.' See also J. S. Trimingham, *Islam in Ethiopia* (London: Oxford University Press, 1952), pp. 45f.

7 Salman Rushdie, *The Satanic Verses* (London: Viking, 1988).

8 These words were recited by Meccans in the 'Days of Ignorance' before Muhammad, as they circled the Ka'ba.

9 Malik Ghulam Farid is in error when he claims (Malik Ghulam Farid (ed.), *The Holy Qur'an* (Rabwah (Pakistan): Oriental and Religious Publishing Corporation, 1969), p. 1139) that Ibn Ishaq makes no mention of the event.

10 See Guillaume, *The Life of Muhammad*, pp. 165f.

11 Farid (ed.), *The Holy Qur'an*, n. 2882, p. 1138.

12 M. S. Seale, *Qur'an and Bible* (London: Croom Helm, 1978), chapter 1.

13 For a restrained yet graphic account of the annual Tenth of Muharram enactment, see G. E. von Grunebaum, *Muhammadan Festivals* (London: Curzon Press, 1951), chapter V.

14 Malise Ruthven, *Islam in the World* (Harmondsworth: Penguin Books, 1984), pp. 158f.

15 See especially Goldziher, *Muslim Studies II*, chapter one, 'Hadith and Sunna'.

16 Winston S. Churchill, *Great Contemporaries* (London: Collins Fontana, 1937), p. 131.

17 See Ruthven, *Islam in the World*, p. 300. Others of these intellectuals were men such as Iran's Mehdi Bazargan and the writer Ameer Ali (whose *The Spirit of Islam* was first published in London in 1890), Sudan's Sadeq el-Mahdi, and a whole generation of leaders in Turkey following the example of Mustafa Kemal (1881–1938), Ataturk as he became, who, in 1924, abolished the Caliphate and introduced sweeping reforms which affected virtually every aspect of Turkish life.

18 For an indication of the details of Khomeini's teaching, see, for example, Ayatollah Sayyed Ruhollah Mousavi Khomeini, *A Clarification of Questions* (Boulder and London: Westview Press, 1984), a translation of Khomeini's *Resaleh Towzih al-Masael.*

19 This is not quite the same as suggesting that the Muslim *must* live under a Muslim government. In L. Barbulesco and P. Cardinal (eds), *L'Islam en Questions* (Paris: Grasset, 1986), a number of Arab writers are questioned about Islamic practice. To the question 'Is it possible for Islam to provide a system of government for a modern State?', Mohammed Arkoun replies: 'Neither historically nor theologically is Islam a system of government . . . The only example which I could identify as pure, spontaneous Islam . . . is that which was associated with the work in Medina by the Prophet' (p. 182; my translation).

20 But see Richard W. Cottam's contribution, 'The Iranian Revolution', in J. R. I. Cole and N. R. Keddie (eds), *Shi'ism and Social Protest* (New Haven and London: Yale University Press, 1986), pp. 55–87. Can a mass movement which overthrew a dictatorship which lacked support even in the armed forces be legitimately termed a revolution?

21 See Cole and Keddie (eds), *Shi'ism and Social Protest.*

22 A. Ehteshami in an obituary assessment of the achievements of Ayatollah Khomeini in the London *Independent*, Monday 5 June 1989.

23 The Ayatollah ('Word of Allah') is the representative, the mouthpiece, of the hidden Imam, on whose authority he speaks. The title is not inherited, nor acquired through advancing through a hierarchy of clerics, but is in a sense recognized and approved by the *umma*, the community. See particularly Shaul Bakhash, *The Reign of the Ayatollahs* (London: Tauris, 1985), especially chapter 2, 'Khomaini'.

24 David Pryce-Jones, *The Closed Circle: An Interpretation of the Arabs* (London: Weidenfeld & Nicolson, 1989).

25 London, *The Times*, Thursday 11 May 1989.

26 Bakhash, *The Reign of the Ayatollahs*, pp. 56–63.

27 ibid., p. 221.

28 ibid., p. 61.

29 cf. Godfrey Jansen's analysis in *The Economist*, 3 January 1981. See also John L. Esposito, *Islam: The Straight Path* (New York and Oxford: Oxford University Press, 1988), pp. 176–83, for an alternative analysis.

30 Which would include the *mujahidin*, from the mid-1970s onward. See Ruthven, *Islam in the World*, pp. 348–52.

31 Responsible in 1988 for the kidnapping and in 1989 for the murder of the American Colonel William Higgins, who had been working with the United Nations.

32 Maxime Rodinson, *Marxism and the Muslim World* (London: Zed Press, 1979), p. 50.

33 Ruthven, *Islam in the World*, p. 30.

34 Rodinson, *Marxism and the Muslim World*, p. 146.

35 See, for example, Ruthven, *Islam in the World*, p. 311.

36 For example, in dealing with the question of the validity of a Muslim's prayer at the mosque, he comments (Ayatollah Khomeini, *A Clarification of Questions*, p. 198): 'When a person mistakenly raises the head from prostration before the imam does, and returns to prostration but the imam raises his head from prostration before he gets to prostration, his prayer is correct, but is void if this event occurs in both prostrations.' The explanation lies in the middle of a section dealing generally with 'Precepts of the Public Prayer' involving twenty variants of the problem posed for a Muslim who fails to synchronize his prayer with that of the imam. There is similarly detailed instruction for the payment of the *zakat* alms, and for the payment of the tax on jewellery gained by accident, say found in the stomach of a fish (p. 241).

37 Sura 4.79 in Farid's translation. But the following verse states the reverse: 'Whatever of good comes to thee is from Allah; and whatever of evil befalls thee is from thyself.' Farid explains that God has endowed man with natural powers and faculties 'by making use of which he can achieve success in life and by making wrong use of them involves himself in trouble. Thus all good is *here* attributed to God and all evil to man' (n. 637).

38 H. U. Weitbrecht Stanton, *The Teaching of the Qur'an* (London: SPCK, 1919), p. 54.

39 Stanton, *The Teaching of the Qur'an*, p. 35.

40 The corruption of Muhammad's name to 'Mahound', 'the devil', in medieval times was resurrected by Salman Rushdie in his allegory *The Satanic Verses*, to the understandable horror of the entire Muslim world.

41 W. Montgomery Watt, *Muhammad: Prophet and Statesman* (London: Oxford University Press, 1961), p. 232.

42 See 'The Alleged Moral Failures', in Watt, *Muhammad: Prophet and Statesman*, pp. 231–6.

43 Incidentally, a wrongly formulated Trinity of Father, Son, and Mary (Sura 5.116f.), a Trinity never acknowledged by the Christian Church anywhere.

44 In A. J. Arberry (ed.), *Religion in the Middle East*, vol. 2 (Cambridge: Cambridge University Press, 1969), p. 401.

45 The details given by Shaul Bakhash in chapters 6 and 9 of his *The Reign of the Ayatollahs* are reminiscent of the Stalinist purges of the 1930s, and of the reprisals taken by the Chinese leadership following the student pro-democracy demonstrations of May-June 1989.
46 Ruthven, *Islam in the World*, p. 227.

17 MARXISM: A POLITICAL ALTERNATIVE

1 L. Kolakowski, *Main Currents in Marxism*, vol. 3, *The Breakdown* (London: Oxford University Press, 1978), p. 523.
2 J. H. Jackson, *Men and Their Times: Marx, Proudhon and European Socialism* (London: English Universities Press, 1958), p. 39.
3 ibid., p. 55.
4 Karl Marx, *Capital (Das Kapital)* (London: Lawrence & Wishart, 1954), in three volumes.
5 ibid., vol. 1, p. 235.
6 ibid., p. 239.
7 ibid., pp. 242f.
8 ibid., p. 247.
9 Marx (*The Communist Manifesto* (Moscow: Progress Publishers, 1965), p. 46) commended the bourgeoisie which had 'subjected the country to the rule of the towns. It has created enormous cities, has greatly increased the urban population as compared with the rural, and has thus rescued a considerable part of the population from the idiocy of rural life.' By contrast, Chinese Communism depended from the start on the peasantry, and this forced a change in Marxist theory in China. See below, pp. 240–3.
10 Marx, *Capital*, vol. 1, Section 5, p. 252.
11 ibid.
12 Quoted in Richard Bernstein, *Praxis and Action* (London: Duckworth, 1972), p. 52.
13 Lenin, 'The Attitude of the Workers' Party to Religion', in *Lenin on Religion* (Moscow: Progress Publishers, 1965), p. 21.
14 ibid.
15 ibid., p. 19.
16 Geoffrey Moorhouse, *The Missionaries* (London: Eyre Methuen, 1973), pp. 88–95. Moorhouse is by no means hostile to Christian mission, but will not produce a mere mission hagiography.
17 Ephesians 2 represents a more-or-less systematic account of the ending of the most intractable racial barrier of all, that between Jew and Gentile, and of a reconciliation between the two which becomes a possibility within the Church.
18 David Barrett, 'Annual Statistical Table on Global Mission: 1985', *International Bulletin of Missionary Research* 9.1 (January 1985), p. 30.
19 During one of the compression periods in Ethiopia many church leaders were imprisoned, and churches destroyed. Of the Kale Heywet Church

alone some 1,600 churches out of a total of 2,700 were closed, some destroyed. But the church continued to grow. One well-known elder was imprisoned for several months. As he walked out of the prison at the end of it his first words were: 'I've read my Bible through four times, and I'm *bursting* to preach'!

20 Dirk J. Struik (ed.), *Birth of the Communist Manifesto* (New York: International Publishers, 1971), p. 13.
21 Kolakowski, *Main Currents in Marxism*, vol. 3, *The Breakdown*, p. 81.
22 ibid., p. 78.
23 In 1988 it was very moving to hear the voice of Alexander Dubcek raised once again in a renewed appeal for the freedom of the peoples of Czechoslovakia – an appeal answered in 1989.
24 According to Barrett, there were 94 Protestant missionary societies in 1907, and by 1926 the number of societies had almost doubled, to 160, with a total of well over eight thousand foreign missionaries.
25 Kolakowski, *Main Currents in Marxism*, vol. 3, *The Breakdown*, p. 54, notes Mao's own admission that not only the 'Leap' itself, but the economic theory behind it, represented a serious error and a major defeat for the Chinese Communist Party.
26 The confrontation between students and the military in Peking's Tiananmen Square in June 1989 represented the most powerful challenge to the Chinese central government to that point. Tanks and Armoured Personnel Carriers were set on fire, and the confrontation was brought to an end only when troops from a distance could be brought in to fire into the unarmed student demonstrators.
27 Kolakowski, *Main Currents in Marxism*, vol. 3, *The Breakdown*, p. 504.
28 See, for example, Donald E. MacInnis, *Religious Policy and Practice in Communist China* (London: Hodder & Stoughton, 1972), Document 28.
29 ibid., p. 253.
30 ibid., p. 249.
31 David Barrett, 'Annual Statistical Table on Global Mission: 1987', *International Bulletin of Missionary Research* 11.1 (1987), p. 24.
32 Julius Nyerere, *Freedom and Socialism* (Nairobi and London: Oxford University Press, 1968), p. 15.

18 LIBERATION THEOLOGY:
AN ALTERNATIVE CHRISTIAN MISSIOLOGY

1 See Emilio Nuñez, *Liberation Theology* (Chicago: Moody Press, 1985), chapter 1.
2 James Cone, *A Black Theology of Liberation* (Philadelphia: Lippincott, 1970).
3 Nuñez, *Liberation Theology*, p. 111.
4 But see Nuñez, *Liberation Theology*, pp. 97ff.
5 But see also the themes identified by J. Andrew Kirk in his *Liberation*

Theology: An Evangelical View from the Third World (London: Marshall, Morgan & Scott, 1979), Part One, 'The Principal Characteristics'.

6 So Juan Luis Segundo writes in *The Liberation of Theology*, trans. John Drury (Dublin: Gill & Macmillan, 1977), first published in Buenos Aires in 1975.

7 J. S. Dennis, *Christian Mission and Social Progress*, vols. I–III (New York: Fleming Revell, 1897–1906). See also the same author's *Centennial Survey of Foreign Missions* (New York: Fleming Revell, 1902).

8 Waldron Scott, *Bring Forth Justice* (Grand Rapids, MI: Wm B. Eerdmans; London: Marshall, Morgan & Scott, 1980).

9 Segundo, *The Liberation of Theology*, chapter 1.

10 Leonardo Boff, *Jesus Christ, Liberator* (London: SPCK, 1980), p. 133.

11 On liberation hermeneutics, see J. S. Croatto, *Biblical Hermeneutics* (Maryknoll: Orbis Books, 1987).

12 J. M. Bonino, *Revolutionary Theology Comes of Age* (London: SPCK, 1975), p. 72.

13 See Richard Bernstein, *Praxis and Action* (London: Duckworth, 1972), pp. 11–12.

14 Lenin, *Collected Works*, vol. 15 (London: Lawrence & Wishart, 1963).

15 Croatto, *Biblical Hermeneutics*, chapter 2, 'Praxis and Interpretation'.

16 Paul Ricoeur, 'Biblical Hermeneutics', *Semeia* 4 (1975), pp. 1–7.

17 Rubem Alves, *What is Religion?* (Maryknoll: Orbis Books, 1984), pp. 24f.

18 See particularly Bas van Iersel and Anton Weiler (eds.), *Exodus – A Lasting Paradigm, Concilium* 189 (Edinburgh: T. & T. Clark, 1987).

19 See Kirk, *Liberation Theology*, chapter 8, 'A Privileged Text: The Exodus'.

20 Rubem Alves, 'From Paradise to the Desert', in Rosino Gibellini (ed.), *Frontiers of Theology in Latin America* (London: SCM Press; Maryknoll, NY: Orbis Books, 1979), pp. 290f.

21 See Alves, *What is Religion?*, especially chapter 3, 'The Exile of the Sacred'.

22 Enrique Dussel, 'Exodus as a Paradigm in Liberation Theology', in van Iersel and Weiler (eds.), *Exodus – A Lasting Paradigm, Concilium* 189 (1987), pp. 83–92, says *eight*, but in fact lists *nine*.

23 Dussel, 'Exodus as a Paradigm in Liberation Theology', p. 86.

24 See especially the judicious and sympathetic rview of liberation theology by Lesslie Newbigin in his *The Open Secret* (London: SPCK, 1978), chapter 8, 'Mission as Action for God's Justice'.

25 Jon Sobrino, *Christology at the Crossroads* (London: SCM Press, 1978), pp. 184–5.

26 ibid., pp. 192f.

27 Boff, *Jesus Christ, Liberator*, pp. 133f.

28 Sobrino, *Christology at the Crossroads*, p. 224.

29 Jürgen Moltmann, *The Crucified God: The Cross of Christ as the*

Notes

Foundation and Criticism of Christian Theology, trans. R. A. Wilson and John Bowden (London: SCM Press, 1974).

30 The same appears not to be true of black theology: for James Cone, at least, 'black' means 'black'.

31 Stephen Neill, *Colonialism and Christian Missions* (New York: MacGraw Hill, 1966), p. 415, quoted in Scott, *Bring Forth Justice*, p. 17.

32 Harold Lindsell, *An Evangelical Theology of Missions* (Grand Rapids, MI: Zondervan, 1949). At the Lausanne Congress in 1974 Lindsell was still totally preoccupied with an ark model of salvation for the world, with a total rejection of the moderating comments of Rubem Alves ('The Suicide of Man', J. D. Douglas (ed.), *Let the Earth Hear his Voice* (Minneapolis: World Wide Publications, 1975), pp. 421–7.

19 MEANINGLESSNESS AND MISSION

1 Arye Forta, 'The New Christian Missions to the Jews: How Should We Respond?', *L'eylah* (April 1988), pp. 22–5. The Noachide laws are deduced from Jubilees 7.20–30, and include the worship of the Creator, honouring parents, abstention from eating blood, and the love of neighbours.

2 Douglas Hare, *The Theme of Jewish Persecution of Christians in the Gospel According to St Matthew*, SNTS Monograph Series 6 (London: Cambridge University Press, 1967), p. 9.

3 P. Sangster, *Doctor Sangster* (London: Epworth, 1962), p. 335.

4 On this subject, see David Burnett, *Unearthly Powers* (Eastbourne: MARC, 1988), chapter 13.

5 Michael Green, *I Believe in Satan's Downfall* (London: Hodder & Stoughton, 1981), p 87. In general it has been the practice among modern theologians to deny the existence of demons; one outstanding exception was Eric Mascall, *The Christian Universe* (London: Darton, Longman and Todd, 1966). Edward Langton's thesis for the degree of Doctor of Divinity of London University dating back to the war (published as *Good and Evil Spirits: A Study of the Jewish and Christian Doctrine*, London: SPCK, 1942), and largely overlooked, while generally holding to the view that spirit 'possession' is a form of delusion, is forced to admit that such a view does not do justice to the full range of evidence for the phenomenon.

6 I. M. Lewis, *Religion in Context* (Cambridge: Cambridge University Press, 1986), p. 24.

7 It is to the advantage of the Muslim societies that personal details of those so persecuted cannot be printed because of the inevitable reprisals that would follow, not only against the individuals concerned, but also against their families. As I write these words I have news of the flight of a Christian (well known to me) from Algeria after not one but several periods of imprisonment incurred entirely as a consequence of that individual's acceptance of Christianity. Islam is in its practice unrelentingly intolerant, whatever may be the import of *some* parts of the Qur'an.

313

8 David Barrett (ed.), *World Christian Encyclopedia* (Nairobi, Oxford and New York: Oxford University Press, 1982), art. 'Haiti'.
9 But see the 1973 Lausanne Covenant (quoted in J. D. Douglas (ed.), *Let the Earth Hear His Voice* (Minneapolis: World Wide Publications, 1975), p. 5): 'In the church's mission of sacrificial service evangelism is primary.'
10 See above pp. 70–1 on conditional immortality, and pp. 72–4 on annihilation.
11 Ray McCauley, *Our God Reigns* (London: Marshalls, 1985). See also Duane Logsdon, *Lord, Let Me Give You a Million Dollars* (Eastbourne: Kingsway, 1985); Colin Urquhart, *Anything You Ask* (London: Hodder & Stoughton, 1978); John Wimber, *Power Healing* (London: Hodder & Stoughton, 1986); John Goldingay (ed.), *Signs, Wonders and Healing* (Leicester: Inter-Varsity Press, 1989); Kenneth Copeland, *The Laws of Prosperity* (Fort Worth: Kenneth Copeland Publications, 1974); Rex Gardner, *Healing Miracles* (London: Darton, Longman & Todd, 1986).
12 *Redemption*, May 1986, p. 32.
13 ibid.
14 ibid.
15 Urquhart, *Anything You Ask*, pp. 111–12.
16 The well-known proponent of divine healing, Francis McNutt, comments: 'As for the people we pray for; it does seem to me that most who have organic disease experience at least some degree of improvement. If we pray for, say, ten people in an hour's period (provided we have the kind of sickness we can check out on the spot), one or two will be completely healed, five or six improved, and for the others not much will happen' (quoted in Gardner, *Healing Miracles*, pp. 165f.).
17 Joni Eareckson, 'Foreword' to Henry W. Frost, *Miraculous Healing* (Grand Rapids, MI: Zondervan, 1979). Frost's book was first published in 1951 by the Overseas Missionary Fellowship.
18 Wimber, *Power Healing*, p. 214.
19 We note the significant context here: 'For to be sure, he was crucified in weakness, yet he lives by God's power. Likewise, we are weak in him, yet by God's power we will live with him to serve you.'
20 Until, it must be admitted, the Church sold itself into a degrading alliance with power, and the 'Holy Roman Empire' was created, casting aside the Pauline weakness in exchange for the illusion of power.
21 See Peter Cotterell, *Cry Ethiopia!* (Eastbourne: MARC, 1988).
22 *The Road to Damascus, Kairos and Conversion* (London: Catholic Institute for International Relations, 1989). The document also carries the imprint of Christian Aid, London, and the Center of Concern, Washington DC.
23 ibid., p. 11.
24 ibid., p. 19.
25 Cotterell, *Cry Ethiopia!* pp. 149–59.
26 See, for example, F. Halliday and M. Molyneux, *The Ethiopian Revolution* (London: Verso, 1981); C. Legum and B. Lee, *Conflict in the Horn of*

Africa (London: Collins, 1977); B. Davidson, L. Cliffe and B. Habte-Sellassie (eds), *Behind the War in Eritrea* (Nottingham: Spokesman, 1980); I. M. Lewis (ed.), *Nationalism and Self-Determination in the Horn of Africa* (London: Ithaca Press, 1983).

27 The San Andreas fault comes no closer than thirty miles, but there are more than forty lesser faults in the Los Angeles metropolitan area.

Bibliography

Achtemeier, P. J., 'Some Things in Them Hard to Understand', *Interpretation*, 38 (1984).

Ahmad, Hazrat Mirza Ghulam, *Jesus in India*, London: The London Mosque, 1978.

Alves, Rubem, *What is Religion?*, Maryknoll: Orbis, 1984.

Ana, Julio De Santa, *Good News to the Poor*, Maryknoll: Orbis, 1979.

Ana, Julio De Santa (ed.), *Towards a Church of the Poor*, Geneva: World Council of Churches, 1979.

Anderson, G. H. and T. F. Stransky (eds), *Mission Trends No. 1*, New York: Paulist Press; Grand Rapids: Eerdmans, 1974.

Anderson, J. N. D., *Christianity and the World Religions: The Challenge of Pluralism*, Leicester and Downers Grove: IVP, 1984.

Arberry, A. J., *et al.* (eds), *Religion in the Middle East*, Cambridge: Cambridge University Press, 1969.

Bailey, F. G., 'The Peasant View of the Bad Life', *Advancement of Science*, December 1966.

Bailey, Kenneth, *Poet and Peasant*, Grand Rapids: Eerdmans, 1976.

Baker, J. A., 'Deuteronomy and World Problems', *Journal for the Study of the Old Testament* 29 (1984).

Bakhash, Shaul, *The Reign of the Ayatollahs*, London: Tauris, 1985.

Ballard, Martin, *Who am I?* London: Hutchinson, 1971.

Barbulesco, L. and P. Cardinal (eds), *L'Islam en Questions*, Paris: Grasset, 1986.

Barnes, Michael SJ, *Religions in Conversation*, London: SPCK, 1989.

Barrett, C. K., 'The Holy Spirit in the Fourth Gospel', *Journal of Theological Studies*, n.s.1 (1950).

Barrett, C. K., *The Gospel According to St John*, London: SPCK, ²1976.

Barrett, C. K., 'Salvation Proclaimed XII: Acts 4.8–12', *Expository Times* 94, 3 (December 1982).

Barth, Karl, *The Epistle to the Romans*, trans. E. C. Hoskyns, London: Oxford University Press,⁵ 1933.⁶

Barth, Karl, *Church Dogmatics*, Edinburgh, T. & T. Clark, 1961.

Barth, Karl, *Theology and Church*, London: SCM, 1962.

Barth, Karl, 'The Revelation of God as the Abolition of Religion', in J. Hick and B. Hebblethwaite (eds), *Christianity and Other Religions*, London: Collins, 1980.

Barth, Markus, *Ephesians 1–3* (Anchor Bible), New York: Doubleday, 1974.

Bauer, David R., *The Structure of Matthew's Gospel*, Sheffield: Almond Press, 1988.

Bavinck, J. H., *An Introduction to the Science of Missions*, Grand Rapids: Baker Book House, 1960.

Beasley-Murray, G. R., *Jesus and the Kingdom of God*, Exeter: Paternoster; Grand Rapids: Eerdmans, 1986.

Beld, A. Van Den, 'Romans 7:14–25 and the Problem of *akrasia*', *Religious Studies* 21 (1985).

Berger, David (ed), *History and Hate: the Dimensions of Anti-Semitism*, London: Jewish Publication Society, 1986.

Bernstein, M., *The Search for Bridey Murphy*, New York: Doubleday, 1956.

Bernstein, R., *Praxis and Action*, London: Duckworth, 1972.

Boff, L., *Jesus Christ, Liberator*, London: SPCK, 1980.

Boff, L. and V. Elizondo (eds), *Options for the Poor, Concilium* 187, Edinburgh: T. & T. Clark, 1986.

Bonino, J., *Revolutionary Theology Comes of Age*, London: SPCK, 1975.

Brierley, Peter, *Mission to London*, London: MARC Europe, 1985.

Bright, John, *Covenant and Promise*, London: SCM, 1977.

Brockway, Allan and Paul Rajashekar, *New Religious Movements and the Churches*, Geneva: World Council of Churches, 1987.

Brown, Raymond E., *The Gospel According to John*, New York: Doubleday; London: Geoffrey Chapman, 1966.

Brueggemann, Walter, *The Land*, London: SPCK, 1978.

Brunner, Emil, *Revelation and Reason*, London: SCM, 1947.

Bultmann, R., *The Gospel of John*, Oxford: Blackwell, 1971.

Burnett, David, *Unearthly Powers*, Eastbourne: MARC, 1988.

Caird, George, *The Language and Imagery of the Bible*, London: Duckworth, 1980.

Carmichael, C. M., *The Laws of Deuteronomy*, Ithaca and London: Cornell University Press, 1974.

Carroll, R. P., *Jeremiah*, London: SCM, 1986.

Carson, D. A., 'Matthew', in Frank E. Gaeberlein (ed.), *The Expositor's Bible Commentary* vol. 8, Grand Rapids: Zondervan, 1984.

Cameron, Nigel M. de S. (ed.), *Embryos and Ethics: the Warnock Report in Debate*, Edinburgh: Rutherford House Books, 1987.

Cassuto, U., *A Commentary on the Book of Genesis*, Jerusalem: Magnes Press, 1961.

Castro, Emilio, *Your Kingdom Come*, Geneva: World Council of Churches, 1980.

Clements, R. E., *Old Testament Theology: a Fresh Approach*, London: Marshall Morgan and Scott, 1978.

Cole, J. R. I. and N. R. Keddie (eds), *Shi'ism and Social Protest*, New Haven and London: Yale University Press, 1986.

Cole, P. and Morgan, J. L. (eds), *Syntax and Semantics*, New York: Academic Press, 1975.

Coleman, R. E. (ed.), *Evangelism on the Cutting Edge*, New Jersey: Revell, 1986.

Cone, James, *A Black Theology of Liberation*, Philadelphia: Lippincott, 1970.

Cook, David, 'Existentialism' in S. B. Ferguson and D. F. Wright (eds), *New Dictionary of Theology*, Leicester and Downers Grove: IVP, 1988.

Copeland, Kenneth, *The Laws of Prosperity*, Fort Worth: Copeland Publications, 1974.

Costas, Orlando, *The Church and its Mission*, Wheaton, Tyndale, and London: Coverdale, 1974.

Cotterell, Peter, *Born at Midnight*, Chicago: Moody, 1973.

Cotterell, Peter, *The Eleventh Commandment*, Leicester: IVP, 1981.

Cotterell, Peter, 'The Nicodemus Pericope: a Fresh Appraisal', *Expository Times* 96.8 (1985).

Cotterell, Peter, 'The Unevangelized: an Olive Branch from the Opposition', *International Review of Mission* LXXVII, 305 (January 1988).

Cotterell, Peter and Max Turner, *Linguistics and Biblical Interpretation*, London: SPCK, 1989.

Craigie, Peter, *Psalms 1–50*, Word Biblical Commentary 10, Waco: Word Books, 1983.

Cranfield, C. E. B., *Romans (International Critical Commentary)*, Edinburgh: T. and T. Clark, 1975.

Bibliography

Croatto, J. S., *Biblical Hermeneutics*, Maryknoll: Orbis, 1987.

Croft, S. J. L., *The Identity of the Individual in the Psalms*, Sheffield: JSOT Press, 1987.

Cullmann, Oscar, *Immortality of the Soul or Resurrection of the Dead?*, London: Epworth, 1958.

Currie, R., A. Gilbert and L. Horsley, *Churches and Church-goers*, Oxford: OUP, 1977.

D'Costa, Gavin, *Theology and Religious Pluralism*, Oxford: Basil Blackwell, 1986.

D'Costa, Gavin, *John Hick's Theology of Religions*, Lanham and London: University Press of America, 1987.

Demarest, Bruce A., *General Revelation*, Grand Rapids: Zondervan, 1982.

Detzler, W., *The Changing Church in Europe*, Grand Rapids: Zondervan, 1979.

Dodd, C. H., *The Interpretation of the Fourth Gospel*, Cambridge: Cambridge University Press, 1953.

Donaldson, Terence L., *Jesus on the Mountain*, Sheffield: JSNT, 1985.

Donovan, Vincent J., *Christianity Rediscovered*, London: SCM, 1978.

Douglas, J. D. (ed.), *Let the Earth Hear His Voice*, Minneapolis: World-Wide Publications, 1975.

Dowsett, Dick, *God, That's not Fair!*, Sevenoaks: OMF; London: Send the Light Books, 1982.

Dupont, Jacques, *Nouvelles études sur les Actes des Apôtres*, Paris: Cerf, 1984.

Eckardt, A. R., *Jews and Christians: the Contemporary Meeting*, Indiana University Press, 1986.

Eddy, Mary Baker, *Science and Health with Key to the Scriptures*, Boston, 1875 and onwards.

Edwards, David, *The Futures of Christianity*, London: Hodder and Stoughton, 1987.

Edwards, David and John Stott, *Essentials*, London: Hodder and Stoughton, 1988.

Eichrodt, W., *Theology of the Old Testament* (Old Testament Library), London: SCM, 1961.

Eichrodt, W., *Ezekiel*, London: SCM, 1970.

Ellul, Jacques, *Money and Power*, Basingstoke: Marshall Pickering, 1986.

England, Edward, *The Mountain that Moved*, London: Hodder and Stoughton, 1967.

Escobar, Samuel, 'Search for Freedom, Justice, and Fulfillment', in G. H. Anderson and T. F. Stransky (eds), *Third World Theologies (Mission Trends No. 3)*, Grand Rapids: Eerdmans, 1976.

Esposito, John L., *Islam: the Straight Path*, New York and Oxford: Oxford University Press, 1988.

Fee, Gordon, *The First Epistle to the Corinthians*, Grand Rapids: Eerdmans, 1987.

Ferguson, S. B. and D. F. Wright (eds), *New Dictionary of Theology*, Leicester and Downers Grove: IVP, 1988.

Flannery, A. (ed.), *Vatican Council II*, Leominster: Fowler Wright, 1975.

Flew, A., 'Theology and Falsification' in A. Flew and A. C. MacIntyre (eds), *New Essays in Philosophical Theology*, London: SCM, 1955.

Forman, Charles W. and Gregory Baum, 'Is there a Missionary Message' in G. H. Anderson and T. F. Stransky (eds), *Mission Trends No. 1*, New York: Paulist; Grand Rapids: Eerdmans, 1974.

Forta, Arye, 'The New Christian Missions to the Jews', *L'eylah*, April, 1988.

France, R. T., 'Herod and the Children of Bethlehem', *Novum Testamentum* 21 (1979).

France, R. T., *The Gospel According to Matthew*, Tyndale New Testament Commentaries, Leicester: IVP; Grand Rapids: Eerdmans, 1985.

France, R. T., *The Evidence for Jesus*, London: Hodder and Stoughton, 1986.

Fitzmyer, J., *The Gospel According to Luke X–XXIV* (Anchor Bible), New York: Doubleday, 1985.

Frost, Henry, *Miraculous Healing*, Grand Rapids: Zondervan, 1979.

Gaeberlein, Frank E. (ed.), *The Expositor's Bible Commentary*, Grand Rapids: Zondervan, 1984.

Gardner, Rex, *Healing Miracles*, London: Darton, Longman and Todd, 1986.

Gibbs, E., *I Believe in Church Growth*, London: Hodder and Stoughton, 1981.

Gibellini, Rosino (ed.), *Frontiers of Theology in Latin America*, London: SCM; Maryknoll: Orbis, 1979.

Gillingham, S., 'The Poor in the Psalms', *Expository Times* 100.1 (October 1988).

Goldingay, John (ed.), *Signs, Wonders, and Healing*, Leicester: IVP, 1989.

Goldziher, I., *Muslim Studies*, London: George Allen and Unwin, 1971.

Green, Michael, *I Believe in Satan's Downfall*, London: Hodder and Stoughton, 1981.

Grice, H. P., 'Logic and Conversation' in P. Cole and J. L. Morgan (eds), *Syntax and Semantics*, New York: Academic Press, 1975.

Grunebaum, G. E. von, *Muhammadan Festivals*, London: Curzon Press, 1951.

Guelich, R. A. (ed.), *Unity and Diversity in New Testament Theology*, Grand Rapids: Eerdmans, 1978.

Guillaume, A., *The Life of Muhammad*, London: OUP, 1955.

Gundry, R. H., *Matthew*, Grand Rapids: Eerdmans, 1982.

Guthrie, Donald, *New Testament Introduction*, London: Tyndale, ³1970.

Guthrie, Donald, *New Testament Theology*, Leicester: IVP, 1981.

Gutierrez, Gustavo, *A Theology of Liberation*, London: SCM, 1974.

Haenchen, Ernst, *The Acts of the Apostles*, Oxford: Blackwell, 1971.

Hare, Douglas, *The Theme of Jewish Persecution of Christians in the Gospel According to St Matthew*, SNTS Monograph Series 6, London: Cambridge University Press, 1967.

Harris, Murray J., *Raised Immortal: Resurrection and Immortality in the New Testament*, London: Marshall, Morgan and Scott, 1983.

Hastings, Adrian, *A History of English Christianity 1920–1985*, London: Collins, 1986.

Hebblethwaite, Brian, *The Ocean of Truth*, Cambridge and New York: Cambridge University Press, 1988.

Hesselgrave, David (ed.), *Dynamic Religious Movements*, Grand Rapids: Baker Books, 1978.

Hick, John, *The Second Christianity*, London: SCM, 1983.

Hick, John, *God and the Universe of Faiths*, London: Collins, 1977.

Hick, John, *God has Many Names*, London: Macmillan, 1980.

Hick, John, *Problems of Religious Pluralism*, Basingstoke: Macmillan, 1985.

Hick, J. and B. Hebblethwaite (eds), *Christianity and Other Religions*, Glasgow: Collins (Fontana), 1980.

Hick, John and P. F. Knitter (eds), *The Myth of Christian Uniqueness*, Maryknoll: Orbis 1987; London: SCM, 1988.

Hill, Monica (ed.), *How to Plant Churches*, London: MARC Europe; British Church Growth Association, 1984.

Hirsch, E. D., *The Aims of Interpretation*, Chicago: University of Chicago Press, 1976.

Bibliography

Hobbs, T. R., 'Reflections on "The Poor" and the Old Testament', *Expository Times* 100.8 (1989).

Hogan, David, 'The Names of God in the Urak Lawoi Scriptures', *The Bible Translator* 35, 4 (1984).

Holloway, David, *The Church of England: Where is it Going?*, Eastbourne: Kingsway, 1985.

Hubbard, B. J., *The Matthaean Redaction of a Primitive Apostolic Commissioning*, Missoula: Society of Biblical Literature and Scholars Press, 1974.

Iersel, Bas van and Anton Weiler (eds), *Exodus: a Lasting Paradigm, Concilium* 189, Edinburgh: T. & T. Clark, 1987.

Jackson, J. H., *Marx, Proudhon and European Socialism*, London: English Universities Press, 1958.

Jaspers, Karl, *Philosophical Faith and Revelation*, Eng. tr. E. B. Ashton, London: Collins, 1967.

Johnston, G., 'The Spirit-Paraclete in the Gospel of John', *Perspective* 9 (1968).

Kane, John, *Pluralism and Truth in Religion*, Chico: Scholars Press, 1981.

Kantzer, Kenneth S., 'The Claims of Christ and Religious Pluralism' in R. E. Coleman (ed.), *Evangelism on the Cutting Edge*, New Jersey: Revell, 1986.

Khan, Muhammad Zafrulla, *Deliverance from the Cross*, London: The London Mosque, 1978.

Kirk, J. Andrew, *Liberation Theology: an Evangelical View from the Third World*, London: Marshall, Morgan and Scott, 1979.

Klaassen, Walter, *Anabaptism, Neither Catholic nor Protestant*, Ontario: Conrad Press, 1981.

Knitter, Paul, *No Other Name?*, Maryknoll: Orbis, 1985.

Knitter, Paul, 'Roman Catholic Approaches to Other Religions: Developments and Tensions', *International Bulletin of Missionary Research* 8, 2 (April, 1984).

Kolakowski, L., *Main Currents in Marxism*, London: Oxford University Press, 1978.

Küng, Hans, 'The World Religions in God's Plan of Salvation', in H. Neuner (ed.), *Christian Revelation and World Religions*, London: Burns and Oates, 1967.

Küng, Hans, *The Church*, London: Search Press, 1968.

Küng, Hans, *On Being a Christian*, London: Collins; New York: Doubleday, 1977.

Kushner, Harold S., *When Bad Things Happen to Good People*, London: Pan Books, 1982.

Langton, Edward, *Good and Evil Spirits*, London: SPCK, 1942.

Leaney, A. R. C., 'The Resurrection Narratives in John 20', *New Testament Studies* 2 (1955–56).

Legum, Colin and B. Lee, *Conflict in the Horn of Africa*, London: Collins, 1977.

Lewis, I. M. (ed.), *Nationalism and Self-determination in the Horn of Africa*, London: Ithaca Press, 1983.

Lewis, I. M., *Religion in Context*, Cambridge: Cambridge University Press, 1986.

Lewis, Norman, *The Missionaries*, New York: Secker and Warburg, 1988.

Lindars, Barnabas, 'The Composition of John XX', *New Testament Studies* 7 (1960–61).

Lindsell, Harold, *An Evangelical Theology of Missions*, Grand Rapids: Zondervan (1949), 1970.

Ling, Trevor, *A History of Religion East and West*, London: Macmillan, 1968.

Loewen, J., 'Translating the Names of God: How European Languages have Translated them', *The Bible Translator* 36, 4 (1985).

Longacre, R. E., *The Grammar of Discourse*, London and New York: Plenum, 1983.

MacGaffey, W., *Modern Kongo Prophets*, Bloomington: Indiana University Press, 1983.

Machovec, M., *A Marxist Looks at Jesus*, London: Darton, Longman and Todd, 1976.

MacInnis, Donald E., *Religious Policy and Practice in Communist China*, London: Hodder and Stoughton, 1972.

Macquarrie, John, *Principles of Christian Theology*, London: SCM, 1966.

Malherbe, A. J., *Social Aspects of Early Christianity*, Baton Rouge: Louisana State University Press, 1977.

Malina, Bruce, 'Structure and Form of Matt. XXVIII.16-20', *New Testament Studies* 17 (1970-71).

Marshall, I. H., *The Gospel of Luke*, NIGTC, Exeter: Paternoster, 1978.

Marshall, I. H., *Jesus the Saviour*, London: SPCK, 1990.

Martin, Marie-Louise, 'Does the World Need Fantastically Growing Churches?', *International Review of Mission* 57 (1968).

Martin, Marie-Louise, 'Confessing Christ in the Kimbanguist Church', *International Review of Mission*, LXIV, 253 (January 1975).

Martin, R. P., *2 Corinthians* (Word Biblical Commentary), Waco: Word, 1986.

Mayes, A. D. H., *Deuteronomy* (New Century Bible), London: Oliphants, 1979.

Mays, J. L., *Amos* (Old Testament Library), London: SCM, 1969.

McCauley, Ray, *Our God Reigns*, London: Marshalls, 1985.

McGavran, Donald, *The Bridges of God*, London: World Dominion Press, 1955.

McGavran, Donald, *Understanding Church Growth*, Grand Rapids: Eerdmans, 1970.

McKane, W., *Proverbs* (Old Testament Library), London: SCM, 1970.

McKane, W., *Jeremiah* (ICC), Edinburgh: T. & T. Clark, 1986.

McKim, Donald, *A Guide to Contemporary Hermeneutics*, Grand Rapids: Eerdmans, 1986.

Miranda, J. P., *Marx and the Bible: a Critique of the Philosophy of Oppression*, London: SCM, 1977.

Moakan, K., 'Seal of the Prophets', *The Review of Religions* LXXIII 9 (September 1988).

Moltmann, J., *The Crucified God*, London: SCM, 1974.

Moo, D. J., 'Israel and Paul in Romans 7.7-12, *New Testament Studies*, 32, 1 (1986).

Moore, Charles, A. N. Wilson and Gavin Stamp, *The Church in Crisis*, London: Hodder and Stoughton, 1986.

Moorhouse, Geoffrey, *The Missionaries*, London: Eyre Methuen, 1973.

Morris, Leon, *The Epistle to the Romans*, Grand Rapids: Eerdmans; Leicester: IVP, 1988.

Motyer, S., *Israel in the Plan of God*, Leicester: IVP, 1989.

Nasr, Seyyed Hossein, *Islamic Life and Thought*, London: George Allen and Unwin, 1981.

Neill, Stephen, *Crises of Belief*, London: Hodder and Stoughton, 1984.

Neuner, H. (ed.), *Christian Revelation and World Religions*, London: Burns and Oates, 1967.

Newbigin, Lesslie, *The Open Secret*, London: SPCK, 1978.

Newbigin, Lesslie, *The Gospel in a Pluralist Society*, London: SPCK, 1989.

Norman, Edward, *Christianity and the World Order*, London: Oxford University Press, 1979.

Bibliography

Al-Nowaihi, Mohamed, 'The Religion of Islam', *International Review of Mission* LXV 258 (April 1976).

Nuñez, Emilio, *Liberation Theology*, Chicago: Moody, 1985.

Nyerere, Julius, *Freedom and Socialism*, Nairobi and London: Oxford University Press, 1968.

Padilla, Rene, *Mission Between the Times*, Grand Rapids: Eerdmans, 1985.

Paget-Wilks, Michael, *Poverty, Revolution, and the Church*, Exeter: Paternoster, 1981.

Penelhum, Terence, *Survival and Disembodied Existence* (Studies in Philosophical Psychology), London: Routledge and Kegan Paul; New York: Humanities Press, 1970.

Pickett, J. Waskom, *Church Growth and Group Conversion*, Pasadena: William Carey Library, 1973.

Popper, K., *The Open Society and its Enemies*, London: Routledge and Kegan Paul, ⁵1966.

Potterie, I. de la, *La Vérité dans Saint Jean*, Rome: Bib. Inst. Press, 1977.

Pryce-Jones, David, *The Closed Circle: an Interpretation of the Arabs*, London: Weidenfeld and Nicolson, 1989.

Rad, G. von, *Deuteronomy* (Old Testament Library), London: SCM, 1966.

Rad, G. von, *The Message of the Prophets*, London: SCM, 1968.

Rahner, Karl, *Theological Investigations*, London: Darton, Longman and Todd, 1976.

Reeves, Donald (ed.), *The Church and the State*, London: Hodder and Stoughton, 1984.

Reid, Gavin (ed.), *Hope for the Church of England?*, Eastbourne: Kingsway, 1986.

Rendtorff, R., *The Old Testament*, London: SCM, 1985.

Ricoeur, Paul, *The Conflict of Interpretations*, Evanston: Northwestern University Press, 1974.

Ricoeur, Paul, 'Biblical Hermeneutics', *Semeia* 4 (1975).

Ricoeur, Paul, *Interpretation Theory: Discourse and the Surplus of Meaning*, Fort Worth: Texas Christian University Press, 1976.

Robinson, J. A. T., *On Being the Church in the World*, London: SCM, 1960.

Rodinson, Maxime, *Marxism and the Muslim World*, London: Zed Press, 1979.

Rowland, Christopher, *Christian Origins*, London: SPCK, 1985.

Rushdie, Salman, *The Satanic Verses*, London: Viking, 1988.

Ruthven, Malise, *Islam in the World*, Harmondsworth: Penguin Books, 1984.

Saeverås, Olav, *On Church-Mission Relations in Ethiopia 1944–1969*, Oslo: Lunde, 1974.

Sanders, J. Oswald, *What of the Unevangelized?*, London: Overseas Missionary Fellowship, 1966.

Sanders, J. T., 'Tradition and Redaction in Luke XV 11–32', *New Testament Studies* 15 (1968–69).

Sartre, Jean-Paul, *Existentialism and Humanism*, London: Methuen, 1948.

Sawyer, John F. A., *Prophecy and the Prophets of the Old Testament*, Oxford: Oxford University Press, 1987.

Schnackenburg, Rudolf, *The Gospel According to St John* vol. 2, London: Burns and Oates, 1980.

Scott, Waldron, *Bring Forth Justice*, Grand Rapids: Eerdmans; London: Marshall, Morgan and Scott, 1980.

Segundo, Juan Luis, *The Liberation of Theology*, Dublin: Gill and Macmillan, 1977.

Senior, Donald and Carroll Stuhlmueller, *The Biblical Foundations for Mission*, London: SCM, 1983.

Sharpe, E. J., *Understanding Religion*, London: Duckworth, 1983.

Shenk, Wilbert (ed.), *Exploring Church Growth*, Grand Rapids: Eerdmans, 1983.

Sobrino, Jon, *Christology at the Crossroads*, London: SCM, 1978.

Stambaugh, John and David Balch, *The Social World of the First Christians*, London: SPCK, 1986.

Starkey, Peggy, 'Biblical Faith and the Challenge of Religious Pluralism', *International Review of Mission* LXXI 281 (January 1982).

Steinmetz, David, 'Theology and Exegesis: Ten Theses', in Donald McKim, *A Guide to Contemporary Hermeneutics*, Grand Rapids: Eerdmans, 1986.

Stott, John, *Issues Facing Christians Today*, Basingstoke: Marshalls, 1984.

Theissen, Gerd, *Shadow of the Galilean*, London: SCM, 1987.

Thomas, Owen C., *Attitudes Toward Other Religions*, London: SCM, 1969.

Thompson, A. L., *Responsibility for Evil in the Theodicy of IV Ezra*, Missoula: Scholars Press, 1977.

Turner, M. M. B., 'Receiving the Spirit in John's Gospel', *Vox Evangelica* XX (1977).

Vaughan, John, *The World's Twenty Largest Churches*, Grand Rapids: Baker Books, 1984.

Vaux, R. de, *Ancient Israel*, London: Darton, Longman and Todd, 1961.

Verduin, Leonard, *The Reformers and their Stepchildren*, Grand Rapids: Eerdmans; Exeter: Paternoster, 1964.

Verkuyl, J., *Contemporary Missiology*, Grand Rapids: Eerdmans, 1978.

Vriezen, T. C., *An Outline of Old Testament Theology*, Oxford: Basil Blackwell, [2]1970.

Wagner, C. P., *Our Kind of People: The Ethical Dimensions of Church Growth in America*, Atlanta: John Knox Press, 1979.

Wagner, C. P., *Leading Your Church to Growth*, London: MARC Europe; the British Church Growth Association, 1984.

Walker, Andrew, *Restoring the Kingdom*, London: Hodder and Stoughton, [2]1988.

Watt, W. Montgomery, *Muhammad: Prophet and Statesman*, London: Oxford University Press, 1961.

Weir, J. E., 'The Poor are Powerless: a Response to R. J. Coggins', *Expository Times* 100.1 (October 1988).

Weiser, Artur, *The Psalms* (Old Testament Library), London: SCM, 1962.

Westermann, Claus, *Genesis 1-11*, London: SPCK, 1984.

Whybray, R. N., 'Poverty, Wealth, and Point of View in Proverbs', *Expository Times* 100.9 (June 1989).

Whybray, R. N., *The Book of Proverbs* (Cambridge Bible Commentary), Cambridge: Cambridge University Press, 1972.

Wilkinson, Alan, *Dissent or Conform?*, London: SCM, 1986.

Wilkinson, Alan, *The Church of England and the First World War*, London: SPCK, 1978.

Wimber, John, *Power Healing*, London: Hodder and Stoughton, 1986.

Wright, C. J. H., 'What Happened Every Seven Years in Israel?', *Evangelical Quarterly* LVI (1984).

Index of Biblical References

Subject Index

Subject Index

Author Index

Author Index

Author Index